DEAD MAN'S CHEST

Robert Louis Stevenson in 1892

DEAD MAN'S CHEST

*Travels after Robert Louis
Stevenson*

NICHOLAS RANKIN

faber and faber

This edition first published in 2008
by Faber and Faber Ltd
3 Queen Square, London WC1N 3AU

A CIP record for this book is available from the British Library

ISBN 978-0-571-24218-4

This book is dedicated to the late Peg Rankin,
and to Maggie Gee and Rosa Rankin-Gee:
my mother, my wife, and our daughter

CONTENTS

ACKNOWLEDGEMENTS

The author is grateful to the following people who gave or lent books, beds, food, friendship, hospitality, ideas and inspiration:
Father Paul Aerts, Daniel Balderstone, Peggy Barb, famille Barrois in Hyères, the Beatties of North Berwick, Neil Berry, Patrick Boland, James Campbell, Esther Caprez and Michael Galvin, John Clark, Frances Coady, Irena Czekierska and Chris Miers, Mike Delahant, Mrs Elisabeth Dennys, Lady Dunpark, Charles Elton, Moris Farhi, Father Nobincio Fernández, the Findhorn community on Earraid, Martin Gayford and Josephine Morrison, Vic and Aileen Gee, Claude Gibelin, Gloucester Road Bookshop, Barbara Goodwin, Sir Hugh Greene, Graham Greene, Sister Mary Laurence Hanley, Father Martin Hayes, John King, María Kodama, Robin Lewis and Alison Dalton, Irene Litoto, Hugh MacDougall, Philip Mason, Robert McCrum, Ernest and Joyce Mehew, Barry Menikoff, John and Carrie Morgan, Northern Lighthouse Board, Ben Okri, Richard and Clara Oliver, Paula J. Peterson, the Phoenix Trust of the Society of Authors who gave a grant of £1000, the Rankin *ainga* of Western Samoa, Lt.-Col. J. T. Rankin, John Rankin, Catriona Rankin, Maureen Rissik, Philip Rose-Taylor, Brian Rotman and Lesley Ferris, John Ryle, Judith Scott and Byron Bartlett, Ellen Shaffer, Anwei Skinsnes Law, Olaf K. Skinsnes, Lance and Sally Stone, Norman H. Strouse, Eleanor Swearingen, Roger and Sarah Swearingen, Joseph and Diane Theroux, the *Times Literary Supplement*, Noel Treacy, John and Alison Waite, Richard Wilson.
The author would also like to pay tribute to the dedicated, friendly and patient staff of public libraries in Bournemouth; London Borough of Camden; Edinburgh; Elko; Honolulu; Hyères-

les-Palmiers; Monterey; New York City; San Francisco; Sydney; and to Mataina T'eo and staff at the Nelson Memorial Library, Apia, Western Samoa.

Special thanks to a beloved great-aunt, Gwynneth Stallard, who has always been my Betsy Trotwood.

For permission to reprint verse and prose extracts from copyright material the publishers gratefully acknowledge the following: E. P. Dutton for 'June 1968' by J. L. Borges; Grove Press Inc. for 'El Sur' by J. L. Borges, translated by Anthony Kerrigan; University of Texas Press for *Other Inquisitions* by J. L. Borges, translated by Ruth L. C. Simms; E. P. Dutton and Penguin Books Limited for *Borges on Writing* by J. L. Borges, edited by Norman Thomas di Giovanni, Daniel Halpern and Frank MacShane; Cause of Mother Marianne of Molokai, Sisters of St Francis of Syracuse, New York for the journal of Sister Leopoldina Burns; The Bodley Head Ltd and Simon & Schuster Inc. for *Collected Essays, A Sort of Life* by Graham Greene; Weidenfeld & Nicolson Ltd and Harcourt Brace Jovanovich Inc. for *Lectures on Literature* by Vladimir Nabokov; Chatto & Windus Ltd and New Directions Publishing Corp. for *Collected Poems* by Wilfred Owen; Oxford University Press for *Eight Modern Writers* by J. I. M. Stewart.

Following Stevenson's practice, the spelling of some Samoan words in this book has been altered, and the nasal *n* written as *ng* instead of *g*. Thus Pago Pago is written Pango Pango. The *ng* is pronounced as in 'singer', not as in 'finger'.

Take not my hand as mine alone –
  You do not trust to me –
I hold the hand of greater men
  Too far before to see.

Follow not me, who only trace
  Stoop-head the prints of those
Our mighty predecessors, whom
  The darknesses enclose.

I cannot lead who follow – I
  Who learn, am dumb to teach;
I can but indicate the goals
  That greater men shall reach.

Robert Louis Stevenson, *Recruiting Songs* (1872)

It has been his fortune . . . to have had to consent to become, by a process not purely mystic and not wholly untraceable – what shall we call it? – a Figure. Tracing is needless now, for the personality has acted and the incarnation is full. There he is – he has passed ineffaceably into happy legend.

Henry James, review of *The Letters of Robert Louis Stevenson* (1899)

I believe that the lesson of his life will only be seen after time has revealed the full meaning of our present tendencies; I believe it will be seen from afar off like a vast plan or maze traced out on a hillside, perhaps traced by one who did not even see the plan while he was making the tracks.

G. K. Chesterton, *Robert Louis Stevenson* (1927)

The steps taken by a man, from the day of his birth to the day of his death, trace an inconceivable figure in time. Divine Intelligence intuits that figure immediately, as man's intelligence does a triangle. That figure (perhaps) has a specific function in the economy of the universe.

Jorge Luis Borges, *The Mirror of the Enigmas* (1940)

Stevenson Family Tree

Alan Stevenson
died 1774

Jean Lillie —— second marriage 1792 —— Thomas Smith
(born 1752–died 1815)
NLB Engineer 1787–1804

Elizabeth Couper
died 1786

Robert Stevenson
(1772–1850)
NLB Engineer 1797–1842

married 1799

Jane Smith
(1779–1846)

Alan Stevenson
(1807–1865)
NLB Engineer 1843–53

David Stevenson
(1815–1886)
NLB Engineer 1853–81

Thomas Stevenson
(1818–1887)
NLB Engineer 1854–87

Robert Alan Mowbray
'Bob' Stevenson
(1847–1900)

David A. Stevenson
(1854–1938)
NLB Engineer 1885–1938

Charles Stevenson
(1855–1950)

Robert Louis Stevenson
(1850–1894)

D. Alan Stevenson
(1891–1971)
Lighthouse Engineer 1919–52

Northern Lighthouse Board (NLB)

PROLOGUE

It all began in a secondhand bookshop in London on 23 April 1983. I had remembered how in Barcelona they celebrate San Jordi – St George's Day – by giving the beloved a rose and a book. A rose is a rose is a rose, but the book is in memory of Cervantes and Shakespeare, who both died on 23 April 1616.

So I went into the dusty shop to buy a book for my wife, and picked up an old grey Longman paperback edition of Robert Louis Stevenson's *The Strange Case of Dr Jekyll and Mr Hyde*. This 1886 novella has entered world myth and, together with Mary Shelley's *Frankenstein* and Bram Stoker's *Dracula*, become so familiar that many people have not troubled to read the original.

Later, browsing in bed, I found other Stevenson stories at the back of the volume; stories first published posthumously in 1896, some as brief as four lines, others only a few pages long. There were twenty *Fables*, and I thought them brilliant. Their insights were modern but the language echoed the Bible, and they did not fit my simple notion of Stevenson as author of boys 'books and 'shilling shockers'. The writer of these consummate pieces was a scrupulous, self-conscious artist. Stevenson's *Fables* reminded me of Jorge Luis Borges.

*

That autumn, J. L. Borges himself came to London to speak to the Anglo-Argentine Society. He was to have come the previous year, but the plan had been torpedoed by the Falklands/Malvinas war of April-June 1982. ('Two bald men fighting over a comb', Borges had commented.) In the event, the famous Argentine writer did not deliver the First Annual Jorge Luis Borges Lecture, but only answered questions.

Among other things, he said:

> Reading is one of the most vivid forms of happiness – I have no memory without reading or writing: my memory is full of quotations. The reader is very important. A book is dead until a reader opens it, and it comes to life when it is read. The reader collaborates, and enriches the book . . .

It was an evening of fascination and frustration. Eighty-four-year-old Jorge Luis Borges, hopelessly blind but still stubbornly living, one of the supreme literary intelligences of the twentieth century, was here, in London, and I was too timid to talk to him. I had spoken to him once on the telephone, a few years before, when he gave me permission to adapt some of his stories for the stage. But I had missed several opportunities of meeting him in Argentina, and I did not want to repeat the mistake.

I thought that since he was blind perhaps he might like someone to read to him, and so I went to his hotel one morning with a bag of books. What do you read to the man who has read everything? My modest selection included the old grey paperback edition of *The Strange Case of Dr Jekyll and Mr Hyde*. In a famous 1960 essay, 'Borges and I', he had written of his preferences: 'shilling I like hourglasses, maps, eighteenth-century typography, the roots of words, the taste of coffee and Stevenson's prose.'

The great man, in dark suit, silk tie and white shirt, was manoeuvred into a hotel lounge armchair by his beautiful secretary and travelling companion, Miss María Kodama.

'It's all right, María, thank you. Well, it's good of you to come, see an old man. You've brought something to read, no?'

'Er . . . yes. Ah, do you know Stevenson's *Fables?*'

'Of course. I have just translated them into Spanish, to be published in Buenos Aires.'

'Which one would you like to hear first?'

' "Song of the Morrow" is a good one, no?'

Borges clasped the blackthorn walking-stick before him with both hands and turned his great head to listen to the strange and circular fable. His face was ugly, then beautiful; luminous with changing emotionsemotions. Words were his element, and being readtowasstilla child's pleasure.

'Borges is spellbound,' he pronounced, happily.

There was only time for four Fables before an interviewer from the *Observer* arrived, together with the photographer who had been jailed in Tierra del Fuego during the South Atlantic war.

'You must come back,' said Borges. 'Bring the essay on dreams.'

*

I searched secondhand bookshops and found a single tome that contained 'A Chapter on Dreams': volume XV of the Thistle edition of Stevenson's works. It was late at night when I next saw Borges and María Kodama. They were sitting over coffee and biscuits in the lounge of their Mayfair hotel.

'I got the book, Borges!'

'Begin! Begin!'

'He's looking for the place, Borges,' scolded María in Spanish, as she brushed some crumbs from his tweed overcoat. My hands shook as I scrabbled for the page.

Stevenson's 'A Chapter on Dreams' should be read by anyone interested in the psychology of writing. The 1887 essay for *Scribner's Magazine* notes 'that strong sense of man's double being, which must at times come in and overwhelm the mind of every thinking creature', and it tells us too of Stevenson's closeness to his own dream-world. All his life he was 'an ardent dreamer' (as a child he had nightmares – a novelist's nightmares – of 'swallowing the populous world'). Stevenson dreamed his Spanish vampire story 'Olalla', as well as the notorious *Dr Jekyll and Mr Hyde*.

A partnership with his subconscious made Stevenson a modest author. 'For myself, he wrote in 'A Chapter on Dreams':

> . . . what I call I, my conscience ego . . . the man with the hat and the boots . . . I am sometimes tempted to suppose he is no story teller at all, . . . so that (by that account), the whole of my published fiction should be the single-handed product of some Brownie, some Familiar, some unseen collaborator, whom I keep locked in the back garret while I get all the praise and he but a share of the pudding. I am an excellent adviser . . .; I pull back and I cut down; . . . I hold the pen too;

and I do the sitting at the table, which is about the worst of it; . . . so that, on the whole, I have some claim to share, though not so largely as I do, in the profit of our common enterprise.

Afterwards, I gave Borges the book, and described its colour as he felt it with his hands. He said it was the volume missing from his own set of Stevenson's works. He was either being kind, or it was a pregnant coincidence.

'What can I give you in return?'

He spoke to María Kodama who went upstairs and returned with the gift.

It was a stone.

I put it in my pocket and said goodnight.

*

'Blessed is the man who finds no disillusion when he is brought face to face with a revered writer', wrote Rudyard Kipling after meeting Mark Twain in 1889.

'Why did you not come and read when you were living in Buenos Aires?' Borges asked.

'Because I was shy.'

'I understand. I too am shy.'

When Borges took your arm to be led, it was not like Blind Pew with Jim Hawkins ('I held out my hand, and the horrible, soft-spoken, eyeless creature gripped it in a moment like a vice'). He had the trustfulness of a child and the charm of a witty old gentleman.

The three of us walked to Shepherd Market, to have lunch in a pub on their last day in London. We talked about films, amongst other things, for Borges had always loved the cinema with an Argentine fervour.

María described the décor of the pub; mock Victorian in flock, plush and brass.

'Are there any *hooligans*?' asked Borges eagerly.

There was laughter at our luncheon table, and eventually Borges called for a toast.

'What shall we drink it in, Borges?'

'I think *brown ale* would be appropriate.'

From the Chesterton-coloured, roaring, winking bar I brought back a small bottle of Forest Brown Ale, and filled the three glasses.

'To Stevenson!' said Borges, and we drank.

Some months later, when I was asked if I should like to go off and write about the travels of RLS I jumped at the offer. I remembered Borges's gift then: a small pockmarked pinkish stone from an ancient city.

'A touchstone,' Borges had said, with a chuckle.

'The Touchstone' was a Stevenson Fable we had read. It was a parable about two brothers seeking a stone that would test quality. The younger finds a mirror that only shows 'the seeming of things'; the elder discovers the touchstone that reveals truth.

And the Fable ends with the words of the elder brother: 'I will go forth into the world with my pebble in my pocket.'

SCOTLAND

I

Robert Louis Stevenson was born in Edinburgh, so I went there first. I travelled from London on a cheap railway ticket advertised by purple and black posters with 'InterCity NIGHTRIDER' emblazoned over the image of a highwayman. His three-cocked hat was stark against the full moon, his long hair was kerchiefed and clubbed, and he wore a bright earring, a froth of jabot. Stars filled the bulk of his shoulders, and a night of moonlit clouds framed a dark castle on a glimmering loch.

The reality was grimy sit-up carriages of single men and plural beercans, but the advertisement wrapped it in a purple cloak of bogus adventure, equating Travel with Romance.

In an 1882 essay, 'A Gossip on Romance', Stevenson remembered the books he feasted on as a boy:

> Give me a highwayman and I was full to the brim; a Jacobite would do, but the highwayman was my favourite dish. I can still hear that merry clatter of the hoofs along the moonlit lane; night and the coming of day are still related in my mind with the doings of John Rann or Jerry Abershaw; and the words 'post-chaise', 'the Great North Road', 'ostler' and 'nag' still sound in my ear like poetry.

A Nightrider leaflet with its 'romantic' image was the bookmark in my borrowed copy of *The Life of William Hazlitt*. Young R. L. Stevenson had loved reading the essays of Hazlitt. 'We are all mighty fine fellows nowadays,' he once said, 'but none of us can write like Hazlitt. 'He even planned to write Hazlitt's biography but did not because, as he explained to Edmund Gosse,' When you take the writer from the man there seems so little left.'

This was hardly my problem with Stevenson. You could take the writer from the man and still be left holding the full-blown cloak of romantic myth that flourished in the twenty years between his death and the First World War. It was the story of an artist from Walter Scott's 'old romantic toun', born into a family of engineers who built lighthouses which shone in the wild dark. Born bourgeois and turned bohemian, he quarrelled with his father's faith and ignored the dress-codes of his caste. Brilliant and ill, he wrote romances, ghost stories, adventures like *Treasure Island and Kidnapped.* He had roughed it to California to marry for love, and later sailed off into the tropical Pacific. In faraway Samoa he made his home among barebreasted women with flowers in their hair and muscular warriors who carried axes for cutting off heads. He became Tusitala, the 'Writer of Tales', and when he died, aged forty-four, they buried him like a chief on the top of a mountain.

It was a stirring legend for the Victorians and Edwardians, and there was an enormous demand for Stevenson's writings after his death in 1894. The 28-volume Edinburgh Edition was followed by *Collected Letters* in 1899 and an authorized biography in 1901. By 1914 four more collected works of RLS had been published: the Thistle and Biographical Editions in the USA, and the 20-volume Pentland and 25-volume Swans ton Editions in Britain.

The tide turned in the Great War. Twenty-five years after Stevenson's death, the eighteen-year-old *Times Literary Supplement* argued in a leading article, 'Stevenson Today' (4 December 1919), that

> the only romanticism generally acceptable today is that of experience . . . [RLS's] constant exhortation to manliness has lost its felicity in the strident company of recruiting sergeants . . . Violence is not the fashion. Nor for that matter is optimism . . . we today have had enough of obvious adventure, and 'brute incident' has cost too much in shattered limbs . . .

Bloomsbury disliked Stevenson, but still new editions of his works kept appearing; the 26-volume Vailima was published in 1923, the 35-volume Tusitala in 1924, the 30-volume Skerryvore in 1926, and the 21-volume Lothian in 1927. The sets may have lacked high intellectual status, but they were read in countless homes and schools.

In the 1930s and 40s Stevenson's critical reputation slumped further. Leavisite critics excluded him from their canon of English Literature as a minor or 'second-rate' eccentric. The centenary of his birth in 1950, however, provoked a flurry of interest and led to an excellent biography, *Voyage to Windward* by J. C. Furnas; but by that time Stevenson had become a minority taste. The academic critics had drawn up the map of 'Eng. Lit'. – here the great peaks, there the mighty rivers – and Stevenson did not figure.

When I was at Oxford, my first tutor in English Literature was J. I. M. Stewart. Dr Stewart was the author of Volume XII of the Oxford History of English Literature, *Eight Modern Writers* (1963), covering the period from 1880 to 1945. The Introduction deals with some of the 'writers of talent and sensibility who do not really command our attention'. RLS appears there in a paragraph on 'Escape Literature': 'Stevenson in himself represents an escape . . . He was an invalid, and his best writing – which is superb – lay in the field of romance . . . '

Fashions change, in literature as elsewhere. In the 1970s several biographies and studies of Stevenson were published, and 1980 opened a new epoch in the scholarly appreciation of his work with the publication of Roger Swearingen's invaluable *The Prose Writings of Robert Louis Stevenson*. It lists chronologically every essay, short story, play or novel that RLS wrote or planned to write.

I had bought a secondhand edition of Stevenson for myself, the 26-volume Waverley edition (1924), a book club version of the Skerryvore edition, which gave me over a metre of books for fifty pounds. There it stood on my shelves, tastefully bound in blue and gold, the dead man's chest of work.

I began reading and rereading the books, and found myself in agreement with Borges: 'If you don't like Stevenson, there must be something wrong with you.'

2

Early morning Edinburgh was raw and cold. The street-lamps bloomed orange haloes in the *haar* or sea-fog, but up above there was a faint gleam of blue sky. I crossed Cockburn Street into Advocates Close and walked up to the Old Town, by foggy steps that led past the boarded-up doors and blinded windows of Stevenson's favourite close or alley. This 'old, black city, which was for all the world like a rabbit-warren, not only by the number of its indwellers, but the complication of its passages and holes', was already dying in Stevenson's youth. But it still had its narrow wynds and closes of tall houses, the tenements or *lands* that had once been crammed with all classes and conditions of humanity, rich and poor living hugger-mugger, nobs above and plebs beneath, sharing the smells and the staircase. With its grim medieval slums nineteenth-century Edinburgh deserved Stevenson's epithet 'eminently Gothic'. In his youth he both loved and hated the place.

I got my breath back in the squat *pend* or archway at the top. The yellow light gleamed on the cobbles; fog sloughed off crumbling stone. The faint steps of a postman, the rattle of a letter-box, the clinking whine of an electric milk-float were the only sounds in the shadows. You could look back through the archway from age to youth, from the decaying Old Town across the cleft of glen to the fine crowns of the Georgian New Town. With my heart beating in the sickly streetlight, I recognized the foggy city of Mr Hyde and Dr Jekyll: 'Half a capital, half a country town, the whole city leads a double existence.'

It was growing lighter and the air smelled of coal-smoke from early morning fires. The city is blackened by generations of chimney-soot from coal burned against the cold, hence the nickname 'Auld Reekie'. I walked down George IV Bridge, and past the statue of the wee dog 'Greyfriars Bobby' the road forked right into Forrest Road where I would be staying. People were going to work, and a *peely-wally* specimen came past, paper under arm, coughing over the first cigarette of the day, his pallor a product of diet and climate, too many chips and not enough sun.

I found the building and went into the dark hallway with its dustbins and worn stairs, the cold echoing communal stair-well of typical Edinburgh flats with each step sagging like a granite hammock. My friend James Campbell had given me a key to the flat he was leaving and the door of my new home from home in Edinburgh opened to a smell of cat and damp. But it was perfectly 'situate', as Stevenson used to write, hard by Greyfriars Church, close to the libraries and the University.

[9]

'Scotland is a nation, but not a state,' Jim had said when I picked up the key from him in London. I had an uncertain relationship to the country. My father was born in Glasgow and I had a Scottish name and mien, but I had never lived there, although I had inherited some sentimental pride in the place.

'Byron said he was born half a Scot and became a whole one,' Jim added.

3

Stevenson's 'precipitous city' is so steep and diverse that it seems larger than it actually is. But as Edinburgh grows familiar it becomes more of a town than a city, and it must have seemed small to Robert Louis Stevenson too. His grandfather's house, his parents' home, his school and university all lie within two square miles. Few have written better of Edinburgh than Stevenson, yet there was no statue, street or monument in the city to honour him. Perhaps he would always be a rebellious son to the City Fathers. When *The Scotsman* reviewed Stevenson's *Edinburgh: Picturesque Notes* in 1878, its critic thought him 'a well-bred lounger, a *flâneur* . . . apt to offend every class in its turn'. *Picturesque Notes* is still a fine introduction to the city, and every local guidebook is indebted to it.

I began my search at his paternal grandfather's house. If you stand by the Scott Memorial in Princes Street and face east, you can see engineer Robert Stevenson's contribution to the New Town of Edinburgh. He planned and executed the eastern access to Princes Street, blasting Regent Road out of the rocky south side of Calton Hill, slicing through the graveyard and bridging the glen. It was 1815, and they named it Waterloo Place.

North, towards Leith, is Picardy Place, once a village of French weavers. Facing it is Baxter Place. The house at No. 1, now called Stevenson House, is tucked under the Greenside lee of Calton Hill. At the beginning of the nineteenth century it was a large, rambling house with a paddock and a horse out the back. The paddock is now a car-park. A group of publishers, Oliver & Boyd, Churchill Livingstone, and Longman, are now housed at 1 Baxter Place. In the hall a brass plaque proclaims:

In this building Robert Stevenson, Engineer, lived and worked. From No. 1 he designed and supervised many works including bridges, harbours, prisons and lighthouses, the most famous of these being the Bell Lighthouse. He was the grandfather of Robert Louis Stevenson, Author.

The chessboard floor reminded me of Stevenson's phrase 'chequered with dreams'. In an unfinished history of his ancestors, *Records of a Family of Engineers*, RLS related a ghost story that happened to his grandfather in Baxter Place. Around dusk on Christmas Day 1806, Robert Stevenson, asleep at his desk, dreamed that his foreman-designate for the Bell Rock, one George Peebles, came staggering into the office. Water streamed from his head and body and flooded the room. A few days later Robert Stevenson learned that George Peebles had drowned at the very hour of the dream when Peebles's Orkney ship sank north of Scapa Flow. The hardheaded engineer was startled by his own possession of 'the second sight', a faculty associated with more impressionable people. The author Graham Greene, for instance, who is also of Scottish descent, had a dream of a ship sinking when he was seven on the night of the *Titanic* disaster.

4

All three of Robert Stevenson's talented sons became engineers and inventors. Thomas Stevenson, for example, the father of RLS, built the first wave dynamometer, designed a new set of portable surveying instruments and improved many lighthouse lamps. In common with other members of the family he never took out any patents on his inventions, however lucrative. The Stevensons believed that good work should benefit the world.

Robert Stevenson, the formidable engineer and patriarch of lighthouses, died a few months before his grandson Robert Louis Stevenson was born; but his talent had already been handed on. His eldest son, Alan Stevenson, was a classical scholar, a linguist who read Dante and Cervantes in the original, a music-lover, a correspondent with Wordsworth, and a brilliant engineer. His Skerryvore lighthouse, on the west coast of Scotland, built between

1838 and 1844, remains the most elegant and daring structure of its kind anywhere around Britain. Highly-strung Alan was a poet at his trade, but after a nervous breakdown, he died relatively young. He had one son, Bob.

Thomas Stevenson, Robert's youngest son and RLS's father, began as an idle and impulsive youth. He eventually conformed at the price of distorting his sensibility into fierce contradictions which caused his only son much pain. After Thomas Stevenson's death, RLS described his father's 'blended sternness and softness that was wholly Scottish and at first somewhat bewildering', and his 'profound essential melancholy of disposition'.

The social advancement of the Stevenson family was dramatic: 'We rose from obscurity at a clap.' Robert Stevenson, the Glasgow-born grandfather, hungered for the university education that he never received; though he married the boss's daughter, he was a classic self-made man. His three sons, all engineers of the second generation after the Industrial Revolution, fitted naturally into the Edinburgh professional class, among doctors, lawyers and professors. *Their* sons, comfortably off, could more easily embrace the ideals of 'the gentleman' that Victorian society promoted. But out of this family of engineers there emerged, in the end, a pair of aesthetes.

Before they grew apart, the cousins were almost like twins, or two halves of the same wildly imaginative person. RAM and RL, Robert Alan Mowbray and Robert Louis, Bob and Louis Stevenson cannot really be understood one without the other. They had the same look and style. In their Bohemian days in France, in the 1870s, they were thought of as brothers. Bob was a brilliant talker, an incandescent improviser of fantasies who graduated from Sidney Sussex College, Cambridge, and studied painting in Paris at the same studio as Sargent. Later he became a crony of Whistler's and, according to the *TLS*, 'the best art-critic in England after Ruskin'. All his life, Bob remained true to the Bohemian ideal. Louis studied engineering, then law, at Edinburgh, and found his feet as a writer first through freelance journalism, then short stories, travel books, plays and novels. 'I do not set out to be a poet,' he wrote of a volume of his verse, 'only an all-round literary man.'

RLS's father Thomas Stevenson married Margaret Balfour on 28 August 1848. He was 30 and she was 19, the youngest daughter of the manse at Colinton. She was a pretty girl with a resolute determination to look on the bright side of things.

I walked downhill from Robert Stevenson's house to the place where Thomas and Margaret had first lived together as man and wife, and where their only child had been born. Across the Leith, cars ripped north along Inverleith Terrace, a dusty run-down street of terraced houses whose first stretch on the right is called Howard Place.

A white van was parked with its offside wheels up on the pavement outside 8 Howard Place. The Rentokil van had WOOD-WORM & DRY ROT SERVICE in big red letters on its side. A dozen Norsk Hydro EEC fertilizer bags, choke-full of rubble and lath, slumped against the fence of the untidy garden where rotted floor-boards and old joists lay piled. A workman came out of the front door and whistled his way down the steps past a black plaque –

> Robert Louis Stevenson
> was born in this house
> on 13th November 1850

– and banged open the back door of the van.

'Oh aye, it's dry rot. Ground floor, at the back.'

He took in a bag of tools and I loitered outside. *Ground floor, at the back* was where RLS had been born a hundred and thirty-four years before. The house had two storeys, a sunken basement, and was close enough to the river to be damp. After a couple of years here the Stevensons moved across the road to Inverleith Terrace, and lived there from 1852 to 1857. But 8 Howard Place was still the honoured birthplace, although the spirit had long departed, like the sap from the wood that crumbled to dust in the front garden.

I was one of many pilgrims to this house, which from 1926 to 1963 had been the headquarters of the Robert Louis Stevenson Club and their museum in Edinburgh. The door was ajar; I pushed it open and entered. Beyond the hall two workmen perched on the edge of a hole in the floor. One dipped his brush in pitch and lavished it on the felt-wrapped end of a yellow beam, like tar on a stump of limb. Then together with his mate he slid it across the gap to slot into a wall-socket. It was someone else's house now, with hideous vases in the hall, a sedgy garden at the back. But I felt encouraged. The reconstruction of the house of RLS was under way.

6

In 1854, Thomas Stevenson joined his brother David as engineer to the Northern Lighthouse Board, and by 1857 his position had improved enough to move to a more substantial house. As I made my way there, every step upward was a reminder of the superior social standing of Edinburgh's New Town. I walked alongside Queen Street Gardens, a series of private parks in the Georgian development. No. 17 Heriot Row had a black door with a knocker and letter-box of polished brass. By the bell-push a small notice said 'Private House Not A Museum'. Carved in stone to the right was

The House of Robert Louis Stevenson 1857–1880.

It was a good solid four-storey Georgian terraced house. Curling ironwork rose from the lanceolate railings to support a globe of electric street-light that had once been gas. A brass plaque at the base of the lamp was engraved with the three palm-trees of the Tusitala edition, and the last verse of Stevenson's poem 'The Lamplighter', from *A Child's Garden of Verses*:

> For we are very lucky with a lamp before the door,
> And Leerie stops to light it as he lights so many more;
> And O! before you hurry by with ladder and with light,
> O Leerie, see a little child and nod to him tonight!

Across the road, on the railings of Queen Street Gardens, a sign said this was the first stop on The Robert Louis Stevenson Heritage Trail. I had a vision of blue-rinsed ladies and querulous men in stetsons following it. Like The Shakespeare Country, it was a tourist package; but also proof of RLS's enduring popularity.

The current householder of 17 Heriot Row, Councillor Mrs Kathleen MacFie, JP, was busy battling to hold Corstorphine South-East for the Tory interest in the forthcoming District Council elections, but she was gracious enough to ask me to tea.

Mrs MacFie, a widow lady with a son at the University, was a handsome ebullient woman from County Monaghan with auburn hair just beginning to turn grey. Despite twenty-seven years in Edinburgh her flamboyant Irishness was unmistakable.

'Aren't you *great!*' she exclaimed, meaning 'lucky', when I said what I was doing. We were in the large dining-room on the ground floor, where tea was laid on white linen and drunk from fine china. Noble names were dropped, and when quizzed about my background I found I was playing the highest cards I could muster.

Mrs MacFie – who is now Lady Dunpark – had just come from lecturing to a group of ladies on the subject of Robert Louis Stevenson. She loved the man, and living in his home gave her responsibilities. She was determined that 17 Heriot Row should always be a family home and not degenerate into offices, or become an arid museum. She felt like the honorary chief of the Stevensonians, most of whom she had met, many of whom she had helped.

'James Pope-Hennessy was a Catholic, a homosexual and an alcoholic. My dear, what a combination!'

She threw back her head in a shout of laughter and gold winked in her jaw.

'Roger Swearingen and his wife Sarah were often here while he was researching Stevenson.'

I realized that I knew the room from Stevenson's 'The Misadventures of John Nicholson', an 1885 story about a fat idler who gets mugged and loses £400 of his father's money. 17 Heriot Row was like that 'citadel of the proprieties', the house of stern David Nicholson, 'the iron gentleman' who would not give his son a proper allowance. The layout of the fictional house corresponded with this real one – fanlight over the door, wide hall with ticking clock, dining-room on the right and next to it Mr Nicholson's study. Mrs MacFie confirmed that the corresponding room at Heriot Row had been Thomas Stevenson's study.

We went up the wide, carpeted stairs under the spacious oval skylight. The first-floor drawing-room was L-shaped with three tall windows overlooking Queen Street Gardens. The bookcase held the Vailima and Tusitala editions of Stevenson's works and there was a black-bordered invitation to Thomas Stevenson's funeral in May 1887 (the cortège left from this house and his only son was' too ill to attend). Yet this was not a museum but a drawing-room of comfortable wealth, with a grand piano, flowers, soft cushions and a large drinks tray. While the décor had changed since Thomas Stevenson's day, the standard of living seemed much the same. Robert Louis Stevenson came from a privileged, upper-middle-class background and his father's money supported him while he was learning to write. He did not become effectively independent until his late thirties.

Out on the landing a bowl of pot-pourri and a guest-book occupied the stand jutting out over the stair-well where the housemaid used to place the breakfast tray before opening Mr and Mrs Thomas Stevenson's bedroom door. A two-foot high statue of Stevenson stood on a table; RLS was slim and elegant, with a jacket half-off one shoulder, an open-necked shirt, a sash round his waist, trousers tucked into calf-length, cross-laced boots with spurs.

Mrs MacFie slept in Robert Louis Stevenson's bedroom on the top floor, overlooking the gardens. He had worked late into the night here, reading, writing, hearing the clocks strike and the wheels of carts and cabs. Mrs MacFie pointed across the trees fuzzed with green to Queen Street.

'That was the Simpsons' house. He could semaphore to Wattie from up here.'

It was a sudden and vivid connection. RLS's friend Walter 'Wattie' Simpson, who paddled the other canoe in *An Inland Voyage*, had lived just across the street.

'If you're going to all those places,' said Mrs MacFie, 'you really must spend a night in this house.'

8

Edinburgh is a city of the dead where the freight of the past lies heavy. The living seem oppressed by a sense of inferiority to the deceased and their illustrious works. The Scottish writer Alasdair

Gray has pointed to Edinburgh's 'ruins and remains and monuments – nostalgia made solid'. Young Stevenson was not untypical when he haunted graveyards at one stage of his life.

His feelings were not reverential, however. In the essay 'Old Mortality', written when he was thirty-three, he looked back on the 'acrid fermentation' and 'divine self-pity' of his adolescence with detachment: 'The ground of all youth's suffering, solitude, hysteria and haunting of the grave, is nothing else than naked, ignorant selfishness.'

The Calton New Burial Ground was a necropolitan suburb of crumbling melancholy. Gravel paths led between family tombs that looked like stone jails with iron bars. The Stevenson family grave was a flat-roofed calaboose close by the eastern wall. The sun, from low behind the Castle, shone red through the bars onto a figurehead on its back wall. I pushed open the rust-pitted gates. Kids had broken in before me; rubbish and the remains of a fire littered the floor; graffiti – 'Sandy B is a cow', 'Sandy B is a immature bitch' – were scrawled on the marble.

The grimy bust at the back of the tomb was of Robert Stevenson, and his repaired nose was the whitest part. I copied into my notebook all the family details, of grandfather Robert and grandmother Jane Smith, of uncle Alan and cousin Bob, from the tablets on the walls. In the middle of the floor was a marble slab in memory of Thomas Stevenson

And of his only son
Robert Louis Stevenson
Essayist, Poet, and Novelist
Born at Edinburgh 13th November 1850
Died in Samoa 3rd December 1894
and buried on VAEA mountain

Six months before he died, Stevenson's thoughts returned from Samoa to Edinburgh and to 'my brother Robert Fergusson'. You can see Fergusson's grave in the Canongate churchyard from the Stevenson family tomb. I walked over to it before the sun set.

'Scotland's three Robbies', according to RLS, were Robert Fergusson, Robert Burns and Robert Louis Stevenson. The second of these poets, Robert Burns, 'is the world's, he did it, he came off, he is for ever'ever'. But Stevenson was strongly drawn to Robert Fergusson,' the poor, whitefaced, drunken, vicious boy that raved himself to death in the Edinburgh madhouse'. Fergusson haunted Stevenson; one born in 1750, the other in 1850:

> Ah! what bonds we have – born in the same city; both sickly, both pestered, one nearly to madness, one to the madhouse, with a damnatory creed; both seeing the stars and the dawn, and wearing shoe-leather on the same ancient stones, under the same pends, down the same closes . . . You will never know, nor will any man, how deep this feeling is: I believe Fergusson lives in me.

A rose grew over the neglected grave whose tombstone had been paid for by Robert Burns:

Here lies
ROBERT FERGUSSON, POET
Born September 5th 1750
Died October 16th 1774

No sculptured Marble here nor pompous lay
No storied Urn nor animated Bust
This simple Stone directs Pale Scotia's way
To pour her Sorrows o'er her Poet's Dust.

Stevenson even thought about dedicating the Edinburgh edition of his collected works to Fergusson, before deciding against it: 'I think my wife is the proper person to receive the dedication of my life's work. At the same time – it is very odd, it really looks like transmigration of souls – I feel that I must do something for Fergusson . . . ' From Samoa, Stevenson asked his old friend and agent, Charles Baxter, to walk down the Canongate and inspect the stone:

> If it be at all uncared for, we might repair it and perhaps add a few words of inscription . . .
> This stone, originally erected by Robert Burns, has been repaired at the charges of Robert Louis Stevenson and is by

him re-dedicated to the Memory of Robert Fergusson as the gift of one Edinburgh lad to another.

In spacing this inscription I would detach the name of Fergusson and Burns but leave mine in the text; or would that look like sham modesty and is it better to bring out the three Roberts?

9

I spent two nights in the Stevenson home in Heriot Row, sleeping in the top-floor room at the back which had once belonged to little Louis's nurse, Alison Cunningham. From the window you could see over the Firth of Forth to the twinkling yellow dots of Fife, where she had been born a fisherman's daughter.

'I was an only child and, it may be in consequence, both intelligent and sickly', wrote Stevenson in San Francisco, aged twenty-nine. He had been a chesty little boy. 'My recollections of the long nights when I was kept awake by coughing are only relieved by thoughts of the tenderness of my nurse and second mother . . . Alison Cunningham.' She was the patient angel of his paroxysms:

> I remember with particular distinctness, how she would lift me out of bed, and take me, rolled in blankets, to the window, whence I might look forth into the blue night starred with street-lamps, and see where the gas still burned behind the windows of other sickrooms.

The Victorians and Edwardians loved this image of the devoted nanny cooling the brow of the infant genius, but there was also a less benign side to the nurse known as 'Cummy'. Young Stevenson suffered from 'high-strung religious terrors and ecstasies. It is to my nurse that I owe these last.' He wept for Jesus and was afraid to sleep in case he went to hell. The Calvinist guilt about pleasure that Cummy instilled in him led the child to renounce one story being read to him, in favour of a religious tract. Out went 'The Soldier of Fortune' and 'instead of something healthy about battles, I continued to have my mind defiled with . . . a whole crowd of dismal and morbid devotees . . . I was sentimental, snivelling, goody, morbidly religious . . . '

[19]

The urge to excess in Scotland is directly related to the Puritan heritage. Stevenson could perceive the bad effect of Cummy's 'over-haste to make me a religious pattern'.

> The idea of sin . . . far from repelling, soon exerts an attraction on young minds . . . until the child grows to think nothing more glorious than to be struck dead in the very act of some surprising wickedness . . . And generally, the principal effect of this false, common doctrine of sin, is to put a point on lust.

*

It is often said that Stevenson could not write about women, but there is no doubt he liked and loved women. 'My ideal is the Female Clan', Stevenson wrote in his forties, when he was 'hopelessly entangled in petticoat strings'. From first to last there were women in his life; Cummy mothered him because Maggie Stevenson herself was sickly, and when he came to die in Samoa, he was surrounded by women – his wife, his stepdaughter, and his mother.

In the 1920s RLS's stepson, Lloyd Osbourne, declared: 'Stevenson was emphatically what we would nowadays call a "feminist". Women seemed to him the victims alike of men and nature.' Stevenson's attitude to women was sympathetic; he hated the men who 'bred' their wives, who abused servants and prostitutes, and he could not abide cheap laughter at women who were old or ill-favoured. He wrote: 'A man should never have been suckled at a woman's breast, he should never have slept in a woman's embrace . . . so far to forget what is honourable in sentiment, what is essential in gratitude, or what is tolerable by other men.'

This old-fashioned and chivalric attitude would not perhaps be called 'feminist' today, for the word has evolved since its usage began in the 1890s. But Stevenson's real feeling for women is amply demonstrated in his life and works. In the early sketch 'Nurses' he criticized the institution of the Nanny, despite his personal affection for Cummy. 'I believe in a better state of things, that there will be no more nurses, and that every woman will nurse her own offspring.'

Stevenson saw how being a professional substitute mother could blight a woman's emotional life. And at the end of his own life he would return to this theme in fiction, creating the memorable charac-ter of the elder Kirstie in his unfinished novel *Weir of Hermiston.*

It was only a few minutes' walk from the family home in Heriot Row to the family business in George Street. One morning I walked up to 84 George Street, headquarters of the Northern Lighthouse Board (NLB). I shook hands with John Clark, their Administration Officer, who was taking me out to the Bell Rock.

The NLB was two hundred years old in 1986. Under its motto *In Salutem Omnium* (For the Safety of All) it maintained beacons, buoys and lights all around Scotland, including fifty-four permanently manned lighthouses. The NLB had two outstanding Pillar Rocks – everybody's idea of what a lighthouse *should* look like – the Bell Rock and Skerryvore.

Robert Stevenson's grandson wrote proudly:

> There is scarce a deep sea light from the Isle of May north about to Lerwick, but one of my blood designed it, and I have often thought that to find a family to compare with ours in the promise of immortal memory we must go back to the Egyptian Pharaohs.

It was on the Egyptian coast that Alexander the Great sited his city Alexandria in 322BC, and on the island just offshore – 'Pharaoh's island' – that he built the first great lighthouse or *pharos* which was one of the wonders of the ancient world.

I leaned on the portside rail of MV *Pharos*, the Commodore Ship of the NLB, and the eighth of its vessels to bear that name. We were slowly sinking in the sea-locks at Leith. The docks seemed deserted. The offshore oil barges *Bergen* and *Neptune* lay moored at a silent wharf, and behind them the bare wide acreage of the Henry Robb shipyard was an empty wasteland. The cranes stood motionless. On the wharf to starboard, rows of stacked pipes for the northern oil-fields gleamed like gun-barrels in the sunlight. Fishing and ship-building were dying here. The ship sank lower.

The *Pharos* is also known as the Commissioners' Yacht. The Lord Advocate and the Solicitor General for Scotland, three Lord Provosts, one Provost, a District Council Chairman, half a dozen Sheriffs-Principal, and a few gentlemen from the marine trade, use the ship on their Annual Tour of Inspection. It is their annual perk for overseeing the NLB's work, and every year there is a dignified scramble as they fight for a good berth and a place at the silver-decorated table with its good food and plenty of drink.

A steward led the way down a passage with teak and brass handrails to the Smoke Room. The cabins were comfortably upholstered in blue leather, with large portholes and belted curtains, big washbasins and triple vanity mirrors. Beyond the Smoke Room, some leather-cased binoculars hung from their straps alongside half a dozen navy-blue boat-capes of fine mackintosh with velvety moleskin collars.

I took a pair of binoculars on deck, and as the ship sank down in the sea-lock, I watched the landmarks of Edinburgh shimmer through the smoke of Leith under a clear blue sky.

The *Pharos* slipped quietly into the Firth of Forth. A steward served coffee in the Smoke Room. While someone told a long story, I noticed a crew member passing by the porthole. His beard, long hair and silver earring suddenly framed was like a daguerreotype of a buccaneer from *Treasure Island*. I remembered how Stevenson drew on his family's lighthouse experience for his fiction. In *Treasure Island*, for instance, Jim Hawkins is in an apple-barrel when he overhears the treachery of Long John Silver, whose two-faced character was partly drawn from a seaman called Soutar who had been employed at the Bell Rock. RLS tells the story in *Records of a Family of Engineers*:

> Soutar first attracted notice as the mate of a praam (stone-lighter) at the Bell Rock, and rose gradually to be captain of the *Regent*. He was active, admirably skilled in his trade, and a man incapable of fear . . . He usually dined on Sundays in the cabin . . . artfully combining the extreme of deference with a blunt and seamanlike demeanour. My father and uncles . . . were far from being deceived; and my father, indeed, was favoured with an object-lesson not to be mistaken. He had crept one rainy night into an apple-barrel on deck, and from this place of ambush overheard Soutar and a comrade conversing in their oilskins. The smooth sycophant of the cabin had wholly disappeared, and the boy listened with wonder to a vulgar and truculent ruffian.

The same book, which Stevenson worked on between 1891 and 1893, also tells of the Bell Rock where the *Pharos* was heading. Once known as the Inchcape Reef, it was a treacherous brown rock cropping up in a principal sea-lane eleven miles south-east of Arbroath. At low water a fifth of its 2000-foot length is above water, but at high tide it is invisible, submerged to a depth of between ten and sixteen feet. This disappearing act had wrecked many ships and prevented any warning signal being placed on the rock's slippery surface.

Robert Stevenson took up the challenge. In early 1800 he went to survey the rock at low tide; while he took measurements his crewmen scavenged metal jetsam from among the crabs and seaweed, 'pieces of a kedge anchor and a cabin stove, crowbars, a hinge and lock of a door, a ship's marking-iron, a piece of a ship's caboose, a soldier's bayonet, a cannon ball, several pieces of money, a shoe buckle and the like'. Robert Stevenson soon began building little models of the stone tower he dreamed of building.

Military spending dominated the Tory budgets of those Napoleonic years. It was not until 1806 that Parliament passed a Bill enabling the Commissioners to raise the £42,000 needed for the scheme. A Royal Navy prize-ship, a captured Prussian fishing dogger, was fitted out as the first *Pharos*, which operated as a 'flotel' for the workers. Aberdeen granite was quarried and cut into 2-to 6-ton blocks and carted to the base at Arbroath, where local workmen were issued with special passes to protect them from roving Navy press-gangs. Work was only possible in summer, and so the historic project began in earnest on 16 August 1807. It was the first time in British industrial history that men were to live and work 'offshore' in the North Sea on an engineering scheme. The roughnecks and toolpushers of today's huge oil and gas platforms and rigs are the heirs of Stevenson's pioneers.

The work lasted four summers. A smithy was set up on the rock complete with forge, vice and bench, in order to repair the tools. The blacksmith with his giant leather bellows became the site's unofficial clocker-out; when the rising tide frothed up under his grate and quenched the fire, the hiss of steam was the signal to down tools and head for the boats. The work was hard, and each man's daily ration included 1½ lb. of beef and six pints of small beer. It was often dangerous, too. Once sixteen men were trapped on the rock, crowding up to the highest point (still called Stevenson's Last Hope). Himself dry-mouthed with fear, Robert Stevenson had to lap a palm of water from a rock-pool before he could speak to the men. Luckily they were rescued by a pilot called James Spink, bringing unexpected mail.

The light that burns to this day was first lit on 1 February 1811, encased in a tower which is 115 feet high and weighs 2076 tons.

*

In the early nineteenth century the greatest painter England has ever produced, J. M. W. Turner, came out in a boat to sketch the Bell Rock lighthouse. The widely reproduced engraving of his drawing – a gigantic wave futilely lashing the proud tower, spray blowing like smoke – catches a heroic romanticism which stands for many things: Art over Nature, Man against the Elements, Light in Darkness, Order from Chaos, 'Let There Be Light', 'For Those In Peril On The Sea'.

The lighthouse also attracted writers. The very first author that RLS met as a boy was R. M. Ballantyne, author of *The Coral Island* (1857) among other works. Ballantyne was researching his novel *The Lighthouse*, which was set around the Bell Rock, and he spent two weeks living there. The young Stevenson found him 'cheerful, good-looking, active, melodious and courageous' and later declared that 'this sight of Mr Ballantyne greatly strengthened an inborn partiality to authors'. He fantasized about future encounters with the writer of adventure books:

> . . . and my ideal, turning to me with that black-bearded, white-toothed smile I had so much admired when it was addressed to others . . . recognized at last my superiority to my fallacious cousins.

11

'You can see the Rock now.'

I put my book down and went out on deck. Dark blue stretched to light blue, and at the band of haze where sea married sky the pink granite shaft of the tower curved to the vertical. Pale as flesh, it wobbled and danced in the binocular lenses as the ship trembled in the cold choppy sea. I heard faint bells, then the rattling clank of the anchor chain. A tiny figure in yellow climbed down the rungs set in the bottom of the tower and then seemed to walk on the water, safe on the invisible catwalk they call the grating.

The Captain said I could go in the work-boat. It was lowered from the davits and, wedged in its bow, I watched the crew loading supplies over the ship's side. The small boat was held by bow and stern ropes but it plunged and bucked like a recalcitrant donkey. It was nimble work stowing the sliding boxes and rolling kegs as we heaved and dropped. 'Mind your fingers,' cried the coxswain, as my white hand gripped the clinkered gunwale swinging in to thud against the ship's iron plates. The last man dropped from the Jacob's ladder and the tarpaulin was dragged over. The bubbling engine slowly moved us out of the shadow and shelter of the ship. Sun and spray burst on the canvas dodgers, and the glistening oilskins and black and white *Pharos* shone out against the sky. We jounced through a jabble of waves towards the lighthouse. Green slime clung to its base. Empty white water kegs were lowered by hoist down the curving tower which stood sharp against the blue sky.

We landed at the Bell Rock. The sea sloshed over the grating, and booted sailors began dragging casks of drinking water to the base of the tower.

'Right,' said the Second Mate, 'you've got five minutes.'

I took Borges's pebble from my pocket, rapped it against the granite and started climbing the iron rungs, not stopping to look down or around, up the curving side through a trapdoor to the platform. The lightkeeper working the hoist greeted me: 'You must be fookin' mad to coom 'ere.'

I crawled through into the building and on up. It must be like living in a bottle; all the rooms are circular, each with its space organized and ship-shape. I carried on climbing up past machinery and cupboards, through a series of hinged steel hatches. On, up, hand over hand. I emerged through the floor in a sunny kitchen, red formica fitted to the round, stools, a colour TV, sink, kettle; but there was no time for tea. I had to go on, gasping and wobbly, back into the dark, up through the topmost floor of the tower, and suddenly it was all light. Stunning, blinding light. A lighthouse gives it out, but the triangular panes in the glass dome also let in a great blaze of sun and sky. At the top, over a hundred feet up, I was the highest thing for miles of blue.

*

Sir Walter Scott had visited the Bell Rock, a hundred and seventy years before. He also came on the Commissioners' yacht, just after the successful and anonymous publication of *Waverley*. But his guide was Robert Stevenson himself, who described their visit on Saturday, 12 July 1814:

> I proposed an early landing and to breakfast in the lighthouse
> . . . The steward was accordingly sent off with his baskets and
> laid on the table of the library or Strangers Room a good
> Scotch breakfast . . . This over, the album kept at the
> lighthouse was produced for signature, but when it came
> round the table to Sir Walter, Mr Erskine laid his hand upon
> the page and said: 'Now, Scott, you must give us something
> more than Walter Scott.' He . . . rather seemed uneasy at the
> proposal; and rising from the table, he turned to one of the
> windows for a short space . . . Sir Walter at length took the pen
> and wrote the following beautiful and expressive lines:

> *Pharos loquitur*
> Far in the bosoms of the deep,
> O'er these wild shelves my watch I keep,
> A ruddy gem of changeful light
> Bound on the dusky brow of night.
> The seaman bids my lustre hail
> And scorns to strike his timorous sail.

*

We dined in the saloon of MV *Pharos* as she headed back to the Firth of Forth. After dinner, an old snuff-horn was passed around the company at table, a ram's horn capped with silver and a mounted grey stone. Round the mouth of the horn was engraved: 'From Sir W. Scott in remembrance of his voyage in the Northern Lights yacht 1814.' I dug out a pinch with the little bone spoon.

It was dark when the *Pharos* anchored off Granton and the small boat ferried us ashore to climb over the pilot cutter to the old jetty steps. A long Mercedes with a chauffeur was waiting for the Bell Rock Lightkccpcrs who had just been relieved after four weeks 'on'. 'Nothing but the best for our men,' said the NLB's Mr Clark.

Back in Hcriot Row, the pass-key let me in Robert Louis Stevenson's old front door. In Cummy's room, overlooking the Firth, I could not sleep for a long time. After twelve hours afloat, my inner car still moved to the swell of the sea.

12

I wanted to sec the garden of Stevenson's maternal grandfather's house at Colinton, a few miles south-west of Edinburgh. On the way, the bus passed St Andrew's College of Education which had tennis courts in front of an ornate nineteenth-century façade. It was a famous place in Edinburgh literary history.

Once Craiglockhart Hydropathic Establishment, it became Craiglockhart War Hospital in the First World War, and under the administration of Dr W. H. R. Rivers came to specialize in the treatment of battle shock. Siegfried Sassoon was sent here after he had protested against the war in July 1917 and thrown the ribbon of his Military Cross into the Mersey. His meeting with Wilfred Owen, editor of the hospital magazine, was a boon for English poetry. Helped by Sassoon, Owen produced some of his best work at Craiglockhart, including 'Dulce Et Decorum Est'. Wilfred Owen was happy in Edinburgh; but he returned to France and was killed a week before the war ended. His family in Shropshire got the news of his death as Armistice bells pealed for victory and peace. His poem 'Anthem for Doomed Youth' was written during his stay at Craiglockhart:

> What passing-bells for these who die as cattle?
> Only the monstrous anger of the guns.
> Only the stuttering rifles' rapid rattle
> Can patter out their hasty orisons.

Further down the road lay the huge Redford Barracks. Two Argyll and Sutherland soldiers at the gate carried self-loading rifles, and the black ribbons of their glengarries danced on their khaki shoulders. A guardhouse notice declared the State of Alertness as BIKINI.

Bikini was an atoll in the Marshall Islands in the Pacific where, after the Second World War, some two dozen nuclear tests took place, including the explosion of the first hydrogen bomb. I thought about Bikini atoll and the foolish French car-engineer, Louis Reard, who named his two-piece bathing suit after the 1946 explosion which blew the middle out of a Pacific island.

Stevenson sailed to the Marshall Islands in 1890 on the ship *Janet Nichol*. I wondered what he would think of them now; places like Kwajalcin, whose huge ring of atoll was depopulated to make a target for MX missiles test-fired from Vandcnbcrg Air Force Base some four thousand miles away in California.

On the outskirts of Colinton there was a butcher's shop that sold *biltong*, the dried meat that Americans call 'jerky', from the Inca word *chcharqui*. I bought some for the taste of my own childhood in East Africa. Settlers' sons had regularly brought *biltong* back to the sandstone prep-school in the Rift Valley, where we little 'white wog' savages stoned each other under the motto *Anglus In Africa Sto*. But it was Stevenson's boyhood I was seeking now, in the garden of Colinton Manse, the house of his mother's family.

*

Margaret Isabella 'Maggie' Stevenson was born a Balfour in 1839. The twelfth of thirteen children, she was the fourth and youngest daughter of the Reverend Lewis Balfour and his wife Henrietta, née Smith. The Balfours were of good provincial stock. Balfours had been lairds at Pilrig since 1718, with ancestors who occasionally made their mark on Scottish history: a bearded minister; a Covenanting fanatic; a family fortune lost in the doomed Scottish colony at Darien in Panama. Balfour was what the Scots term a *kent* name, a 'known' name in a country where names are tribal maps across time and space.

'The Balfours, I take it, were plainly Celts', Stevenson wrote late in his life, 'their name shows it – the "cold croft" it means.' RLS had long been interested in the relationship between heredity and character. He called it 'the romance of destiny'. In a letter of May 1891, he wrote: 'The ascendant hand is what I feel most strongly; I am bound in and in with my forebears.'

His own name was made up from the names of his two grandfathers. He was christened Robert *Lewis Balfour* Stevenson, one name kernelled in the other, the moralist inside the engineer. He chose to become Robert Louis Stevenson; the middle name was still pronounced *Lewis* though spelled in the French style. His grandfather, Lewis Balfour, son of the 3rd Laird of Pilrig, became Minister of Colinton Parish in 1835 and remained so until his death in 1860, when the family dispersed and little Lewis Stevenson's visits to the Manse came to an end.

13

Colinton Manse was big and grey, with a bay window over the lawn and six sash windows facing the church. Set in an oxbow of the River Leith as it carved out Colinton Dell, it reminded me of certain English Regency vicarages, with their large trees, lawns and rhododendrons. But in Scotland nature is harsher; winter had shabbied the grounds, and though the river ran musically it did not seem an ideal place for the frail and chesty.

Mrs Johnston, the Minister's wife, came out to weed, in headscarf and coat, carrying a cardboard box for a trug. I introduced myself.

'Somebody else came for a book, about ten years ago.'

'James Pope-Hennessy?'

'Yes, I think that was him.'

'It was the last book he wrote before his, ah, unfortunate end.'

The author of the 1974 biography of Stevenson had been murdered by a rent-boy.

Mrs Johnston went back into the hall and rummaged in her handbag for a small booklet.

'It's the last copy I'm afraid, so you can't take it away.'

Colinton Manse and RLS had selections from the various pieces that Stevenson wrote about his childhood at Colinton. 'Out of my reminiscences of life in that dear place all the morbid and painful elements have disappeared. That was my golden age – *et ego in Arcadia vixi.*' It is the first important place in the imagination of this most topographical of writers, where he felt an 'animal' happiness:

> I have been happier since . . . but I have never again been happy in the same way . . . The sense of sunshine, of green leaves, and of the singing of birds, seems never to have been so strong in me as in that place.

As a young boy, Stevenson played in the garden; sometimes alone, but often with his sallow young cousins back from India where his Balfour uncles flourished. He was an excited and intensely imaginative child: 'I usually insisted on the lead, and was invariably exhausted to death by evening.' At twenty-nine he could still remember 'what a fury of play would descend upon me'.

The garden at Colinton is a perfect size for a child, almost an island, in a rough rectangle of eighty yards by forty. A low wall on the south and east sides protects it from the river, and to the west a long wall holds back the graveyard. I ducked through the shrubbery by the gate to a gap in the mossy granite wall:

> Over the borders, a sin without pardon
> Breaking the branches and crawling below,
> Out through the breach in the wall of the garden,
> Down through the banks of the river, we go.

Stevenson's poem 'Keepsake Mill' in *A Child's Garden of Verses* continues:

> Here is the mill with the humming of thunder,
> Here is the weir with the wonder of foam,
> Here is the sluice with the race running under –
> Marvellous places, though handy to home!

There had been a snuff-mill behind the wall, one of seventy along the Leith; it burned down in 1916. The untidy bank and the steep slope across the stream was still exactly as he had described it.

Across the gravel of the drive there was a yew tree. My footsteps crackled on a carpet of brown needles:

> Below the yew – it still is there –
> Our phantom voices haunt the air
> As we were still at play,
> And I can hear them call and say:
> *'How far is it to Babylon?'*

Beyond this tree ran the wall of the churchyard, where 'after nightfall "spunkies" might be seen to dance, at least by children'.

[30]

Below the wall had been a path called 'the Witches' Walk' where young Stevenson had pressed his ear to the stones to listen for the voices of the dead. No child with a stick of a sword could run there now. Holly, laurel and elder had grown up into thick brush, clammy with cobwebs. Near the kirk's chancel elder roots had broken part of the graveyard wall which had now collapsed in a tumble of rocks and dirt.

I found myself looking for some carved initials in the wall, or even a long lost toy. Such an absurdly literal quest had been foreseen by the author of *A Child's Garden of Verses* in the final poem, 'To Any Reader'; in lines addressed to 'You, hunting in the garden rows . . . Where other children used to play':

> So you may see, if you but look
> Through the windows of this book,
> Another child, far, far, away
> And in another garden, play.
> But do not think you can at all,
> By knocking on the window, call
> That child to hear you. He intent
> Is still on his play-business bent.
> He does not hear, he will not look,
> Nor yet be lured out of this book.
> For long ago, the truth to say,
> He has grown up and gone away,
> And it is but a child of air
> That lingers in the garden there.

14

When Stevenson wrote *A Child's Garden of Verses* (first published in 1885), he was as far from his childhood as I was from mine, in his early to mid-thirties, and living elsewhere, at Hyères and Bourne-mouth. What seems natural and simple and childlike is actually the product of art and a complex adult mind. However, the verses' charm is not condescending. They are entirely believable as a child's view of the world, and catch a youthful mixture of egotism and wonder in a startling and original way. Nor is the melancholy of some of the poems an adult preserve: even a young child has a notion of the passing and the passed.

What was new and fresh in its time swiftly became familiar, and within thirty years it would be sneered at in the *TLS* and described as tired. Yet generations of adults and children have read or heard the poems and felt them quite true to their own experience. When my wife read the poems as an asthmatic six-year-old, confined to bed, she thought they were all about her.

Some poems evolved over the years.

> The world is so great and I am so small
> I do not like it at all, at all

became in print the ambiguous 'Happy Thought':

> The world is so full of a number of things
> I'm sure we should all be as happy as kings.

*

I jumped over the wall on to a garden rubbish tip; the river bounced over the rocks, swirling like bitter:

> Dark brown is the river,
> Golden is the sand.
> It flows along for ever,
> With trees on either hand.

I threw stones after a bobbing stick that drifted away down the wooded dell; floating on down RLS's 'dirty Water of Leith' towards Craiglockhart, Slateford, Stenhouse and Murrayfield, Dean Village and Stockbridge, through Canonmills by the house where RLS was born, on north of Bonnington and the Balfour House at Pilrig, past the Custom House, down into the harbour at Leith and from the Firth of Forth out to the sea:

> Away down the river
>   A hundred miles or more,
> Other little children
>   Shall bring my boats ashore.

*

Maggie Stevenson had written of her son at seven: 'Louis is getting very wild and like a boy.' He was an imaginative savage. 'Once, as I lay, playing hunter, hid in a thick laurel, and with a toy gun upon my arm, I worked myself so hotly into the spirit of my play, that I think I can still see the herd of antelope come sweeping down the lawn and round the deodar; it was almost a vision.' In 'A Gossip on Romance' Stevenson wrote: 'Fiction is to the grown man what play is to the child.'

I stood on the lawn listening to the rushing river, a wood-pigeon somewhere in the tall trees. One summer evening, when the parlour was being cleaned and all its furniture and contents were ranged on the lawn, Stevenson's Aunt Jane showed him the wing-bone of an albatross, and she 'told me of its largeness, and how it slept upon the wing above the vast Pacific, and quoted from the *Ancient Mariner*: ' . . . With my cross-bow/I shot the albatross . . . ' I do not believe anything so profoundly affected my imagination.'

I paced the lawn of green and springy turf. 'Never dare to tell me anything about "green grass",' Stevenson once scolded young Adelaide Boodle, correcting the writing exercise she had done for him in Bournemouth. 'Tell me how the grass was flecked with shadows. I know perfectly well that grass is green. So does everybody else in England. What you have to learn is something different from that. Make me see what it was that made your garden distinct from a thousand others.'

The ghosts of his lost childhood made Colinton different.

15

Outside the kirk there was another Robert Louis Stevenson Heritage Trail noticeboard. I read how at Colinton 'Louis enjoyed playing with the toy soldiers his aunt had bought him, setting them upon the dining-room table to recreate famous battles . . . '

He also played these games in Edinburgh, in 'the purely visionary state' shared with his cousin Bob, when Louis was five and Bob eight. 'We had countries (his was Nosingtonia, mine Encyclopaedia) where we ruled and made wars and inventions, and of which we were perpetually drawing maps.'

Most small boys play with soldiers. Young Graham Greene, for example, used H. G. Wells's book on the subject, *Little Wars*, to organize his nursery battles. Stevenson, however, never really stopped. In his thirties, he drew chalk maps on the floor of a Davos attic for the intricate *Kriegspiel* or war game with his twelve-year-old stepson, Lloyd Osbourne. The campaigns took weeks, with imaginary dispatches, dice and foot-rules, tin soldiers and carts of printers' ems for ammunition. Edmund Gosse remembered meals prolonged 'while General Stevenson marched his troops between the mustard pot and the salt box, and dashed out to crush a flanking party from behind a dish of olives'.

The noticeboard said . . . 'as an adult, he never lost his pleasure in war games, and it is said that had his health allowed RLS might have become a soldier'.

In Davos, Stevenson read Sir Edward Hamley's *The Operations of War Explained and Illustrated* and wrote to his father: '"O that I had been a soldier" is still my cry.' It was a common enough cry in the age of Empire. But if Stevenson had lived to seventy he would have survived the First World War, and seen 'honour' and 'glory' trampled by total war into so much blood and mud. *A Child's Garden of Verses* (1885) has a poem, 'The Dumb Soldier', innocently imagining the experiences of a tin soldier hidden under the lawn of Colinton Manse. Some thirty years later, in the Great War, Adelaide Boodle, the girl who had once written the 'green grass' exercise for Stevenson, gave young friends in the Bournemouth Officer Training Corps some of Stevenson's old lead soldiers, 'which I asked them to bury in the mud of the trenches.'

*

I walked round the graveyard of Colinton kirk. Stevenson had wondered, in his essay 'The Manse', what he might have inherited from his ancestor the Reverend Doctor Balfour: 'even as I write the phrase he moves in my blood, and whispers words to me, and sits efficient in the very knot and centre of my being.' RLS was intrigued by 'this *homunculus* or part-man of mine that walked about in the eighteenth century with Dr Balfour in his youth.' He believed that in family history we could 'be reminded of our ante-natal lives. Our conscious years are but a moment in the history of the elements that build us.'

This consciousness of heredity, which is also a consistent theme in the poetry of Jorge Luis Borges, would recur to Stevenson when he came to write a pair of adventure novels set in a crucial period of Scottish history. Stevenson never fathered a son; he only created characters. It is interesting that he should choose to give his family name to one of these fictional offspring: the eighteenth-century hero of *Kidnapped and Catriona* is called David Balfour.

I found the Balfour tomb north of the kirk. It was in the Scottish unadorned style – three stone walls, a plain doorway, a floor of cinders open to the sky, and a tablet, green with age, that read

UMBRA LABITUR ET NOS UMBRAE

It was In Memoriam grandfather Reverend Lewis Balfour DD; grandmother Henrietta Scott Smith; four dead infants; James Melville Balfour, civil engineer, drowned off the coast of New Zealand in 1869; and the Balfour uncles who went to India.

A new stone stood proud from the right-hand wall, with cut letters sharp in the morning light:

In memory of
Lt-Cdr David Ian Balfour RN
killed in action in
HMS Sheffield
The Falklands
1982

The date of death of Stevenson's distant cousin was not on the stone, but I already knew it. On 4 May 1982, in revenge for the sinking of the cruiser ARA *Belgrano*, the destroyer HMS *Sheffield* was hit by an Exocet missile; and David Balfour was among the dead.

I stood on the threshold of the Balfour tomb for a long while. Beyond the wall, the wintry sun shone on the trees of Colinton Dell. A dark cedar of Lebanon tilted its planes in the wind. The ripple of gunfire from the Army ranges on the Pentlands faded away, and you could hear the river again.

16

The upper-middle-class families of Edinburgh and Glasgow traditionally took a house for the summer at one of Scotland's many resorts. The Stevensons visited several resorts, but one which made a lasting impression on RLS was North Berwick in East Lothian (formerly Haddingtonshire). He described it in 'The Lantern-Bearers', an essay written some twenty-five years after his first visit in 1862. Far away, in a small wintry town in upstate New York, he clearly recalled the fishing village with its drying nets, scolding wives, the smell of fish and seaweed, and the blowing sands. He remembered the small 'shops with golf-balls and bottled lollipops; another shop with penny pickwicks (that remarkable cigar) and the *London Journal*, dear to me for its startling pictures, and a few novels'.

North Berwick was then confined to a rocky spit between two sandy bays, with sand-dunes full of rabbits and gulls to the west and a range of cliffs to the east. It overlooks the Firth of Forth with its little islets and, prominent among them, the great Bass Rock, 'tilted seaward like a doubtful bather, the surf ringing it with white'. The Bass is still the home of thousands of gannets, or 'solan-geese' as Stevenson called them, 'hanging round its summit in a great and glittering smoke'.

In *Catriona* (1893), David Balfour is imprisoned on the Bass Rock. His jailer (whose name, Andie Dale, is by way of a family joke – the Dales were cousins of the Stevensons) tells him 'The Tale of Tod Lapraik', a creepy short story of the supernatural in the Scots vernacular. Tod Lapraik is a warlock: while he sits in a *dwam* or trance by his weaver's loom at home in the town, his *fetch* or evil double can be seen on top of the Bass Rock, where it 'lowped and flang and danced like a daft quean at a waddin". Sandie Fletcher loads his fowling-piece with lead and 'a siller tester' (a silver sixpence), 'bein' mair deidly again bogles'. When he fires at the fetch on the Rock, it vanishes, and Tod Lapraik is found 'a bluidy corp' at home in North Berwick, with a silver sixpence in his heart.

North Berwick has changed. When I visited it there were many more 'villas', golf-courses on the once wild links, and a swimming pool in the rocks near the harbour. But some things are just as they were described in 'The Lantern-Bearers'. The hollyhocks and lupins in the small gardens are still 'more than usually bright' in the clear sea air, and the rocky foreshore where Stevenson had paddled and fished for 'podleys' or young pollack is as yet unspoiled. I went to The Quadrant, a few minutes from the small harbour, a terrace of small houses with a clear view of the Bass from the upper windows. Local belief has it that the Stevensons once rented No. 6, but there was no indication of this fact, and it was not on the 'Heritage Trail'. Few of the inhabitants of that pleasant and placid little town appeared to have read 'The Lantern-Bearers'.

Stevenson's most vivid memories of North Berwick were of life in the open air. He was thirteen or fourteen years old, and climbed the rocks, explored, went swimming ('the sand scourging your bare hide, your clothes thrashing abroad from under their guardian stone'); he enjoyed digging houses in the sand-dunes, having a secret smoke, lighting fires with driftwood and 'Crusoeing' ('a word that covers all extempore eating in the open air'). Sometimes he and the other boys would climb North Berwick Law, an old volcanic plug just south of the town, to see the whale's jaw-bone at the top and the view for miles around. He went riding on donkeys and ponies, racing his cousins. He may not have been a robust child, but he adored activity. 'I was the best player of hide-and-seek going.' Severe illness came much later in life, and even then, he hated immobility. Frail and sickly at Hyères, aged thirty-three, he still sustained his boyhood fantasies. He wrote self-mockingly, but revealingly, about growing old to Cosmo Monkhouse in 1884:

> Never! After all boyhood's aspirations, and youth's immoral daydreams, you are condemned to sit down, grossly draw in your chair to the fat board, and be a beastly Burgess till you die. Can it be? . . . Shall we never shed blood? This prospect is too grey . . . To confess plainly, I had intended to spend my life (or any leisure I might have from Piracy upon the high seas) as the leader of a great horde of irregular cavalry, devastating whole valleys . . .

'The Lantern-Bearers' suggests that everyone has such fantasies: 'The clergyman, in his spare hours, may be winning battles, the farmer sailing ships, the banker reaping triumph in the arts . . . ' Stevenson thought that these ideal other selves were a person's 'set treasure'; and Chesterton wrote of Stevenson that 'the true private life is to be sought not in Samoa but in *Treasure Island*; for where the treasure is, there is the heart also.' The invalid writer had the heart of a boy and could 'still, looking back, see myself . . . turning in the saddle to look back at my whole command (some five thousand strong) following me at the hand-gallop up the road out of the burning valley: this last by moonlight.'

17

Stevenson's first 'book' was a 16-page pamphlet, privately printed by his father, called *The Pentland Rising*. It recounted an incident in the hills just south-west of Edinburgh, in a historical period that would continue to fascinate him. He had been writing stories set in the late seventeenth century since he was thirteen, and for his bicentennial account of the Covenanter uprising he read authentic narrative sources; a habit he would stick to when preparing his later historical novels. 'After all', he wrote, aged twenty, 'what one wants to know is not what people did, but why they did it – or rather, why they *thought* they did it; and to learn that, you should go to the men themselves.'

The Covenanters were Puritan fundamentalists who saw themselves as the Lord's Chosen People. They had refused to accept bishops or take the Oath of Allegiance after the restoration of the monarchy in 1660. They held their own religious meetings or 'conventicles' up in the hills, and were fined and persecuted by the State. The first rising was bloodily put down at the Battle of Rullion Green on 28 November 1666; fifty Covenanters were killed in battle and thirty were later executed in Edinburgh.

When he was forty-three, RLS looked back on *The Pentland Rising* as 'trash', 'an absurdity written by a schoolboy', and he did not want it reprinted in his collected works. However, it foreshadowed many of his characteristic interests and techniques as a writer of historical novels. *The Pentland Rising* also shows the topographical novelist-in-the-making. Stevenson's imagination required a map or an actual place to start working. His fictions are rooted in real terrains like the Pentlands, where he could walk for himself over the battlefield at Rullion Green and put to use what Virginia Woolf would later call his 'exact, quick glance at visible things'. *The Pentland Rising* also shows a capacity to choose the telling detail. When Covenanter Paton tried to kill General Tam Dalyell of Binns, his first shots 'hopped off Dalyell's buff coat . . . into his boot'; and so Paton had to cram silver coins into his horse pistol as a last expedient against the man he feared was the Devil.

Stevenson was on the side of the underdogs in this conflict, the Covenanters, and throughout his life he would support those who, with 'paucity of numbers and Spartan poverty of life', defied the big battalions. In the late nineteenth century, the age of imperialism, he would see and sympathize with other causes ground under by the wheel of history: American Indians, Polynesians and, especially Samoans, the people among whom he ended his days, at a time when they were struggling for independence against three contending empires – British, American and German.

Written at the age of sixteen, *The Pentland Rising* may also be read as siding with the sons against the fathers.

18

The Pentland Hills themselves began to play an important part in Stevenson's life from 1867, when his parents rented a house in Swanston, a village at their foot, as a summer cottage. You could close the black door of 17 Heriot Row and walk to Swanston in a couple of hours. Stevenson did so regularly and described the walk in the last chapter of *Edinburgh: Picturesque Notes*. In his day the villa-builders had only come part way; he recorded 'the chisels tinkling on a new row of houses'. It is all built up now, through Bruntsfield and Morningside, streets of neat dwellings all the way to Fairmilehead and Bowbridge. Where RLS saw 'sea-birds skim the tree-tops and fish among the furrows of the plough', there is now a roundabout and the plastic Pentlander Restaurant. In sight of Swanston, a Glasgow company has erected a large sign beside Swanston Road: 'Building Commencing Soon! Homes With The Built-In Plus!' Swanston Road now not only crosses the valley but also a dual carriageway and a double course of giant electricity pylons.

Swanston itself is still a village of thatched and whitewashed cottages. A bench on the green is dedicated to the memory of the poet Edwin Muir, who liked to come and meditate here. Muir wrote, in 1931: 'Stevenson has simply fallen out of the procession. He is still read by the vulgar, but he has joined that band of writers on whom, by tacit consent, the serious critics have nothing to say.'

Swanston Cottage, which the Stevensons rented, is not directly signposted by the Heritage Trail and has a large 'PRIVATE' notice on the gate. Stevenson loved the house – set apart, low built, facing the hills, with a walled garden surrounded by green fields – and incorporated it in his fiction. In *St Ives: The Adventures of a French Prisoner in England*, the hero, Monsieur le Vicomte de Saint-Yves, who escapes from Edinburgh Castle, makes his way to Swanston Cottage and hides in a hen-house there.

St Ives was the set book when Wilfred Owen taught English for a time at an Edinburgh school in 1917, and he brought a party of schoolchildren to see the place they had read about. 'It is beautiful', wrote Owen, 'that the children of Tynecastle School are able to get nearer the romantic heart of Stevenson.' Lord Guthrie gave them tea at the cottage, and displayed his Stevenson memorabilia: a rifle, spurred riding-boots, framed letters and photos, a lock of hair, a golfball with RLS carved in it, and the house itself, largely unchanged since the Stevensons' tenancy.

I stood under a window ledge where Guthrie had carved RLS 1867 RLS 1880. A broken window pane was patched with cardboard and Sellotape. The house's current owner worked in advertising; in his garden a half-dug swimming pool had been abandoned.

Swanston still had a shepherd. Stevenson's essay 'Pastoral' (1887) is about John Todd who was shepherd there in his day: 'the oldest herd in the Pentlands . . . all his life faithful to that curlew-scattering, sheep-collecting life'. Todd, with his snuff-stained beard and long plaid, was an artist at his trade and the skinny young Stevenson plagued him. 'C'way oot amang the sheep!' Todd would bellow from the hillside. In the end, however, he became used to Stevenson wandering the hills – Halkerside, Caerketton, Allermuir-and unbent enough to tell the young writer dog stories and memories of the drove-road. Swanston's shepherd in 1984 was Adam Blake, and he and his slinking dogs had won many medals and prizes, and even appeared on TV.

19

Glencorse Church, in the Pentlands, also took a hold on Stevenson's imagination. He had walked there often with his father on Sundays, over the hill from Swanston Cottage. It is not an easy place to find today. The Ministry of Defence seems to have taken over all the land.

It was quiet and deserted near the ruin of the church, with only the sound of water trickling under the deep shade of the trees. There is a bridge over the burn now, but in Stevenson's day there used to be a ford. 'Go there', Stevenson told S. R. Crockett in a letter from Samoa the year before he died:

> . . . and say a prayer for me: *moriturus salutat*. See that it's a sunny day . . . stand on the right-hand bank just where it goes down into the water, and shut your eyes, and if I don't appear . . . well, it can't be helped.

Glencorse Church sat on a tump of hill, shrouded by trees, with an overgrown path and a churchyard gate that screeched with rust. The church was roofless, with a tower of gaunt struts, and set in the walls were crumbling Campbell armorials and blank-eyed windows. In the vanished aisle and pews a bumble bee droned among willowherb and nettles. 'GBH' was scrawled on the west wall, and a Carlsberg Special tin lay next to a glue-sniffer's crisp-packet. Skinheads' communion. I felt uneasy, and remembered Stevenson's horror story 'The Body Snatcher', where dissectors dig up a corpse in Glencorse churchyard, fumbling it into a wet sack in total darkness.

I stood by a plain headstone among the grass and dockleaves.

> ICI REPOSE CHARLES
> COTIER DE DUNKERQUE
> MORT LE 8 JANVIER 1807

Stevenson had noticed the grave of this desolate stranger and felt curious: 'I suppose he died prisoner in the military prison hard by.' Cotier may have been the starting-point for *St Ives*, Stevenson's novel of another Napoleonic prisoner-of-war.

Wind shivered the leaves and sudden sunlight lit up the wrecked church. I remembered Stevenson's last novel, *Weir of Hermiston*, and the scene of love at first sight that was set at this very spot. Clouds covered the sun and it felt very cold.

20

Stevenson took up the then new sport of canoeing in his early twenties and went regularly to the old Hawes Inn at the Queen's Ferry, a few miles west of Edinburgh. It was not only where the Firth of Forth narrowed to make a good stretch for canoeing, but the Inn itself was the sort of place that could provide proper inspiration for a story. 'There it stands,' Stevenson wrote in 'A Gossip on Romance', 'apart from the town, beside the pier, in a climate of its own, half inland, half marine – in front, the ferry bubbling with the tide and the guardship swinging to her anchor; behind, the old garden with the trees.' Stevenson said he had lived at the Hawes 'in a perpetual flutter', on the heels of some adventure that should justify the place. 'Some day, I think, a boat shall put off from the Queen's Ferry, fraught with a dear cargo.' And when the 1882 essay was published in book form in 1887, a footnote had been added: 'Since the above was written I have tried to launch the boat with my own hands in *Kidnapped*.'

From Dalmeny railway station I could still see the Hawes Inn, which Stevenson found so romantic. But it has shrunk now, dwarfed by the two thrusting symbols of progress and technology it lies between. The skyline is now dominated by the red trellis of the Forth Railway Bridge, an epic of Victorian engineering, premiered in 1890, which Stevenson never saw. Further west is the duller concrete span of the Forth Road Bridge. Any superseded technology may become romantic. People admire early motor-cars, or feel nostalgia for the sort of steam-trains that once puffed across the Forth. Yet even they were hatefully modern once. The opium-eating romantic Thomas De Quincey, for example, loathed early steam-trains, scorning 'the pot-wallopings of the boiler' and travel 'by culinary process'. He lamented 'the electric sensibility' of the superseded horse, and the great days of the English Mail-Coach. 'On the new system of travelling, iron tubes and boilers have disconnected man's heart from the ministers of his locomotion.'

The picturesque Hawes Inn was already drawing romantic-minded tourists in Stevenson's day. Americans sought out the 'quaint, old' inn where Lovel and Jonathan Oldbuck had dined in Walter Scott's novel *The Antiquary* (1816). The Robert Louis Stevenson Heritage Trail noticeboard stands outside now, for few

Americans read Scott these days; only the Russians remain loyal to Sir Walter.

The inn itself has the neutral amenities of a modern hotel but the Clansman Restaurant Menu boasted spuds with pretensions: *Pommes Natures, Pommes Frites, Pommes Berrichonnes, Pommes Dauphines, Pommes Sautées, Pommes Lyonnaises*. Room No. 13 (the R. L. Stevenson Room) had twin beds and a washbasin; a view of the Forth and the legs of the Cantilever Railway Bridge from the windows either side of the fireplace. The window panes were scratched with names, a drawing of a ship. Next door was 'the David Balfour Room'.

The Menu said: 'Robert Louis Stevenson was to immortalize the Hawes Inn in *Kidnapped* (1886). Gazing out to sea from his bedroom (No. 13) he formulated the plot for this exciting adventure.' (This is not strictly true: Stevenson wrote *Kidnapped* in Bournemouth, hundreds of miles away.) 'In the book, the old Ebenezer arranges the kidnap of his nephew David Balfour with the help of Captain Hoseason in "a small room, with a bed in it, and heated like an oven by a great fire of coal".'

At South Queensferry, the kidnapping in *Kidnapped* takes place. Innocent David Balfour goes aboard the brig *Covenant* of Dysart, is knocked on the head and taken to be sold as a slave in the Carolinas plantations. It is June 1751. The ship sails out of the Forth, and north round the rocky coast of Scotland, bound for America. Alan Breck Stewart is picked up; there is the fight in the roundhouse, and then the ship is wrecked on the lighthouseless Torran Rocks, which lie south-west of the island of Mull.

21

Robert Louis Stevenson is particularly associated with islands because of his first novel *Treasure Island*, but they were a joy to him all his life. Partly this was a literary pleasure: Defoe's *Robinson Crusoe* was a work he was familiar with by his early teens. 'Were you ever *marooned*?' he once asked another boy at North Berwick, who didn't even know what the word meant. But every child understands the magic of an island, and can make one in a bed, a bath, a box, up a tree; a place where it can be safely isolated, as it once was, in the womb. An island is limited in size, a definite territory: this appeals to a child, whose life is bounded by rules and restrictions anyway. An island encloses, but it also excludes, like a charmed circle.

Stevenson loved many islands: one in a pond in Queen Street Gardens near 17 Heriot Row; one at Bridge of Allan, 'a little eyot of dense, freshwater sand, where I once waded deep in butterburs, delighting to hear the song of the river on both sides, and to tell myself I was indeed and at last upon an island.' Some thirty years later he wove this island into *Kidnapped* as the 'little sandy islet' where David Balfour and Alan Breck Stewart hide from the redcoats of Stirling Castle.

But there was another island which he thought of as peculiarly his. This was the small, tidal island of Earraid (pronounced Erid) which lay just under the toecap of the island of Mull. 'My isle. (I call it mine after the use of lovers.)' The memory of it haunted him from the first time he saw it, aged eighteen, through the porthole of the lighthouse steamer; and the spell was cast forever when he returned and spent three weeks there. His father, Thomas Stevenson, was supervising the construction of the Dubh Artach lighthouse for the Torran Rocks, using Earraid as a base. The summer of 1870 on Earraid was a time Stevenson would never forget.

22

It was dark when I got off the Bowman's bus at Fionnphort, at the western tip of the Ross of Mull. Down the slipway, the last ferry to Iona swashed at its moorings under a yellow light. I slung my bag and ran for its ramp grinding impatiently on the wet concrete. The ferry's name was *Morvern*. I sat among schoolchildren returning home for the weekend, for the only secondary school is on the mainland, and the island pupils have to board in Oban for the week. There was no boat back that night, and pushing west in total darkness on the brief trip felt like stepping off the edge of the world.

The ramp clanked down on Iona. When Dr Johnson had been in the Hebrides he arrived by day on the 'illustrious Island, which was once the luminary of the Caledonian regions, whence savage clans and roving barbarians derived the benefits of knowledge, and the blessings of religion'. Now it was dark; the hotels were shut for the winter and the local people had melted away to their own homes. But help was at hand. A woman unlocked first the guest-house, then a shop which sold tinned food, for there are no pubs or restaurants on Iona. A cheerful blonde couple from North Wales were in the same boat and, as the only guests, we took over the place and improvised a meal together in the bright kitchen.

'I hope you don't mind,' she said with a grin, 'but we smoke dope.' He plonked a half-full bottle of red wine on the table. The 'dope' was Nigerian, the wine French, the woman an actress and the man a diver. We talked of dredging, wrecks, precious metals, fishing, sharks and sunken ships.

*

I found myself at last on the diver's platform, twenty pounds of lead upon each foot and my whole person swollen with ply and ply of woollen underclothing. One moment, the salt wind was whistling round my nightcapped head; the next I was crushed almost double under the weight of the helmet . . . The attendants began to turn the hurdy-gurdy, and the air to whistle through the tube; someone screwed in the barred window of the vizor; and I was cut off in a moment from my fellow-men . . . the weights were hung upon my back and breast, the signal-rope was thrust into my unresisting hand; and setting a twenty-pound foot upon the ladder, I began ponderously to descend.

Robert Louis Stevenson was the only Victorian novelist of note who ever went down in a diving-suit. One cannot imagine Henry James doing it, but it shows the greed for physical experience that marked young Stevenson. He was seventeen and helping his father build the ultimately unsuccessful breakwater for the harbour of Wick, in the bleak north-east of Scotland:

Some twenty rounds below the platform, twilight fell. Looking up, I saw a low green heaven mottled with vanishing bells of light; looking around, except for the weedy spokes and shafts of the ladder, nothing but a green gloaming, somewhat opaque, but very restful and delicious . . .

Stevenson had paid 'a certain handsome scamp of a diver, Bob Bain by name' five shillings to let him have a go in the suit, and wrote this account twenty years later in 'The Education of an Engineer':

And presently, Bob motioned me to leap upon a stone . . . Up I soared like a bird, my companion soaring at my side. As high as the stone, and then higher, I pursued my impotent and empty flight. Even when the strong arm of Bob had checked my shoulders, my heels continued their ascent; so that I blew out sideways like an autumn leaf, and must be hauled in, hand over hand, as sailors haul in the slack of a sail, and propped upon my feet again like an intoxicated sparrow.

*

In the morning I wandered among the worn tombstones of Scottish kings and the blackened walls that testify to fourteen centuries of Christianity since Saint Columba came to convert the Picts. 'Perhaps,' Dr Johnson wrote, 'in the revolutions of the world, *Iona* may be sometime again the instructress of the Western Regions.'

Dr Johnson was still with me when I took the ferry back across from Iona to Mull. People of my name, ancestors or relatives, came from this part of the Hebrides. I saw the grave of a ferryman called Maclean, a common name too in Mull. The Rankins were a sept of the Macleans, and in clan times had been henchmen and pipers to their Maclean chief. Dr Johnson heard a Rankin's pibroch on Coll in 1773 and wrote: 'The bagpiper played regularly, when dinner was served, whose person and dress made a good appearance; and he brought no disgrace upon the family of *Rankin*, which has long supplied the lairds of *Col* with hereditary musick.' But I was a child of the Scots diaspora; although my face fitted in these western islands I had no history there, only the yearnings of the deracinated. 'Where do you come from?' has always been a hard question. 'London' is the easy answer now; the white lie of the immigrant.

23

In Fionnphort's only shop Mrs Hanson was curious of my business. I told her I wanted to go to the island of Earraid and she gave me a telephone number. I knew that the people who lived there were an off-shoot of Findhorn, a 'spiritual education community' near Inverness. The Findhorners spoke with the angels and devas of plants, and had turned a sandy desert into an oasis of giant vegetables.

A deep American voice answered the phone, and after I had explained who I was he told me to stop the white bus that would pass soon, and get a lift down to the ferry at Fidden Point. The minibus stopped beside a haystack and we all got out above the rocky shore. A quarter of a mile away across the Sound, the island of Earraid rose. Under the lee of the hill, a tight line of slate-roofed cottages with smoking chimneys were penned behind grey walls.

We loaded the boat with bags and supplies. The bus-driver, Will Reed, ripped the outboard motor into action and we crossed the Sound to a jetty of fine granite ashlars. I climbed some iron rungs and a hand pulled me to the top.

'Welcome to Earraid.' The American voice I had heard on the phone now came from a thick black beard. 'Hi! I'm Loren,' he said. Will asked for volunteers to fetch hay for the cattle, and I humped bales from boat to tractor to stalls by the mangers in the long byre-It was a community where you had to work your way.

The single row of nine semi-detached one-storeyed houses was made of grey granite. With its slate roofs and smoking chimneys it was like any Scottish fishermen's terrace. But these cottages had been built in 1868–9 by skilled artisans of the Northern Lights as dwellings for five families of lightkeepers. The brass handles and bolts on the wooden doors still bore the stamp NL. Before the doorsteps was a muddy street, and drystone walls that enclosed the vegetable gardens running towards the Sound. A girl in clogs walked up the street past the old Earraid post-box in the wall, now plugged with wood, ringing the handbell for lunch. I was invited to eat, and we had thick lentil soup and fresh wholemeal bread in the communal dining-room at the end of the row.

I got down early and asked permission of Loren the black-bearded cook to roam over Earraid, the island of *Kidnapped* and 'The Merry Men'.

'Go ahead. The boat leaves at three.'

24

At the age of nineteen, Robert Louis Stevenson was an engineering student, duly expected to follow his father and uncles into the family lighthouse and harbour-work business. He already had his 'own private determination to be an author', but the matter was not yet settled with his father, on whose indulgence and allowance the boy depended.

In the summer of 1870 RLS came back to the island where his father's workmen had the shore station for the building of the Dubh Artach lighthouse. Earraid is not quite an island because it is tidal, regularly linked to Mull when the sea ebbs, one of RLS's 'marvellous places, though handy to home'.

RLS found surprising changes on the little island that year:

> behold! there was now a pier of stone, there were rows of sheds, railways, travelling-cranes, a street of cottages, an iron house for the resident engineer, wooden bothies for the men, a stage where the courses of the tower were put together experimentally, and behind the settlement a great gash in the hillside where granite was quarried.

Although Stevenson was meant to be an engineer, he seems to have spent his three weeks engaged in other activities: writing poems, 'sea-bathing and sun-burning . . . clambering on the boulders, trying to sail a boat', and thinking about what he was going to do. 'It was a long look forward; the future summoned me as with trumpet calls, it warned me back as with a voice of weeping and beseeching; and I thrilled and trembled on the brink of life, like a childish bather on the beach.'

Leaving the settlement I found the treeless, sheep-cropped, tussocky, hilly island the same as it must have been in Stevenson's day. Time was short, and I sprinted up and down hillocks and leapt across boulders, trying to make a quick circuit of the island. I admit I got lost on Earraid. It looks small on the map, about a square mile, but it has Protean qualities. 'Earraid's about five square miles if you ironed it flat,' a member of the community had remarked. Earraid deceives because there is nothing to mark proportion. With no tree or human figure to give it scale, a forty-foot cliff could be two hundred feet. Distances become uncertain. Stevenson had the kind of imaginative focus, a spy-glass effect, that could make the miniature leap into the larger-than-life; and when you are alone on Earraid this phenomenon seems literal. This distortion of space partly explains how Stevenson transformed the real Eilean Earraid into the fictional 'Eilean Aros' of his 1881 story 'The Merry Men', where the cliffs are huge and the rocks deadly.

'The Merry Men' is in some ways a rehearsal for the novel *Kidnapped*: their opening sentences are similar, and the heroes of both – Charles Darnaway and David Balfour – are each Lowland orphans with a crazed uncle whom they visit, and both discover evidence of murder. Both plots involve them with wrecks and Earraid, and the story of a 'kelpie' or water spirit. There are parallel details – Charles has a shoe-buckle, David a coat-button – and both of them eventually succeed at the end of their adventures. Charles marries his uncle's heiress, while David catches his uncle out, and gains his inheritance.

The summer of 1870 which Stevenson spent on Earraid saw the outbreak of the Franco-Prussian War. Stevenson was obsessed by 'the loudness of these far-away battles, and the pain of men's wounds, and the weariness of their marching'. Twenty-four years later, to the month, in Samoa, he remembered that war as he sat writing a letter in his big house, regularly interrupted by the sound of German, British and American warships shelling the Atua rebels in their thatched houses along the coast.

> It is odd, though, I can well remember, when the Franco-Prussian War began, and I was in Eilean Earraid, far enough from the sound of the loudest cannonade, I could *hear* the shots fired, and I felt the pang in my breast of a man struck. It was sometimes so distressing, so instant, that I lay in the heather at the top of the island, with my face hid, kicking my heels for agony.

Stevenson's childlike capacity for total imaginative involvement – here, hunted and shot by invisible soldiers – was remarked on by many who knew him. If sometimes it was an 'excess of sensibility' which he outgrew, he also retained a delight in action: walking, sprinting, riding, sailing. Stevenson determined to write 'physical sensations plainly expressed'. In *Kidnapped* David Balfour remarks: 'By what I have read in books, I think few that have held a pen were ever really wearied, or they would write of it more strongly.' And in *Kidnapped*, for the first time in English literature, in what Henry

James called 'the really magnificent chapters of "The Flight In The Heather"' Stevenson describes utter exhaustion. Through those six chapters Stevenson found, according to James, 'a wonderfully exact notation' for David Balfour's sensations of fear, stitches, heat, cold, thirst, pain, giddiness and the staggering bone-tiredness that leads to his collapse at Cluny's Cage and the ensuing quarrel. Nowadays, such descriptions are a commonplace of the action genre, and a host of popular writers, including John Buchan and Graham Greene, owe no small debt to Stevenson.

25

I missed the boat and had to stay overnight in the settlement, where I heard about the regeneration of Earraid. In 1870 there had been 180 people on the island, but this gradually dwindled to number only the families of the Dubh Artach lightkeepers. The lighthouse was mechanized in the 1940s, and by 1961 Earraid had a population of one and the houses fell into disrepair. In 1977, a Dutchman bought the island for £90,000, but Henk Vendersluin only wanted to use the island for a few weeks in the summer and came to an arrangement with the Findhorn Community, who were looking for a retreat. Everyone was happy: locals were glad to see lights and smoke return to the cottages, and the Findhorners repaired the cottages and worked the land in lieu of rent.

The community seemed quite used to paying guests, and I was placed in a room with three spare males including a morose youth, the only Scot there, who treated his spell on the island as a jail-term, to be endured in bed. I soon got used to finding in the sitting-room, warmed by a wood-burning stove, a Kiwi kneading a Californian's foot in a diagnostic therapy called Reflexology, and someone else immersed in a book about the Great Pyramid.

The people were decent, idealistic, largely middle-class and apolitical. They didn't drink and I saw no drugs. They hoped they were helping the planet, and were certainly not harming it. People were friendly, but not proselytizing. The clearest definition I gained of their life was 'a practical expression of the spirit', and the best thing about the Findhorners on Earraid was that everyone worked; in the kitchen, in the garden, in the house. They were 'self-sustaining, but not self-sufficient'. Sanitation was improving: they had clean water and a hot shower. There was no electricity, but lamps and candles sufficed. The lavatories were out the back, wooden dunnies complete with heart-shaped little window. The Americans in particular did not like pioneering with a torch in the cold and dark.

My host, Will Reed, had grown up on a farm in New Zealand where the regular killing of sheep had made him a vegetarian. When he came to Britain, curiosity drew him to Findhorn. A rangy type in overalls and *llucho* – an Andean hat with ear-flaps – Will was ferryman, bus-driver, fisherman, builder and mechanic. He knew about timber and peat-cutting, the uses of seal-oil, and the benefits of killer whales. Unsentimental about animals, he regretted that a rare sea-otter should have got itself into a creel and drowned, but when it happened he cured the skin and kept it to hand on his desk.

Will took a party of city people out over the island. We went to the old Northern Lights observatory, a rusting hut where Earraid could signal to Dubh Artach, fourteen miles south-west. We went up Knockmore, Earraid's highest point, and looked out over the smaller rocky green islands where sheep were left to graze in summer. We saw Tinker's Hole, the best anchorage, and the natural amphitheatre of Otter Bay, and then the sandy inlet that is called Balfour Bay, after David Balfour who crawled ashore there from the shipwreck in *Kidnapped*. Just out from Balfour Bay some black granite rocks, foaming with surf, were well-placed to have wrecked a ship close enough to shore for the principal characters to have survived. I pointed them out and asked Will what they were called.

'Those are Rankin's Rocks.'

Will took me across the Sound of Earraid when I left. I rowed, unhandy at first, across the smooth water. It was a cold and cloudy day; the land looked bare and windswept. It had never been easy living here, and Will was wondering whether to leave or remain for another two years. 'I miss the sun,' he said. 'It's too cold and wet.'

We talked about the Falklands War. Will said there had been intense local feeling during those weeks in 1982. 'Some people had relatives down there. But others just identified with the Falklanders. You see, it's so like here.'

The bus bumped on the track through moss and moor, past sea and sheep, a landscape of melancholy, bleak beauty.

Six months later, on my way to America, I bumped into a girl from Earraid by the post-office at Heathrow Airport. We chatted, and I asked what Will had decided. 'Oh, he stayed,' she said.

26

After Stevenson had read a paper called 'Notice of a New Form of Intermittent Light' to the Royal Scottish Society of Arts, for which he won a silver medal, he was encouraged to tell his father that he wanted to be a writer, not an engineer. Thomas Stevenson, ever the anxious parent, insisted that the boy have something to fall back on, and so, in 1871, RLS dropped out of engineering and began studying law.

It was a compromise acceptable to both sides; RLS in due time passed his legal exams, though he never practised, and Thomas Stevenson could look to the Edinburgh tradition of lawyers who wrote in their spare time: Kames, Scott, Jeffrey, Cockburn, etc. Law had replaced war in Scottish history as the means of settling feuds and disputes. The rise of the lawyer, in the two centuries leading up to the Reform Bill, had been one of the civilizing pillars of the Enlightenment. Case-law is also a rich historical record, and the reading proved invaluable to the kind of historical writer that Stevenson would become. Lawyers pepper his books: Prestongrange, Rankeillor, Stewart, Utterson, Mr Johnstone Thomson WS, the 'hanging judge', Weir. Law could be cynically and politically abused too: David Balfour sees it as part of a system of 'fraud and violence'.

*

Law, engineering and medicine are three notable Edinburgh professions, and Stevenson studied the first two and experienced the third only as a patient. The dedication to his 1887 book of poems, *Underwoods*, thanks eleven doctors. 'Doctors is all swabs,' Billy Bones tells Jim Hawkins, but they are also one of the high castes of Edinburgh; Scottish doctors, surgeons and research scientists have been major contributors to Western medicine. The pub on the corner of Forrest Road, where I was staying, was called 'The Doctors' and the bookshop round the corner had a skeleton in the window, with open textbooks of hideous oral diseases, and hardcore pathology inside.

Long before he came to write *Dr Jekyll and Mr Hyde*, the medical atmosphere influenced young Stevenson. As a student he underwent a curious dream-adventure (related in 'A Chapter on Dreams') where he dreamed in sequence, thus leading 'a double life – one of the day, one of the night – one that he had every reason to believe was the true one, another that he had no means of proving to be false.' In his dream-life,

he passed a long day in the surgical theatre, his heart in his mouth, his teeth on edge, seeing monstrous malformations and the abhorred dexterity of surgeons. In a heavy, rainy, foggy evening he came forth into the South Bridge, turned up the High Street, and entered the door of a tall *land*, at the top of which he supposed himself to lodge. All night long, in his wet clothes, he climbed the stairs, stair after stair into endless series, and at every second flight a flaring lamp with a reflector. All night long, he brushed by single persons passing downward – beggarly women of the street, great, weary, muddy labourers, poor scarecrows of men, pale parodies of women – but all drowsy and weary like himself, and all single, and all brushing against him as they passed. In the end, out of a northern window, he would see day beginning to whiten over the Firth, give up the ascent, turn to descend, and in a breath be back again upon the streets, in his wet clothes, in the wet, haggard dawn, trudging to yet another day of monstrosities and operations.

This is a nightmare of horror and ambition. The nineteenth-century doctor goes up the staircase, and the poor and sick descend. An ambitious social-climbing surgeon could go far, and perhaps too fast. The rise and fall of the anatomist Dr Robert Knox is exemplary, for he was destined for greatness and doomed to disgrace. Brilliant with the scalpel, he had to rely on 'resurrectionists' or 'body-snatchers' to supply him with fresh corpses, because although there had been a Chair of Anatomy in Edinburgh since 1705, the question of materials for dissection was not regularized until the Anatomy Act of 1832 – legislation hastened by Dr Knox's misfortunes.

Knox paid £7 10s for a fresh corpse, and Mr William Burke, who ran a doss-house, went into partnership with a Mr Hare to speed up the production of dead bodies from the city's poorer classes. He gave a new word to the English language: the transitive verb 'to burke' means to murder without marking, usually by suffocation. Burke and Hare were eventually caught in 1829, amid scenes of popular revulsion and indignation. Hare turned King's evidence, and Burke was hanged. Justice was poetic too; after he was cut down from the gallows, his body was cut up. Hare was given a new life in America, where a mob caught and quicklimed him. He returned to Britain, and as late as 1855 was a familiar blind beggar outside the Langham Hotel in London.

Nothing was proved against Dr Knox, but his career suffered, and the mob howled for his blood. He is the basis of 'Mr K—' in Stevenson's 1881 story 'The Body Snatcher', the tale of two young Edinburgh doctors caught up in the traffic of corpses. Like the dream, it is also a tale of horror and ambition: one doctor rises, and the other falls.

Fettes, a weak and self-indulgent character, lodges over the dissecting-rooms, and it is his job to receive the bodies. 'Here, after a night of turbulent pleasures, his hand still tottering, his sight still misty and confused, he would be called out of bed . . . by the unclean and desperate interlopers who supplied the table.' Fettes covets 'consideration' from his masters and fellow-pupils, and has 'that modicum of prudence, misnamed morality, which keeps a man from inconvenient drunkenness or punishable theft.' Like Dr Jekyll, who has his 'secret pleasures', Fettes is selfish: 'For his day of work he indemnified himself by nights of roaring, blackguardly enjoyment; and when the balance had been struck, the organ that he called his conscience declared itself content.'

Fettes's moral test comes when he recognizes one of the cadavers and detects signs of violence on her body. He confides in the racy and handsome class assistant, 'a young doctor, Wolfe Macfarlane, a high favourite among all the reckless students, clever, dissipated and unscrupulous to the last degree'. Water-weak Fettes and 'Toddy' Macfarlane become confederate in crimes that end in horror in the rain by Glencorse Church. Poor Fettes goes mad, or 'succumbs to a state of melancholy alcoholic saturation', but Macfarlane rises in society, going to London, and attending the bedsides of the higher gentry. Years later, they meet again by chance. Fettes is a drunk, 'bald, dirty, pimpled'. Dr Wolfe Macfarlane, on the other hand, is 'alert and vigorous . . . richly dressed . . . with a great gold watchchain . . . breathing, as he did, of wealth and consideration'. When Fettes reminds him of the secret of their past, Macfarlane flees in terror, leaving behind his 'fine gold spectacles broken on the threshold'.

27

Edinburgh doctors also experimented on themselves. Professor Sir Robert Christison once swallowed a calabar bean from toxicological curiosity and only avoided death by using his shaving water as an emetic. Professor Sir James Young Simpson handed out tumblers of chloral at home until he and his guests were insensible upon the floor. This dramatic empiricism helped develop modern anaesthetics. I noticed a wall-plaque in North Bridge Street in Edinburgh which said:

In 1847 in a pharmacy on this site
Duncan Flockhard & Co made the chloroform used by
Sir James Young Simpson
in his historic experiments on the relief of pain.
This plaque was erected on the occasion of the 3rd
World Congress of the International Association for
the Study of Pain held in Edinburgh in 1981.

The Simpsons lived just the other side of Queen Street Gardens from the Stevensons, and the families were friends. RLS had known Sir James before he died in 1870, and the doctor's son and heir, Sir Walter Simpson, Bart, was to be his travelling companion over the next few years, up to and including the canoe trip of *An Inland Voyage* in 1876. Stevenson must have known of the Simpson experiments, and the eager butler who passed round 'champagne chlory' below stairs and had to run to his master crying: 'For God's sake, sir, come doun! I've poisoned the cook!' The Simpson experience is one source for that notorious self-experimenter, Dr Henry Jekyll MD, DCL, LL D, FRS.

Other Edinburgh doctors entered popular literature at the end of the nineteenth century. Dr Arthur Conan Doyle, also born in Edinburgh, and who studied medicine there, created the great detective Mr Sherlock Holmes. Holmes applied scientific principles to the solving of clues, and experimented on himself by injecting cocaine. Holmes, though, was not a doctor but he was based in part on a famously observant Edinburgh physician. Stevenson admired the Holmes and Watson stories, and on 5 April 1893 wrote to Conan Doyle about the great sleuth: 'Only the one thing troubles me: can this be my old friend Joe Bell?' Conan Doyle had acknowledged that Dr Joseph Bell, who could make astonishingly accurate guesses about his patients' lives and habits from their dress and deportment, was a basis for Sherlock Holmes.

28

In 1869, when Stevenson was elected to 'The Spec' (the University's elite Speculative Society), the weekly meetings were from eight until twelve pm. At nine, some of the members would leave 'to buy pencils', which meant, in fact, a drink at Rutherford's in Drummond Street. This branch of the Rutherford's chain had opened as a *howf* or grog and grub shop in 1834 and a century and a half later is the only survivor bearing the name.

Where grey Drummond Street meets South Bridge is as trivial as any T-junction. Across from Rutherford's red teak front is Khushi's Lothian Restaurant, offering Punjabi Curry Dishes; next door, Stewart's Bar is proclaimed on the glass of a street-lamp; over No. 12 is the bloody-bandage pole of Wood's Barber Shop, founded in 1890, when it was The Empire Toilet Saloon ('All-work-done-on-hygienic-principles'); then Pasquale Café-Restaurant; the Drummond Café and Barbarelia Hairdressers. An ordinary corner of Edinburgh, unremarkable but not forgotten. From the South Seas Stevenson wrote a letter to his old Edinburgh crony Charles Baxter:

> *Yacht 'Casco', at sea near the Paumotus*
> *7am September 6th, 1888, with a dreadful pen.*

My dear Charles, – Last night as I lay under my blanket in the cockpit, courting sleep, I had a comic seizure. There was nothing visible but the southern stars, and the steersman out there by the binnacle lamp; we were all looking forward to a most deplorable landfall on the morrow, praying God we should fetch a tuft of palms which are to indicate the Dangerous Archipelago; the night was warm as milk, and all of a sudden I had a vision of– Drummond Street. It came on me like a flash of lightning: I simply returned thither, and into the past. And when I remember all I hoped and feared as I pickled about Rutherford's in the rain and the east wind; how I feared I should make a mere shipwreck, and yet timidly hoped not; how I feared I should never have a friend, far less a wife, and yet passionately hoped I might; how I hoped (if I did not take to drink) I should possibly write one little book, etc. etc. And then now – what a change! I feel somehow as if I should like the incident set upon a brass plate at the corner of that dreary thoroughfare for all students to read, poor devils, when their hearts are down.

There is no brass plate, high or low, at the end of Drummond Street.

*

The public bar of Rutherford's was packed; a row of old regulars with their pints under the moulded cornices, a crowd at the bar, and through the smoke and chatter the sound of gunfire and squealing tyres from the TV over the door. A youth tangoed with the one-armed bandit, and a man in the far corner mauled blues and jigs from a harmonica in the warm fuggy air. The barman took a break with a small whisky and the *Evening News*, a heroin scare headlined in bold. Bob Turnbull had been the landlord and owner of Rutherford's for twenty years. He had put up the partition that split the old single room with its boxes round the walls into the saloon and public bars. He pointed out a large oil-painting of Rutherford's red teak front that hung on the wall, done by an art-student. 'There's one thing odd about that painting: there are no locks or door-handles,' he remarked. 'Must have thought it was a Free House.'

Rutherford's is genteel compared to some of Edinburgh's pubs, one of which is nicknamed 'Vietnam' because of all the fights. Leith still has the reputation it had in Stevenson's day, as a place of shebeens and sailors 'dives.' Oh aye,' said one informant, pint glass in hand, 'they're a' chinkies and darkies doon there.' He gave me the names of three pubs where there were prostitutes: 'The hoors are young lassies, ye ken, but eh, a bit rough-like.'

I thought of young RLS sitting in a drinking den with his notebook. His nickname was 'Velvet Coat' from his favourite jacket. He was a young gentleman who thought himself 'a dead hand at a harridan, I never saw the one yet that could resist me'. He was also, in his own words, 'a heartless drunken young dog', or wanted to be.

Drinking and fornicating are also traditions of Edinburgh, which once had two hundred brothels in the Royal Mile; and Stevenson as a young man of the early 1870s certainly drank and probably fornicated, for it was part of growing up.

> I walk the streets smoking my pipe
> And I love the dallying shop-girl
> That leans with rounded stern to look at the fashions;
>
> . . .
>
> I love night in the city,
> The lighted streets and the swinging gait of harlots.
> I love pale cool morning,
> In the empty bye-streets,
> With only here and there a female figure,
> A slavey with lifted dress and the key in her hand,
> A girl or two at play in a corner of waste-land
> Tumbling and showing their legs and crying out to me loosely.

Stevenson, at this time 'careless of a town's abusing', also dressed eccentrically, in blue-black flannel shirts with a red tie, salt-and-pepper trousers and patent leather shoes. He was a skinny spindle-shanks, and must have looked a fright to the respectable. Once he was seen walking up to the Old Town carrying an armchair on his head, taking it to his new friend, the poet William Ernest Henley, a poor patient in the Edinburgh Infirmary just behind Rutherford's.

*

Henley was a patient of Dr Joseph Lister's and was languishing in bed after his tubercular foot had been amputated. His sonnet-sequence 'In Hospital' had been published in *Cornhill Magazine*, and it was the editor of that periodical who brought RLS along to the Infirmary one black afternoon in early 1875. The two contributors liked each other, became close friends, collaborators and readers of each other's work.

Henley was a bellowing Tory who was determined not to be disabled by illness. With his great red beard and tangled hair he played the role of a belligerent warrior. He once knocked down Oscar Wilde with his crutch. 'It was the sight of your maimed strength and masterfulness that begot John Silver in *Treasure Island*', Stevenson confessed to him in May 1883. Henley's *Lyra Heroica – A Book of Verse for Boys* is an imperialist primer, or First Steps in Jingo – an anthology with pages of what Wilfred Owen was to call 'the old lie'. Henley also became an important editor, whose literary judgement, at least, was sound. The political bully also had his softer side. He adored his daughter, who died tragically young, and who became the basis for Wendy in J. M. Barrie's *Peter Pan*. Pain, life and letters embittered Henley, and he turned against Stevenson in later life.

29

In the 1870s life at home became irksome for Stevenson. Henry James later noted the 'friction and tension' in RLS's early life, when 'the unjustified artist' was 'fermenting . . . in the recusant engineer'. Stevenson also had difficulties with his father. God the Father is a strong motif in Presbyterianism and Stevenson's own troubled relationship was a familiar Scots predicament. It was not a simple matter of Thomas the tyrant and Louis the liberator. 'He had learned in childhood that salvation is always for the other man. In the years of adolescence he had rebelled, but he had never regarded himself as innocent and his father as guilty', wrote Graham Greene.

Yet Stevenson had to define himself in opposition to his father, much like his friend and contemporary Edmund Gosse, who produced the classic account of the Victorian 'filial relation' in *Father and Son* (1907). Indeed, when Edmund Gosse met Thomas Stevenson in September 1880 he was reminded strongly of his own father, Philip. Perhaps most sons of that generation experienced the splitting that Gosse describes, when he first deceived his parents by his 'crafty silence'. The child runs into the back garden: 'There was a secret in this world and it belonged to me and to a somebody who lived in the same body with me. There were two of us and we could talk with one another.'

Stevenson loved his father, a man he described as 'shrewd and childish, passionately attached, passionately prejudiced; a man of many extremes, many faults of temper, and no very stable foothold for himself among life's troubles.' Thomas Stevenson also loved his son, and was in many ways indulgent. Some Edinburgh folk were shocked to see the son cheeking his father at the dinner-table. In the end though, there were ideas that Thomas Stevenson could not tolerate, and disbelief in God was the principal one.

Archibald Bisset remembered a walk to Cramond with the Stevenson *père et fils*. Louis was praising Herbert Spencer's *Theory of Evolution* to the skies.

At length his father said:

> 'I think, Louis, you've got Evolution on the brain. I wish you would define what the word means.'
>
> 'Well, here it is *verbatim*. Evolution is a continuous change from indefinite incoherent homogeneity to definite coherent heterogeneity of structure and function through successive differentiations and integrations.'
>
> 'I think,' said his father with a merry twinkle in his eyes, 'your friend Mr Herbert Spencer must be a very skilful writer of polysyllabic nonsense.'

And yet Thomas Stevenson would cry in rage, 'I blame Herbert Spencer!' when his son told him that he did not believe in God. It was a bombshell; the same explosive that detonated in countless Victorian households after Darwin. Thomas Stevenson was narrowly religious, with 'a clansman's loyalty to the Church of Scotland'; his son was an arrogant, adolescent freethinker. There were terrible scenes of melodrama and emotional blackmail: 'You have rendered my whole life a failure,' the father told his twenty-two-year-old son; 'I had thought to have had someone to help me when I was old.'

His mother wept, near hysteria, and the son felt the weight of his parents 'damnation; the guilt of a 'horrible atheist'. Bob Stevenson was banned from the house as a malign influence and gloom descended on 17 Heriot Row. Out of the conflict there was to come a fine Fable, 'The House of Eld', but in the meantime, nothing but pain.

'It was really pathetic to hear my father praying pointedly for me today at family worship, and to think that the poor man's supplications were addressed to nothing better able to hear and answer than the chandelier.'

The tensions of home and the oppressive milieu of small town Edinburgh played on Stevenson increasingly in the first half of 1873. He needed an escape. 'One thing, indeed, is not to be learned in Scotland, and that is, the way to be happy.'

He went down to Suffolk, on what he called 'a certain very fortunate visit . . . to England in the summer of 1873'.

COCKFIELD

I

My visit to England was to a country rectory, the house of a
cousin of mine and of her husband, the delightful Churchill
Babington; I knew what I had to expect, croquet parties, the
parsons' wives, the ecclesiastical celebrations . . .

Stevenson's cousin, Maud Wilson, only six years his senior, was
one of Maggie Stevenson's many nieces and the daughter of her
eldest sister Marion Balfour. Maud had married the Reverend
Churchill Babington in 1868 and they lived at a spacious rectory in
Cockfield, about eight miles south of Bury St Edmunds, Suffolk.
Louis Stevenson arrived one August day with a knapsack on his
back, walking up the hill from the little station at Cockfield. He was
free of home and on the move. Two years before, he had come across
Walt Whitman's *Leaves of Grass*, 'a book which tumbled the world
upside down for me, blew into space a thousand cobwebs of genteel
and ethical illusion . . .'.
Stevenson knew 'The Song of the Open Road':

> I think whatever I shall meet on the road I shall like, and
> whoever beholds me shall like me,
> I think whoever I see must be happy.

There was an interesting guest at the rectory who was beautifully
unhappy. She was Mrs Frances 'Fanny' Sitwell, then thirty-four, the
mother of a ten-year-old boy called Bertie. Stevenson found her very
attractive and sympathetic, maternal and yet somehow erotic. Her

tinge of sadness was from her failed marriage to the man she had married at seventeen, the Reverend Albert Sitwell, described by one writer as a person of 'unfortunate temperament and uncongenial habits', which Pope-Hennessy took to mean either 'drink or choir boys'. Fanny Sitwell had broken away from him a few months earlier, and found herself a job as Secretary of the College for Men and Women in Queen Square, London. She could not divorce, but she was emancipated and intelligent; she reviewed for the *Manchester Guardian*. RLS had never met such a woman, and fell in love. He entertained her son, hoping perhaps to win the mother's affections.

Fanny Sitwell was 'a lady', Stevenson wrote later, 'whose generous pleasure – perhaps, I might almost say, whose weakness – it was to discover youthful genius. With a little goodwill and a little friendship, genius is mightily easily supplied. Mrs Sitwell found it or supplied it in my case, and announced the discovery . . . ' She announced it to her friend, mentor and protector, the literary and art critic Sidney Colvin. His existence may have helped her to decide to leave her disagreeable husband, and yet it was not for another thirty years, after the Reverend Sitwell and Colvin's mother had both died, that Fanny Sitwell was to marry Sidney Colvin. By then she was sixty-four and he fifty-eight.

Colvin was Slade Professor of Fine Art at Cambridge when Fanny Sitwell summoned him to meet the youthful genius she had known only a few days. Colvin belonged to a world that Stevenson wanted to enter; he had already read Colvin's signed reviews in the *Fortnightly Review*, and knew he contributed to *Cornhill*, *The Globe*, *The Portfolio* and *Pall Mall Gazette*; Colvin also knew Burne-Jones and Rossetti, and had been an early member of the New Club (which had become the Savile in 1871). Stevenson went to meet him at the little station in a state of agitation. But the 'great man' was prepared to notice him with favour. This predisposition was important:

> I do not know, I do not think, that Colvin would have taken to me by nature; I am doubtful whether I should have taken to him. Meeting as we did, I the ready worshipper, he the ready patron, we had not got up the hill to the rectory before we had begun to make friends.

Sidney Colvin remembered that August day in 1873 too.

[63]

I had landed from a Great Eastern train at a little country station in Suffolk and was met on the platform by a stripling in a velvet jacket and straw hat, who walked up with me to the country rectory where he was staying and I had come to stay . . . I could not wonder at what I presently learned – how within an hour of his first appearance at the rectory, knapsack on back, a few days earlier, he had captivated the whole household.

Colvin too was charmed by the manic young Scot and noticed how fast time seemed to pass in his company.

Pure poetic eloquence (coloured always, be it noticed, by a strong Scottish accent), grave argument and criticism, riotous freaks of fancy, flashes of nonsense more illuminating than wisdom, streamed from him inexhaustibly . . . .

Cockfield Station has been closed for over twenty years. Weeds now grow on the platform and the waiting-shelter had broken windows and rubbish inside. From the place where Stevenson and Colvin met the trees of the rectory are visible at the top of the hill. But I could not follow their footsteps yet; I had an appointment first.

2

I stopped by a big house, parked the car outside the gate and walked across the gravel. Through the french window I could see a tall bespectacled man with a sunburned bald head reading The Times. He was wearing a cardigan, grey flannels and old Dunlop tennis shoes, and when he opened the front door I could see just how big Sir Hugh Carleton Greene was.

'Ah. You found the place. Come in.'

'Thank you. Lovely garden.'

'It's full of aconite. Did you know aconite is only supposed to grow where Roman soldiers shed their blood?'

'Really? Boudicca's territory began just north of here, Ixworth, Ickworth, all Ickeni country. Maybe some of the legions did die here.'

We chatted about Suffolk. He pointed out the old railway line from Lavenham to Bury that ran across the bottom of the garden.

'Oh, and this place gets a mention in Drayton's *Polyolbion* too.'

Inside, Sir Hugh Greene showed me a copy of the parish magazine *Green Links* with an article he had written in December 1979.

'In 1963 I started to look for a house in West Suffolk, the country from which many of my ancestors, particularly those connected with the Greene King Brewery in Bury St Edmunds, had come.'

Sir Hugh had been Director-General of the BBC and Chairman of Greene King. In 1984 his brother Graham Greene was asked by the *Observer* what he felt about the celebration of his eightieth birthday. 'One thing I did enjoy was going up to Bury St Edmunds to the Greene King Brewery and doing a mash – the first stage of brewing. By October there will be 100,000 bottles with a special label with my signature on it. It's their strongest beer. They're very good, Greene King. Now that I liked

In *Green Links*, Sir Hugh described the family connection with Cockfield. 'My great-uncle by marriage, Dr Churchill Babington, was Rector of Cockfield from 1866 until his death in 1889 . . . '

I had my notebook out, scrawling notes.

'Let me get this right. Churchill Babington's wife – Maud Wilson – was your great-aunt.'

'That's correct. Great-aunt Maud. She married again after Churchill Babington died, Colonel Henry Wright, and we used to visit them at No. 11 Belgrave Road in London. Graham writes about it in *A Sort of Life*?

'So great-aunt Maud is the sister of your . . . ?'

'My grandmother, Jane Whyte Wilson, who married the Reverend Carleton Greene. They married here, you know, and Stevenson was at the wedding.'

'Stevenson was at your grandmother's wedding?'

'Yes he was. And the daughter of that marriage is my mother Marion.'

'So the relationship of you and your brother Graham Greene to RLS is –?'

'First cousin, twice removed.'

Sir Hugh showed me *The Family of Greene*, an unpublished work by his older brother Raymond, from which the following sketch of the family tree is derived.

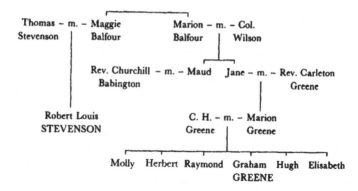

Robert Louis Stevenson had attended the wedding of Graham Greene's grandmother, which took place in St Edmundsbury Cathedral in Bury St Edmunds on 4 October 1870. Two days later RLS wrote to his mother:

> The marriage went off exceedingly well, and the persons in question were sent off in triumph . . . Maggie [Wilson] is not bad looking: the belles of the marriage party were May and Nora Piers.
>
> After the marriage we all went off to Risbygate Street, where we had refreshments and a photographer . . . All then came out to Cockfield where we had a luncheon and four croquet sets. The day including 16 miles drive lasted from 7.30 to 7; and, at the end of it, the greater part of us felt as though the Labours of Hercules were at last eclipsed.

This first visit to Suffolk, coming just after his weeks on Earraid, was a shock to Stevenson. It was all so different from Scotland. 'Nothing is the same; and I feel as strange and outlandish here as I do in France or Germany.' His essay 'The Foreigner at Home' (1881) recalls: 'A week or two in such a place as Suffolk leaves the Scotsman gasping . . . The first shock of English society is like a cold plunge.' It helped confirm his Scottish identity, and all his life he would retain 'a strong Scots accent of the mind'.

Sir Hugh and I drove over to Cockfield Rectory. Like so many East Anglian villages, Cockfield has lost a lot of life. Before the Great War it had its own railway station, five pubs, three coal-merchants, three blacksmiths, two butchers, two carpenters/undertakers, a news-agent, a carrier, a milkman, a game-merchant, a fishmonger, a baker and a fruit and vegetable man. Now there is electricity and TV, but the businesses have vanished. People drive to supermarkets in Bury; the youth injure themselves on motorcycles.

From a white gate the long drive curved back through trees and parkland to the eighteenth-century parsonage. Disease had killed the elms that Pope-Hennessy saw and now there were only limes and hornbeams, together with rectory exotica, a cedar of Lebanon and a redwood.

We passed the fine Georgian entrance – a red pair of panelled doors with sidelights, two stone Doric columns, a classical pediment framing the fanlight – and walked round the left side of the house. An expansive lawn yielded to a crescent of lilied moat with ducks and a large paddock where a white horse browsed under a blossoming cherry. It was Colinton with class: a big, brickfronted house with a hem of flagstone walkway and a magnolia and a yellow rose growing up by the tall sash windows. You could imagine the croquet parties on summer evenings, long dresses trailing over the lawn, a little flirtation after tea. I slipped inside, into a fine bare drawing-room with tall generous-paned windows overlooking the lawn. The graceful room spoke of greater ease and wealth than Scotland's: in place of Colinton's kirkyard, the view stretched over grass, ducks and daffodils under the willow, to a green field and the open Suffolk sky.

*

Stevenson's world opened up at Cockfield. To Fanny Sitwell, his 'Consuela' and 'Madonna', he wrote ardent letters over the next couple of years, confiding his hopes and yearnings, rehearsing the pressures at home. And to Sidney Colvin, Stevenson would feel a great debt. 'It is very hard for me . . . to say what I owe . . . this most trusty and noble-minded man. If I am what I am and where I am, if I have done anything at all or done anything well, his is the credit. *It was he who paved my way in letters.*'

This is the generous view of Colvin. There is an uncharitable one: that he was prim, narrow and in later years a poor editor of Stevenson's work and letters. Kipling, in brutal vein, supplies an unforgettable portrait of him: 'an all-fired prig of the first water . . . [who] suffers from all the nervo-hysterical diseases of the nineteenth century . . . A queer beast with matchstick fingers and a dry unwholesome skin.' But when Stevenson at twenty-three needed a hand on the old Grub Street route to his profession, it was the maligned Sidney Colvin who gave it.

4

Over lunch at the Three Horseshoes in Cockfield (a Greene King pub) Sir Hugh Greene confirmed that his brother thought of Robert Louis Stevenson as 'one of the family'. I had read Graham Greene's first volume of autobiography, *A Sort of Life*, where he wrote of RLS: 'I had lived as a boy on the fringes of his world: his relative and biographer, Graham Balfour, had come to our house . . . Names which appeared in his *Collected Letters* were photographs in our family album. In the nursery we played on the bagatelle board which had belonged to him.'

Sir Hugh told me about going with his brother and Graham's biographer, Professor Norman Sherry, to their old home in Berkhamsted: 'the place where everything was born'. They found a bagatelle table in one of the rooms and Graham became very excited. The story ended in anticlimax; the table was someone else's, a later addition. But his excitement showed what the original board had meant.

A Sort of Life and 'The Lost Childhood' have much to say about early reading. The Greene brothers are great book-collectors; Graham and Hugh went around secondhand bookshops trying to get volumes remembered from the nursery. Graham Greene has attributed his own later travels in Africa to the childhood experience of reading Rider Haggard's 1886 novel *King Solomon's Mines*. I reminded Sir Hugh that Haggard had written that as a bet with one of his brothers that he could write a better book than *Treasure Island*, published in 1883. Graham Greene also collected books about lighthouses, and owned a copy of Alan Stevenson's account of the building of Skerry vore. I wondered what being related to Stevenson meant to the writer, and asked Sir Hugh how I could get in touch with his brother.

'Write to our sister Elisabeth. She works as Graham's secretary and will pass things on.'

The Greenes seemed a close-knit family. There was a Spectator competition in 1980 for a parody of Graham Greene which they all entered under pseudonyms: Hugh won, Elisabeth came third, Graham came nowhere.

5

I drove the dozen or so miles north from Cockfield to my parents' home at Grimstone End along one of the oldest roads in England. Peddars Way, a series of tracks running from London to north Norfolk via Braintree, Sudbury, Lavenham, Ixworth, East Dereham and holy Walsingham, was there before the Romans came. They metalled parts of it to march their troops against Boudicca, the Ickeni queen, and the road was still there when the Angles and Saxons settled into North Folk and South Folk. Peddars Way skirts Coney Weston, named not for rabbits but for a king' s town – Old English cyninges tūn – and the road was still there when the Normans put Pakenham Mill into their Domesday Book, as it is still there now, buried under tarmac, posted with other names and numbers.

On Suffolk walks with Colvin in late August 1873, Stevenson talked through what was to become his first paid piece of writing, called 'Roads'. Colvin got it placed in *The Portfolio*, where it appeared in December 1873 under the name L. S. Stoneven. R. L. Stevenson got £3 8s od for his professional début. 'How full it is of Cockfield!' he wrote to Fanny Sitwell. Few writers forget their first paid acceptance, when all promise lies before them. 'The road is already there – ' Stevenson wrote in 'Roads', 'we shall not be long behind.'

'Roads' was Stevenson's beginning, and another road was his end. Twenty-one years later, he made his last public and political utterance after the building of a road in Samoa – *O Le Ala O Le Loto Alofa*, 'The Road of the Loving Heart'. My own trail's end was far over the sea, under the mountain where Stevenson stood a few weeks before his death and made a speech in Samoan which ended:

Chiefs! Our road is not built to last a thousand years, yet in a sense it is. When a road is once built, it is a strange thing how it collects traffic, how every year as it goes on, more and more people are found to walk thereon, and others are raised up to repair and perpetuate it, and keep it alive; so that perhaps even this road of ours may, from reparation to reparation, continue to exist and be useful hundreds of years after we are mingled in the dust. And it is my hope that my faraway descendants may remember and bless those who laboured for them today.

'FARAWAY DESCENDANTS'

I

In a 1951 essay on Kafka, Jorge Luis Borges observes: 'The word "precursor" is indispensable in the vocabulary of criticism, but one should try to purify it from every connotation of polemic or rivalry. The fact is that every writer creates his precursors. His work modifies our conception of the past, as it will modify the future.'

When Graham Greene began to write, he regretted that Stevenson was not still alive to be his mentor: 'Perhaps I would have found the courage to consult him in distant Samoa and have sent him my first book.' That was a novel called *The Man Within*, whose title (actually from Sir Thomas Browne) might well describe Mr Hyde. Greene's second book, the novel called *The Name of Action*, has been suppressed by its author, and a 1930 first edition with dustcover can now fetch over 500 guineas. Greene wrote of its failure in *A Sort of Life*:

Action can only be expressed by a subject, a verb and an object, perhaps a rhythm, little else. Even an adjective slows the pace or tranquillizes the nerve. I should have turned to Stevenson to learn my lesson: 'It came all of a sudden when it did, with a rush of feet and a roar, and then a shout from Alan, and the sound of blows and someone crying as if hurt. I looked back over my shoulder, and saw Mr Shuan in the doorway crossing blades with Alan.' No similes or metaphors there, not even an adjective.

Greene's first successful novel was *Stamboul Train*, a political thriller. The division that Greene has drawn between his 'entertainments' and his other novels may be artificial, but it reflects his curious status as a writer who is both popular and serious. It is a status that Stevenson had before him. Indeed, Greene's early Penguin books mention his family relationship to Stevenson on the jacket.

Like Stevenson, Greene began as a journalist, and he has tackled the same literary forms: reviews, poetry, plays, short stories, novels, and travel books. Like Stevenson he is restless and manic-depressive, close to his own dream-world. Like Stevenson he is a dual creature, drawn to paradox. Greene has been a lifelong 'double agent' since he lived both sides of the green baize door of the School House at Berkhamsted, as pupil and headmaster's son. He has said that the writer's job is to betray, yet he has stayed most loyal to the principles of his leftist generation. He is a believer and a sceptic, and, like Stevenson, a hoaxer. Elusive, shy, the odd man out, Greene has also been haunted by a fraudulent *doppelgänger*, an incident of imper-sonation that the author of *The Third Man* related in a book of conversations called *The Other Man*: 'I do not mean to say I do not fear life still; I do; and that terror (for an adventurer like myself) is still one of the chief joys of living.' That is Stevenson, but it could be Greene. Perhaps Greene's life is a secret emulation of Stevenson's. He has travelled further than Stevenson ever went, seen more danger and death, taken more drugs. As Stevenson went to the leprosy colony at Molokai, so Greene went to the *léproserie* in the Congo for *A Burnt-Out Case*. And both have been associated with leaders of small tropical countries struggling for independence against imperial pressure. Greene is not only a relative but a true twentieth-century heir of Robert Louis Stevenson.

2

Several of Greene's books have been filmed, as have Stevenson's. Film-makers have readily seen their visual possibilities, even if the eventual films were a travesty. Greene, who grew up in the heroic age of cinema and has been a film critic, was once asked about the influence of cinema on his writing and replied:

When I describe a scene, I capture it with the moving eye of the cinecamera rather than with the photographer's eye – which leaves it frozen . . . Authors like Walter Scott or the Victorians were influenced by paintings and constructed their back-grounds as though they were static and came from the hand of a Constable. I work with a camera, following my characters and their movements. So the landscape moves. When I turn my head and look at the harbour, my head moves, the boats move, don't they?

Bertolt Brecht had already spotted the same techniques in Stevenson. His 1925 'Notes on Stevenson' observes that filmic vision *(die filmische Optik)* had existed in Europe long before the technology to make films. Brecht thought that Rimbaud's approach was purely optical, and that 'with Stevenson events are quite clearly visually ordered'. He pointed to Chapter IX of *The Master of Ballantrae*, where the description of the rolling ship as Mackellar tries to kill the Master is completely cinematic.

G. K. Chesterton, in 1927, was also impressed by Stevenson's clarity of vision: 'All his images stand out in very sharp outline; and are, as it were, all edges.' The chip cut into the Admiral Benbow's inn-sign by Billy Bones's cutlass chasing Black Dog was a symbol, Chesterton thought, of Stevenson's literary and visual attack, the bright cut and the homely vivid point.

The emphasis Stevenson placed on visual effects is clear from his description of *reading* in 'A Gossip on Romance', which almost seems apter for the video age:

> We should gloat . . . be rapt clean out of ourselves . . . our mind filled with the busiest, kaleidoscopic dance of images, incapable of sleep or of continuous thought. The words . . . should run . . . in our ears like the noise of breakers, and the story . . . repeat itself in a thousand coloured pictures to the eye.

Stevenson wrote the sort of stories he would like to read, and his 'thousand coloured pictures to the eye' pointed the way to techniques that later film-makers would use. The 'shots' in Stevenson are sometimes so clear it is difficult to remember that he lived before there were moving pictures. On 1 February 1892 he told Colvin how he wanted to tackle his new novel *Sophia Scarlet*: 'The problem is exactly a

Balzac one, and I wish I had his fist – for I have already a better method – the kinetic, whereas he continually allowed himself to be led into the static.'

3

Graham Greene's *Collected* Essays are drawn from thirty years of journalism, and there are references to Stevenson in about a sixth of them. The only other author who approaches that frequency is Henry James. Greene calls James 'the superior artist', but it is Stevenson who seems to haunt his imagination.

In 1948 Graham Greene was forty-four, the age at which Stevenson died. Perhaps it was a climacteric for the ex-Russian Roulette player to outlive his cousin. In that year Greene wrote two articles about Stevenson. The first, 'Two Friends', was a review of *Henry James and Robert Louis Stevenson: A Record of Friendship and Criticism*, edited by Janet Adam Smith. He describes James's domed brow and his resemblance to the Prince of Wales. Then there was Stevenson,

> the other, the man with the hollow nervous face, the thin gangling legs, the over-publicized moustache, splashing through fords at midnight, risking a bullet in parochial politics, endangering his life every day he lived for no apparent purpose except perhaps a desperate desire to prove he could be something other than a writer.

Greene's review of Lettice Cooper's *Robert Louis Stevenson*, published in the same year, focuses on late RLS, 'the tired disheartened writer of the last eight years, pegging desperately away at what he failed to recognize as his masterworks'. Greene sees his own concerns in Stevenson: 'Suffering like literature has its juvenilia – men mature and graduate in suffering.' He picks out a piece from one of Stevenson's letters on the spirit of the anarchists in 1890s Europe, men 'who commit dastardly murders very basely, die like saints, and leave beautiful letters behind 'em . . . people whose conduct is inexplicable to me, and yet their spiritual life is higher than that of most'. This foreshadows Greene's fictional territory. He has chosen lines from Browning as a possible epigraph for all his work:

> Our interest's in the dangerous edge of things,
> The honest thief, the tender murderer,
> The superstitious atheist . . .

The review ends with this image of Stevenson. 'He was on the eve of *Weir*, the old trim surface was cracking up: the granite was coming painfully through. It is at this point, where the spade strikes the edge of the stone, that the biographer should begin to dig.'

*

On 24 June 1949 a letter appeared in the *Times Literary Supplement*.

> Sir, – I have been commissioned by Messrs William Heine-mann to write a biography of Robert Louis Stevenson, and I should be grateful if any of your readers who have unpublished letters of Stevenson's, or letters dealing with his family and friends, would allow me to inspect them. They would be promptly returned.
>
> *Graham Greene*
> 5, St James's Street, London SW1.

This fascinating biography was never completed, and I wondered why. The centenary of Stevenson's birth, 1950, saw a renewal of critical interest, and I thought it likely that Greene had adandoned the work because he came across J. C. Furnas writing his book *Voyage to Windward*, which was published in 1952. I wrote to Greene's sister, Mrs Elisabeth Dennys, to ask if this was so, and if anything had survived which I might be able to see. She replied: 'The answer to your first query is "yes", he did abandon his projected biography because of Furnas's biography. Secondly, I do have a file of letters and jottings from when Graham was working on the project . . . '

4

The orange folder had 'R. L. Stevenson' on the top right corner and '1949–50'pencilled on the cover. I enjoyed undoing the string.

Greene had got off to a vigorous start, firing letters from St James's Street to Balfour relatives, contacts of Janet Adam Smith and G. B. Stern, collectors like Edwin Beinecke, libraries, publishers and universities. He envisaged a long job, going through the unpublished material, collating the censored letters, interviewing people who had met Stevenson, or their descendants, and trying to turn up new evidence. Inevitably there were wild goose chases; one after a story that Sidney Colvin had been systematically defrauding Stevenson of monies from his publishers, which turned out to be a fabrication of Lloyd Osbourne's first wife, another after an old man called Howard who claimed to have been under-cook at Vailima in Samoa.

In early July, Greene was 'rather dismayed' to hear that there was an American on the same trail. A letter from New York confirmed that a J. C. Furnas, author of *Anatomy of Paradise*, a book about the South Seas, had been commissioned to do a biography and his manuscript was expected in the fall of 1950. Greene wrote back to say that there should be no conflict, as he would not expect to publish until 1953.

The *TLS* letter had drawn other responses, some more helpful than others: Roger Lancelyn Green sent transcripts of excised portions of Stevenson's letters to Fanny Sitwell, and the hand-written notes of his own abandoned life of Stevenson; Moray Maclaren, who was enjoying the serialization of *The Third Man* in the *Daily Express*, offered a galley of his own centenary study, *Stevenson and Edinburgh*; a Frenchman sent a booklet on Puy; a Jesuit from Indiana wrote to offer his Loyola University Master's thesis on Stevenson's changing attitude to the Catholic church.

Greene flew to Edinburgh on what he called 'the Stevenson quest' on 19 July 1949, arriving by the morning plane for a three-day stay at the North British Hotel. In the Scottish National Library, reading the letters to Fanny Sitwell, he worked through lunch. He also went to 8 Howard Place, then still the Stevenson Museum. It would have been wonderfully bizarre if, at Stevenson's birthplace, Greene had bumped into the other notable visitor of that month – Walt Disney, who was preparing to film his version of *Treasure Island*.

There were interesting letters in the file. Lady Leslie (born Marjorie Ide) was the younger sister of Annie Ide – a girl to whom Stevenson made the gift of his birthday, in a comically official document, because she had been born on Christmas Day. Lady Leslie wrote to Greene from Santa Barbara, California, where she was staying with an old friend from her Samoan childhood, Mrs Salisbury Field, known as 'Teuila'. This 'Teuila', now over ninety and still alert, was none other than Stevenson's step-daughter, born Isobel Osbourne, later Mrs Belle Strong.

Lady Leslie gave Teuila a copy of Greene's *Nineteen Stories*. Teuila wrote two letters to Greene and sent him a copy of her autobiography *This Life I've Loved* with annotations and extra photographs. His thank you letter of 30 August 1949 told her of the family connection: '"Aunt Maggie" is, or I should say was, my great-great-aunt, so I am satisfying a certain family pietas in writing about Robert Louis Stevenson.' The unpublished material he had seen, he told her, 'only increases one's respect and admiration for the writer'.

The letter also contains interesting information about the novel *The Wrong Box*:

> Scribner's sent [RLS] proofs to Samoa [sic: in fact Hawaii] and after waiting and receiving no corrections went ahead and published the book. On the day of publication the proof sheets returned, containing heavy corrections throughout, and the last chapter completely re-written in manuscript. Scribner's apologized and told Stevenson that they would make the changes in the next edition, but in fact this has never been done and the proof sheets rest in Scribner's archives. I tried to buy these the other day without success, and earlier when I was a publisher I tried to persuade them to issue the book in the form Stevenson intended. What seems to me odd is that Scribner's should still be able to prevent the publication of the book that is still in copyright and owned, I suppose, by your brother's children. I would be very interested to hear whether you were aware of this situation.

Twenty-one years later Graham Greene wrote again to the *TLS* (30 October 1970) repeating this story and asking: 'Where are those proofs now and will we ever read *The Wrong Box* in its true version?' Further correspondence ensued; the last letter was from E. J. Mehew, the Mycroft Holmes of Stevensonians, who had the facts at his fingertips and had examined the manuscript and proof sheets at Yale. In 1985, Ernest Mehew told me he hoped to edit the true version of *The Wrong Box* for Bodley Head, Graham Greene's publisher.

In 1981 Graham Greene won the Jerusalem Prize. He spoke in his acceptance speech about Freedom of Thought. Greene said he was honoured by the prize and that he had known and admired some of its earlier winners:

> They have spoken up in situations far more dangerous than I have had to encounter. Ignazio Silone against the Fascists, Borges against the Peronists. You probably know the story of how a telephone rang in Borges's apartment in Buenos Aires after the return of Perón. His old mother answered. A voice said, 'We are coming to kill you and your son.' She replied, "It will be easy for you to kill my son because he is blind, but for me you will have to come quickly for I am ninety years old." Like mother, like son.

Later in his speech, talking of gangsterdom, Greene said: 'The victims have no Solzhenitsyn to describe their oppression: there is no Amnesty to take up their cause. It is left to the individual to fight alone for himself. In the words of Robert Louis Stevenson: "With the half of a broken hope for a pillow at night/That somehow the right is the right."'

The words are from Stevenson's 1893 poem 'If this were faith' (which Kipling may have half-recalled when he wrote 'If – 'in 1910). It is a poem which seems close to Greene's own hopeful scepticism.

> God, if this were enough,
> That I see things bare to the buff
> And up to the buttocks in mire;
> That I ask nor hope nor hire,
> Nut in the husk,
> Nor dawn beyond the dusk,
> Nor life beyond death:
> God, if this were faith? . . .
>
> To go on for ever and fail and go on again,
> And be mauled to the earth and arise,
> And contend for the shade of a word and a thing
>   not seen with the eyes:

With the half of a broken hope for a pillow at night
That somehow the right is the right
And the smooth shall bloom from the rough:
Lord, if that were enough?

The triangle between Stevenson, Borges and Greene is perhaps an artificial construct. The Stevenson-Borges and Stevenson–Greene connections are documented. But what about the third side of the triangle, Borges-Greene?

In 1971 Greene was in Argentina to research his novel *The Honorary Consul*, which was published in 1973. I myself read the book early the next year in Argentina, a copy borrowed from the lending-library of Harrod's department store on Florida Street, Buenos Aires. A character in *The Honorary Consul*, Dr Plarr, has tea with his greedy mother at the Richmond tea-room on the same street. But since the novel was written, Florida Street had been permanently closed to traffic, a welcome relief in Buenos Aires, where drivers do not always believe in traffic lights and think it *macho* to accelerate at pedestrians trying to cross the street.

In Buenos Aires, Greene met Borges for the first time, at the flat of Silvina Ocampo, wife of Borges's friend and collaborator Adolfo Bioy Casares. Greene and Borges descended to the street. The two writers were talking about Robert Louis Stevenson. Greene said he thought that Stevenson had written at least one good poem. Borges, perhaps remembering his own military ancestors, began to recite

Say not of me that weakly I declined
The labours of my sires, and fled the sea,
The towers we founded and the lamps we lit,
To play at home with paper like a child.
But rather say . . .

and, bravely blind, stepped off the pavement into the insane Buenos Aires traffic. Greene pulled Borges back, and saved him from the fate of Blind Pew.

*

I wish I had also been at the Second Annual Jorge Luis Borges Lecture in London on 1 October 1984, because it was delivered by

Graham Greene. I could not ask him any questions because I was on a mountain in Western Samoa that day. But I thought about Greene up there by Stevenson's grave, holding in my hand the small, pinkish, pockmarked pebble that Borges had given me before I set out on the quest.

FRANCE

I

The world that Cockfield opened up was closed down again in Edinburgh. The old tensions and worry about his future helped make the thin, nervous youth ill. A scheme to study in England might have given him the necessary independence and distance from family conflict, but Stevenson collapsed in London before he could take his examinations for the English Bar. Colvin arranged for him to see Dr Andrew Clark, who recommended rest for his patient, *alone*, in the South of France. Illness legitimized the escape from 'a gloomy family, always ready to be frightened by their precious health'. For his twenty-third birthday in November 1873 Stevenson was recuperating in Menton at the eastern end of the Riviera.

*

Stevenson already knew Menton, having been there with his mother in 1863 when she suffered from lung-trouble. The Calvinist conscience made illness a moral punishment, but Stevenson could joke about it, wanly. 'My whole game is morality now', he wrote to his Edinburgh friend Charles Baxter, 'and I am very serious about it. Indeed I am very serious about everything, and go to the boghouse with as much solemnity as another man would go to church.'

It was no fun to be an invalid with suspected tuberculosis. Despite the romantic military metaphor, Stevenson found a deadly languor 'among the wounded soldiery of mankind . . . all shut up together in some basking angle of the Riviera, walking a dusty promenade or sitting in dusty olive-yards within earshot of the interminable and unchanging surf – idle among spiritless idlers; not perhaps dying; yet hardly living either . . . '.

A doctor in Nice told him he did not have TB, but RLS still felt weak and depressed. Then Colvin came out for Christmas – they went to Monaco and the casino at Monte Carlo – and Stevenson moved to another hotel in Menton where there lived a French painter and some cheery and flirtatious Russian ladies. Things began to look brighter.

At the end of January 1874, Colvin introduced Stevenson to Andrew Lang, another Scot recuperating in Menton from lung-trouble. Lang, born in 1844 in Walter Scott country near Selkirk, was a Fellow of Merton College, Oxford, who had published a collection of poems. RLS and Lang did not like each other at first. Lang thought Stevenson's cloak the affectation of a romantic poseur; Stevenson thought Lang too prim and delicate, fluting his Oxford vowels. But their dislike was probably due to their similarity. Eventually they became friends; the next summer Stevenson visited Lang at Oxford, got drunk and threw up in his rooms. They kept in touch until Stevenson's death two decades later.

Andrew Lang was a contradictory character. One of his first stories proposed that Queen Elizabeth I was really the Earl of Darnley in drag. A classical scholar who worked on Homer, Lang also once said: 'I might have been an anthropologist if I could have made a living out of it.' Sigmund Freud said Lang's work was of 'capital importance' to his own book *Totem and Taboo*. Lang was a prolific and influential critic; his revealing statement 'The modern element in literature disturbs' led him to reject the great Russian, French and American novelists for the likes of Rider Haggard, A. E. W. Mason and Anthony Hope. He advocated 'More claymores, less psychology' for literature, and his taste for brutality flavoured with sentimentalism intensely irritated Henry James. Lang is probably best remembered today for the series of multi-coloured Fairy Books. He was shy, self-evasive, fey and perceptive, and wrote of RLS in *Adventures Among Books*:

> Mr Stevenson possessed, more than any man I ever met, the power of making other men fall in love with him. I mean that he excited a passionate admiration and affection, so much so that I verily believe some men were jealous of other men's place in his liking.

Some kind of jealousy, perhaps, can be seen in an 1898 essay by

John Jay Chapman, an American who Stevenson had once been kind to in Bournemouth. Brilliant and disturbed, Chapman mutilated his own hand in a fit of writer's self-hatred. He saw RLS as a complete sham, of'capitalthe most extraordinary mimic that has ever appeared in literature . . . He is ephemeral . . . the mistletoe of English literature whose roots are not in the soil but in the tree.' Chapman was interested in the popularization of literature since 1850 – 'the age of the Distribution of Knowledge' – and he linked RLS and Andrew Lang to this industry for the American market. 'Andrew Lang heads an army of workers who mine the old literature and coin it into booklets and cash . . . While Lang culls us tales and legends from the Norse or Provençal, Stevenson will engage to supply us with tales and legends of his own . . . The two men serve the same public'

At least one South American, however, reacted to their efforts with a gratitude bordering on love. A poem by Jorge Luis Borges, 'June 1968', is about the happiness of a man sorting his books on to new shelves. 'To arrange a library is to practise, in a modest way, the art of literary criticism':

> the satisfaction given by
> the anticipation of a habit
> and the establishment of order.
> Stevenson and that other Scotsman, Andrew Lang,
> will here pick up again, in a magic way,
> the leisurely conversation broken off
> by oceans and by death.

In a 1971 seminar at Columbia University, after Norman Thomas di Giovanni's translation of the poem had been read to the class, Borges added a gloss: 'These are two men whom I love personally, as if I had known them. If I had to draw up a list of my friends, I would include not only my personal friends, my physical friends, but I would also include Stevenson and Andrew Lang.'

2

From his time in Menton, Stevenson wrote an essay that is a footnote to the history of Victorian invalidism, 'Ordered South' (1873). Eighty years later, Borges wrote one of his best short stories, 'El Sur' or 'The South'. At first sight they have nothing in common but a point of the compass. But as Borges writes in his story, 'Reality favours symmetries and slight anachronisms.'

John Sturrock has pointed out that many of Borges's characters become confined, which paradoxically liberates the authorial imagination. Stevenson's stepson Lloyd Osbourne once wrote of the imprisoned life 'of Stevenson, who did much of his writing in bed. Stevenson's 'Ordered South' is an account of his semi-invalidism at twenty-three; Borges's 'The South' is a fictionalizing of an accident and illness he experienced at thirty-nine.

On Christmas Eve 1938, Borges banged his head on a window, got septicaemia and nearly died. After a period of delirium, he feared his mind had gone, and to prove his sanity began to write a new kind of story – 'Pierre Menard, Author of the Quixote'. In the fictionalized accident in 'The South' the protagonist Juan Dahlmann is carrying a copy of *The 1001 Nights* upstairs to his apartment when he bangs his head on an opened window, gets septicaemia and nearly dies.

When he wakes from fever, Dahlmann is in the same sort of feeble stupor as the narrator of Stevenson's 'Ordered South'. Both of them notice it is autumn. Both are from the Protestant North and travel by train to the liberating South to recuperate. Stevenson writes of 'the indefinable line that separates South from North'; and Borges specifies: 'Every Argentine knows that the South begins on the other side of Rivadavia.' In Stevenson's essay the South is 'an estate out of which he had been kept unjustly'; in Borges's story the South is 'the empty shell of a ranch'. The Stevenson invalid feels split: 'He is like an enthusiast leading about with him a stolid indifferent tourist. There is someone by who is out of sympathy with the scene . . . and that someone is himself.' And the Borges invalid shares the same condition: 'It was as if he were two men at a time: the man who travelled through the autumn day and across his native geography, and the other one, locked up in a sanatorium . . . '

In both essay and story the invalid longs for heath and an active life. In November 1873, while he was writing 'Ordered South', Stevenson wrote to Fanny Sitwell: 'If you knew how old I felt! . . . I am a man of seventy: O Medea, kill me, or make me young again!' 'Ordered South' echoes the letter:

He has outlived his own usefulness, and almost his own enjoyment; and if there is to be no recovery; if never again will he be young and strong and passionate . . . he will pray for Medea: when she comes, let her either rejuvenate or slay.

In 'The South' Dahlmann has the chance of rejuvenation or slaughter; he is insulted by rural toughs and challenged to fight; an old gaucho throws him a knife which lands at his feet. 'There go many elements', Stevenson wrote in 'Ordered South', 'to the making of one moment of intense perception.' Dahlmann's moment is when he picks up the knife – without hope, but without fear. As readers, we do not really know if Dahlmann is actually still in the hospital, being stuck with needles. But to die in a knife-fight is perhaps better than dying in a bed. 'He felt that if he had been able to choose, then, or dream his death, this would have been the death he would have chosen or dreamed.' And Borges's story ends with Dahlmann, holding the knife that he might not know how to use, going out into the flat pampas plain.

> Or, Lord, if too obdurate I,
> Choose thou, before that spirit die,
> A piercing pain, a killing sin,
> And to my dead heart run them in!
> RLS, 'The Celestial Surgeon' (1882)

A fellow has to die fighting, you know.
RLS in conversation, Manasquan, New Jersey (1887)

3

In April 1874, Robert Louis Stevenson made his 'first independent acquaintance with Paris'. He came to see his cousin Bob Stevenson, who was studying painting, and their earliest haunts were on the Left Bank, in the fifth and sixth *arrondissements*. Bob lived at 81 Boulevard de Montparnasse, and Louis stayed in hotels: one on the corner of Rue St Jacques and Rue du Val-de-Grâce, another in the Rue de Racine. Both hotels have now vanished.

Paris in the 1870s offered the Stevenson boys freedoms that

Edinburgh could never match. According to Andrew Lang they were playing 'the wild Prince and Poins' at this epoch, in the city which was the original place to be 'Bohemian'. The word had been introduced to England by Thackeray in 1848, with the sense of unconventional social gypsy. These romantic and sponging vagabonds with artistic pretensions caught the European imagination through Henri Murger's novel *Scènes de Bohème*, a work both derided and emulated by later art-students. Stevenson himself thought the book 'sugar-candy pastorals . . . written in rose-water'.

Lloyd Osbourne wrote of his stepfather, R. L. Stevenson:

> What he praised most in the French as a national trait was their universal indulgence towards all sexual problems – their clear-sighted toleration of everything affecting the relations of men and women. He often said that in this the French were the most civilized people in Europe.

Stevenson loved the 'frankness' and 'lack of hypocrisy' of the French. He thought the British were better governed, but their outlook was 'blinkered by caste, puritanism and prejudice'. Late in life Stevenson still deplored these British constraints. He told Osbourne:

> How the French misuse their freedom; see nothing worth writing about but the eternal triangle; while we, who are muzzled like dogs, but who are infinitely wider in our outlook, are condemned to avoid half the life that passes us by. What books Dickens could have written had he been permitted! Think of Thackeray as unfettered as Flaubert or Balzac! What books I might have written myself. But they give us a little box of toys, and say to us, 'You mustn't play with anything but these.'

Stevenson's novel *The Wrecker* (1892) gives us some idea of art-student life in the 1870s, though the book is more about chasing dollars than girls. Two characters in the book seem close to Bob and Louis (the madcap Stennises, 'Stennis-*aîné* and Stennis-*frère*'), and one incident in the book may account for some of the £1000 which Stevenson was given by his father after passing his Law exams in

1875. A proposal to visit the country by some art-students causes some to wonder if they have time to pack:

> But the Stennis boys exclaimed upon our effeminacy. They had come from London, it appeared, a week before with nothing but great-coats and tooth-brushes. No baggage – there was the secret of existence. It was expensive to be sure; for every time you had to comb your hair, a barber must be paid, and every time you changed your linen, one shirt must be bought and another thrown away; but anything was better (argued these young gentlemen) than to be the slaves of haversacks. 'A fellow has to get rid gradually of all material attachments; that was manhood' (said they); 'and as long as you were bound down to anything, house, umbrella or portmanteau, – you were still tethered by the umbilical cord.'

Life was not all fun and folly. Bob was studying painting at Carolus-Duran's studio near Montparnasse, where the notable American portrait painter John Singer Sargent was also a pupil. It was Carolus-Duran who first directed Bob's attention to the paintings of Diego Velázquez, and R. A. M. Stevenson was to write an influential book about the great seventeenth-century Spanish painter in 1895. Bob suggested that Velázquez was important to modern art because he trusted his eye, not 'traditional rules or scientific study', and his paintings were unified, tonal 'impressions' rather than 'pattern [s] of lines and tints'. His book also stresses that Velazquez's 'effect of realism' was really 'the most consummate finesse of art'.

The Stevenson cousins became apprenticed to their crafts in Paris, and they were close enough for their aesthetic concerns to interpenetrate. The chapter of Bob's *Velazquez* called 'The Dignity of Technique' seems to apply almost equally to what Louis was learning: 'When he leaves nature for art, a man leaves bright boundless space where he has no dominion for a dark cloistered place where he is master . . . But he must learn to obey what, for want of a better word one may call the law of decorative effect.' RLS appreciated technique as much as his cousin. 'There is something . . . in the very air of France that communicates the love of style. Precision, clarity, the cleanly and crafty employment of material, a

grace in the handling . . . seem to be acquired by the mere residence . . .
The air of Paris is alive with this technical inspiration.' Both
cousins also found it outside the capital, near Fontainebleau;' to
leave that airy city and awake the next day upon the borders of the
forest is but to change externals'.

4

The village of Barbizon on the western edge of the Forest of
Fontainebleau became the most important place in France for the
two Stevensons. Here, Bob had his eyes opened by Corot and the
Barbizon school of landscape painters, and he remained loyal to
them for the rest of his life. Louis was enchanted by 'the poetry of life
and earth' that the Forest came to represent, a green 'fairyland' in
direct contrast to the modern world of 'gin and steamhammers'. It
was a good place for an apprentice writer and Stevenson wrote two
essays about Barbizon and its environs: 'Forest Notes' (1875) and
'Fontainebleau: Village Communities of Painters' (1883). In the
second essay, RLS looks back on his younger self:

> He enjoyed a strenuous idleness full of visions, hearty meals,
> long, sweltering walks, mirth among companions; and still
> floating like music through his brain, foresights of great works
> that Shakespeare might be proud to have conceived, headless
> epics, glorious torsos of dramas . . . visions of style that repose
> upon no base of human meaning; the last heart-throbs of that
> excited amateur who has to die in all of us before the artist can
> be born . . . We were all artists; almost all in the age of illusion,
> cultivating an imaginary genius . . . small wonder, indeed, if
> we were happy!

*

I read on the train from the Gare de Lyon. I had bought, from a Left
Bank *bouquiniste* near tourist-packed Notre Dame, one of the
excellent 10/18 volumes of Stevenson called *La France que j'aime*,
which contained all his essays on France and French writers. The
introduction by Francis Lacassin pointed out that Stevenson could
and did pass as French among Frenchmen, and called him *le plus
français des écrivains anglais*'. Stevenson reads well in French; the

wordier bits emerge with Gallic aplomb. His work is more easily available in France than in England.

I got off the train at Bois-le-Roi and walked the five miles to Barbizon. It was a fine breezy day in May, and the shadows of clouds ran over lilac blossom as I walked out past the gardens and gates of villas along the road towards Fay. After crossing a thundering highway, I was suddenly at the edge of the forest, on a dead straight road dwindling away through the trees to a point. Cars shot past at a speed which seemed mindless in the Forest of Fontainebleau. One has to go slowly, preferably on foot, to appreciate something of the 40,000 hectares of breathing woodland.

*

The old royal hunting forest of Fontainebleau is, as Stevenson points out, a preserve rather than a wilderness, but its size and variety make it seem 'natural'. Close to Paris, it had been favoured since the 1830s by Romantic writers and painters who visited the villages on its western edge. Theodore Rousseau settled at Barbizon in 1836, followed by Jean-Francois Millet in 1849, and both men lived there for the rest of their lives. They took to gardening and *la vie naturelle*; they were socialists and pacifists who disliked hunting and protested at the destruction of the forest, conservationists ahead of their time. Around them grew up the Barbizon school of painters whose influence extended far beyond the forest. Painters came from all over Europe, Scandinavia, North America, even Australia, and took back ideas, techniques and a new attitude to the natural world.

R. L. Stevenson first came to Barbizon a few months after Millet's death in 1875 where there was still a crowd of international expatriates trying to be painters. Years later he was grateful for their company:

> This purely artistic society is excellent for the young artist. The lads . . . are at that stage of education . . . when a man is too occupied with style to be aware of the necessity for any matter; and this, above all for the Englishman, is excellent . . . Here, in England, too many painters and writers dwell dispersed, unshielded, among the intelligent bourgeois . . . [who] prate to him about the lofty aims and moral influence of art. And this is the lad's ruin. For art is, first of all, and last of

all, a trade. The love of words and not a desire to publish new discoveries . . . mark the vocation of the writer . . .

5

A kilometre down the straight road I came to a firing range, signposted *DANGER DE MORT*. But one was only in danger when the red triangle was displayed. This was *le weekend*, and there was no gunnery practice. The large brown areas on the map were the same in Stevenson's day; areas set aside for the military.

I cut off the road down a sun-baked track of white crushed limestone that ran through clearings and over culverts draining the sedgy ground. Machine civilization began to fade with the zip of cars on the asphalt far behind. The last reminder of modern technology was a nodding donkey-pump behind a square of fence, quietly extracting petroleum. The Paris basin yields around a million metric tons of crude oil every year.

The path became clayey and soft, twisting under the branches, winding into a denser green world unchanged from when Stevenson described it:

> Ants swarm in the hot sand; mosquitoes drone their nasal drone; wherever the sun finds a hole in the roof of the forest, you see a myriad transparent creatures coming and going in the shaft of light . . . you are conscious of a continual drift of insects, an ebb and flow of infinitesimal living things between the trees . . .

Deep in a European hardwood forest, it is still easy to forget where you are and what century you are in. It could be Sherwood or Arden or any of the 'Greenwood States' that Stevenson loved to imagine. My own mind began to wander; I slowed down, stopped, and lay down for a long while in a sunny ring of birches away from the path.

*

Waking out of the dream of the forest gradually, I walked towards a humming buzz of traffic and the high voices of children. Suddenly there was the shock of a bourgeois family in their smart pale clothes, and their Alsatian bounding forward in great sand-spurting lopes, thin-chested as a wolf . . . I braced myself for a savaging but the man called out 'Viens, Vodka!' and in a spray of dirt the beast spun round, turned lolling tongue to waving tail, and raced back again. Soon there were picnic tables by a carpark of campers' vehicles, solid people seriously eating and drinking, footballers washing at a tap, a snarling highway. I crossed it fast and plunged into the trees again, heading for Barbizon.

*

'Forest Notes' opens in the flat fields behind Barbizon:

> The sun goes down, a swollen orange, as it were into the sea. A blue-clad peasant rides home, with a harrow smoking behind him among the dry clods. Another still works with his wife in their little strip. An immense shadow fills the plain; these people stand in it up to their shoulders; and their heads, as they stoop over their work and rise again, are relieved from time to time against the golden sky.

Stevenson is painting with words.

The last two sentences of the extract are a direct reference to J.-F. Millet's famous 1859 picture *The Angelas*, painted on the spot that Stevenson describes.

*

Beech gave way to oak as I walked down through the leaf-mould towards the eastern side of Barbizon. The music seeping between the tall trunks grew louder; brash rock music, with gunfire, and shrieks. Barbizon, *village des peintres*, had a travelling fair this Sunday, and 'the companionable silence of the trees' had been overtaken by roaring modernity. Bumping dodgems and bright merry-go-rounds with loudspeakers whose bass made your guts vibrate. Leather-clad bikers gunned their motors, and 22s cracked from the shooting-gallery. Louts hurled wooden balls at pyramids of tins and darts at trapped balloons. Among all the frazzled parents and wailing kids, bare-chested men with bad teeth, gypsyish touts and gum-chewing girls with cheap handbags, I saw an old man in army boots and green-stained clothes shuffling his sit-up-and-beg bicycle through the mob. His hump bent him almost double and, as he raised his muttering head to look around, the effort twisted his face into a painfully angry rictus.

6

Barbizon had changed from a small village of Bohemian painters into a villa'd town of bourgeois punters. Along La Grande Rue, Mercedes-Benzes were parked outside expensive restaurants, and the pavements in front of antique shops were packed with day-trippers and art-loving tourists.

I made my way along the street, looking for Siron's Inn. Here Stevenson and the young painters had lived for five francs a day, and helped themselves to wine and beer from the cellar. In 'Forest Notes' he had described painters on chairs out in the street in the early evening, waiting for the *patache* or horse-drawn omnibus from Melun, other drinkers in the billiard-room, doves in the dove-cot, Hortense drawing water from the well, the *chef* in his kitchen off the courtyard and a painter jangling a waltz on the old piano in the dining-room.

The Hôtellerie du Bas-Bréau was a half-timbered house on the right of the street. A brown plaque on the front wall said:

R. Louis Stevenson
while at this hotel wrote
Forest Notes

I walked under the broad coach entrance, bristling with the heads of dead animals. A rich and wrinkled American couple passed me, talking loudly. It was a Four Star Hotel and the reception had a telephone, computer and VDU in matching tasteful tan. In the inner courtyard, a red-faced man with a fat cigar and a brandy snifter the size of a boar's testicles lounged in a linen suit across the table from his *poule de luxe*. She stared at me in frank disdain. I was out of place, and hot from walking and running in the woods.

'*Monsieur?*' said the receptionist. I scooped sweat from my brow, smiled ingratiatingly and showed a press card.

'I'm interested in him,' pointing to a small photograph of Stevenson that hung in a frame by the counter. Someone had stuck a sprig of boxwood from Palm Sunday over it. 'Can I have a look at it?'

Stevenson wore a velvet jacket, held a pen in his hand and stared straight at the camera. I recognized the picture from the cover of the Stevenson/Baxter letters book. There was no date on the brown paper back, but M. Fava the hotel proprietor had written his name upon it, and the erroneous information that Stevenson's first visit to the hotel had been in 1879. He was four years out of date.

'Have you got any information about the history of the hotel?'

She passed over a slim brown folder: Hôtellerie du Bas-Bréau, Barbizon, Seine-et-Marne. Inside there was a blue and white booklet, 'Extracts from the Golden Book'. I opened the first page and started laughing.

There she was, on Stevenson's old stamping ground of Siron's Inn, frowning into the sunlight at another irritating photo-call, gripping the balcony rail like a captain on the ship's bridge: the Rt Hon. Margaret Thatcher MP, Prime Minister of the United Kingdom of Great Britain and Northern Ireland.

On the opposite page, the Stevenson plaque on the wall outside was visible over the head of Bettino Craxi of Italy, then, in order: Francis Mitterrand of France, Wilfrid Maertens of Belgium, Helmut Kohl of Germany, Andreas Papandreou of Greece, Ruud Lubbers of Holland, Poul Schluters of Denmark, Pierre Werner of Luxembourg, and Garret Fitzgerald of Ireland, walking in the street with name-tagged security men and interpreters and police motorcyclists.

It was taken after the Fontainebleau Summit, La Reunion du Conseil Européen, 25-26 June 1984, attended by the ten European leaders. The centre photo in the booklet showed them at table for *le dîner qui a dégelé l'Europe* (the meal that thawed Europe), sitting round the candlelit white napery and gleaming crystal, great bowls of blurred pink, white and violet flowers; the presidents and prime ministers of the European Economic Community, ranged in suits and ties and hankies in top pockets, the single woman in her queenly pearl necklace.

Stevenson described a rather less formal meal in 'Forest Notes':

Under these works of art so much eating goes forward, so much drinking, so much jabbering in French and English, that it would do your heart good merely to peep and listen at the door. One man is telling how they all went last year to the fete at Fleury, and another how well So-and-So would sing of an evening; and here are a third and fourth making plans for the whole of the rest of their lives; and there is a fifth imitating a conjuror and making faces on his clenched fist, surely of all arts the most difficult and admirable! A sixth has eaten his fill, lights his cigarette, and resigns himself to digestion. A seventh has just dropped in and calls for soup. Number eight, meanwhile, has left the table, and is once more trampling the poor piano under powerful and uncertain fingers.

7

On another sunny day I took a train to Fontainebleau, hired a bicycle at the station, and rode to what RLS called 'the glaring crossroads' by the gorge of Franchard in the middle of the forest.

Stevenson came with a wagon-load of painters on their way to Grez-sur-Loing. On the way they met the colour-man, M. Desprez, and put in their orders for paints and chalks. On the Route Ronde they were stopped by a mounted trooper: the artillery were practising on the Quadrilateral range just ahead. The doctor in the wagon-party – 'his speech is smooth and dulcet, his manner dignified and insinuating' – talked them past the sentry and they drove quickly across the range. 'At any moment we may meet the sergeant who will send us back. At any moment we may encounter a flying shell, which will send us somewhere further off than Gretz.'

Their ghostly party went south. I cycled a few hundred yards west under the trees to Franchard, whose chapel Stevenson had incorporated into an 1882 short story which contains a pompous doctor called by the real-life colour-man's name, Dr Desprez.

I rode past the Franchard inn where the doctor had celebrated with a bottle of Bass Pale Ale. The restaurant was drifted over with leaves and chairs were leaned forwards onto rusting tables. Furious dogs ran barking behind the chain-link fence. I freewheeled through the twisty tree-roots and bald dirt of the Franchard car-park, past a group of policemen in tracksuits lounging by the edge of a long open glade. The barking died away. Near the fire-watchers' tall derrick tower a school bus was disgorging a party of students with their science teacher.

The chapel was locked. Rooks quarrelled in the trees. I walked round the back where there was a boarded-up well and a plaque commemorating *The creation of the International Union for the Conservation of Nature and Its Resources*, founded in 1948.

Much of Franchard has been conserved as Stevenson described it, with 'rocks and birches standing luminous in the sun'. I followed the track west, down a long deep gorge, a limestone fault cleaving through heather and pine with strange boulders rearing from yellow clay. You could still see its romantic possibilities for a painter or writer.

Idly cycling back past the Franchard inn I gave a V-sign to the same barking dogs as they hurled themselves at the fence. In an instant they were no longer running parallel to the wire, but wheeling away, and before I realized what was happening all three were out and racing at me in a three-pronged attack led by a vicious Dobermann pinscher.

Lyndon Johnson once said of Gerald Ford that he couldn't walk and chew gum at the same time. Three potentially rabid French dogs induced a frenzy of simultaneity: I bellowed and balanced, pedalled and lashed out with my feet at the barking snapping jaws. My heart was pounding madly by the time I got safely to the crossroads. The three dogs ran cockily back and forth under the trees, strutting triumphant tails.

Stevenson's wagon-party of artists from Siron's were bound in the end for Grez-sur-Loing. 'Gretz lies out of the forest, down by the bright river. It boasts a mill, an ancient church, a castle, and a bridge of many sterlings.'

It was at Grez-sur-Loing in the summer of 1876 that Robert Louis Stevenson first met the woman he was to marry.

8

Fanny Vandegrift was born in Indianapolis, Indiana, on 10 March 1840. She was the daughter of Jacob Vandegrift, a builder of Dutch descent who spent a lot of money and died poor, and Esther Thomas Keen, a tiny but vigorous woman of Swedish ancestry. Fanny was a dark, curly-haired, lively tomboy of a child, good with her hands and endowed with a Gothic imagination. At seventeen she married a handsome lieutenant on the State Governor's staff called Samuel Osbourne, and their first child Isobel, known as Belle, was born the next year. Osbourne went off to the Civil War, returned, then set off again in 1863 to escort a tubercular friend to California. His friend died in Panama, but Osbourne went on to San Francisco and thence to Nevada to try and get rich in the silver mines. Once settled in, he sent for his wife and child.

Fanny had grit. With a five-year-old child she travelled to New York to take a boat south, and then a train across the isthmus of Panama, another ship up to San Francisco, and went on by wagon and stage-coach to the mining camps on Nevada's Reese River, and the crude town of Austin in Lander County. There were few women among the miners and Paiute Indians would peer in through the windows of their small cabin. Fanny learned to cook beef in fifteen different ways, use a frying pan as a mirror, shoot with a revolver and roll her own cigarettes. Little Belle remembered extraordinary happenings: the murderer who made her little animals of sour-dough and molasses; the band of Indians who brought in the heart of a prospector who had died in Death Valley, returning it to his widow.

The family moved to Virginia City, Nevada. (Mark Twain's *Roughing It* (1872) gives a good idea of what it was like.) Sam Osbourne began going with saloon girls, while Belle made friends with a mulatto Cherokee gambler and barber called Billy Bird. In 1866 Sam Osbourne took off to go prospecting in the Coeur d'Alène mountains, and Fanny and Belle took the Wells Fargo stage to San Francisco. Rumour came that Sam had been killed by a grizzly, but in the end he turned up safe and sound, and he and Fanny had another child named Samuel Lloyd in April 1868. Sam embarked on new romantic affairs and Fanny went home to Indianapolis.

In 1869 they were reconciled again, for Sam was a charmer, plausibly contrite, and they lived in a cottage in Oakland, across the bay from San Francisco. Fanny took up painting and gardening, and gave birth to a second son called Hervey. Sam Osbourne soon returned to his philandering ways and, in 1875, Fanny left him, and took herself and her three children to Europe. They lived in Antwerp for three months but it was difficult for women to study art there, so they moved to Paris and an apartment in Rue de Naples near St Lazare station. Mother and daughter enrolled at the Julien Atelier in Passage des Panoramas.

Belle was seventeen and as beautiful as her name. She was thrilled to find that a sister of Louisa M. Alcott, the original of Amy in *Little Women*, was in her class. Seven-year-old Lloyd went to a French school where, with the siege of Paris still fresh in everyone's memory, he was nicknamed 'Prussian' for his blonde hair. But the five-year-old Hervey was ill, suffering from scrofulous tuberculosis.

The winter of 1875–76 turned out to be a grievous one for Fanny

Osbourne. She summoned her husband by telegram from America, and he came in time to see their youngest boy die on 5 April 1876. Hervey was buried at Père Lachaise, in a temporary grave because they could not afford a proper one. The loss of her child turned Fanny's mind for a while. She lost weight, and suffered hallucinations. A doctor said she needed a change, and an American sculptor called Pardessus recommended Chevillon's Inn at Grez-sur-Loing, 60 kilometres south-east of Paris, as a fine and peaceful place to spend the summer. They left the flat and travelled by train and diligence to Grez, to the old inn whose garden led down to the bright river and the grey arching bridge.

*

I took the train to Bourron-Marlotte and walked the mile and a half to Grez through wheatfields and carolling larks. At the entrance to the town there was a sign by the cemetery warning any 'nomads' against fixing their abode. Dusty wreaths lay on the war memorial to the 'children' of Grez, and the long hot street through the sleepy small town was empty.

Chevillon's Inn has long gone, but you can walk over the bridge that generations of art-students, including Fanny Osbourne, have painted, and sit on a bench in the willow-hung park on the opposite bank, to look back over the same flowing river.

*

It was July 1876 when the lads at Siron's heard that women from across the Atlantic had invaded Grez. Bob Stevenson went down to check, and if necessary chuck them out. The first one he met was seventeen-year-old Belle, in the courtyard of the Inn. Years later, in her impressionistic biography *This Life I've Loved* (1937), she remembered:

> A stranger appeared; an artist, evidently, from his velvet jacket and flowing tie. He was slim and dark and so odd and foreign-looking that we thought he was a Pole, or a sort of gentleman gipsy, and were surprised when he greeted us somewhat formally in English.

Her younger brother Lloyd was to recall:

> A dark, roughly dressed man as lithe and graceful as a Mexican

vaquero and evoking something of the same misgiving . . . In my innocence I thought he might suddenly strike Isobel . . . Then she ran up to our room, laughing with excitement, to tell us that 'Bob' was a most agreeable and entertaining man . . . and my sister's eyes were shining at the obvious impression she had made.

Bob had never met any American women and he was charmed. American males were already a new source of fun and Bob quoted for months what he claimed an American painter had said to him of the Loing Valley: 'Seems mighty settled round here, stranger.' For her part, Fanny was attracted to Bob: 'He is exactly like one of Ouida's heroes, with the hand of steel in the glove of velvet.'

As Bob had not reported back, Walter Simpson, Stevenson's neighbour from Edinburgh, was the next to arrive. 'The Bart' as he was nicknamed was equally struck by the two lively attractive women. Next scout in was Frank O'Meara, a handsome twenty-year-old Irishman who Belle fell for in a big way. Eventually Louis Stevenson himself arrived. Legend has him stepping through the window from the garden in the evening lamplight, and falling in love with Fanny Osbourne at first sight.

In fact, Fanny Osbourne's letters to her friend Timothy Rearden in San Francisco show a greater initial interest in RLS's cousin. They also demonstrate the Stevenson boys' tendency to romanticize themselves for eager American ears. Fanny wrote excitedly:

Bob Stevenson is the most beautiful creature I ever saw in my life . . . He spent a large fortune at the rate of eight thousand pounds a year, and now he has only a hundred pounds a year left; he graduated from Cambridge with high honors and won all the boat races and everything of that sort, studied music and did wonderful things as a musician, took holy orders to please his mother, quit in disgust, studied painting and did some fine work, and is now dying from the effects of dissipation and is considered a little mad . . .

Louis, his cousin, the hysterical fellow . . . is a tall, gaunt Scotchman with a face like Raphael, and between over-education and dissipation has ruined his health, and is dying of consumption. Louis reformed his habits a couple of years ago, and Bob, this winter. Louis is the heir to an immense

[98]

fortune which he will never live to inherit. His father and mother, cousins, are both threatened with insanity, and I am quite sure the son is . . .

Life at Grez was entertaining, with boats and water sports, and Fanny and Belle both entered into the spirit of the place in the summers of 1876, 1877 and 1878. Gradually Fanny's emotional interest shifted its focus. Bob told her: 'You must have nothing to say to *me*, for I am only a vulgar cad, but Louis is a gentleman, and you can trust him and depend upon him.' Louis thus supplanted his older cousin, and Fanny was grateful to Bob for it: 'He is right about his cousin, whom I like very much, and who is the wittiest man I ever met.' But Fanny also found RLS very emotional. He had a flaming temper, and a matching Scots over-sensitivity: 'I do wish he wouldn't burst into tears in such an unexpected way; it is so embarrassing. One doesn't know what to do, whether to offer him a pocket handkerchief, or to look out of the window.'

In November 1876, four months after meeting Fanny Osbourne, Stevenson wrote an essay called 'On Falling In Love'. He said: 'the ideal story is that of two people who go into love step for step, with a fluttered consciousness, like a pair of children venturing together into a dark room. From the first moment when they see each other, with a pang of curiosity, through stage after stage of growing pleasure and embarrassment, they can read the expression of their own trouble in the other's eyes . . . '

But Fanny Osbourne, mother of two children and mourning a third, was still married to her feckless husband Sam. No doubt Stevenson minded. Elsewhere in 'On Falling In Love' he wrote: 'Jealousy, at any rate, is one of the consequences of love; you may like it or not, at pleasure, but there it is.'

9

In 1876, not only did Stevenson meet his future wife, but he also made the canoe-trip that was to result in his first book, *An Inland Voyage* (1878). His companion was his old friend Sir Walter Grindlay Simpson, Bart. Seven years older than Stevenson, he was a stolid man 'of a sincere and somewhat slow nature', a good balance for Stevenson's nervous temperament. They had travelled together before: to Brussels and Hamburg in 1872; through the Hebrides in the yacht *Heron* in 1874; and on a walking tour through the Loing Valley in the summer of 1875, when Stevenson got himself arrested for a few hours in Châtillon, accused of vagabondage, and had to be rescued from the police-station by his titled friend.

Canoeing was a new sport, popularized by an eccentric barrister called John MacGregor whose canoe *Rob Roy* went on waterways from Baalbek to the Baltic. MacGregor first wrote about his exploits in 1866, and Stevenson not only corresponded with the pioneer, but took to the sport himself, exploring with Baxter and Simpson and various cousins the little islands of the Firth of Forth that can be seen from the upper windows of 17 Heriot Row – Cramond, Inchmickery and the Oxcar Rocks.

An Inland Voyage has been described by Bruce Chatwin as 'the prototype of the incompetent undergraduate voyage'. It was more than that: Simpson in his 'solid English oak' canoe *Cigarette* and Stevenson in his 'French cedar' craft *Arethusa* managed to cover over 200 miles from Antwerp to Pontoise, just north of Paris. But the tone of the book is very much that of the worldly-wise undergraduate with a self-conscious pipe, proud to be attracting attention along the canals while duller folk earn their livings in stuffy offices. Stevenson is not quite sure who he is writing for; perhaps leisured youth who share his gentlemanly contempt for trade. For the first and last time, he is posing as 'an Englishman'.

An Inland Voyage tends to show off and is precious in parts. It failed to sell even half its first print run of 1000 copies, but it got twenty long reviews which noticed something new and fresh, and it was a dozen years ahead of the slightly similar *Three Men In A Boat*.

*

In September 1876, Simpson and Stevenson (calling themselves by the names of their canoes *Cigarette* and *Arethusa*) slid along the Willebroek Canal from Antwerp to Brussels: in May 1984 I took a train from Ostend to Brussels to follow their route. The pollarded trees by the canal were shooting green, calves rocked across a meadow, and the houses looked English, but squeezed taller. I fell asleep on the train, and in the hypnagogic twilight the Flemish chatter in the compartment sounded like English with weirdly concertina'd vowels.

I woke up hungry at Brussels. On the Channel ferry I had read a Belgian tourist brochure that sounded hurt:

> If French cuisine has a very good name and is known everywhere, Belgian cuisine is not lacking. And let us, once and for all, destroy the myth that Belgium is exclusively a realm of chips.

Stevenson had been here before me:

> The food, as usual in Belgium, was of a nondescript occasional character; indeed I have never been able to detect anything in the nature of a meal among this pleasing people; they seem to peck and trifle with viands all day long in an amateur spirit: tentatively French, truly German, and somehow falling between the two.

Brussels station had a subway full of small bars dispensing hotdogs and fritters. Belgium is a beer-drinking country. I bought a box of big red matches – *dikke rode lucifers*, in Brueghel's tongue. The grey concrete platforms had little metal and glass waiting-rooms like spartan bus-shelters. Each bore a floral sticker in either of the country's two languages, Flemish (Dutch) or Walloon (French):

> *Vrije toegang met fair-play dank u*
> *Accès libre avec fair-play merci*

'The Anglo-Saxon is essentially dishonest', Stevenson once observed in Augustinian mood, and 'the French is devoid by nature of the principle that we call "fair play".'

It was interesting that *fair play* should be a loan-word in Belgium, that sports-mad country. The concept had broadened in meaning to imply 'civic decency'. But competitive sport seemed to be intensifying the aggression it was meant to sublimate. The month before I was in Brussels, shots fired from a bar had killed one and wounded another English football fan. And in the summer of 1985, thirty-nine football fans died after fighting broke out at a match between Liverpool and Turin, played in Brussels, administrative centre of the new Europe.

Stevenson and Simpson took a train south from Brussels, across the French frontier to Maubeuge. I followed in their wake. Now, as then, the customs and immigration men work their way down the train, and as the *douanier* in well-pressed uniform and immaculate *képi* handed back my passport I thought of Stevenson, who always had trouble at borders. 'To pass the frontier, even in a train, is a difficult matter for the *Arethusa*.' Stevenson thought of himself as 'a marked man for the official eye'. He was rarely believed to be British, and sometimes he was taken for a spy, with his long hair and Indian smoking cap. Nowadays his bags would be regularly searched for drugs etc; then he was the only one on the train who was asked for his papers. 'Although I clung to my rights, I had to choose at last between accepting the humiliation and being left behind by the train. I was sorry to give way, but I wanted to arrive at Maubeuge.'

The train passed through Mons, where the first battle of the Great War of 1914–18 had been fought.

10

Maubeuge is an industrial city five miles south of the Belgian border. In the 1939–45 war Allied bombers pounded the factories and railway yards, and as 'precision-bombing' was its usual messy business, 90 per cent of the town's centre was destroyed. It was rebuilt after the war, but its soul had gone, and it now mimics animation. With its annual *Kermesse de la Bière* that dates back as far as 1962, Maubeuge has pretensions to pseudo-medieval jollity. But, like Raymond Chandler's Los Angeles, it is a city with all the personality of a paper cup.

Avenue Jean Mabuse, with its cinemas and cafés, was full of kids out of their overalls and into tight shirts, medallions and a haze of aftershave, all looking for a good time. I could not find Stevenson's hotel Le Grand Cerf; it must have been bombed or demolished. But I saw an Army tank on a rockery and many unlovely buildings. In the Place des Nations two Arab youths, stretched over a car bonnet, were being searched by police, and people stopped to stare. The move from the Mahgreb to Maubeuge seemed all loss: an old man in a burnous walking painfully round a car-park as though it were an exercise-yard. After dark the streetlights did not all work, and I stumbled over broken pavements. Dogs were barking, Arab music wailed from a block of flats and every car that passed had its radio blaring rock. Walking with my hands in my pockets, I found my fists were tightly clenched.

On Maubeuge's Avenue Franklin Roosevelt two untended monuments are face to face.

9 Nov 1918: *Délivrance de Maubeuge par la division de la garde*
britannique.

2 Sep 1944: *Délivrance de Maubeuge par le groupe A de la 3ème*
division blindée américaine.

Behind the monument to the First World War a llama was masticating. The big-eyed cameloid with delicate lips wadding grass seemed wholly surreal until I realized I was outside Maubeuge Zoo.

The zoo occupies the old fort. Wild beasts are penned in the remains of the fortress first built by Vauban after the town became French under the terms of the 1648 Treaty of Nijmegen. Stevenson wrote: 'The troops drum and trumpet and man the ramparts, as bold as so many lions.' Now there are real lions.

The dirty, slavish condition of the animals in Maubeuge Zoo made me ashamed to belong to the human race. Through a window smeared with faeces I stared at a moulting chimpanzee in a two metre cube of tiled space with a metal bed. It was like a totalitarian hospital, and she was in the foetal position, rocking, rocking, rocking.

At the top of the fortified zoo an area was fenced in to make what they called '*une promenade agréable*' where the animals were '*en liberté*'. A peacock screamed above the noise of traffic, in a city ringed by industrial smokes. A sullen lynx was in a muddy, barred cave at the summit and we stared at each other through the grille. Stevenson always hated cruelty to animals. Once he stopped some men from tormenting a dog. 'It's not yours,' they said. 'No,' he replied, 'it is God's creature and I am here to protect it.'

Shrieking schoolchildren passed under the huge walls. This whole dispiriting display of other species was meant to be *pédagogique, scientifique, éducatif, récréatif*. There were distorting mirrors on some trees that made the 'humans' look grotesquely fat or freakishly thin. At the exit there was a bear in a pit, then the Boulevard d'Europe with red flats and the city abattoir.

While I was sitting in the railway station buffet a child was suddenly sick on the floor. The mother cleaned it up with a mop and bucket provided by the contemptuous barman. I was glad to board the first train leaving Maubeuge.

11

The train south skirted the Forest of Mormal. It was raining, as it had rained on Stevenson and Simpson paddling along this stretch of the river. The Forest of Mormal – 'a sinister name to the ear' Stevenson admitted – was a bad place to be in August 1914. It split the British Expeditionary Force retreating from Mons, forcing General Haig's I Corps to the east. It was a sweltering hot afternoon when they reached Landrecies.

'Landrecies', Stevenson observed in 1876, 'is not the place one would have chosen for a day's rest, for it consists almost entirely of fortifications . . . [Landrecies] was a point in the great warfaring system of Europe, and might on some future day be ringed about with cannon smoke and thunder, and make itself a name among strong towns.'

That day came on 25 August 1914 when the Brigade of Guards marched into Landrecies, which Rudyard Kipling in *The Irish Guards in the Great War* called 'an unlovely, long-streeted town'. The retreat was chaotic; Corps HQ was mixed up with the Guards and some of its senior officers were feeling the strain. An over-excited Colonel fired his revolver at some British remounts, thinking they were German Cavalry in pursuit.

Things were worse at the very top. General Sir Douglas Haig with his trousers round his boots was not a happy man. Medicine for a stomach upset had given him violent diarrhoea. 'If we are caught, by God we'll sell our lives dearly!' Orders went out from the General's lavatory to organize the whole town for defence. Barricades were made of furniture, mattresses, carts, the regimental tool-limbers, chopped down trees. Bayonets gouged loopholes in the walls of private houses. Soldiers and civilians waited in the heat for the German Army that had punched through Belgium.

Around seven o'clock in the evening men of the 14th Regiment of the German IV Korps ran into the northern pickets. They had no idea the British were there, but were hoping for a billet in Landrecies for the night. What Kipling called 'a night-fight of some splendour' took place. A haystack caught fire; a howitzer knocked out a German field-gun; infantrymen fired many rounds. General Haig thought the Brigade was doomed. At 1.35 am he reported to GHQ that the situation was 'critical', then fled south in a staff-car.

Landrecies was to become one of the first legends of the Great War; here diarrhoea and desperation were fabricated into high heroism. Sir John French's dispatch to Lord Kitchener on 27 August 1914 has caught Haig fever. 'A German infantry column, about the strength of a brigade [a brigade is 3000 to 5000 men] emerged from the wood north of the town and advanced south in the closest order, filling up the narrow street. Two or three of our machine-guns were brought to bear . . . The head of the column was checked and stopped, a frightful panic ensued, and . . . in a very few minutes, no less than 800 to 900 dead Germans were lying in the streets.' The novelist John Buchan's version in *Nelson's History of the War* further elevates the bodycount: 'In the main street of Landrecies alone there were nearly a thousand of their dead and wounded, and one Jaeger battalion had ceased to be.'

In fact, German losses at Landrecies were fifty-two dead and around seventy-five wounded: the British figures were twenty dead and one hundred and sixty-one wounded. Compared with what was to come it was a mere skirmish. And the 'frightful panic' was not German, but General Haig's.

*

Henry James wrote of RLS in 1887: 'If things had gone differently with him, he might have been an historian of famous campaigns – a great painter of battle pieces.' If Stevenson had lived, the end of the First World War would have almost coincided with his sixty-eighth birthday. Perhaps he would have written a history of the war, like Kipling or Sir Arthur Conan Doyle, who was seventy-two when his *British Campaigns in Europe 1914–1918* was published in 1928. I wonder what RLS would have made of the action at Landrecies.

In the Landrecies section of *An Inland Voyage* the young Stevenson had had a lot to say about the 'stirring music' of military drums: 'each dub-a-dub goes direct to a man's heart, and puts madness there, and that disposition of the pulses which we . . . nickname Heroism'. An unheroic detail in Kipling's history of his dead son's regiment could be an ironic reply to Stevenson: 'One of the Regimental drums was seen and heard going down Landrecies main street in the darkness, strung onto the foreleg of a gun-horse who had stepped into it as a battery went south.'

12

Everyone was thinking about war at the time I was in Landrecies. In early June 1984, the lenses and microphones of the Western media were pointed at the beaches of Normandy for the fortieth anniversary of the D-Day invasion in the 'Good War' against fascism. The President of the United States (who had served in Hollywood) was receiving great coverage for the veteran vote in Presidential election year. The ferries were full of men remembering.

Ours is the American century, as the nineteenth had been Britain's. I could not but remember that 1984 was also the seventieth anniversary of the Retreat from Mons, and those seven decades had seen Britain's long retreat from imperial power, moving from the stature of Romans to the status of Italians in three generations.

*

At Landrecies, the weather hadn't changed in 108 years. The rain was 'simply bedlamite' for Simpson and Stevenson too. I ran into the station and put on Wellingtons and waterproofs. Rain flailed the streets and I walked into the first hotel I found; a pool of water gathered round my feet as I asked for a room. The Hotel Dupleix was named after the last French Governor-General of India, who was defeated by Clive, and it stood across from the Glarke barracks, named after a soldier who was a Duke under Napoleon, and a Marshal under the Bourbons. Dupleix and Clarke are Landrecies's most famous sons.

The barracks were big and shabby, occupied at weekends by lounging recruits in fatigues, yawning and spitting out of the upper windows. At night their shaven heads and sprawling bodies filled the small cafés. A sergeant with calf-length boots and a beard like a Spanish legionnaire stood drinking Jupiter beer with his slick corporal at a bar decorated with waggish slogans. The jukebox played '99 Luftbalons' and four bawling recruits shouldered each other round a shuddering bar-footy table. The next day they were hurtling importantly about in jeeps, jungled with camouflage hacked from local flora, their long radio aerials whipping like dry-fly rods.

I wanted to go south down the canal and hired an elderly bicycle. The bike-shop man pumped the tyres up tight as a drum. I walked the bike a hundred yards to the lock and down on to the tow-path which stretched ahead for a mile, a muddy path on the right of a gunmetal canal pointing straight across fields and swampy ground. It was a wobbly ride, under the grey sky, and after some half a mile I stopped to watch a barge approach, pushing up the Sambre-to-the-Oise canal. It was precisely on this stretch just south of Landrecies that Stevenson saw long lines of barges painted white and green with bright iron railings, flower-pots, children playing, men fishing, women washing and mongrel dogs keeping watch. Stevenson and Simpson fantasized about life on a barge:

> We had projected an old age on the canals of Europe . . . We should be seen pottering on deck in all the dignity of years, our white beards falling into our laps. We were ever to be busied among paint-pots . . . There should be books in the cabin, and tobacco-jars, and some old Burgundy as red as a November sunset and as odorous as a violet in April . . . All this, simmering in my mind, set me wishing to go aboard one of these ideal houses of lounging.

In his dedication to *An Inland Voyage*, Stevenson taxed his companion, Sir Walter: 'My dear *Cigarette*, . . . That, sir, was not a fortunate day when we projected the possession of a canal barge . . . ' For they did later acquire a barge at Moret-sur-Loing, and a carpenter called M. Mattras to refit the hulk. She was grandiloquently christened *The Eleven Thousand Virgins of Cologne* and money and sweet champagne were poured into her. Then funds and enthusiasm dwindled. Bob Stevenson, another hopeful partner in the scheme, wrote to Henley from Cernay in October 1878: 'Nobody has heard of Sir Walter and the Barge in which I have adventured mine estate, my person and my time. I fear it is a "fichu" affair also the canoes quite decidedly "flambé".' The barge rotted at her moorings, and the unpaid carpenter sold it, together with the two original canoes, *Cigarette* and *Arethusa*.

The barge chugging up towards me held a shiny Fiat car amidships, foursquare on dainty yellow blocks. I stood astride the bike by the grey canal watching the barge nosing up, its bow-wave trembling the reeds, and then I heard a bang like a gunshot. The front forks of the bike sank with a sigh and I dismounted to examine the four-inch gash of a blow-out. The tyre had been pumped too hard, and exploded when I leaned on the handlebars. I left the useless machine outside the cottage of a sympathetic woman and walked down the canal from Landrecies to Ors.

After a mile, the canal makes a sharp zig-zag past the eastern tip of Bois l'Eveque, where Erwin Rommel had run out of gas in the 1940 blitzkrieg, and narrowly escaped capture by a French tank unit. There were blackbirds and a cuckoo in the tall poplars. I watched a goods train clanking along beside the canal southward to Ors. It began to rain again and I pulled the waterproofs out of the haversack and put them on. Raindrops pitted the metallic surface of the smooth canal. A slow barge came past the dripping trees.

It was along this stretch of canal that Wilfred Owen had died in the last Big Push of the Great War. In 1918, the war had returned to Landrecies. The British attacked along a sixty-mile front, crossing the Sambre—Oise canal, and Wilfred Owen's 2nd Battalion Manchester Regiment were assigned to the stretch north of Ors. Zero hour was 5.45 am on 4 November 1918. British infantry assembled in darkness three hundred yards west of the canal with mist covering the low, wet ground. First, artillery shelled the Germans who were dug in on the eastern side of the canal; then Lieutenant Wilfred Owen MC led his platoon across the wet fields carrying planks and duckboards to the shelter of the canal bank. The British shelling was unsuccessful and heavy machine-gun fire still came from the German side, aimed at the engineers attempting to bridge the forty-foot canal. Owen's messmate, 2nd Lieutenant James Kirk, paddled across the canal with a Lewis gun to cover them, firing continuously until he was killed.

At 8.30 am word came up that it was easier to cross south of Ors, over a bridge of kerosene cans. By that time the Manchester Regiment had eighty wounded and twenty-five dead on this stretch of canal – including Lieutenant W. E. S. Owen, killed by machine-gun fire while encouraging his men.

13

The sun broke through the clouds and gleamed on the canal stretching down to Ors. There was blue wood-smoke, the snarl of a chain-saw, the clear thock of an axe. Across the meadow I could see a low wall and branches hazed with blossom where the map marked a British cemetery. There was a deep ditch on the right of the canal, but a tree lay across it. One of the workmen logging came over to ask what I was doing.

'*Je suis anglais. Je vais au cimetière.*'

He nodded and smiled.

'*Vas-y, monsieur.*'

I walked over the trunk of alder and jumped down into the spongy green meadow whose wet grass was sprinkled with buttercups. Nine trees were spaced across the field and the wind blew gently in my face. Ors British Cemetery lay behind grey drystone walls, underneath pink flowering cherry trees.

This Cemetery was built and is maintained by the Commonwealth War Graves Commission. The land on which this cemetery stands is the free gift of the French people for the perpetual resting-place of those of the Allied Armies who fell in the war of 1914–18 and are honoured here.

I walked among the graves of South Africans, Sappers, Highlanders, Lancashire Fusiliers. It was a peaceful place. I had a quiet smoke on a stone seat where cherry blossom floated in pools of rain water. The buttercups shone across the hundred yards of field to the canal where a plume of smoke rose from the loggers' burning of trash. There was no sign of Wilfred Owen at Ors British Cemetery.

I turned the bronze handle of the safe in the wall and took out the Cemetery Register. There was no W. E. S. Owen marked in any of the nearby cemeteries either. I looked through the Visitors 'Book, bound in green plastic. Other pilgrims helped more than the authorities. On 25 August 1980, T. Spagnoly from London had written:' Looking for England's greatest war poet Wilf Owen? Found him in village communal grave. Stone unkempt. Why no signs or registry book?'

Two weeks later a regular soldier wrote: 'I too came in search of the grave of Lt. Owen. Surely we are not ashamed to recognize what he said and to accord him the honour he deserves.'

In the Visitors' Book were thanks from locals; complaints from schoolchildren who had got their feet wet; lone signatures and people in groups; gruff words, proud words, sad words. A shaky line by an unknown relative I shall not forget: *I have found him at last as I promised you Dad.*

I sat among the dead men in the quiet meadow that Robert Louis Stevenson had paddled peacefully past in the rain, forty-two years before the battle.

*

The sun was shining hotly as I marched into Ors. Two joggers from the Army Camp passed me on the humpback bridge. Ors church is red brick with a spire and the *patron* of the Café des Arcades nearby said the cemetery was through the village, up by the station. I picked flowers from the wayside – buttercups, heartsease, speedwell – and twisted a stalk of grass round the stems. A horse cantered in a muddy field, happy in the sun.

Ors Village Cemetery had shiny black headstones with inset photos and plastic wreaths. At the end of the gravel avenue is a bronze sword set in a tall cross, the sign of a war grave. Wilfred Owen is in the back row by the low wall with the church spire straight ahead when you look south-east. The air was loud with bird-song and the life of the village, a cock crowing, barking dogs, a braying donkey, whinnies from the horse in the field. I put the flowers by the poet's headstone in the sunshine and stood back. Wilfred Owen from Shropshire lies between two young men of my grandfather's regiment, the Lancashire Fusiliers, aged eighteen and twenty-one.

Lieutenant
W. E. S. Owen MC
Manchester Regiment
4th November 1918 age 25

In the same Row A of the dead at Ors are 2nd Lieutenant James Kirk aAnd Lieutenant-Colonel James Neville Marshall, who both won the Victoria Cross on that day.

*

I had a beer and a sandwich at the café in the square. It was the sort of place where you shake hands with everyone who comes in. An old man in a beret sat over a glass of red wine loudly discussing duck-shooting with the *patron*, who had a string vest and a heat rash. His small son Wilfred clamoured for an ice-cream so Papa took a five franc piece from the till.

I shook hands with everyone again when I left, especially the kid with chocolate round his mouth.

'*Au revoir, monsieur,*' he piped.

'*Au revoir, Wilfred.*'

*

Stevenson wearied of *An Inland Voyage* after paddling himself into a stupor. A tree had taken him out of the *Arethusa* and he got soaked and chilled, though he clung to his paddle. The two men retreated by train, taking their canoes with them. I felt oppressed by war and rain and took the train back, in search of Fanny Osbourne and the love with which RLS ended his book:

> You may paddle all day long; but it is when you come back at nightfall, and look in at the familiar room, that you find Love or Death awaiting you beside the stove; and the most beautiful adventures are not those we go to seek.

Fanny, Belle and Lloyd awaited him at Grez-sur-Loing. *Cigarette* and *Arethusa* were finally moored at the bottom of Hotel Chevillon's garden. The seven-year-old Lloyd Osboume noticed the attraction between RLS and his mother; the two 'would sit and talk interminably either side of the dining-room stove while everybody else was out and busy, under vast white umbrellas, in the fields and woods'. The boy was overjoyed when his mother told him, as they prepared to go back to Paris in the autumn, 'Luly is coming too.'

14

Stevenson was to spend more and more time in France over the next two and a half years, flitting between Edinburgh, London and Paris. He would turn up unexpectedly, Edmund Gosse noticed, 'piratical descents, staying a few days or weeks and melting into air again'.

The French influence showed strongly in his writing at this time. In 1877 Stevenson wrote an essay for *Cornhill Magazine* called 'François Villon, Student, Poet, Housebreaker' as well as a fictional account of the fifteenth-century outlaw poet called 'A Lodging for the Night'. Another story of the same year, 'The Sire of Malétroit's Door', was also set in fifteenth-century France.

In early 1877, Robert Glasgow Brown founded a new weekly paper called *London* and Stevenson contributed to the first seven issues. Three of his essays were about Paris life. 'In the Latin Quarter No. 1 – A Ball at Mr Elsinare's' described a party at a studio on Rue Notre Dame des Champs,' not a hundred miles from the Boulevard Montparnasse'. The belle of the ball is Fanny's daughter, 17-year-old Isobel Osbourne:

> She is a Californian girl, and has spent her childhood among Bret Harte's stories, petted by miners and gamblers, and trappers, and ranche-men, and all the dramatis personae of the new romance . . . Belle is frank and simple and not at all like an American miss. She looks like a Russian – a South Russian I mean . . . Tonight she is dressed in gilt, like a stage fairy, and her hair is full of gold powder; her dark face is flushed, and her eyes shine with happiness.

It is hard to find anything romantic today in the area around Rue Douai, where Fanny and her children were then living. It is a block below Place Pigalle and the streets are full of tarts, pimps, massage parlours, and the insistent hissing, '*Tsss, tsss, m'sieur*', of touts for porno shows and films like *Jeunes Filles a Sodomiser; a danse macabre* of punters, crooks and policemen.

*

In early 1878 Stevenson's boisterous friend from the Edinburgh Infirmary, W. E. Henley, took over the editorship of *London* magazine and relied on Stevenson for copy. Small magazines are probably more important to their editors and contributors than the great world which refuses to buy them; *London* folded in 1879, after two years of life and 114 issues. Probably the only full original set of it is in the British Library at Colindale, and all the other copies have gone to dust. But *London* lives in literary history: it was the first place where Stevenson published the stories of the 'Latter-Day Arabian Nights', gathered into book form four years later as New *Arabian Nights*.

'It may seem a paradox', wrote G. K. Chesterton, 'to say that his most original work was a parody.' In his perceptive book Robert Louis Stevenson (1927) Chesterton calls *New Arabian Nights* 'the most unique of his works . . . unequalled . . . He invented a genre which does not really exist outside his work . . . an atmosphere where incongruous things find a comic congruity . . . a sort of solid impossibility.' This genre, which the Spectator in 1882 called 'grotesque romance', was a form that Stevenson invented, and others continued. Chesterton himself recreated the atmosphere in *The Man who was Thursday: A Nightmare* (1908) and in some of the Father Brown stories from 1911. In a BBC Home Service talk on 26 August 1963, Jorge Luis Borges said that both Stevenson and Chesterton had 'the idea of thinking of London as a kind of fairy-land where anything may happen'.

Some of Stevenson's ideas for *New Arabian Nights*, notably that of 'The Suicide Club', come from fantasies expounded by or shared with his cousin Bob. The genre seems to flourish with collaboration, two minds spurring each other on to ever more fantastic details – like Borges and Bioy Casares, for example. Another cousin of Graham Greene's, Christopher Isherwood, evolved a similar kind of fantasy around Cambridge, the Mortmere stories, working together with his friend and fellow-undergraduate Edward Upward.

The 'Latter-Day Arabian Nights' ran in seventeen instalments of *London* from June to October 1878. The seven interlinked stories of 'The Suicide Club' and 'The Rajah's Diamond' combine metaphysics with pure silliness and defy a realistic reading. In apparently real places – Leicester Square, Charing Cross, Trafalgar Square – solid cigar-smoking, champagne-drinking gentlemen in evening dress inhabit a world of fantastic events and secret societies, whose byways are explored by Prince Florizel of Bohemia and his Master of Horse, Colonel Geraldine. Prince Florizel (based on that king of the *demi-monde*, Bertie Prince of Wales) is a secret benefactor and righter of wrongs. At the end, this *deus ex machina* becomes the tobacconist Theophilus Godall.

'The spirit, sir, is one of mockery,' says The Young Man With The Cream Tarts, and the *New Arabian Nights* question and tease the idea of 'adventure'; they are about story-telling, the tricks of narrative, what is revealed and what withheld. Stevenson was 'an artifex', declared G. K. Chesterton, and the stories seemed preposterous to the first publisher to whom they were submitted, and he promptly rejected them. A modern critic has called them 'sham'. But all stories are 'sham' in the end; even Naturalism and Realism are 'sham'. Stevenson points to the fact. The stories in New *Arabian Nights* were a new kind of fiction.

The fantastic events in 'The Suicide Club' and 'The Rajah's Diamond' are set in real streets in London and Paris, and some of them contain private or sentimental references. In one story, a character runs down the steep Rue Ravignan, in Paris. Stevenson knew the Montmartre street well; Fanny Osbourne and her children lived in rooms at No. 5 in 1877.

There seems no doubt that Fanny Osbourne and Robert Louis Stevenson were lovers in the three summers from 1876 to 1878, in the time they spent together in Grez, Paris and London. There are few clues: an erotic poem; a reference in a Stevenson letter to missing 'the dear head on the pillow'. But there were many problems for them. A woman's reputation could still be 'ruined'. She was married and ten years older than RLS. He was poor and still dependent on his father for supplements to his meagre earnings from writing. Although Thomas Stevenson claimed to believe that any woman should have a divorce just for the asking, it was another matter altogether to expect him to approve of this particular match. In 1878, RLS had been writing for money for five years, but his literary career was only just establishing itself: *An Inland Voyage* was published early in the year, and *Edinburgh: Picturesque Notes* at the end. The only certainty was that RLS and Fanny Osbourne loved each other.

Then, her husband stopped sending her money, and demanded that she return; and on 15 August 1878 Fanny Osbourne and her two children went back to America.

16

Missing Fanny is the subtext of RLS's next travel-book, *Travels With a Donkey In The Cevennes*. The dedication (to Sidney Colvin) hints as much: 'Every book is, in an intimate sense, a circular letter to the friends of him who writes it. They alone take his meaning; they find private messages, assurances of love, and expressions of gratitude dropped for them in every corner.' Above all, as he later confessed to Bob, these were 'protestations to F.', messages of love for Fanny Osbourne.

Stevenson went down to the Massif Central of France and arrived in Le Puy on 28 August. He set out from Le Monastier-sur-Gazeille on Sunday, 22 September, and walked 120 miles south with Modestine his donkey to Saint-Jean du Gard, arriving on Thursday, 3 October 1878.

*

It is a famous journey; even people who have not read the book have heard of *Travels With a Donkey*. But I decided not to go to the Cevennes. Too many people have already followed RLS and his mouse-coloured donkey; for example, the critically acclaimed Richard Holmes in *Footsteps: Adventures of a Romantic Biographer*. Nor was Holmes the first to track Stevenson in the Cevennes; J. A. Hammerton did the trip in 1903, Robert T. Skinner in the 1920s and Andrew J. Evans in the 1960s, and there were others. A travel-book which becomes the *topos* for other travel-books must be remarkable.

The centenary of *Travels With a Donkey*, in 1978, raised it to the status of an industry. A Franco-Scottish Stevenson Centenary Committee was set up; the French National Tourist Board became interested; the approximate route was cleared and marked. The Committee published a 'bilingual French – Englich edition: *Sur les traces de STEVENSON – topoguide de l'itinéraire/In Stevenson's footsteps – a guide to his jorney'*.

A man started a business hiring out donkeys at exorbitant rates; the Stevenson exhibition at Monastier town hall and the memorial to him in the convent buildings were visited by journalists and filmed by TV crews; and Stevensonian experts from around the world were invited to drive and feast along the route. In the end there wasn't a schoolchild along the Haute-Loire, Ardèche, Lozère and Gard way that did not know about Stevenson, *le célèbre écrivain écossais*.

A South London travel company that specializes in walking tours, Waymark Holidays, sent John Sheringham to scout out the original route and find suitable inns and hotels along the way. Waymark Holiday 252 'Travels Without a Donkey' began in 1979, and over four hundred people have subsequently walked the route with them in groups of a dozen. Stevenson is the theme and the 'selling-point' of the holiday; the volunteer leader carries a copy of the book and so do most of the middle-aged people who go on the fortnight's trip. The route is exactly Stevenson's wherever possible; the holiday is not expensive; you could go yourself one summer.

The centenary year also produced a fascinating book. *The Cevennes Journal: Notes on a Journey Through the French Highlands* was the first publication of Stevenson's original notebook on the journey, together with eight of his more than competent sketches, jotted notes, lists of expenses and counts of how many words he had written. *The Cevennes Journal* gives several insights into how the final travel-book is made. 'The only art is to omit', Stevenson wrote in 1884, and what Stevenson omitted from his *Journal* when he came to write Travels *With a Donkey* is instructive. He left out quite how cruel he had to be to get Modestine moving, and also how deeply affected he was by the Trappist monastery at Our Lady of The Snows. Travel-writers also add to their accounts what they have subsequently read about the region where they travelled; *Travels With a Donkey's* historical matter is a result of library rather than leg-work.

Very different books are produced by travellers who write, and writers who travel. Stevenson's *Travels With a Donkey* is among the first of a genre of literary travel-writing which has become a British speciality. One piece of rhetoric in the book seems to place RLS in the camp of the pure travellers: 'For my part I travel but to go; I travel for travel's sake. The great affair is to move; to feel the needs and hitches of life a little more nearly, to get down off this feather-bed of civilization, and to find the globe granite underfoot and strewn with cutting flints.' But *The Cevennes Journal* contains what Stevenson originally wrote, and shows that he omitted from his published book the real reason for his trip: 'I travel for travel's sake. *And to write about it afterwards, if only the public will be so condescending as to read.'*

Many of the long line of travel-writers who succeed Stevenson have no other reason for going away than getting a book out of it. The traveller is often the true subject of the post-Stevenson travel-book, and is of more interest to us than the terrain. A note that Stevenson made during his night at the monastery on Thursday,

26 September 1878 could be an epigraph to the genesis of the modern self-conscious travel-book: '*A voyage is a piece of autobiography at best.*'

Stevenson's gift is to strike up a personal relationship with the reader, sharing every experience, even down to the glow of his night-time cigarette reflected in the silver ring on his hand. He is a palpable self in the darkness; an immediate living presence throughout the book. RLS has also become a Pied Piper with the power to make others follow him. And those who pursue another writer have to grapple with more than one self as they write their travels.

AMERICA

I

The year of the Zulu War, 1879, would be the year of decision and departure for Robert Louis Stevenson. Fanny was far away in California, trapped in an unhappy marriage, and Stevenson, wavering between mistress and family, was tormented into work. His writing in the first eight months of 1879 worries away at his personal and ethical concerns.

'The Truth of Intercourse' (January) is about lies. 'The cruellest lies are often told in silence . . . And how many loves have perished because, from pride, or spite, or diffidence, or that unmanly shame which withholds a man from daring to betray emotion, a lover, at the critical part of the relation, had but hung his head and held his tongue?' This sounds like regret at having let Fanny go.

'Lay Morals' (March) presents 'a young man . . . conscious of vague powers and qualities, and fretting at the bars of life'. Pope Hennessy called these essays 'rather unattractive', but RLS writes interestingly of his reaction to society's inequality, its respectable hypocrisy, and the general relentless urge to material profit: 'We have a sort of blindness which prevents us seeing anything but sovereigns'. Privilege made him feel guilty; his response was that we should take the words of Christ and Walt Whitman to heart and live them absolutely.

The sense of conflict in 'Lay Morals' contains the germ of *The Strange Case of Dr Jekyll and Mr Hyde*:

It follows that man is twofold at least; that he is not a rounded and autonomous empire; but that in the body with him there dwell other powers, tributary but independent . . . Pascal laid aside mathematics; Origen doctored his body with a knife; every day someone is thus mortifying his dearest interests and desires, and, in Christ's words, entering maim into the kingdom of Heaven . . . But there is another way, to supersede them by reconciliation . . . [and] . . . not live with our opposing tendencies in continual see-saw of passion and disgust, but seek some path on which the tendencies but serve each other to a common end.

Stevenson longed to resolve his own contradictions, between dutiful son and reckless lover. 'The soul demands unity of purpose, not the dismemberment of man.'

'Some Aspects of Robert Burns' (May-August) finds RLS, exalted by his love for one woman, rejecting Burns's lechery and infidelity. Criticizing Burns for being 'something of the vulgar, bagmanlike, professional seducer' took courage in Scotland. Of course, Stevenson had his own past as 'Velvet Coat' to repudiate.

In August he began 'The Story of a Lie', a fable of a strong parent and a weak child whose powers are reversed, so the tyrant becomes dependent and the impotent magnanimous. The author wrote keenly of 'the daily want of comprehension and daily small injustices, through childhood and boyhood and manhood, until you despair of a hearing, until the thing rides you like a nightmare, until you almost hate the sight of the man you love, and who's your father after all'.

At twenty-eight, Stevenson was too old to be living with his parents. He was in the same state as six years ago, before he escaped to Cockfield. He had to get away.

*

The stroke of destiny fell at the end of July 1879. Back in Edinburgh after Paris and London, Stevenson received a telegram from Fanny in California. It has not survived and we do not know what it said. But Stevenson knew at once what he had to do. In 'Lay Morals' he had written how 'the perfect man . . . was never torn between conflicting impulses, but . . . submitted in every action of his life to a self-dictation as absolute and unreasoned as that which bids him love one woman and be true to her till death'.

Secretly, in Hanover Street, a few hundred yards from his home in

Heriot Row, a young man with the feeble alias 'Robert Stephenson' bought himself a one-way second-class ticket to New York from the Edinburgh agents of the Anchor Line of Steam Packet ships. Telling his parents only that he had 'business' down south, Stevenson took the train to London on 30 July. There Gosse and Colvin and Henley thought his decision was a mad whim and tried to dissuade him, but Stevenson was adamant: he was off to see Fanny in California.

On 6 August 1879 he met his fellow-passengers on the Broomielaw of Glasgow Docks and went by lighter down-river to Greenock where the SS *Devonia* lay moored, on the eve of sailing for America. Once aboard, Stevenson wrote to Baxter, 'I am in fair spirits but a little off my nut and quite off my feed.' He sent Colvin a letter for Thomas Stevenson, the contents of which are not known, and told his friend he was 'detached from life . . . I feel as if I cared for nobody . . . I cannot believe fully in my own existence . . . I never was in such a state. I have just made my will.'

The convulsion of leaving had taken a week, and he had thrown himself forward into the future like dice. With the Atlantic and all of America to cross he was wide open to the buffetings of chance. 'Danger, enterprise, hope, the novel, the aleatory, are dearer to man than regular meals', he wrote later.

Stevenson was not 'a consistent First Class Traveller in life'. On the *Devonia* he was neither in the smart Saloon, nor in the Steerage, the poorest accommodation. He had taken 2nd Cabin, so he would have a table to finish writing 'The Story of a Lie': 'For he had fallen into that stage when men have the vertigo of misfortune, court the strokes of destiny, and rush towards anything decisive, that it may free them from suspense though at the cost of ruin. It is one of the many minor forms of suicide.'

2

I wanted to get a ship from Glasgow to New York to follow in his wake, but there were no passenger boats in 1984. In 1870 the Anchor Line was shipping 25,000 passengers over the Atlantic, and in 1879 there were daily sailings to New York. But Glasgow is no longer the Babylon of the Industrial Revolution; this century the Clyde has died, and even the whisky is driven in containers down to English ports.

Stevenson's ticket to America cost eight guineas on a 3500-ton emigrant ship. A hundred and five years later the cheapest fare was £99 on a mass-tourism jumbo jet. We both left on 7 August.

I did not actually take off till the eighth. The Virgin Atlantic plane from Gatwick broke down, and the grumbling passengers were driven in the rain to a hotel, a touristic limbo, with the Olympics on TV. *Out of my country and my self I go.* On the *Devonia* Stevenson palled up with an ex-blacksmith, 'my excellent friend Mr Jones'. I teamed up with a Junker punker from Brixton, a student with green studs in one ear. He had an American passport, was called Frederick Wolf Werner S— Graf von der S—, and his great-uncle had tried to kill Hitler and had been hanged with piano-wire.

At Heathrow the next day there was a distraught woman who said she had been there for three days. I was frisked from head to toe when my spectacles case triggered the alarm of a metal detector. I sat on the British Airways plane next to a nurse going to pick up a patient in North Carolina. She talked cheerily of BIDs – the Brought In Dead – and rescuing smashed tourists and dying businessmen from eastern Bolivia or northern Nigeria.

The film was *Romancing the Stone.* With my pebble in my pocket I slept fitfully as we flew west, clutching a slipping copy of *From Scotland to Silverado*, James D. Hart's unexpurgated edition of Stevenson's *The Amateur Emigrant.*

3

The book was never published in Stevenson's lifetime as he first wrote it. It was to have been a two-part work, *The Emigrant Ship* and *The Emigrant Train*, but his treatment of the experience led family, friends and publishers to suppress it. *Across the Plains* did appear in a magazine four years later, but *The Emigrant Ship* was not printed until the Edinburgh Edition of 1895, after Stevenson's death. He and Colvin had revised it by then, and 30 per cent of the text had been cut.

Pope-Hennessy thought that what Stevenson saw and heard on the emigrant ship shocked the refined upper-middle-class sensibilities of the publisher, Kegan Paul, and Sidney Colvin. Thomas Stevenson, embarrassed by his son's embracing of poverty, said in

1880: 'I think it not only the worst thing you have done, but altogether unworthy of you', and he paid back the publisher's advance of £100 to block the book at galley-proof stage.

What is upsetting about *The Amateur Emigrant?* Ostensibly, the realist details: the horrible cheesy smell of the Steerage, the poorest accommodation; people being sick, etc. But the social comments also bite. *The Amateur Emigrant* is all about class. The narrator, who by all the rights and advantages of breeding, caste, class, education and taste should be in the Saloon (with 'my equals and inferiors') is in the 2nd Cabin and spending his time with the rock-bottom Steerage passengers.

'I found I had what they call fallen in life with absolute success and verisimilitude.' Only a brass plate on a lavatory door – GENTLEMEN – recalled his peers. 'The sailors called me "mate", the officers addressed me as "my man".' His vanity was chagrined to be ignored by the young ladies on board, none of whom paid him 'the tribute of a glance', but passed him 'like a dog'. 'What are called the upper classes may sometimes produce a disagreeable impression in what are called the lower.' Stevenson was a good mixer, however. 'The Steerage conquered me; I conformed more and more to the type of the place, not only in manner but at heart, growing hostile to the officers and cabin passengers who looked down upon me, and day by day greedier for small delicacies.'

4

I found out more about the Steerage people after I got to New York City. Upstairs in the New York Public Library I looked up the *Devonia*'s passenger-list, which, as far as I know, no scholar or biographer of Stevenson has examined. I fitted the microfilm roll into the machine and was winding the handle past ships from Bremen, Havre, Hamburg, Glasgow, Liverpool, Palermo, Rio de Janeiro, with my head bent agonizingly to one side, pitying the professional academic, when a kindly woman stopped and showed me how to tilt the image to the vertical. Suddenly there was ship no. 915. Name of Vessel: Devonia, *Port of Embarkation*: Glasgow, *Date of Arrival*: 18 August 1879.

The passenger manifest was in a very legible hand. I remembered that the purser of the *Devonia* had offered Stevenson 'some other kind of writing, "for which", he added pointedly, "you will be paid". This was nothing else than to copy out the list of passengers.' What I saw did not look like Stevenson's writing, but I was grateful for its clarity.

The eleventh name on the list of 256 passengers was 'Robert Stephenson'. *Age:* 29. *Occupation:* Clerk. *Country to which they ... belong:* Scotland. *Country in which they intend to become inhabitants: USA. Died on the voyage:* None. *Part of the vessel occupied by each Passenger during the voyage:* 2nd Cabin.

I pored over the list. There were fifty-one in the Saloon and their occupations were given as Clerks, Divines and Nil – the idle rich. There were twenty-two in the 2nd Cabin; fifteen Scots including six women, four Norwegians, a Dane, a Swede and an Irishman.

The 2nd Cabin as Stevenson knew it was

a modified oasis in the very heart of the steerages. Through the thin partition you can hear the steerage passengers being sick, the rattle of tin dishes as they sit at meals, the varied accents in which they converse, the crying of their children terrified by this new experience, or the clean flat smack of the parental hand in chastisement.

There were 183 passengers crammed in the five Steerages – Scots, Irish, German, Scandinavian, one Russian. There were many occupations listed in the ship's manifest: Brewer, Carpenter, Chemist, Clerk, Draper, Engineer, Farmer, Grocer, Joiner, Labourer, Lawyer, Marble Cutter, Mason, Merchant, Miner, Moulder, Nil, Plate-Layer, Seaman, Servant, Sheet Iron Roller, Silk Weaver, Teacher, Tenter, Watchmaker, Weaver, Wife.

Stevenson talked and sang with them; these are the people he wrote about in the chapter 'Steerage Types'. The chemist, for example, was identified in the manifest as Isodor Bruhs, twenty-seven. The only Russian on board, he looked a desperado, but Stevenson learned from him (in broken German) that he had been an apothecary. He sang a solo at a concert, 'his Kalmuck head thrown back . . . a suitable piece of music, as deep as a cow's bellow and wild like the White Sea.'

The voyage was an eye-opener for Stevenson. He saw the drunk, the idle and the incompetent as well as the victims of the recession of the 1870s, 'a prolonged and crushing series of defeats' for working people. It made him conscious of his own 'fortunate beginning'. His sympathies are clear: 'We must see the rich honest, before we need look hopefully to see the poor considerate.' The *Devonia* confirmed what he had already observed about 'tramps and morality' in An *Inland Voyage*: 'As long as you keep in the upper regions, with all the world bowing to you as you go, social arrangements have a very handsome air; but once get under the wheels and you wish society were at the devil.'

Unsentimental about the working classes, Stevenson took a critical interest in their thinking. The bigoted materialist MacKay 'had an appetite for disconnected facts which I can only compare to the savage taste for beads'. This was a general characteristic of avid newspaper readers:

> One and all were too much interested in disconnected facts, and loved information for its own sake with too rash a devotion . . . They did not perceive relations but leaped to a so-called cause, and thought the problem settled. Thus the cause of everything in England was the form of government, and the cure for all evils was, by consequence, a revolution. It is surprising how many of them said this, and that none should have had a definite thought in his head as he said it. The true reasoning of their souls ran thus – I have not got on; I ought to have got on; if there was a revolution I should get on. How? They had no idea. Why? Because – because – well, look at America!

The full version of *The Amateur Emigrant* is well worth reading. To read the vivid and characterful text carefully is to understand the social education that RLS underwent, and it is worth remembering that no other writer of his generation and class did anything like it. In this trip were the seeds of what he told Lloyd Osbourne in the last years of his life: 'The saddest object in civilization, and to my mind the greatest confession of its failure, is the man who can work, who wants work, and who is not allowed to work.'

5

I had not been in New York City for fifteen years and it took me a while to readjust to its noise and filth. I stayed with my old friend

Robin Jared Lewis and his wife, Alison Dalton, on the Upper West Side by Columbia University, and it was good to have a haven. Down on Broadway, the brazen muggy heat of the August streets hit you like a foul towel. The sights were the same: yellow cabs bouncing on rutted asphalt; sun-burned bag-ladies; gasping joggers; the panhandler lurking by the bank cash-dispenser. But there were changes: a very black Ethiopian selling sunglasses on a street-corner; a Korean in a singlet unloading vegetables; a woman in a sari at the newspaper kiosk in the subway.

New York has an amazing variety of immigrants, and two out of its seven million are fresh from elsewhere. The radio said NYC had 200 ethnic minorities. 'That include the two Nauruans?' asked Robin. Immigration reflected world turmoils and it seemed to me there were more brown, black and yellow faces on the streets than in 1969. 'Know what it reminds me of?' Robin said as we dodged through hot crowded streets one night. 'Calcutta. New York is a third world city now.'

Immigration made America. In the nineteenth century they came in waves to New York City, Irish, German, Scandinavian. Stevenson's emigrant ship arrived just as the influx was increasing: from 1877 to 1882 immigration quadrupled to 800,000 people a year. Stevenson came just before the new waves of Poles, Czechs, Italians, and shtetl Jews fleeing pogroms. He came three years before the racist, panicky Chinese Exclusion Act was passed to keep out the 'Yellow Peril', seven years before the Statue of Liberty was dedicated in New York harbour, thirteen years before the huge immigration centre opened on Ellis Island to receive the millions. There would be 24 million immigrants to the USA between 1880 and 1900, and another 20 million by 1914.

Aprenda a Hablar Inglés, ¡Ven, es la hora Miller!, Food Stamps/ *Cupones de Alimentos*, I managed to read through the blue-black-green aerosolled haze on the screeching downtown express. The whole carriage was a jungle of illegible, illiterate spray-paint, like a tube of camouflage netting.

I got out at the southern tip of Manhattan and walked through Battery Park, whose lavatories were called 'Comfort Stations'. I stood on reclaimed land, looking south-south-west to the Statue of Liberty. It was a solid block of scaffolding and tarpaulin, under-going cleaning and repair.

I was looking for Castle Garden, where the immigrants used to come ashore. It had been a fort to fight the British in 1812, then a theatre and public hall, and from 1855 to 1890 the nation's principal immigration depot ('the Gateway to the New World') that admitted seven million future citizens.

Castle Garden was now an empty cylinder in a park, like the bare shell of an amphitheatre. A buxom National Park Ranger in a tight uniform told me it had been a two-storey building housing customs and immigration officials as well as doctors and interpreters. The place had swarmed with land-scheme agents, ethnic friendly societies and sharks. Among the boarding-house runners who met the boats would be smiling men who greeted compatriots in their own language, offering advice and accommodation.

'Allow me to take the luggage,' they would say. 'You follow on behind to the address on this printed card.' With relief the frightened immigrants yield – such kindness in America, such good luck. The address on the card is an empty lot; their baggage has been stolen, and everything from the old country is gone. Imagine the rage, the tears. Welcome to the New World.

6

These 'cautions and grisly tales' had reached the immigrants on SS *Devonia* in August 1879. 'You would have thought we were to land upon a cannibal island', wrote Stevenson of the approach to New York. 'You must speak to no one in the streets, as they would not leave you till you were rooked and beaten.' Worse things were rumoured to go on in hotels.

The *Devonia* tied up at Pier 20 on the Hudson River waterfront on the evening of Sunday, 17 August 1879. Only the Saloon and 2nd Cabin passengers disembarked; the Steerage had to pig it for another night before being processed through Castle Garden. RLS stuck with his shipboard friend Mr Jones, who was experienced in these matters.

They took a baggage wagon in pouring rain down to the Lower West Side, to a place that Jones knew. The streets were like Liverpool. They got out at 'Reunion House, No. 10 West Street, one minute's walk from Castle Garden . . . lodging per night 25 cents . . . satisfaction guaranteed to all persons; Michael Mitchell, Proprietor.' After a bad cigar and a drink they set out to eat, and celebrated in a French restaurant like sailors ashore.

At Reunion House they shared a room, Jones in the bed, Stevenson on the floor. The lavatory was across a rainy yard. 'There were three basin-stands, and a few crumpled towels and pieces of wet soap, white and slippery like fish.' By now Stevenson had met three Scots lads who had been in New York City for months, and none of them had found a job or earned a penny. 'I began to grow sick at heart for my fellow-emigrants.'

*

There is no trace of No. 10 West Street now, just a huge building called 17 Battery Place, whose hundreds of offices from Able Shipping to Morton Zuckerman carry on the business of banking, containers, shipping, stevedoring, warehouses, etc. I had a hero sandwich in the ground floor coffee shop; office workers carried out lunch in brown paper bags wax-crayoned with the price. An obese man with a strong Brooklyn accent was loudly describing an effete neighbour:

'He's wert ya cwll a paeansy eyass.'

It was a couple of blocks from Stevenson's old boarding house to Broadway. I walked up the packed lunchtime street in the sunshine, past Bowling Green, where Peter Minuit 'bought' Manhattan from the Indians for $24 worth of beads in 1626. Stevenson had a hellish day on the wet Monday of 18 August 1879. His mackintosh was soaked inside and out. 'I went to banks, post-offices, railway-offices, restaurants, publishers, booksellers, money-changers, and where ever I went a pool would gather about my feet.' Stevenson found the people 'all surprisingly rude and surprisingly kind', a characteristic of New Yorkers that has not changed.

Some time that day he managed to write to Henley: 'I have passed the salt sea with comparative impunity, having lost only a stone and got the itch. I could not eat, and I could not sh— hush! – the whole way; but I worked . . . '

There must have been a message from California at the Post Office, for his letter to Henley continued: 'My news is bad and I am wet to the skin. F. has inflammation of the brain, and I am across the continent tonight . . . '

The 'itch' Stevenson referred to was 'an unparalleled skin irrita-tion' – he deleted the words 'very similar to syphilys' – which 'sometimes stings like a whiplash; and sleep is impossible to me. Last night I did not close an eye, but sat on the floor in my trousers and scratched myself from 10 pm to seven, when I arose much the better for the exercise.'

Stevenson went to a chemist on Broadway for a salve. 'The gentleman in fine linen told me, with admirable gravity, that my liver was out of order, and presented me with a blue pill, a seidlitz powder and a little bottle of some salt and colourless fluid to take . . . He might as well have given me a cricket bat and a copy of Johnson's dictionary.'

*

I went to look at the headquarters of US capitalism, Wall Street, named after the fortified stockade the Dutch erected across the south of Manhattan island in 1653 to keep out the Indians. As Stevenson wrote, 'Old, red Manhattan lies, like an Indian arrow-head under a steam factory, below Anglified New York.' It was hard to remember or imagine in the cosmopolis of concrete, glass and steel that Wall Street was where the Stock Exchange began, under a buttonwood or sycamore tree in 1792. Now millions of unreal, invisible dollars shuttled electronically around the financial markets of the planet, linked by chattering, green-faced computers.

Out on the narrow, dusty street itself, the action was more immediate. In front of shuttered building sites with noisy dinosaur machinery, three different black 'Spot-The-Lady' teams were hustling from the tops of cardboard boxes. The three-card trick looks simple; you are sure you can follow the Queen as it is shuffled together with two other cards. But it is an elaborate con, and most of the players clustered round hollering and peeling off bills are in on the scam, not fellow punters, but 'coney-catchers'.

Stevenson had already seen the irony in the distinction we vir-tuously make between different forms of speculation. His 'pea and thimble' is another version of the three-card trick. In 'The Misad-ventures of John Nicholson', 'Fatty' Nicholson befriends a fellow in California: 'This young man was the nephew of one of the Nob Hill magnates, who run the San Francisco Stock Exchange, much as more humble adventurers, in the corner of some public park at home, may be seen to perform the simple artifice of pea and thimble: for their own profit, that is to say . . . '

*

Stevenson set out to travel the 3000 miles west to Monterey in California. His nightmare trip on the emigrant train began at 5 pm on Monday, 18 August 1879, at the Ferry Depot on Manhattan where he took the boat across to Jersey City. 'The porters charged among us like so many maddened sheep-dogs', violently discharging barrow-loads of boxes, and Stevenson had to save a child from being crushed. The stupefied emigrants were packed on a listing ferry that crossed the Hudson in wind and rain. On the other shore there was a stampede to the platform. They were locked out of the train, without refreshment, and RLS bought some oranges:

> As only two of them had a pretence of juice, I threw the other four under a car, and beheld, as in a dream, grown people and children groping on the track after my leavings.

7

The railways have sadly declined in 1980s America. The country is so big that it is faster and frequently cheaper to take a plane, and so I flew to Chicago Midway.

'We reached Chicago in the evening', wrote RLS. 'I was turned out of the cars, bundled into an omnibus, and driven off through the streets to the station of a different railroad. Chicago seemed a great and gloomy city.'

In the morning I walked the few blocks from the University of Chicago's International House to the bus-stop, passing a prowl-car with a grumbling radio, a shotgun rack and pair of blackshirted cops drinking coffee out of styrofoam cups. Stevenson romantically claimed that in America, 'Even the shotgun, the navy revolver and the Bowie knife seem more connected with courage than with cruelty.' I remembered that one of the commonest complications of pregnancy in Cook County was gunshot wounds.

I took a bus to get to Stevenson's railroad station in central Chicago. The grass was tawny under a hot blue sky, and as the No. 6 went north on Lake Shore Drive, metallic Lake Michigan looked as big as the sea. Near the Museum of Science and Industry a minor character straight out of a Saul Bellow novel got on, and stood straphanging next to a pregnant Hispanic. The Chicago-natty or Runyon-sporty style was all checks and stripes, from light tattersall jacket to two-tone brogues. His pink tie was pulled down from the unbuttoned green shirt collar, and he hadn't shaved for three days.

I walked west to Union Station. Chicago is 'great and gloomy', especially under the elevated railways of the Rapid Transit System. Deep in the canyons of the financial district, suddenly the sun on Wabash Avenue is filtered and corrugated through the corroded metal 'Loop' as trains batter overhead, shuttling light and shade like a mad jenny.

I bought a ticket for the 477-mile trip west to Omaha, Nebraska, and went out to look at the city.

Two blocks east of Union Station is the tallest office building in the world, the Sears Tower. Staring up at the black triple-stemmed ziggurat guarantees neck-ache. It dominates the city and as an obedient tourist I went to pay homage. In the lobby was the Information Chicago computer.

'Welcome!' read the 16-inch screen. 'Touch me, and I'll tell you all about Chicago – My Kind of Town.'

Up popped the 1980 Census figures at a stroke: Chicago had a population of 3,005,072; just under 1.5 million were white, nearly 1.2 million were black, 422,000 were Spanish-speaking and 6,072 were American Indian. 242,593 were 'Other'. Cook County had 5¼ million people, the State of Illinois nearly 11½ million.

The etymology of Chicago was obscure: *chicaugou* meant 'strong' or 'great' in the Illinois language, but *shegahg* meant 'wild onion' in Chippewa. 'Windy City' was really 'Garlic Breath'.

Then it was History's turn on the screen. On 9 October 1871, Mrs O'Leary's cow knocked over a kerosene lamp near a westside lumber yard and in the subsequent 'Great Chicago Fire' some 17,000 buildings were destroyed and 100,000 people made homeless. Stevenson arrived in Chicago eight years after the Great Fire:

> I remember having subscribed, let us say sixpence, towards its restoration at the period of the fire; and now when I beheld street after street of ponderous houses and crowds of comfort-able burghers, I thought it would be a graceful act for the

corporation to refund that sixpence, or, at the least, to entertain me to a cheerful dinner. But there was no word of restitution. I was that city's benefactor, yet I was received in a third-class waiting room, and the best dinner I could get was a dish of ham and eggs at my own expense.

I prodded the garrulous computer for 'facts' about the world's largest private office building. The answers were instantaneous; a blizzard of American grandiosity. I went up to the Skydeck on the 103rd floor, which was open fifteen hours a day, seven days a week. Aliens, out-of-towners, sightseers, strangers, tourists, vacationers and visitors disgorged from busy lifts, old and young, black and white, *chino* and *latino*, bearded Amish and fat Veterans of Foreign Wars; they had all come to stare at grimy urban sprawl to the limits of the heat-hazed horizon.

My telescope drooped and I found myself looking at the railroad tracks out of La Salle Street Station where a tiny figure, a working man, was stepping over rails and ties. Though he was flattened by the telephoto effect, shimmered by heat haze and diminished by distance, walking with his oilcan by the twinkling lines he was living and human.

Back on the ground level, frightened people scuttled out of another lift. A man with a purple face and blood running from his nose and mouth lay on the floor, his legs thrashing in spasms.

'Heart attack, you reckon?' said a pleased old man to his lizardy friend.

'Move on, *please*!' cried the panicking elevator-man.

'C'mon!' A man with buck teeth and crazy eyes dragged his son through the crowd for a closer look. The boy had a baseball cap on back to front and his mouth wide open in a grin of tremendous joy.

Stevenson was 'dog-tired' in Chicago, 'hot, feverish, painfully athirst.' The journey was telling on him. He took the train west towards the Missouri. I followed.

8

Train 5 to California, an 'Amtrak Superliner', was my first double-decker train. As red-capped porters busybodied below I listened in puzzlement to an endless stream of officious instructions to passengers over the tannoy. Amtrak was protecting itself against the most litigious citizenry in the world. Law firms advertise their staffs with pictures in the Yellow Pages, all capped teeth and careful coiffure. No poor lawyers in America.

The rusted bridges and weedy shunting-yards receded with the Sears Tower, and clouds melted in the hot blue sky as the train ran west through the trees and houses of suburban Riverside, LaGrange Park and Western Springs. There were tennis courts and swimming pools and expensive cars in Highlands and Hinsdale and Clarendon Hills. The Stars and Stripes were much in evidence, still flaunting the chauvinism of the Los Angeles Olympics. I had seen an 'In God We Trust' sticker on a garbage truck and now I saw the US flag over a sewage plant. At Downers Grove a man slept along a pile of cut planks in the shade. The long train moaned desolately in the hot afternoon through the flat lands and the cornfields, and I dozed until Aurora.

The train thumped over the Fox River. Illinois seemed all Indian corn, miles of maize, cob after cob, acre after acre of sweet-corn. Beyond Somonauk and Mendota, staring through the window became a slow trance. Farm-houses spaced regularly over the wide fields all blended into one; a clapboard house with a TV aerial, a whitewashed cartwheel by the porch, wooden shutters by the curtained windows and a stone chimney at one end. There would be Lombardy poplars, a horse in the paddock, a grain silo or two, a barn with a corrugated iron roof and a pick-up truck out front.

Kewanee, Galva, Oneida: the land began to swell, like sea towards shore. Galesburg, Illinois, explained itself on giant signs – 'The Home of the Poet Carl Sandburg' – 'Fire-brewed BLATZ now at local prices!' Two men slowly painted the glans of a giant silo.

We were heading for Iowa now, speeding through curves. The train looped so you could see the front cars and the shadows lengthened along back-country dirt roads and willows glowed down by the creek and the melancholy hoot of the train set five deer off across a green pasture.

Then there were quick changes: swampland; dead trees poking up from brush; a belt of lush green; and suddenly the Mississippi stretching wide and brown between banks of tanned mud and green trees. There was a tug-boat, and men in caps stared from a barge with a crane. Though I only glimpsed it for a few seconds, that passage across the Mississippi meant I could put my finger on the map that August afternoon and know exactly where I was in space, 125 miles north of where Mark Twain was born at Hannibal, Missouri.

The train pulled up at Burlington, Iowa. Stevenson had been here before me: 'When I awoke next morning I was entirely renewed in spirits, and ate a hearty breakfast of porridge, with sweet milk, and coffee and hot cakes, at Burlington upon the Mississippi. Another long day's ride followed.'

Ottumwa, Charlton, Osceola; Creston at 9.11 pm. The fat man across the aisle wore an ostrich-patterned shirt and a baseball cap with 'REESE'S' on it. He stared into a paperback called *Death's Angel*. It was near here that Stevenson realized that he 'had come among revolvers'.

It grew dark and I was left with the map of Iowa on my lap, tracing our three-hour journey ahead through counties called Lucas, Clarke, Union, Adams, Montgomery and Mills. I tried to imagine all the towns and villages of Iowa, from Larchwood to Keokuk, New Albin to Hamburg, Clinton to Blencoe, Pleasanton to Rake, and to imagine all the people and all the busy days of their lives, in the fields and feedlots, offices and gas-stations, workshops and supermarkets. Perhaps Walt Whitman's singing of epic lists, the shuttering of slides, the cramming in of everything's name was the only way to capture the huge variety of'the sacred Union';' All these States compact, every square mile of these States without excepting a particle.' But I could not even imagine all Iowa. Perhaps you could go mad contemplating the map of Iowa, in the train running across its darkness.

9

Around midnight I got off the train in Omaha, Nebraska. The night was warm, thrilling with cicadas. I stood on a bridge overlooking the sodium-lit railway yards with my pack on my back, and the hums and clanks reminded me of nights at home near the cutting north of Euston, and my wife asleep in our bed, so far away.

I walked into the city to find the bus station, and asked directions. A couple walked me there. Bob was in advertising and Rita worked for Union Pacific. She told me, as we passed black kids break-dancing on flattened cardboard boxes to ghetto-blaster music, that the railroad company had a museum on Dodge and Fourteenth 'with lampshades made out of Indian skin'. We passed the fancy restaurants of Omaha, and I thought of railways and genocide.

Outside Omaha lies the Strategic Airborne Command Headquarters: computers and omnicide.

A drunk lurched up to cadge a light for a fumbled cigarette and sat down heavily opposite me in the yellow seats of the Burger King at Omaha's Greyhound bus station. Poor, shambling Chuck had a twitchy face that slid from eagerness to bafflement and a lower lip that quivered between truculence and tears. He called himself 'a Bohunk' (a contemptuous term for Bohemian or Czech), and slipped gear from pride to self-hatred as he said it. He loved his father (maudlin tales of athletic prowess); he hated his father (bitter tales of bullying and beating). Chuck's brother had been a Rhodes Scholar, 'at Oxford University, you heard of that, right?' He admired his brother; he hated his brother. Chuck had failed at the American Dream, he had not stood for Congress like his father or won a scholarship like his brother. He had failed at high school, failed to get on to the basketball team, failed to get married, failed to stop drinking. He was fresh out of jail for trespassing and vagrancy, defiantly banging his fist on the table then cowering in case a nearby fat-assed and po-faced cop should eject him from the diner. Chuck spilled change on to the formica, and I got him a soda and a pack of cigarettes from the machines.

'Do you hear me, do you understand what I'm saying?' he pleaded as I drooped with sleeplessness.

'I hear you, Chuck.'

Then he began to tell me how great the American athletes had been at the Olympics, and his eyes filled with tears as he described their prowess in gym, track and field. I never met a more patriotic man.

At 3.45 am I got a bus going west and slept right through dawn on the plains of Nebraska.

10

Omaha is west of the Missouri River, facing Council Bluffs, Iowa, on the eastern bank. Stevenson arrived there on Thursday, 21 August

1879, where the Union Pacific's 1000-mile stretch of railway track began its western run to Ogden, Utah. At the Emigrant House in Council Bluffs, human being were 'sorted and boxed for the journey'. The train had twenty cars of freight, baggage and cattle, a car for the Chinese, a car for single men (where Stevenson travelled) and one for women and children. When their names were called the hundred or so people piled aboard. Long, narrow and wooden, the cars had 'a stove and a convenience, one at either end, a passage down the middle and transverse benches upon either hand'. The lamps were dim and the seats too short for anyone to lie down, but they had reversible backs, like those on Argentine trains, so a passenger could choose which way to face. On the Union Pacific you chummed up with the person opposite and then hired, at an extortionate rate, a board and three cushions to put across your two seats upon which you could sleep.

They made up the train in the afternoon. 'At last, about six, the long train crawled out of the Transfer Station and across the wide Missouri to Omaha, westward bound.' It was Friday, 22 August 1879, 'a troubled uncomfortable evening in the cars. There was thunder in the air, which helped keep us restless.' A boy with whooping-cough made it no jollier.

Ogden, where they changed to the Central Pacific, was ninety hours away; nearly four days and nights. The train moved slowly, about fifteen miles an hour, with frequent stops for freight and animals. August is a hot month, and by the end of the trip the train stank abominably:

> a whiff of pure menagerie, only a little sourer, as from men instead of monkeys . . . I do my best to keep my head the other way, and look for the human rather than the bestial in this Yahoo-like business of the emigrant train. But one thing I must say: the car of the Chinese was notably the least offensive, and that of the women and children by a good way the worst. A stroke of nature's satire.

The railway line to California had only been open ten years, after the famous driving of the Golden Spike at Promontory, Utah. The Spike marked the end of seven years' work laying 2500 miles of track. It was a great American saga of courage and chicanery, energy and greed, as two companies raced each other to lay the most track; the Union Pacific built from the east, Central Pacific from the west.

Stevenson was filled with wonder, 'how at each stage of the construction, roaring, impromptu cities, full of gold and lust and death, sprang up and then died away again, and are now but wayside stations in the desert'. His imagination was excited by the mix of people, 'how in these uncouth places pig-tailed Chinese pirates worked side by side with border ruffians and broken men of Europe, talking together in a mixed dialect, mostly oaths, gambling, drinking, quarrelling, and murdering like wolves'.

In fact the 15,000 Chinese were sober and extraordinarily hard-working men, heroes of two terrible winters in the Sierras when they tunnelled through solid granite and carved the sides out of mountains. Leland Stanford, one of the 'Big Four' of the Central Pacific, completely changed his racist attitude to the Chinese when he saw that their industry had saved his wealthy hide.

Stevenson thought the achievement cried out for some Homer to chronicle it. When he remembered:

> . . . that all this epical turmoil was conducted by men in frock coats, and with a view to nothing more extraordinary than a fortune and a subsequent visit to Paris, it seems to me, I own, as if this railway were the one typical achievement of the age in which we live, as if it brought together into one plot all the ends of the world and all the degrees of social rank, and offered to some great writer the busiest, the most extended, and the most varied subject for an enduring literary work.

Saturday, 23 August 1879 was clear after the thunder, and Stevenson – who had been nicknamed 'Shakespeare' by other passengers – climbed up on the roof of the train trundling through Nebraska under a cloudless blue sky. 'I made my observatory on the top of a fruit-waggon, and sat by the hour upon that perch to spy about me.' He was with a baccy-chewing, juice-spitting man from Missouri and slowly scribbled a letter to Henley to pass the time.

> Desolate flat prairie upon all hands. Here and there a herd of cattle, a yellow butterfly or two; a patch of wild sunflowers; a wooden house or two; then a wooden house alone in miles of

waste; then a windmill to pump water. When we stop, which we do often, for emigrants and freight travel together, the kine first, the men after, the whole plain is heard singing with cicadae.

I I

It was strange to wake up hours out of Omaha and see the parchment of Nebraska scrolling past, its colours uncertain through the tinted windows of a Greyhound bus on Route 80. Stevenson had travelled too slowly, and now I was going too fast, trapped in the irrevocable speed and unreality of the modern tourist, a condition that some try to arrest with manic photographing. I stared out the window of the air-conditioned bus as at a TV screen. There were long monotonies of highway, trucks and cars, glimpses of the railway, cattle behind fences, clouds in the enormous sky.

I envied Stevenson, perched on the 'dirty and insecure' train roof in the sunshine, in his shirtsleeves and Derby hat: 'I wear nothing but a shirt and a pair of trousers, and never button my shirt. When I land for a meal I pass my coat and feel dressed.'

In the middle of America Stevenson and I coincided. Between Kearney and North Platte it was 1540 miles back east to New York and 1540 miles on west to San Francisco. It was a hundred and five years to the day since RLS was there, and by the side of the road and the railway track there were still 'innumerable wild sunflowers, no bigger than a crown piece'.

*

At a wayside halt before North Platte, Stevenson noticed a handsome woman who was selling milk:

> The place where she lived was to me almost ghastly. Less than a dozen wooden houses, all of a shape and nearly of a size, stood planted along the railway line . . . This extreme newness, above all in so naked and flat a country, gives a strong impression of artificiality . . .

RLS saw houses 'still sweating from the axe', but the modern towns are as incongruous, with advertising signs on high stilts, neon

[137]

tubes dusty by daylight, glitter rubbed down to tackiness. Against the landscape, human artifice looked both absurd and fragile.

North Platte itself had been the end of the line a dozen years before Stevenson passed through. The Indians wanted the whites to go no further, and in September 1867 a US government commission travelled there to talk 'Peace' with the Native Americans. Sioux and Cheyenne sat down with white army officers, recent veterans of a brutal Civil War.

One of the reporters covering the talks was Samuel Clemens, who later became Mark Twain. Another was Henry Morton Stanley, the ambitious Welshman who later found Dr Livingstone and introduced automatic weapons into the heart of Africa. Stanley said later that he learned how to handle 'natives' from watching General William T. Sherman 'inhaling with befitting gravity three distinct whiffs' from a Catlinite peace-pipe.

'You must submit and do the best you can,' General Sherman had warned the Amerindians. 'If you continue fighting you will all be killed . . . Live like white men and we will help you all you want.' But they did not want to live like white men, and the Indian Wars continued until 1890.

*

The bus made its lunch stop in Cheyenne, capital of Wyoming. Stevenson had had his lunch stop here too, for forty minutes on Sunday, 24 August 1879. The town was then a decade past its roaring railway beginning and settling to the big money of land and cattle barons.

The town dozed. Three Indians sitting in the shade shared a brown paper bag. The Gothic railway station looked like a parody of an Oxbridge college gatehouse and had 1885 carved in its sandstone portal. The State Capitol's gilded dome gleamed on a postcard inside a dim shop that sold boots and belts, hats and feathered hat-bands, vulgar jewellery and *COWBOYS MAKE THE BEST LOVERS* belt-buckles.

12

Stevenson called his next chapter 'The Deserts of Wyoming'. It took forty-four hours to cross the Territory of Wyoming, steadily climbing higher. The gloomy landscape and the altitude 'in that God-forsaken land' depressed Stevenson, and this was not helped by his drinking and smoking. He had got drunk with two companions nicknamed 'Dubuque' and 'Pennsylvania', and his itch had become appalling:

> The hot weather and the fever put into my blood by so much continuous travel, had aggravated these symptoms until they were strangely difficult to bear. When the fit was on me I grew almost light headed. I had to make a second cigarette before the first was smoked, for tobacco alone gave me self command under these paroxysms of irritation.

This was deleted from the 1895 edition of The Amateur Emigrant, which continues:

> I had been suffering in my health a good deal all the way; and at last, whether I was exhausted by my complaint or poisoned in some wayside eating house, the evening we left Laramie I fell sick outright.

*

After Cheyenne I sat on the bus next to a girl from LA with a bag full of spiritual tracts. I read about an elderly woman called Peace Pilgrim who had walked 27,000 miles through the States preaching non-violence before she died in Indiana in 1981. I read a five-point programme, *One Person Revolution For World Peace: Won't You Join Me Now?*, and looked out the window at outcrops of red shale rocks bristled with green pines. JESUS CARRIES MY LOAD said a Mack truck. Religion favours desert places: the numinous grows in the emptiness.

At Medicine Bow National Park the road reached 8640 feet, then coasted down to Laramie on its high plain. It was a name I had known since boyhood when there was a song on the radio called 'The Man from Laramie': 'He had six notches on his gun' we were told. But Laramie was no romantic Western town, with its 30-foot high Marlboro Man, Quick Draw Optical, Hardee's Drive-Thru Service, signs on stilts, neoned motels, chrome, concrete, and brandnames. Dusty bushes and slummy trailer parks at the edge of town soon gave way again to the blowy highway and the brown hills.

These long bare hills, dotted with cattle, were mottled by running shadows of clouds. Cloud ruled the high places of the North American West. Under the swelling belly of the nearest cumulus, along its shirred perspective to the billowing sides of distant thunderheads, the city-dweller's stare is awed by what natives call The Big Sky. Unlike Laramie, the clouds did not disappoint.

13

When the Union Pacific train left Laramie at 9 pm on Sunday, 24 August, RLS was exhausted. What followed was an unforgettably dreadful night among the passengers slaughtered by sleep: ' . . . here two chums alongside, flat upon their backs like dead folk; there a man sprawling on the floor, with his face upon his arm . . . '. Stevenson 'passed to and fro, stepping across the prostrate', probably heading for the convenience at one end of the car, reduced to the lowest indignity of the traveller, diarrhoea on public transport. He wrote to Henley: 'What it is to be ill in an emigrant train let those declare who know. I slept none till late in the morning, overcome with laudanum, of which luckily I had a little bottle.'

At the high point of the country, the continental divide, Stevenson's spirits were at their lowest. And it is at this point in *The Amateur Emigrant* that he distances himself from actuality by inserting a boy's account of worse horrors undergone on the Oregon Trail. For all his woes, RLS at least was not dead, and 'scalped upon the deserts'.

*

The gleaming lanes of road ran ahead and dived under a great curtain of rain across the western horizon, a darkness veined with sudden scars of lightning. The wind moved ahead of it, blowing sand in faint snakes over the road, whipping up the far dust into a brown edge to the blue-grey shadow moving over the land. Beyond the North Platte river the bus entered the penumbra and a banner of flame from a refinery flared bright orange in the gloom.

In Rawlins, Wyoming, the motels, the stores, the trailer parks, the pick-ups at Deb's Bar and the empty lot by McDonalds all waited for rain. The bus made a fifteen-minute stop under the darkening sky. I stood in the door of a takeaway with a mug of coffee as the girl from LA danced to Bruce Springsteen on the juke-box, waiting for her onion and *jalapeño* pizza. Way off under the shadow of the clouds I could see down to where faraway shafts of sunlight shone on the distant plain, an ache of childhood Bible pictures. The first fat drops of rain arrived with a cold wind, and the Stars and Stripes thumped and snapped on its rope. As we ran for the bus the rain came straight and hard, and the smell of wet earth was the last gulp of freshness before the door of the air-conditioned Greyhound sighed shut, and the tinted view and the swash of the wipers found us back on the highway once more, hissing on wet asphalt towards Rock Springs.

14

The Omaha woman who ran the inexpensive Rose Motel in Rock Springs, Wyoming said the town was getting rough again, with fights and stabbings at the Cowboy Bar when the boys from the oil-rigs were liquored up. Wyoming licence plates depicted a brown kicking horse on a yellow field, and every pick-up seemed to have spotlights on the cab-roof and a man in a hat revving it round town with the muffler off. Bar-stool cowpunchers teetered out of dark saloons with loudly maudlin Country & Western music; there was whoopin 'and hollerin' till late.

I switched TV channels from the sycophancy of the Republican Convention in Texas, through an inane game show and a self-righteous and ungrammatical preacher, to find Marlon Brando taking a vicious flogging in *One-Eyed Jacks*. Later in the film Ben Johnson spelled out G-R-E-A-S-E-R to a Mexican's face before shooting him.

That night I re-read the chapter in *The Amateur Emigrant* called 'Despised Races'. 'Of all stupid ill-feelings', it began, 'the sentiment of my fellow-Caucasians towards our companions in the Chinese car was the most stupid and the worst.' Stevenson's own attitude to the Chinese was one of wonder and respect: 'Their forefathers watched the stars before mine had begun to keep pigs.' It was not an attitude shared by many whites in America, especially California, where any depression prompted cruelties from the older immigrants who feared the newcomers would steal their jobs.

*

Stevenson came to America at a crucial time for the Chinese. They had been attacked since the early days of the Gold Rush, but there were severe anti-Chinese riots in San Francisco in 1877, and the Chinese Exclusion Act was finally passed by Congress in 1882. Racist 'Yellow Peril' scaremongers had a field day, although the fears of 'swamping' were actually absurd. In 1880 the US population was over 50 million, of which only 0.2 per cent were ethnic Chinese. But they were an identifiable target for hate and fear, and one of the worst incidents took place in Rock Springs itself, in September 1885, when twenty-eight Chinese miners were murdered.

The other despised race was the American Indian. Stevenson himself wrote:

> If oppression drives a wise man mad, what should be raging in the heart of these poor tribes, who have been driven back and back, step after step, their promised reservations torn from them one after another as the States extended Westward, until at length they are shut up into these hideous mountain deserts of the centre . . .?

'The only good Indian I ever saw was dead,' General Phil Sheridan had said a dozen years before Stevenson travelled across 'their hereditary continent'. 1879 was three years after Custer had died at the Little Big Horn.

> I saw no wild or independent Indian; indeed, I heard that such avoid the neighbourhood of the train; but now and again at way-stations, a husband and wife and a few children, disgracefully dressed out with the sweepings of civilization, came forth and stared upon the emigrants. The silent stoicism of their conduct, and the pathetic degradation of their appearance, would have touched any thinking creature, but my fellow-passengers danced round them with a truly Cockney baseness. I was ashamed for the thing we call civilization.

15

Drinking intoxicants on coach prohibited. Smoking on buses is prohibited by law in Oregon, Utah, Los Angeles county, cities of Oakland, Berkeley, San

Francisco. In other areas cigarette smoking is permitted in last 4 rows only. This coach is restroom equipped for your convenience. Your Operator: JOHN MAHAFFEY: Safe, reliable, courteous.

The Greyhound driver, wearing aviator's sunglasses, turned his head towards the seat behind him.

'Sir? Could you locate that noise?'

I jammed the rattling window.

'I thenk ye too,' said a wizened old lady who was sitting on the other front seat. 'Hed thet all night. Sounded like a chipmunk tryin' to git in.'

It was a good ride to Salt Lake City, Utah. The bus was empty, the driver in a mood for talking, and when awake the old lady joined in too.

'I'm seventy years old 'n' I live in the San Joaquin Valley in California. Originally from Missoura. We went west 'cause my husband had asthma, real bad. He was coughin' up *blood.*'

Operator John Mahaffey had traced his ancestors back to the MacPhees or MacFies who had emigrated from Colonsay in the Hebrides after the '45, the second Jacobite rebellion. I thought of Mrs MacFie, keeper of the Stevenson home in Heriot Row, Edinburgh.

Below our road, a long freight train ran along the Green River. A skunk that had not made it was smeared across Route 80, and a blown tyre lay curled like a black alligator on the shoulder of the road. It was empty country under a blue sky with a wash of feathery high clouds. There were snow-drift fences with overlapping palings, and an eagle sitting on one pole. In the mountains to the south smoke plumed from industries down towards places with beautiful names like Lonetree and Burntfork.

When we passed an old trading-post John Mahaffey told me the story of the mountain-man Jim Bridger. The fort, established by Bridger on Black's Fork of the Green River in 1843, is now restored and whitewashed, and is the site of a fake trappers' annual rendez-vous when nostalgists dress in buckskins and fire black powder weapons. Jim Bridger played his own part in an American tragedy. One of the original Rocky Mountain Fur Company trappers, he explored the West, found the Great Salt Lake and the geysers of Yellowstone, and knew the lie of the land better than any white of his generation. He lived with Indians and had several Indian wives, yet Bridger was an agent of the forces that would destroy the West he loved. His place on the Green River had a forge to repair the wagons of emigrants moving west along the Oregon Trail that he himself had mapped. Too late, he began to understand the future; when at last he came out of retirement in Missouri to warn General Sheridan not to attack the Sioux and Cheyenne, nobody listened. Bridger died in 1881, poor, blind and forgotten, and the whites overran the Indian lands like locusts. In our century a pollutant-belching power-plant was named in his honour.

The bus rolled through land dotted with sagebrush, fibrous grey juniper, yellow wild mustard and green Mormon tea. As John told me about the elk, antelope, moose, badger, coyote and raccoon, a squad of F-16 jets from Hill Air Force Base flew high overhead.

We went through Ogden, Utah, and passed the factory where John Mose Browning invented the automatic pistol in 1897. By then the age of the bow and arrow in the West was over, 'the enemy within' was defeated, and the United States of America could begin to look overseas for new foes to conquer.

16

The bus from Salt Lake City left Utah across the Bonneville Salt Flats, glaring white under the hot sun. After miles of alkaline desert I began to think it was snow and that the gathered pools of bitter water were broken ice – a weird Siberia in Utah. The bus bounced behind a water wagon spraying down dust. The proper road was half closed; construction crews were elevating it above the Salt Lake which had itself risen dramatically. Many of the road-gang workers were women.

My edition of the *Salt Lake Tribune* had an interview with Clint Eastwood. He was asked what he thought about being called a feminist film-maker. 'It's very simple,' Eastwood replied,

> I've always been interested in strong women. When I was growing up the female roles were equal to the men, and the actresses were just as strong as the actors. Now, in a lot of movies, you seem to have half a cast. The guy will be a big macho star. The woman will be a wimp. Women in the

audience don't like to see that, and I believe men don't either. Isn't it going to be twice as interesting to have two strong characters?

It made me think of Fanny Osbourne, waiting for Stevenson in Monterey. She was certainly a strong character. Monterey was just north of Carmel where Eastwood lived. I wondered who you could get to impersonate whom in a film about Robert Louis Stevenson and Fanny Osbourne. I burst out laughing at the thought of Clint Eastwood in the role of Sidney Colvin.

*

At Wendover we crossed from Utah into Nevada, and from 3 pm Mountain Standard Time to 2 pm Pacific Standard Time. In a second we gained an hour and promptly gambled a quarter of it away. Everyone poured off the bus and went from bright sunshine into a dim casino filled with slot-machines personalized by Christian names, place names or zodiac signs, and which also played electronic jingles and silvery fanfares to the winners. Nickels, dimes, quarters and silver dollars were scooped from paper cups and jumbo icecream tubs and frenziedly fed into the maws of one-armed bandits owned by mobsters. One man won $100 and the whole bus cheered him when he got back on. For a moment it seemed as if we were all on holiday, but the mood was ephemeral. We drove on up into desert country through the Pequod and the Independence mountains, and the bone of salt-flats disappeared behind us.

Nevada is a big, empty state, useful to the military. North-east of Death Valley and an hour's drive from Las Vegas is the Nuclear Testing Site where the US military tested atom bombs on their own troops. Radioactive fall-out from the 1950s tests had drifted east over Utah and other states. Under the Nevada desert near Skull Mountain, Britain's own nuclear bombs have been developed and tested since public outcry stopped the messy atmospheric explosions in the Pacific.

People used to call the American West 'God's Own Country'; then it became the country where men played at being gods. When Robert Oppenheimer saw the first atomic mushroom darkening the sky above Alamogordo in New Mexico he remembered a line from the *Bhagavad Gita*: 'I am become Death, the shatterer of worlds.'

The natural clouds that towered above me in Nevada that day were still magnificent, lined with silver and green and purple and gold. I daydreamed through Wells; the driver chewed tobacco; Star Valley had green alfalfa fields; and the light was soft as we crossed Mary's River and death seemed further away than it really was.

17

From Toano we travelled all day through deserts of alkali and sand, horrible to man . . . and came by supper-time to Elko. As we were standing . . . outside the station, I saw two men whip suddenly from under the cars, and take to their heels across country. They were tramps . . . who had been riding on the beams since eleven of the night before . . . These land stowaways play a great part over here in America, and I should have liked dearly to have become acquainted with them.

Gentleman-of-the-road RLS saw his first hoboes in the town of Elko which was then only ten years old. A newcomer wrote in February 1869: 'I arrived in Elko and it is a fine place of about sixty canvas tents. All sorts of games and vices are in progress. There were only two men killed this afternoon.'

The Central Pacific railroad, pushing east from Sacramento, dragged teamsters, muleskinners, bullwhackers, woodcutters, cowboys and prospecting miners in its wake. Elko had cheap liquor and ten brothels with from six to twenty women in each, and pimps who beat them into obedience. A community mushroomed out of the desert; by December 1869, the town had nearly five thousand inhabitants, and boasted saloons, hardware stores, banks and blacksmith shops, a school, a court-house, a church and a newspaper – The Elko Independent. By the time canvas tents became frame houses land values had quintupled, and when in 1871 a fire burned down the business section of town, an enterprising man set up an adobe brick machine that turned out 30,000 mud bricks a day. In 1874 the first University of Nevada was founded, and there was piped municipal water the next year. The Chinese community settled south of the railroad tracks with a joss-house, a Tong hall, laundries and wash-houses, and a water-wheel in the Humboldt River to irrigate their vegetable gardens and sugar-cane fields.

*

The thousands who drive through Elko on I-80 have no real need to leave Idaho Street with its motels, gas-stations, banks, eateries and casino. I wandered down to Railroad Street to find the original station where RLS had stopped briefly for supper on 27 August 1879. I was a few months late: the old tracks running through town had been torn up, and Project Lifesaver was going to turn the wide stretch of gravel into an enormous parking-lot.

An odd thing happened to Stevenson after his supper in Elko. He was stopped by three red-faced men who asked if he was travelling on the train, and if he would like a job. 'I'm running a theatre here,' said one of the men, 'and we're a little short in the orchestra. You're a musician I guess?' Stevenson said that he was not and the man looked put out. Then one of his companions asked him, on the nail, for five dollars.

'He bet you were a musician; I bet you weren't. No offence, I hope?'

'None whatever,' said Stevenson, and the strangers 'withdrew to the bar, where I presume the debt was liquidated.'

*

Three blocks along Commercial Street from the now vanished station I was offered the cheapest room I had found in America. 'Doc' Moore's place was an old-fashioned wooden building with Chinese elms and twisty box-elders outside. I sat down to read the *Elko Daily Free Press* and its small ads. In Elko you could get baton-twirling lessons from Charlotte, buy an Appaloosa gelding or an Appaloosa mare, swap your 12-gauge shotgun for a Suzuki dirt bike, or trade your Vespa motor scooter – 'no mopeds!' – for a Colt.22 pistol, 'nice shape'.

I was writing at the table in my shabby room when 'Doc' Moore knocked and came in, cap on the back of his head, holding a couple of cans of beer. 'Doc' had knocked off for the day, though his vigorous old Basque neighbour was still busy. We popped the cans and talked. The door of the room was open; from the look of his other guests 'Doc' was a one-man Statue of Liberty, taking in the 'wretched refuse' and 'huddled masses', some of whom had lived there for years. He was an easy-going, kindly man of sixty-five, raised on a ranch eighty miles south of Elko, and who talked rather like Walter Brennan. His real name was actually Cedric, after his English grandfather, a stonemason who had gone from Derbyshire to the copper mines of Chile, then goldrushed to California and afterwards to Eureka in Nevada. He had put up a store, started a stagecoach line and married the daughter of an Italian charcoal burner before settling at the ranch where Doc's dad had grown up before him.

'Doc' Moore knew the ways of the West; like placer mining, where you run the water in sluices so the gold catches in riffles at the bottom of the trough; and how the sheep and cattle survive the Nevada winter without hay. The cold kills the bitterness of the button brush and the white sage, so the critters eat what they don't touch in summer.

18

The last pages of *The Amateur Emigrant* light up with longing to see Fanny and the joyous rush down into California. Stevenson woke up by Emigrant Gap early on Friday, 29 August 1879.

> I had one glimpse of a huge pine-forested ravine upon my left, a foaming river, and a sky already coloured with the fires of dawn . . . You will scarce believe how my heart leapt at this. It was like meeting one's wife.

As they dropped down through Blue Cañon, Alta and Dutch Flat, the passengers went wild with joy 'and bawled like schoolboys':

> At every turn we could see further into the land and our own happy futures . . . The day was breaking as we crossed the ferry . . . the bay was perfect – not a ripple, scarce a stain, upon its blue expanse . . . and suddenly . . . the city of San Francisco, and the bay of gold and corn, were lit up from end to end with summer daylight.

So *The Amateur Emigrant* ends, on the upbeat of exultation. But San Francisco was not Stevenson's destination. From the Davis Street

Wharf he made his way to another station for another train going south, over a hundred miles down the coast. It was 4.30 pm on Saturday, 30 August 1879 when Stevenson got off the train at Monterey. The journey was not yet over. The station was out of town and he hitched a ride on Manuel Wolter's cart which took him over the last stretch. In three weeks of almost continuous travel RLS had covered some six thousand miles from Britain to the west coast of America. The plodding cart dropped him outside the Bohemia Saloon, and Stevenson limped inside for a brandy.

> *Monterey Californian* September 1879
> Those boss mixologists, the Sanchez Brothers, keep a standing invitation in this paper to friends, acquaintances, and strangers in town, to visit them at their liquidating establishment, the Bohemia Saloon, and sample their brands. They keep the best of everything – prime cigars, delightful cigarittes and consoling beverages. Drop in and see 'em.

Monterey was an old Spanish town and fishing-village with adobe houses, iron balconies, red-tiled roofs, sandy streets and sidewalks made of planks and whale bone. Some street-corners had old Spanish cannons stuck upright to serve as hitching posts. Monterey had already attracted writers and painters. The poet Charles Warren Stoddard told his painter friends about it; and one of them, Joseph Strong, was to meet Fanny's daughter Belle in Monterey and later elope with her. Joe liked a drink and was probably a *habitué* of the Bohemia Saloon with its 'consoling beverages'. He had an ally in one of the bar's owners, for Adolfo Sanchez was, at the time, courting Fanny's younger sister Nellie Vandegrift. When Stevenson arrived, therefore, the women living at the Casa Bonifacio, a few doors away from the Bohemia Saloon, had three suitors in town.

It is not known if Stevenson went straight to see Fanny. He arrived on a Saturday and Samuel Osbourne, Fanny's undivorced husband, still sometimes came down from San Francisco for the weekends to visit his wife and children.

'Things are damned complicated', Stevenson wrote to Baxter. It is possible that Joe Strong headed off an embarrassing meeting by finding Stevenson his dollar-a-day room at Rosanna Leese's house nearby, and telling him to lie low for a day or two.

Lloyd Osbourne later remembered how Stevenson arrived in Monterey. One day Fanny looked at her twelve-year-old son with a curious brightness in her eyes. 'I have news for you,' she said. 'Luly's coming.' Osbourne wrote:

> I think RLS must have arrived the next day. I remember him walking into the room, and the outcry of delight that greeted him; the incoherence, the laughter, the tears; the heart-welling joy of reunion. Until that moment I had never thought of him as being in ill-health . . .

[Stevenson had been vigorous in Grez-sur-Loing. No invalid could have paddled from Antwerp to Paris, or walked with the donkey Modestine through the Massif Central.]:

> Now he looked ill even to my childish gaze; the brilliancy of his eyes emphasized the thinness and pallor of his face; his clothes, no longer picturesque but merely shabby, hung loosely on his shrunken body, and there was about him an indescribable lessening of his alertness and self-confidence.

Fanny Osbourne was in a fix. She was trapped in an unhappy marriage, but was uncertain if she wanted to divorce the father of her children, the man who helped support them. She had been ill, with what Stevenson called 'inflammation of the brain', but had sent her desperate telegram, and now her 'literary friend from Scotland' had come 6000 miles to be with her. It was a gallant but embarrassing act. In Spanish-speaking Monterey decorum had to be preserved, and she now had not only an irregular husband visiting but a scarecrow of a *gringo* from over the seas, 'the one object of scandal, gossip, imaginative history'. Moreover, he had not arrived on a white charger with pockets full of money, but exhausted and poor, wrecked by pleurisy, eczema and malnutrition. It was too much.

Some sort of scene occurred. Dejected, Stevenson took what he thought was the healthy way out of the fogs of Monterey; he went camping in the hills as he had in France when Fanny left for America the year before. He wrote to Charles Baxter on 9 September:

My dear Charles,
Address me c/o Jos D Strong, Monterey, Monterey Co., Cal.
This is not a letter, for I am too perturbed . . . My news is
nil. I know nothing, I go out camping that is all I know.
Today I leave, and shall likely be three weeks in camp. I
shall send a letter from there with more guts than this, and
now say good bye to you, having had the itch and a broken
heart.

Joe Strong and RLS set off in a buggy down the Carmel Valley
to the home of an English fruit farmer called Edward Berwick.
After spending a night there, Stevenson set off alone on horseback
up into the tawny Santa Lucia mountains. He was not at all well,
and somewhere along the San Clemente creek, about fifteen miles
south of Monterey, he collapsed:

> Two nights I lay out under a tree in a sort of stupor, doing
> nothing but fetch water for myself and a horse, light a fire
> and make coffee, and all night awake hearing the goat-bells
> ringing and the tree-frogs singing when each new noise was
> enough to set me mad.

Two small girls, Sarah and Dolly Wright, found him there, still
lying under a tree. He was so thin that they later nicknamed him
'Splinters'. They summoned an ex-bear-hunter called Captain
Anson Smith who was the partner in their father Jonathan
Wright's angora goat-ranch. Stevenson was pronounced 'real sick'
and ordered up to the house. Two more days followed in which
Stevenson 'scarcely slept, or ate, or thought'.

19

I went to look for the angora goat-ranch where Stevenson had lain
ill a hundred and five years before. It was 85 degrees in the shade,
and some 250 miles to the south, Los Angeles was enduring its
highest temperatures since 1882. Robinson Canyon Road winds
up from Carmel Valley, well above the sea-fog that sometimes
shrouds the Monterey Peninsula; the newly gravelled surface had a

25 mph speed limit to protect windscreens. The reddish earth shimmered in the heat, and the grass was burned brown so the hollow stalks were dry and crunchy. Even the butterflies seemed dazed with heat. The road wound through pines and redwoods in the folds between rounded hills, their tawny curves dotted with oak and cork trees.

Spotting the silvery timbers of a ruined cabin below and to the left of the road, I climbed through a three-strand barbed wire fence and trespassed down through the dry meadow. Burrs stuck to my socks and my trouser turn-ups filled with grass-seed.

Smith and Wright had picked a good place for a house, close to shade and water, at the junction of four small valleys on a site neither too exposed nor shut away. But now it was as ruined as Glencorse Church. The stone chimney was still standing, but half the roof was down, and the light cross-hatched through shattered laths and cracked planks. Vandals and weather have done their work; soon it will be gone.

I wandered around, down to the small creek, under the trees, among the remains of the two room cabin. It was not hard to visualize it as a small goat-ranch, with an Indian servant cooking over a wood fire, a bear-hunter's rifle leaned up in the corner, and Stevenson lying in an exhausted trance on a blanket, as David Balfour would lie at Gluny's Gage in *Kidnapped*.

Stevenson did not die, and only rested up for a couple of weeks at the ranch. He passed the time telling stories to Sarah and Dolly Wright, helping them with their homework and working fitfully on his *Amateur Emigrant* notes. Then he made his way back down to Monterey.

He still had the stinging rash and his landlady disliked it. She upped the rent to force him out, and then burned all his bedding; RLS moved on to the Girardin French House, a $4 a month sailors' flophouse with thick adobe walls and a floor of beaten earth, just across the stream from the town jail. The Girardin House was saved from destruction in 1927 by two ladies and was given to the State of California in 1941. It is now Stevenson House, a prosperous museum dedicated to the memory of one who had slept on the floor there in poverty.

I had gone straight to Stevenson House when I got off the bus in Monterey. It was late at night and the town seemed to be all banks, real-estate offices and empty parking lots under harsh light. There were few people in the cool quiet streets, but I spoke to the gardener as he let himself in the wooden door of the building. He said I couldn't sleep in the garden and when I asked if he knew a cheap place to stay shook his head and said: '*Es todo para millonarios aqui* ('It's all for millionaires here').

The gardener was right. As Stevenson had foreseen, Monterey had gone under to 'the millionaire vulgarians of the Big Bonanza'. It was no longer a place for Hispanics, Stevenson's 'poor, quaint, penniless, native gentlemen'.

The nearest motel was far too expensive, and the Armed Forces YMCA was closed. Monterey is a garrison town, and the 17,000 soldiers of the 7th Infantry Division at Fort Ord are as important to the town's economy as tourism.

The man who gave me a lift to a motel on the outskirts was indignant at my scorn for 'millionaire vulgarians'.

'Monterey is top dollar, man. We may not like it, but that's progress.'

I thanked him as I hauled out my bag, borrowing words from an English beggar, 'You're a gentleman.'

'Well,' he sang, 'I wouldn't say tha-a-at!'

The motel was run by Indians from India. I watched TV in my room. Seventy per cent of those polled thought the B-1B Bomber was worth the money. Ronald Reagan, wearing a daft cap, made a speech to the American Legion. 'Alka-Seltzer!' urged an advertisement, 'ease symptoms of stress that can come from success'. Priscilla Presley pouted Quench lipstick. A Georgia redneck killed an eagle with a baseball bat and was interviewed, grinning and shuffling. Mark Twain's 'The Mysterious Stranger' was adapted on PBS:

'Who are you?' someone asked. 'Your dream' was the reply.

No longer real, I fell asleep.

I joined a guided tour of the Monterey Stevenson House. It was all very pleasant there now; the squalid yard had yielded to a sunny garden bright with flowers. A quavery-voiced tourist said: 'Oh my, isn't it lovely? Is this where he wrote *A Child's Garden of Verses?*'

Museums are strange; fictions made of objects, not words. It was odd to stand by the thirteen-foot mahogany table and know that it had gone from its original tropical forest to the dining-room of 17 Heriot Row, that it was dismantled and shipped to Samoa, re-assembled at Vailima, then shipped and stored again before ending up in Monterey, where it was touched and admired by ladies with blue hair. A bookcase of Thomas Stevenson's was also there, containing gift copies of Henry James's *Lesson of the Master* and *The Real Thing*. What was 'the real thing' on the heritage trail of objects? Everything in the museum was both solidly real and quite unreal, because divorced from history and function. A cabinet held Stevenson's pocket-knife, a silver hip-flask engraved *Coelum Non Solum*, a purse, spurs, binoculars, a conch shell, a valise, a carpet bag, some fine tapas and spears. There was a desk from Hyères, a rocking chair from Saranac, and photos from Samoa. Henry James had called Stevenson 'a Scotchman of the world' and now there were bits of his possessions scattered round the globe. If you joined up all the dots, would any figure that emerged be anything to do with the man?

*

The child in Stevenson had a field day in California. Perhaps researching for his projected 'western' novel *Arizona Breckinridge: A Vendetta in the West*, or perhaps for the fun of it, Stevenson had a go with a percussion-cap revolver. His pistol had been 'useless' on *Travels With a Donkey* and now it was almost disastrous, for when he fired six charges the bullets all remained in the barrel, choking it from muzzle to breech with solid lead that took a man three hours to drill out. 'Another shot', he wrote to Henley, 'and I'd have gone to kingdom come.'

His most irresponsible exploit in the dry summer of 1879 was starting a forest fire. Actually there was already a fire in progress, but RLS helped to spread it. He wanted to know if it was the pale wispy beard of Spanish moss that burned, and instead of pulling a piece off just walked up to a pine tree and applied a match to one of the hanging tassels. 'The tree went off simply like a rocket; in three seconds it was a roaring pillar of fire.' Then he ran like hell. That night he went out to have a look at his handiwork. 'It was a good fire, though I say it that should not.' He later turned the incident into one of his *Fables*, 'The Two Matches'.

22

I went to the library, got out a microfilm of the old weekly newspaper the *Monterey Californian* and read through the issues from September to December 1879 to see what Stevenson had contributed. RLS got $2 a week helping the polysyllabic editor Crevole Bronson, and took a wry view of both him and his paper – 'a losing business'. There were many advertisements:

> . . . and the only original matter which awoke much interest was in the form of personals. These take . . . one of two classical forms. As thus: 'Jack Smith came over Tuesday, from Tres Piños where he is doing a great hardware business. He was looking splendid and left a bottle of whiskey at our office. Call again, Jack!' Or again as thus: 'It is not true that Alexandro Gomez lost his way going home from the Fan-dango.' The first ministers to the vanity of Jack; the second to the mirth of Alexandro's friends.

In the issues I read, the personals often appeared in a column called *DOTS from Freelance*:

> Freelance says there is no truth in the report . . . – That Joe thinks there is $50 a week in it. – That the dance was gotten up expressly for 'them' and because they never put in an appearance the boys are mad. – That G. N. has a strawberry mark on his arm, but says he knows nothing of the Grampian Hills. – That she says 'O, Jamie! Jamie! You'll break my heart!' – That you may expect soon to hear again from 'FREELANCE'.

I sat for a time over this. 'Joe' could be Joe Strong; the Grampian Hills are in Scotland; the strawberry mark could be eczema; the initials G. N. could be George North, the pseudonym that Stevenson was to use for the first appearance of *Treasure Island*. And then I checked myself, on the verge of cryptomania.

The one article Stevenson definitely wrote in the *Monterey Californian* was 'San Carlos Day – A Barbarian at the Carmello Mission' in the issue of 11 November 1879. On its saint's day the week before, he had visited the ruined eighteenth-century Franciscan Mission of San Carlos Borromeo del Rio Carmelo which had over 3000 Indians buried in its cemetery. RLS was struck by the terrible state of its fabric. 'Here, in America,' he wrote, 'on this beautiful Pacific coast, you cannot afford to lose what you have . . . I am moved, by sentiment, to pray for restitution or at least repair.' His appeal struck a note, a subscription was raised and repair work began the next year. The Carmel Mission is now lovingly restored and much visited by tourists: and a dusty picture of RLS is unprominently displayed in an obscure music case.

What impressed Stevenson at the Carmel Mission on San Carlos Day was the Indians singing Mass in Latin: 'the old, mediaeval civilization and your old primeval barbarian, hand-in-hand'. The scene impressed Stevenson enough to write about it in three different pieces. He watched the Indian who conducted the singing, about eighty years old, stone-blind, with his eyes bandaged and leaning on a staff, being led to his place in church by a little grandchild:

> He had seen changes in the world since he first sang that music sixty years ago, when there was no gold and no Yankees, and he and his people lived in plenty under the kind priests . . . who had now passed away from all authority and influence in that land – to be succeeded by greedy land-thieves and sacrilegious pistol-shots. So ugly a thing may our Anglo-Saxon Protestantism appear beside the doings of the Society of Jesus.

San Carlos Day was 4 November, and the *Monterey Californian's* editorial that day reads like a Stevenson piece. Provoked, the Ute Indians of Colorado had killed some soldiers and their intolerant agent; it was an ugly time; and the editorial is scathing about the treatment of Native Americans.

Pen them up and starve them to death if you can; if not, make drunkards of them, they will be more easily robbed . . . The government is blind – intentionally blind – or it would at once turn its eyes upon the Indian ring, a combination of heartless thieves who rob the savages of their land and their food and who are responsible for every Indian outbreak.

23

In Monterey, Stevenson noted, 'the smallest excursion is made on horseback'. Then, Spanish was the language of the streets and all males considered themselves *caballeros*. Now, English is the principal language and cars are as compulsory as horses were once. Buses are infrequent and the sidewalks peter out so the pedestrian is trapped on a highway and has to scramble down embankments and through fences to get home. Urban walking is an 'Un-American' activity, while the consumption of fuel and goods appears to be a patriotic duty.

When Stevenson was not ill in bed or reading Thoreau, or spending time with Fanny, he walked a lot. He would set out north-west through the Chinatown that later became Steinbeck's Cannery Row (now a ghetto of tourist shops and restaurants) to the woods behind Lovers 'Point and the lighthouse. There he found the little wooden houses of 'The Pacific Camp Grounds, the Christian Seaside Resort' where crowds came in the summer 'to enjoy a life of teetotalism, religion and flirtation'. Pacific Grove is now a secular small town, and no longer teetotal.

Stevenson found the long beaches 'enticing to the idle man'. The coast of the Monterey Peninsula was a pungent reminder of North Berwick and Earraid. The adventure story he wrote in Monterey, 'The Pavilion on the Links', is set in Scotland, but the landscape owes something to Monterey:

> The country . . . was mixed sand-hill and links; links being a Scottish name for sand which has ceased drifting and become more or less solidly covered with turf . . .

Fanny's sister, who later settled in Monterey, named her first son

Luis or Louis after RLS, and six years after he had been in Monterey, Stevenson published a poem for his name-child in *A Child's Garden of Verses*:

Now that you have spelt your lesson, lay it down and go and
play,
Seeking shells and seaweed on the sands of Monterey,
Watching all the mighty whalebones, lying buried by the
breeze,
Tiny sandy-pipers, and the huge Pacific seas.
And remember in your playing, as the sea-fog rolls to you,
Long ere you could read it, how I told you what to do;
And that while you thought of no one, nearly half the world
away
Someone thought of Louis on the beach of Monterey!

West of Monterey I walked across sand-dunes down to the strong-smelling beach at Spanish Bay. 'Strange sea-tangles', that Stevenson had noticed, 'new to the European eye' lay like corded clubs and ropy spars and gave off clouds of tiny insects and hopping sand-lice when I approached. The fog drifted in tatters over Point Joe and behind were creaking green pines. The foghorn sounded like someone blowing into a deep-bellied bottle.

A ground squirrel dashed down a hole in a puff of dust. There is plenty of wildlife around the Monterey Peninsula – gulls and cormorants, sand-pipers and brown pelicans, starlings and crows. I missed the sea-otters, but heard the barking laugh of the harbour seals long before I watched them jostle each other on Seal Rock. The Monterey cypress trees were bent back by the prevailing wind, their greenery like a flash-photo of storm-blown hair. On the golf-course under the Scots pines deer cantered away from electric carts bearing obese sportsmen.

24

California is eager to be identified with *Treasure Island*. Stevenson did say that the scenery of his first novel's imaginary island was 'in part Californian', but California stakes a stronger claim – it actually wants to *be* Treasure Island. One of the golf-courses on the Monterey Peninsula is called Spyglass Hill Golf Course, after Spyglass Hill in *Treasure Island*. The road just behind it in Del Monte Forest is called R. L. Stevenson Drive, and it runs through Pebble Beach, the richest and most exclusive private community in northern California. Pebble Beach has only four gates leading into it, but it is an island of wealth, with a Lodge that boasts 'intimate French cuisine . . . in an elegant setting', half a dozen golf-courses and a maidan for chukkas of polo. It enjoys a quasi-aristocratic status in style-conscious California, and has become a snob's heaven. The snobbery is rooted in unreality. California was already a fiction when Stevenson arrived. The name 'California' was taken from a sixteenth-century novel, *Sergas de Esplandián*, which was the fifth volume of the popular romance *Amadís de Gaula*: 'At the right hand of the Indies there is an island named California.'

California and *Treasure Island* share a common mythic appeal. You get a map, travel west, land on an island and after a spot of bother find unlimited wealth. California, after 1849, also meant gold at the end of the rainbow. The treasure in *Treasure Island* is actually blood-money which has been laundered by time and magicked into Instant Old Money – 'doubloons and double guineas and moidores and sequins'. It is money severed from social relations, morally neutral, the treasure of a child's world of finders-keepers. The slaves who mined and minted it, the pirates who murdered to get it, the real price of Flint's treasure no longer matter when the righteous get their hands on it.

Money has the same apparent innocence in California. 'It's beautiful, man.' And so it is – everything green, clean, rich and fine in Pebble Beach; kept that way by a full-time private security force. It's an island of wealth with the brown faces and bright weapons of the pirates kept outside. Pebble Beach is owned by Columbia Pictures, which is in turn owned by Coca-Cola – a company that sells a fantasy product which it calls 'the real thing'.

Graham Greene has said: 'I would rather end my days in the Gulag than in – than in *California*.'

*

I took a last look at Alvarado Street before leaving Monterey. The house where Fanny, Nellie, Belle and Lloyd had lived was now a branch of Crocker Bank. The Bohemia had become the Bourbon Street Saloon. Bronson's two-bit newspaper had become a cinema showing *The Revenge of the Nerds* and *CHUD (Cannibalistic, Humanoid, Underground Dwellers)*. Whale bones had given way to Woolworth's.

It was incredibly hot. On the bus I lost my temper with the drugged youth lolling in the next seat who kept smearing blood from a cut hand on my trousers. I stared angrily out of the window at the inhumanly vast vegetable fields of Salinas.

25

As I came into San Francisco over the six-lane Bay Bridge from Oakland, I could see the hilly city aspiring upwards like Chicago. To the right, over the blue bay dotted with white sails, was the island of Alcatraz, once a prison whose most famous inmate, Robert Stroud, taught himself ornithology in his cell and became known as the Birdman. In the early 1970s radical American Indians seized the island as a protest against US government policies for their people. Also visible was a flat artificial island which the map tells you is called Treasure Island.

Treasure Island in San Francisco Bay was man-made for the Golden Gate International Exposition of 1939. A full-time 'Theme Girl' was hired, a dancer called Zoe Dell Lantis. The theme was romantic piracy – a garbled mixture of Stevenson and J. M. Barrie – and Zoe Dell was dressed in a Peter Pan suit with thigh high boots to pose prettily with spyglasses and treasure chests as a pouting buccaneer.

Treasure Island is now a world novel, with interesting things to say about nineteenth-century imperial attitudes. But in our own century there is a new twist: the responsibilities vested in the Squire, the Captain and the Doctor have been largely usurped by the military-industrial complex of which Eisenhower warned. In the name of 'National Security' the pirates have taken over the ship and all the treasures of the earth.

Treasure Island in San Francisco Bay now belongs to the US Navy.

26

Stevenson lived in San Francisco from Christmas 1879 to May 1880. The dominant note of his letters to Charles Baxter at this time is illness, and the strongest motif in his essay on the city is instability. San Francisco is in a zone of earth tremors and as it was a largely wooden city the other great fear was fire. In 1906 both would devastate many districts.

Monterey had been 'a hole', RLS wrote to Henley. In October he had told him:

> I have had an awful time. I got a telegram to come home because my father was ill. This I will not do anyway. He would be better or dead ere I got there anyway, and I won't desert my wife. That same night, F. nearly died; and I have the worst account of her health.

Stevenson called Fanny 'my wife', although she was still married to Osbourne. He wrote to Baxter in the same month:

> . . . there is to be a private divorce in January . . . and yrs truly will himself be a married man as soon thereafter as the law and decency permit. The only question is whether I shall be alive for the ceremony.

The feckless Osbourne lost his job as a San Francisco court reporter and the financial responsibility for Fanny fell squarely on RLS's thin shoulders. He asked Baxter to sell his books in Edinburgh, where his parents were threatening to cut him off, and continued writing.

Fanny lived with her sister at the rose-trellised cottage across the bay in Oakland, but Stevenson stayed in San Francisco and took a room at Mrs Carson's house at 608 Bush Street, paying $4 a month.

*

It was not the original building, but it had the plaque:

ROBERT LOUIS STEVENSON

Lodged at 608 Bush Street
December 1879 to March 1880

and there wrote essays, poems, A
autobiography and fiction.

Plaque placed by admirers of the author
in co-operation with
the California Historical Society July 26 1972

When the plaque was put up you could rent an apartment in the
building for $130 a month. As I was copying details in my notebook,
in 1984, a man was inquiring about the apartment available for rent.
The 'super' in grey overalls told him it was $800 deposit and $450 a
month – a hundred-fold price rise in a century.

*

In a January 1880 letter to Sidney Colvin, Stevenson described his
daily routine, how every morning between 8 and 9.30 a.m. 'a slender
gentleman in an ulster with a volume buttoned into the breast of it'
would emerge on to Bush Street and make his way down Powell,
past Union Square, across Market and down Sixth Street to the Pine
Street Coffee House for a 10-cent breakfast of coffee, roll and butter.

I followed his footsteps. A bleeding man lay on the corner of
Powell and O'Farrell Streets. A black wino stood beside him with
his hands outstretched dramatically.

'Some-BAD-y call the e-MER-gency!' he hollered.

It is not a smart area: there are winos, the bus station, porn shows
and cheap restaurants. The alley called Stevenson is actually named
after Colonel J. D. Stevenson, who led a bunch of East Coast
hooligans and Bowery toughs out west to help 'liberate' California
from the Mexicans; their brand of patriotism meant pistol-whipping
Hispanic miners. I saw a shop selling militaria and T-shirts with
slogans like: Airborne – Death From Above; Kill A Commie For
Mom; Mercenaries Don't Die, They Just Go To Hell To Regroup.
Tolerant San Francisco has many veterans from Vietnam and
strange detritus from the 1960s and early 70s, heavily bearded
longhairs in camouflage fatigues and dark glasses who would gather
with other street-people round a preacher or singer. The veterans of
the war America lost had been treated shabbily, dishonoured by the
chauvinism that only cheered winners at the Olympics.

*

Soon after his 10-cent breakfast Stevenson could be seen with a little hatchet at his window-sill, splitting kindling and breaking lumps of coal for his fire. After three or four hours of writing *The Amateur Emigrant*, or his unfinished western *Arizona Breckinridge* ('about as bad as Ouida, and not so good'), or his essay 'Henry David Thoreau: His Character and Opinions', Stevenson would go for lunch at Donadieu's, a few blocks east on Bush Street. His meal was consumed while reading some racy French romance, like Ponson de Terrail's *Rocamble*. He would then take a walk before starting work again at 4.30 pm.

He had tightened his belt even further by the time he wrote to Henley early in 1880:

> As for my poor people, I cannot help that, God knows; and I am glad they mean to disinherit me; you know, Henley, I always had moral doubts about inherited money and this clears me of that forever. I enjoy my economy. Think of 45 cents a day for all food and drink. Less than two shillings including wine and what not! Is it not a cheap place?

27

On his afternoon walks Stevenson sometimes sat in Portsmouth Plaza near Bush Street, and there is a monument to him there. When I visited it, a very old Chinese man sat nearby on a red bench under the poplars and Chinese elms.

TO REMEMBER ROBERT LOUIS STEVENSON

The 13-foot granite shaft was unveiled on 17 October 1897 by the RLS Fellowship. On top is a greenish bronze of a sixteenth-century galleon by George Piper, 'emblematical of Stevenson's wandering and romantic tastes'. A bracing paragraph from RLS's 1887 essay 'A Christmas Sermon' is also carved on the shaft. But not its final sentences, perhaps because their stoical sentiment is 'Un-American':

> Whatever else we are intended to do, we are not intended to succeed; failure is the fate allotted. It is so in every art and study; it is above all so in the continent art of living well.

There is a photograph of the monument in J. A. Hammerton's *Stevensoniana*, published in 1910. In it, the galleon is sailing south. When I saw it in 1984 it was sailing north. After it was cleaned, they had put it back on the wrong way round.

*

Portsmouth Plaza boasts the Chinese Cultural Centre and is really part of Chinatown. Chinese were packing into the Golden Phoenix restaurant. On a sidewalk three men were being chatted up by a pair of hookers in a car, clichés of inscrutability turning to half-embarrassed delight.

I walked up Grant Avenue, and the windows were full of teak, ivory, jade, silk and porcelain. San Francisco's Chinatown is the biggest outside Asia and in Stevenson's time parts of it were a ghettoized slum. Tong or Chinese gang wars had started in 1875, and as there were twenty Chinese males to every female, prostitution, gambling and drug-smoking were the common resorts of men so far from their families. To Stevenson, however, it was as romantic as the Baghdad of *The Arabian Nights*. 'Chinatown by a thousand eccentricities drew and held me', he wrote in *The Wrecker* (1892):

> I could never have enough of its ambiguous, interracial atmosphere . . . never wonder enough at its outlandish necromantic-looking vegetables, set forth to sell in common-place American shop-windows, its temple doors open and the scent of the joss-stick streaming forth on the American air, its kites of Oriental fashion hanging fouled in Western telegraph-wires . . .

Nearly a hundred years later, the contribution that the clever, hard-working Chinese have made to America is even clearer. Abused and excluded, sometimes beaten and shot, they were at the foundations of all Californian wealth – fishing, fruit and vegetables, mining, light and heavy industry, the admirable services of cleanliness and good food. Many of the brightest students at Berkeley are now Chinese Americans, a shift of characteristic acumen from cooliedom to super-computers in three or four generations. I read in the paper that T. Y. Lin of Berkeley was proposing a vast and elegant bridge across the Straits of Gibraltar to solder Africa to Europe. But a Chinese boy told me, outside the

[164]

British Consulate, how very hard it was to get a visa into that other British outpost, Hong Kong.

*

San Francisco sometimes seemed like America at its best, eclectic and welcoming. On to the groaning humming tram stepped a stocky figure in cape and mask with a Star of David on his chest. 'Captain Chutzpah is here!' he announced, and handed out his cards (available for parties, etc.). At the back of the tram sat a blonde youth, truly Californian with both surf-*and* skateboard. A wrinkled Chinese grandmother in blue peasant blouse pinged chattily at a beautiful child with a satchel; a long-haired white woman was reading *Cutting Through Spiritual Materialism* by a Tibetan Buddhist. Out of the window it was just as Stevenson described: 'The streets lie straight up and down the hills, and straight across at right angles, these in sun, those in shadow, a trenchant pattern of gloom and glare.' Flowering eucalyptus blazed in the sunlight by bright clapboard houses. It was not hard to feel suddenly happy in that vivid city.

28

I was looking for Garuda Airlines when I came across GAY in the San Francisco phone-book. Here was an entire economic community, every conceivable profession and service identified by sexual prefer-ence – gay accountants, gay butchers, gay dentists, gay lawyers, etc. I remembered seeing a T-shirt with the slogan

San Francisco!
my favourite city
where the women are strong
and the men are pretty

But in the subway I read a poster stuck uncomfortably under another advertising Life Insurance:

AIDS has already killed over 200 San Franciscoans. If you're gay – protect yourself and your partner by having only safe sex. This message sponsored by the Harvey Milk Lesbian and Gay Democratic Club.

A grizzled old tramp swayed next to me on the platform. 'How about that!' he roared, waving at the poster. I wore dingy whites and carried a black notebook. The tramp looked me up and down. 'You a doctor?' he asked hoarsely. I fled before he began listing symptoms.

*

In San Francisco, a man who, nowadays, would have been called 'gay' greatly helped Stevenson. This was Charles Warren Stoddard (1843–1909), a California literary figure who began writing in the Golden Era of Bret Harte, Mark Twain and Joaquin Miller and who ended up as a patron of Jack London. In 1869, he became a roving correspondent for the *Overland Monthly*, and set off on seven years' travel around the world. His book *South Sea Idyls* was published in 1873. Critic Roger Austen has described the book as 'brimful of unabashed homoeroticism'. Stoddard lived a long time before there was a gay section in the San Francisco phone-book: 'When he began falling in love in the 1860s, there was no word in the dictionary to define the sort of person he was becoming', says Austen. 'He only knew that when he had a "Kid" he was happy, and that when there was no young man in his life he was forlorn.'

Stoddard visited Stevenson once at his lonely lodgings in Bush Street:

> . . . submerged in a billow of bedclothes; about him floated the scattered volumes of a complete set of Thoreau; he was preparing an essay on that worthy, and he looked at the moment like a half-drowned man – yet he was not cast down. His work, an endless task, was . . . to become his life-preserver and to prolong his years. I feel convinced that without it he must have surrendered long before he did.

The two men did not share sexual tastes. Stoddard wrote of Stevenson's work: 'I fail to find a pronounced flesh-tint – I fail to find even the suggestion of one.' The frail but tenacious Scot had a supremely intellectual view. 'I take him to have been the last man in the world to awaken or invite passion.' Stoddard thought Stevenson 'more likely to be revolted than appealed to by carnality. A man unfleshly to the verge of emaciation.'

Stoddard's influence is important because it was he who first turned Stevenson towards the great Pacific. *The Wrecker*, the novel where Stevenson incorporated much of his early life, features both Stoddard and the call of the Pacific. In the chapter 'Faces on the City Front' the hero and narrator Loudun Dodd meets 'a certain San Francisco character' who is clearly Stoddard. His apartment was full of Pacifica:

> a museum of strange objects – paddles and battle-clubs and baskets, rough-hewn stone images, ornaments of threaded shell, coconut bowls, snowy coconut plumes – evidences and examples of another earth, another climate, and another (if a ruder) culture . . .

Dodd, like Stevenson in 1880, had already noticed with interest among the tall ships of San Francisco harbour, 'another class of craft, the Island schooner . . . '.

San Francisco still keeps the doors of the Pacific. The East Coast of America looks to Western Europe, but in California the faces on the street and the TV airline advertisements clearly show a Pacific orientation. The economic facts are clear: the USA and Canada today exchange more goods with Asia and the Pacific than with Europe, and a third of modern US trade now flows west. But in Stevenson's time looking out over the Pacific was like standing 'on the verge of the Roman Empire (or, as we now call it, Western civilization) . . . gazing onward into zones un-romanized'.

Charles Warren Stoddard lent Stevenson some instructive reading, his own book *South Sea Idyls* and two other novels: Herman Melville's *Typee* (1846) and *Omoo* (1847). When finally, eight years later, RLS sailed out from the Golden Gate into the Pacific on the yacht Casco, his first island landfall was Nuku Hiva in the Marquesas, where Melville had first landed from the *Acushnet* in 1841. Stevenson would follow him into the Pacific, and never return.

29

The top Stevenson scholar in the USA smokes Camels and drives a classic 1957 Chevrolet Bel Air, the first and only car he has ever had. Roger G. Swearingen – Literary Sleuth – got out of the blue Chevy to shake hands.

He was a tall, clean-shaven man with a serious face and horn-rimmed spectacles but, as Stevenson wrote of a different hunter, 'when this grave man smiled, it was like sunshine in a shady place'. I met his attractive wife Sarah, a 'magnolia blossom' from North Carolina, and then we went cruisin', Chevy to the levee.

We drove through sunny Golden Gate Park, up to Clifftop House and then down to Santa Cruz through fields of Brussels sprouts and pumpkins, talking all the way. After a good dinner we played the machines in the fairground and watched the snoring barking seals from the old wooden pier as lights twinkled on the dark waters of the bight of Monterey.

Swearingen is a Dutch name, and his ancestors have been in the States for 350 years, from the days when New York was Nieuw Amsterdam. Roger was born in Hawaii and had grown up in San Francisco. His 1970 PhD at Yale was The Early Literary Career of Robert Louis Stevenson, 1850–1881: A Bibliographical', and he had been working on Stevenson for seventeen years. He earned his living, while working on his scholarly biography of RLS, as a technical writer for a large computer firm.

The Swearingens opened both fridge and study to my needs and greeds. It was a privilege to sit at Roger's desk, under an N. C. Wyeth illustration from *Treasure Island*, a palm tree outside the window, free to loot his books and notes. I was hectic with enthusiasm, but Roger, a calm man of dry wit, was an intelligent and corrective influence. He answered all my queries, showed me slides, and played a tape of Orson Welles's terrific 1938 radio adaptation of *Treasure Island*, done by the same Mercury Theatre team that had panicked half New Jersey with a realistic adaptation of H. G. Wells's *The War of the Worlds*. Orson Welles was already a genius of his craft at twenty-three. He narrated the radio *Treasure Island* as well as playing Long John Silver – a part close to his heart – in a tribute by one of cinema's *enfants terribles* to one of its literary forebears.

30

In his Bush Street lodging, Stevenson practised thrift and kept on scribbling. In February he went down with an unpleasant 'pleuritic fever'. He was 'very very sick' and described his illness in a letter to Edmund Gosse as 'a toss-up for life or death'. For the first time, aged twenty-nine, Stevenson coughed blood. Whatever the disease – whether malaria, pleurisy or incipient tuberculosis – RLS carried on heavily and happily smoking roll-up cigarettes.

After a spell in an Oakland hotel, he at last moved into the house where Fanny and Nellie were living. Fanny was now divorced, and she and Dr Bamford kept Stevenson alive. An Oakland dentist took all Stevenson's teeth out, and the replacement false ones changed the lines of his face. His parents meantime had telegrammed saying 'Count on £250 pounds annually.' As he was preparing to marry Fanny Osbourne, Stevenson was being made into a new but frailer man, constantly aware of his own mortality.

*

'In sickness and in health . . . till death us do part.'

On Wednesday, 19 May 1880, RLS kissed Fanny Stevenson in the front room of the home of Presbyterian Minister W. A. Scott at 521 Post Street, San Francisco.

All marriages contain a private mystery, and the Stevensons' is no exception. They married for life, in every sense, and were loyal to each other till death. RLS wrote lovingly of his wife; the criticisms of her as bossy and neurotic, a bad influence, come from others and are one of the more tiresome forms of intrusive biographical speculation. Who has the right to question someone else's choice of mate, especially when the marriage lasts? Fanny was an unusually strong woman for her day; her influence on RLS was great; and she performed the thankless role of writer's spouse admirably. But jealousy, like love, can persist long after death – even in biographers.

Stevenson had written about marriage before he even set eyes on Fanny Osbourne. In 'Virginibus Puerisque', written in May 1876, he had said: 'Marriage is a step so grave and decisive that it attracts light-headed, variable men by its very awfulness . . . They think it will sober and change them.' He already knew, in theory, that marriage was 'a field of battle and not a bed of roses', but after a couple of years' practical experience of the institution he could write with insight:

> Marriage is one long conversation, chequered by disputes. The
> disputes are valueless; they but ingrain the difference; the

heroic heart of woman prompting her at once to nail her colours to the mast. But in the intervals, almost unconsciously and with no desire to shine, the whole material of life is turned over and over, ideas are struck out and shared, the two persons more and more adapt their notions one to suit the other, and in process of time, without sound of trumpets, they conduct each other into new worlds of thought.

After two nights at San Francisco's giant Palace Hotel, Fanny and Louis set off northward on 22 May 1880 for the rest of their honeymoon in and above the Napa Valley. Stevenson began keeping a diary, 'The Silverado Journal', which he was to write up two years later as *The Silverado Squatters*. Saturday night they spent in South Vallejo and then the newly-weds, with their setter-spaniel Chuchu, took the train north through Napa and St Helena to the hot-springs resort of Calistoga at the end of the line.

31

I woke up on the bus north of Napa. There were big old eucalyptus trees with crackly strips of bark, and vineyards stretching in rows across the tilth of grey volcanic dirt. At Yountville the bus stopped in the shade of trees near the Veterans' Home, and a towheaded man with a beard and bib-overalls hollered deafening greetings to a friend getting off. The grass on the hillsides under the blue sky was burned lion-coloured by the hot bright sun, and Mexican-looking men worked in the fields, driving tractors and trailers.

We came into the outskirts of St Helena. The half-timbered Harvest Inn set the tone for a genteelly prosperous town with gourmet delicatessens and antique shops. Commerce here had pretensions to history: over the picture of a stage-coach was emblazoned 'Wells Fargo – since 1852'; then 'Taylor's Refresher – since 1949'.

St Helena has no bus depot. The heat hit me in a blast as I stepped off the air-conditioned vehicle into the hottest summer for years. There was so much sun that the grape harvest was three weeks early. Heading for the Stevenson Museum I passed a plaque commemorating St Helena's war dead – two in the First World

War, seven in the Second, one in Korea, and five in Vietnam. I crossed two sets of rusting railroad tracks that led north through pink oleander to the deserted and decrepit station. The new Mr and Mrs Stevenson had stopped here for a couple of minutes on Sunday, 23 May 1880 on their way to Calistoga a few miles further up the valley. Later they went to live on the blue mountain at the end of the tracks for their 'squatters' honeymoon.

The middle of the valley was flat, with piny hills along the side and a hot smell of resin, herb and dust. I found the Silverado Museum in a complex of whitewashed buildings surrounded on three sides by vines with dusty black grapes.

32

When I told the Silverado Museum's small, white-haired curator Ellen Shaffer that I was a journalist she shook her head and said, 'Oh dear.' It did not help matters much to quote RLS's dictum (as if to deny its truth in my own case) that 'the practice of journalism is liable to leave a man wedded to cheap finish' for she merely nodded. But she happily told me about the museum.

It had been founded fourteen years previously by Mr Norman H. Strouse and his late wife Charlotte. Miss Shaffer had known him for fifty years. In the 1920's, she said, Mr Strouse had bought John Henry Nash's fine edition of *The Silverado Squatters*, and the writing gave him such pleasure that he began buying Stevensoniana and related memorabilia. Strouse rose to become chairman of the Board of J. Walter Thompson, the largest advertising agency in the world, and after his retirement moved to the St Helena area to build a house called 'Skerryvore' on a part of Glass Mountain they had renamed 'Spy-Glass Knoll'. With local roads called 'Swanston' and 'Bournemouth', he made a world of Stevensonian names; and the charitable trust he set up to run the Museum was the 'Vailima Foundation'. Ellen Shaffer told me that Yale University had the best collection of Stevenson material, from the bequest of another business tycoon, Edwin J. Beinecke – 'Mr Green Shield Stamps' – but Strouse was not far behind. In 1968, the Silverado Museum had 800 items and by 1984 around ten times as many.

Miss Shaffer had spent much of her life in the antiquarian book trade; she once saw Rudyard Kipling, the year before his death, unsuccessfully bidding for back copies of the Lahore *Civil and Military Gazette* and Allahabad *Pioneer* at a sale in London. She was a mine of information about the Stevenson world, and she enjoyed its gossip too. Fanny's son, Lloyd Osbourne, had been 'a rake', in her opinion; his first wife, Katharine Durham, was 'a psycho' and Fanny had been glad to pay for the divorce. Lloyd's second child, Louis, ended up living with a woman called Conchita in a Mexican trailer park, and Joe Strong, Belle's husband, had been 'a drunk'.

The museum had some rather good watercolours and oils by the same Joe Strong; landscapes of Monterey, Honolulu, the Gilbert Islands and Samoa. I was pleased to see for the first time one of Bob Stevenson's oil paintings, using the same chiaroscuro technique as Whistler's *Nocturnes*. There was a wealth of photographic material from Isobel and Joe's son, Austin Strong; seven volumes of Fanny's letters; manuscripts of *The Strange Case of Dr Jekyll and Mr Hyde, The Master of Ballantrae* and Chapter 1 of *Travels With a Donkey*. All sorts of orphaned objects lay in the Museum: a pair of gloves Henry James had left behind at the Stevensons' house in Bournemouth; a set of RLS's visiting cards from late in life, with two addresses – The Athenaeum Club, London, and Vailima, Samoa; locks of hair, and lead soldiers buried in glass cabinets. A photo of Stevenson's grave, taken before the First World War, had a note from Count von Bülow to Lord Rosebery:

> Mr Stevenson was at times a stern critic – but we always honoured him, and feel no shame today in admitting that much he wrote and said was well deserved. The grave on Mt Vaea shall ever be honoured as would be the resting place of one of Germany's most distinguished dead.

33

Four in the afternoon was closing time but outside the museum it was still stunningly hot. I bought bread and cheese and a can of soda and decided to lie in the shade in Lyman Park till the sun was lower, re-reading *The Silverado Squatters*. A group of Mexican workers lay near me on the grass, quietly talking. At 5 pm I watched a man in a yellow shirt reverently lower and fold the US flag from the Post Office pole. Then I set off to walk and hitch out of town to find a cheaper place to stay.

St Helena was the kind of town where the rich whites did not like backpackers, and the Hispanics in pick-ups were none too keen on *anglos* either. I had reached the avenue of elms between Beringer Brothers Winery and the vineyards of Charles Krug before a young man, in a car the size of a small tennis-court, picked me up and dropped me on the Silverado Trail. I walked north beside a brown hillside till I saw a chalet-type house standing back from the road. The kennel-on-a-pole that passes for an American mailbox said 'Oliver House: Bed and Breakfast' and as B&B is the cheapest accommodation in my country I walked up the drive to give it a try. The big man hosing the lawn turned a friendly face and stuck out his hand.

'Hi! I'm Richard Oliver!'

We chatted. Richard told me he used to work for Mr Strouse as a caretaker; the hill behind us was Glass Mountain, named for the shiny black obsidian the Indians had made into arrow-heads, and Mr Strouse's lovely home 'Skerry vore' was just over the other side. I was introduced to Richard's wife Clara, who appeared smiling on the deck of the chalet, and two blond sons called Orlin and Jonathan, whose current hero was Mr T of *The A-Team*. Everyone was very friendly; but Bed and Breakfast in America was nowhere near as cheap as I had hoped, and I set off again northwards up the Silverado Trail.

I had not gone more than a few hundred yards when with a pip on the horn a Volvo drew up beside me and Richard Oliver was looking across the front seat.

'Give you a ride?'

'Great! Thanks.'

'Say, Clara and I just talked. Why don't you stay with us? Room'll be empty otherwise. Ten bucks a night, with a good breakfast.'

'Are you really sure?'

'Sure I'm sure.'

And so I found a home from home in the Napa Valley. They fed me, cared for me, urged me to phone my wife seven thousand miles away, and would not let me, in the end, pay a penny. Richard and Clara Oliver were Mormons, Latter Day Saints, and their true Christian charity deeply touched me.

When I asked 'why?' one day, Richard sang me Prophet Joseph Smith's favourite hymn:

> A poor wayfaring man of grief
> Hath often crossed me in my way
> Who sued so humbly for relief
> That I could never answer, Nay.

Bed and Breakfasts were a controversial matter that summer in St Helena. When the Olivers started theirs they were the eighth in the area, but now Napa County had 160 and the Council was cracking down. One opponent of Bed and Breakfast in the *St Helena Star's* street poll was spectacularly frank: 'We need to maintain St Helena's small-town image. And to preserve the sewer system. We can't afford to have any more John hook-ups.'

There was a simmering feud between the tourist interests and the farm lobby. Some thought the Valley was changing too fast. There had once been a mixture of agriculture here: dairy ranching; walnut groves; orchards of pears, apples, plums and citrus fruits; fields of wheat, and grapes on the hillsides. But the California wine boom of the 1970s meant grapes everywhere. There were 165 wineries in Napa Valley, and the absurd TV soap-opera called *Falcon Crest* – a corked *Dallas* or *Dynasty* – is based on the industry.

Observing Napa's wine-growing business in 1880, Stevenson foresaw that 'the smack of California earth shall linger on the palate of your grandson'. He was right; nowadays you can readily buy Californian wine in Europe, and it travels well.

34

Louis and Fanny Stevenson visited Mr Schram's winery in late May 1880, coming by horse and carriage south from the cottage they were renting in Calistoga. It was the oldest vineyard in the valley. The former Rhinelander Jacob Schram had worked at it for eighteen years, and now his establishment was 'the picture of prosperity; stuffed birds on the verandah, cellars dug far into the hill-side, and resting on pillars like a bandit's cave'.

Fanny sat on the verandah with Mrs Schram, a large jolly woman, and talked about underwear: 'Mr Schram wishes her to wear corsets, God help us, in this hot weather; she has to wear them when she goes to pay a visit, hence pays no visits, hence as she says "people hate her".' The menfolk kept busy down in the cellar. Stevenson's Journal the next day recorded: 'One way and another, I tasted eighteen different liqueurs yesterday, and my feelings today incline towards the temperance extreme.'

*

Teetotal Richard Oliver drove me up to the present Schramsberg Winery one morning. It was on the western slope of the valley; the car rumbled over a deer-grid set in the road that wound up among tall sequoia, maple and Douglas fir trees, with purple periwinkles and orange poison-oak at their feet. The original white clapboard house with its first-floor verandah and geraniums in pots is still there, but a large new winery stood under the pines and eucalyptus. The Mexican workers' white football rose through the air and went into the pond with a splash.

The burrowing insect pest *Phylloxera*, whose devastating effects RLS had seen in the Cevennes in 1879, finally wiped out Jacob Schram. His winery had been out of operation for fifty years when Jack and Jamie Davies bought it in 1965. Their Schramsberg Winery became famous as the place that revolutionized California sparkling wines, using Chardonnay, Pinot Noir and Pinot Blanc grapes and *méthode champenoise* with all its arts of *terrage*, riddling and disgorging. History added the Presidential seal of approval. President Reagan's banquets feature Schramsberg wines, and President Ford toasted Queen Elizabeth II in Schramsberg in July 1976. When President Nixon and Dr Kissinger flew to Beijing for the rapprochement with China in 1972, they took Schramsberg Blanc de Blancs. (They may not have realized how appropriate the gesture was: Chinese workers had slaved for two years to hew Schram's caves out of the rock.)

California champagne is such a success that the French themselves have been buying land in Napa and other Californian valleys to compete. Moët et Chandon were followed there by Piper Heidsieck, Deutz, Roederer and Mumm's.

In Stevenson's day, wine in California was still experimental. 'We look forward, with a spark of hope, to where the new lands, already weary of producing gold, begin to green with vineyards.' His vision has come true, of 'those virtuous Bonanzas, where the soil has sublimated under sun and stars to something finer, and the wine is bottled poetry.'

35

The Olivers arranged for me to have lunch with Mr Strouse and his party at La Belle Hélène Restaurant in the Hatchery, an 1884 building in St Helena owned by the Vailima Foundation. The silver Ford parked outside with its yellow-on-blue California licence plates was clearly Norman Hulbert Strouse's car: RLS NHS.

Mr Strouse was a frail-looking man of seventy-seven, with a grey moustache, wearing a western-style check shirt and a jade stone necktie. Despite his success in J. Walter Thompson, he seemed more interested in fine binding and printing than Madison Avenue. Stevenson preoccupied other members of his family too. His daughter, Patricia Beresford, had written an unpublished biography of Fanny – the manuscript, unfortunately, was in New York.

Mr Strouse was also a member of the all-male San Francisco Bohemian Club; the same club to which Virgil Williams and Charles Warren Stoddard had admitted RLS as a temporary member a century before. It now had 2000 members internationally, and a fourteen-year waiting list to get in. The Bohemians of today are rich and powerful men; presidents of corporations and people like Henry Kissinger come to their annual junketings on Russian River. I thought of Barbizon and how Mrs Thatcher and the other European leaders had dined in state at Siron's Inn where once poor painters and writers had broken bread. Mr Strouse reminded me that the old Bohemian Club were responsible for saving the widowed Fanny Stevenson's house from the great fire in San Francisco after the earthquake of 1906. *The Overland Monthly* of September 1906 describes what happened:

> When the fire that destroyed five square miles of the best of San Francisco swept out of bounds, it surged out to North Beach and besieged Russian Hill . . . The home of the widow of Tusitala seemed doomed to perish in the holocaust. Just at this crucial moment a party of Bohemian and Press Club

members . . . arrived on the scene . . . Realizing that Mrs Stevenson was at that time in Mexico, and that her home and prized belongings were at the mercy of the flames . . . they seized buckets and wet sacks, and dipping the remaining water from the nearly dry reservoir, they rallied round the threatened residence till the east side of Hyde street lay in smouldering ruins . . . This episode of the fire is one of the many indications of the devotion of the friends of Robert Louis Stevenson to his memory . . .

Mr Strouse was not even born at that time, but earlier members of his club had saved some of the things he would eventually own.

36

Fanny and Louis Stevenson spent the first two weeks of their honeymoon in Calistoga. Today's town has a fake frontier feel to it, with red-brick banks and wooden sidewalks, a view of hills dotted with chaparral and palisades tufted with pines. Although they are only seven miles apart, St Helena and Calistoga are very different: St Helena is genteel while Calistoga is vulgar, with its mud baths and massage parlours and signposted 'sights' like the Petrified Forest and Old Faithful Geyser. America has a deep love of shows. If you dug a hole in the ground and put a fence around it with a gate and a sign, people would pay a dollar to peer into it. Stevenson was never attracted to this kind of tourism for its own sake. 'Sightseeing is the art of disappointment,' he wrote of Calistoga. Yet it was not so for Jorge Luis Borges when he went up happily in a hot-air balloon over the Napa Valley, and called his experience 'a voyage through the lost paradise that is the nineteenth century'.

Calistoga's nature is clear from its museum, which is not restrained like St Helena's but brash with vivid dioramas made by a one-time Walt Disney collaborator. Yet the showmanship is apt for a town which owes its very existence to an archetypical 'millionaire vulgarian of the Big Bonanza', the semi-legendary Sam Brannan.

*

Brannan was an Irish adventurer, a renegade Mormon who helped found Sacramento and ran California's first newspaper, the one which announced the Gold Rush to the world – but only after Brannan had made his killing. He set up stores to supply the miners, and they paid for his goods in gold-dust which clerks poured into chamber-pots under the counters till they overflowed. In 1851, at a time of American expansionism – the USA had just acquired Arizona, New Mexico, Texas and California – Brannan led an unsuccessful party of rowdy filibusters to try and take over the Hawaiian islands from the rightful King Kauikeaouli. Brannan was four decades ahead of his time: it would be Stevenson who would witness the end of the imperial process.

One of the original big spenders, Brannan purchased 2000 acres of land in the upper Napa Valley around the hot springs where the Wappo and Pomo Indians used to pitch their sweat-lodges, where he built a resort which opened in 1862. It was meant to be like one of the *haut bourgeois* places back east that had so impressed him, and its name was a spoonerism that stuck. Grandiosely drunk, he tried to say he would build the Saratoga Springs of California, but what came out was 'the Calistoga of Sarafornia'.

Calistoga had a large hotel with cottages for guests, stables and a racetrack for Brannan's thoroughbreds, a Birnam wood of imported plants and shrubs, a tea-plantation, 9000 mulberry trees complete with Japanese attendants for his silk-worm project, a skating-rink, herds of Merino sheep, the best food and gallons of fine wine and spirits.

Grog and girls took their toll; after 1869 Brannan's fortunes went downhill. Financially over-extended, drained by an expensive divorce, and half-crippled from eight bullets received in a shooting affray, Brannan appealed to his friend, rail magnate and millionaire Leland Stanford, to rescue him by siting his proposed Stanford University at Calistoga. But Stanford's emissary was accidentally thrown out of a coach on a rough Calistoga road, and Stanford chose Palo Alto instead. Had it gone otherwise, Napa Valley might have become Silicon Valley, famous not for grapes but microchips and computers. It was not to be, and Brannan's dream went sour. When he tried it again with 1.6 million acres in Sonora, Mexico, the valiant Yaqui Indians blocked his plans, and Samuel Brannan died broke in 1889.

37

Calistoga's Sharpsteen Museum has evidence of other California dreams. Nearby Silverado City mushroomed when silver was found on Mount St Helena. But the vein ran out in 1875, and after only three years of life Silverado itself vanished. In June 1880, Stevenson could write to Sidney Colvin:

> We hope to get a house at Silverado, a deserted mining-camp eight miles up the mountain, now solely inhabited by a mighty hunter answering to the name of Rufe Hansome, who slew last year a hundred and fifty deer.

An old photo on the wall of the Sharpsteen Museum shows a stagecoach and its eight horses outside the Magnolia Hotel, Calistoga. It was a wooden building of a style familiar from countless westerns and had played an incidental part in the history of modern technologies.

In October 1874 an English photographer was locked in a room of the Magnolia Hotel with a deputy sheriff on the door. His name was Eadweard Muybridge and he had just shot his wife's lover dead. At the subsequent murder trial in Napa, his lawyer's impassioned defence of *crime passionel* won a 'Not Guilty' verdict, and he was saved for his life's work. In 1878, using twenty-four synchronized cameras and one of Leland Stanford's trotting-horses, Eadweard Muybridge caught the moment when all four hoofs of the horse were off the ground. His books – *Animal Locomotion* (1887), *Animals in Motion* (1899) and *The Human Figure In Motion* (1901) – atomize time, turning movements and moments into objects that could be held and studied. His work was a prelude to the cinema: it was only a step from pictures of motion to motion pictures.

In the Magnolia Hotel photo you can make out the owner's name on the fascia – J. A. Chesebro, 1876. In June 1880, Stevenson 'dropped into Cheeseborough's' one evening, and was asked if he would like to speak to 'Colonel' Clark Foss, the famous local stagecoach-driver:

> Next moment, I had one instrument at my ear, another at my mouth, and found myself, with nothing in the world to say,

conversing with a man several miles off among desolate hills
. . . It was an odd thing that here, on what we are accustomed
to consider the very skirts of civilization, I should have used
the telephone for the first time in my civilized career. So it goes
in these young countries; telephones, and telegraphs, and
newspapers, and advertisements running far ahead among the
Indians and the grizzly bears.

It is the beginning of the modern world. Kipling would
incorporate new technologies in his short stories – cinema, motor
cars, wireless – and Stevenson did likewise. RLS disliked the
telephone but was aware of its importance; his 1892 novel *The
Wrecker* is one of the very first to use the telephone – men talking, but
not seeing each other – as an integral part of the plot.

38

The man who found the Stevensons their place to camp at the
deserted Silverado mine was a bearded Russian-Jewish storekeeper
in Calistoga called Morris Friedberg. He is referred to in *The
Silverado Squatters* as Mr Kelmar, and also called 'the village usurer'
from his practice of extending credit. The Kelmar family are comic
figures, but Stevenson was never an anti-semite. In a letter of 1891
he wrote:

> Isaiah and David and Heine are good enough for me . . . Were
> I of Jew blood, I do not think I could ever forgive the
> Christians; the ghettos would get in my nostrils like mustard or
> lit gunpowder.

Napa Valley has had its anti-semitic visitors, notably that complicated descendant of a French-Jewish merchant, the writer Hilaire
Belloc. He married Elodie Hogan, a local girl, in Napa, on 16 June
1896; they passed through Calistoga heading northward to honeymoon in Geyserville. Belloc must have seen the mountain dominat-
ing the valley and surely known who had been there before him.
There is still rabid anti-semitism in Calistoga. A stupid and
garrulous woman was telling me about the town after 1945. 'You

know it was becoming a Jewish resort with the terrible San Francisco type Jew, the vulgar kike type, really Jewy Jewy, walking around with nothing on so the nice people quit coming . . . '

She was married to a policeman.

39

I read to Richard from *The Silverado Squatters* as he drove the car up to Silverado, twisting up the old Lawley Toll Road that Stevenson had taken:

> In one place it skirts along the edge of a narrow and deep canyon, and I was glad, indeed, not to be driven at this point by the dashing Foss . . . Vineyards and deep meadows gave place more and more . . . to woods of oak and madroña, dotted with enormous pines. It was these pines, as they shot above the lower wood, that produced the pencilling of single trees I had so often remarked from the valley . . . Each fir stands separate against the sky no bigger than an eyelash; and all together lend a quaint, fringed aspect to the hills.

'That's just it, isn't it?' said Richard. 'Pencilled, like eyelashes.'

We reached the Robert L. Stevenson Memorial Park, Historical Landmark No. 710, and got out at where the old Toll House had stood. Only a few stones remained, and the 'brown, beaten earth' of the stage-coach halt was overgrown with grass.

Richard gave me what Stevenson's driver had given him – 'a lecture by the way in California trees . . . He taught me the madroña, the manzanita, the buck-eye, the maple.' We climbed up through the woods still dripping from early morning rain and there was a pungent smell of pine as the sun warmed the moist air. I peered at a madroña tree whose smooth yellow limbs seemed rusted; it was reddish bark peeling in short strips off a waxy butter-coloured trunk. Richard said it made good firewood. The path led on up into dappled shade, with lizards scuttling away among the low sage and manzanita bushes. A gloomy clearing among tall trees marked the place where the Silverado mine had once been.

*

When the Stevensons first came here they saw a triangular platform of rock and rubble wedged into a canyon. They clambered up and saw a brown wooden house to their right, the old Assay Office and bunkhouse. It was wrecked and rubbishy and poison oak grew up through the floorboards, but it had two floors and three rooms, and they realized it could be inhabited. There was sun, the smell of bay and nutmeg, and a great view. They moved in.

The house has vanished, leaving in its place a monument erected by the Women's Clubs of Napa Valley in 1911, a pale marble book lying open on blocks of granite and engraved with a morbid verse which is by RLS but is inappropriate to his life at this period:

> Doomed to know not Winter, only Spring, a being
> Trod the flowery April for a while,
> Took his fill of music, joy of thought and seeing,
> Came and stayed and went, nor ever ceased to smile.

Across the canyon from where the old house had stood was the mine that failed, a slanted slit of quartz and cinnabar the colour of dried blood, and much as RLS saw it, with 'the strata propped apart by solid wooden wedges', a wound in the side of the mountain.

*

There were four squatters – Louis and Fanny 'the King and Queen of Silverado; Lloyd, the Crown Prince; and Chuchu [the dog], the Grand Duke'. Lloyd had come from school to join them, and together they cleared out the house. Stevenson deepened the little spring that was to be their well. 'I liked to draw water. It was pleasant to dip the grey metal pail into the clean, colourless cool water; pleasant to carry it back, with the water lipping at the edge, and a broken sunbeam quivering in the midst.' They lit a fire at the old blacksmith's forge. Rufe Hanson and his 'Caliban' brother-in-law brought up their baggage, but Fanny had left the trunk keys behind in Calistoga. Everything was higgledy piggledy; they put fresh hay in the old bunks and went to bed by candle-light, in their 'shattered, moon-pierced barrack'.

Slowly the pair made a rough home – their first married home.

The door was repaired with hinges of old boot-leather and the windows were hung with muslin curtains. Game hung inside and bottles were cooled in the nearby spring. They were at the top of the timber-line; above was bald rock, below was the dense forest, and around them plants were creeping back over the miners' wreckage, calcanthus, azaleas, white heath and aromatic bay. Crickets sounded at night, under the stars, and by day the buzz of rattlesnakes frightened the dog. RLS loved it. He was always first up in the mornings, and boiled the water for porridge and coffee. Lloyd did have lessons, but played the rest of the time, trundling an old wagon for ore along the railway.

There was 'a melancholy interregnum' when Fanny and Lloyd suffered from diphtheria and they went down to Calistoga temporarily. When they returned Joe Strong came with them – he was both entertaining and a great hand at an omelette. Later he drew the frontispiece for *The Silverado Squatters*. Stevenson's health apparently improved; high on his mountain, only once did he have to take laudanum, for a stomach complaint.

The six weeks at Silverado were a delightfully eccentric start to the marriage. The newly-weds'happiness brightens *The Silverado Squatters*:

A single candle in the neck of a pint bottle was their only illumination; and yet the old cracked house seemed literally bursting with the light. It shone keen as a knife through all the vertical chinks; it struck upwards through the broken shingles; and through the western door and window it fell in a great splash upon the thicket and the overhanging rocks.

The Robert Louis Stevenson Memorial Park is dark and overgrown now, and Richard and I had to scramble up higher above the mine, grasping the roots of pines, to get above the timber-line and enjoy the view that Stevenson had. I was told that if the conditions were right, it was still possible to see the phenomenon that Stevenson brilliantly describes in his chapter 'The Sea Fogs' where he looks down from Mount St Helena and sees the whole Napa Valley filled with fog that flows and streams like a body of water. The sun was melting clouds as we watched, high over the green and brown miles of land.

40

It was a long way home, back to Britain, and the Stevensons went swiftly after they left Silverado in July 1880. There had been warm letters from Thomas and Maggie Stevenson, encouraging them to return to Scotland. Louis, Fanny and young Lloyd boarded a Pullman from San Francisco to New York on 29 July 1880 and crossed the continent in a little over a week. On 7 August they went aboard SS *City of Chester* bound for Liverpool; it was a year to the day since RLS had left Glasgow on the *Devonia*.

The Stevensons would spend the next couple of years summering in the Scottish highlands and wintering in Davos, Switzerland. RLS had lung trouble, and Fanny had gall-stones and intestinal complaints. Davos was full of tubercular cases, and death was a constant presence in the cold bright air. Fanny Sitwell brought her son Bertie to Davos because of his tuberculosis. He was eighteen, had just left Marlborough, and died in his mother's arms. It was for Fanny Sitwell, his first love, grieving in Davos, that RLS wrote the poem inscribed on the Silverado monument up Mount St Helena.

*

I lay in a hammock between two pines at the back of kindly Oliver House on the Silverado Trail, watching the sun go down and thinking about home. A crescent moon appeared as the light drained from the sky, crickets sawed shrilly and the frogs made a silvery bubbling sound.

I reached down to the ground to push the hammock into a swing again, and picked up a flake of shiny black obsidian from among the dust and pine-needles. It was strange what cultures value: old arrowheads or bits and pieces of Stevenson in glass cabinets. Museums became mausoleums, and life was locked away. The wedding-rings of Fanny and Louis Stevenson were in a bank-vault that the curator was unwilling to open. But the spirit of Stevenson was in his writing, not in his possessions – the books were the real dead man's chest. I looked up at what RLS had called 'the nameless colour of the sky'. Nobody owned that yet.

41

In the summer of 1881 the Stevensons were in Scotland and RLS returned to fiction writing. In June 1881 he and Fanny were scaring each other by writing and reading aloud supernatural stories or 'crawlers' – including 'Thrawn Janet' and 'The Body Snatcher'.

In August 1881 the family moved to a cottage in Braemar, on Royal Deeside. During that wet summer they regularly saw Queen Victoria on the road outside the back windows, taking her constitutional drive from Balmoral Castle, with a pair of 'anxious, not to say cross' ladies-in-waiting. Her Majesty showed 'true Scottish spirit in her indifference to the weather'.

The summer was so wet that much time was spent indoors, and among the entertainments at the cottage was a box of watercolours for young Lloyd, then aged thirteen. He began the map of an island. Stevenson joined in and elaborated it, naming various places and calling the whole 'Treasure Island'. It was like childhood again, when he and Bob had made maps of their countries Nosingtonia and Encyclopaedia. Stevenson later wrote:

> I am told there are people who do not care for maps, and find it hard to believe . . . here is an inexhaustible fund of interest for any man with eyes to see, or tuppence worth of imagination to understand with . . . As I pored upon my map of *Treasure Island*, the future characters in the book began to appear there visible among imaginary woods; and their brown faces and bright weapons peeped out upon me from unexpected quarters, as they passed to and fro, fighting and hunting treasure, on these few square inches of a flat projection. The next thing I knew, I had some paper before me and was writing out a list of chapters.

He called his romance *The Sea-Cook* and wrote a chapter a day for fifteen days; every day he read it out to the family, including his father. Thomas Stevenson loved it as much as Lloyd. He called it '*his* kind of picturesque' and actively collaborated, suggesting the name *Walrus* for Flint's ship and listing the contents of Billy Bones's sea-chest on the back of a legal envelope:

> a quadrant, a tin cannikin, several sticks of tobacco, two braces of very handsome pistols, a piece of bar silver, an old Spanish watch and some other trinkets . . . a pair of compasses

mounted with brass, and five or six curious West Indian shells . . . an old boat-cloak, whitened with sea-salt . . . a bundle tied up in oilcloth and looking like papers, and a canvas bag, that gave forth, at a touch, the jingle of gold.

But after fifteen chapters Stevenson dried up. The first half was sold to the magazine *Young Folks*, and when the first instalment of 'Treasure Island; or, The Mutiny of the Hispaniola by Captain George North' appeared on 1 October 1881, the tale was still unfinished. Yet in November, back at Davos, the rest flowed, at the rate of a chapter a day, and the seventeen-instalment serialization was completed smoothly on 28 January 1882. It was not a great success with the readers of *Young Folks* but it appeared in book form in November 1883 after W. E. Henley urged Cassell & Co to accept it. Stevenson was paid a £100 advance on royalties and the first edition was 2000 copies. *Treasure Island* has never been out of print since.

*

Why has *Treasure Island* been so popular? The title brilliantly evokes two universally shared day-dreams; for wealth and irresponsible freedom. And while the book is not 'realistic' it is very visual: the reader actually 'sees' the characters, the setting and the action. This is hardly remarkable now, in the age of cinema and TV, but in the nineteenth century Stevenson's 'thousand coloured pictures' were the nearest equivalent of a first-rate action movie.

The novel is about escape, and may have been tinged unconsciously with an ideal version of imperialism: on the other side of the sea vast wealth awaits discovery by bold sailors, and there are no awkward natives to make the dream turn ugly. *Treasure Island* is an escape in time, back from the industrialized nineteenth century to a semi-mythical eighteenth century ('the year of grace 17–'). And it is an escape from women: Jim's fussy mother and Silver's black woman are left behind.

Treasure Island is a day-dream with some of the brutal qualities of a nightmare; scarred, soiled, deformed pirates curse and murder. Blind Pew's tap-tapping stick has real terror and, as RLS said, it includes 'stunning violence'. A certain decorum rules, however: oaths are mentioned but not quoted, and from the very first sentence of the book we have been reassured that the hero will survive. Men can escape to great adventures, and come safely home. Boys can become men, and in reading the story, men can be boys again.

Treasure Island is also a kind of rapid *Bildungsroman*. Jim Hawkins has to become a man soon after the death of his father, and duly navigates treachery, greed, pain and death before finding that the treasure means only 'blood and sorrow'.

For Jim, the island is 'accursed'; for us it is one of the most memorable settings. English literature is peculiarly strong in books about islands: More's *Utopia*, Shakespeare's *The Tempest*, Defoe's *Robinson Crusoe*, Swift's *Gulliver's Travels*, Wyss's *The Swiss Family Robinson*, Ballantyne's *Coral Island* (and its twentieth-century complement, Golding's *Lord of the Flies*), Marryat's *Masterman Ready*, Butler's *Erewhon*, Barrie's *Peter Pan*, Huxley's *Island* – the list could go on forever. Yet *Treasure Island* is perhaps the most famous; and the late Roy Plomley, deviser of the popular BBC radio programme *Desert Island Discs*, thought it 'the very best desert island/pirate/ buried treasure story ever written'.

It is not just the islander British who have responded to the book. Whatever its critics may have thought, all over the world *Treasure Island* has been abridged, adapted, cartooned, dramatized, edited, filmed, illustrated, musicalized, parodied, retold in Basic English, simplified to Pitman's Shorthand and endlessly translated – into Afrikaans, Croat, Czech, Dutch, Esperanto, French, Gaelic, German, Italian, Kamba, Luganda, Polish, Portuguese, Russian, Spanish, Swahili, Swedish, Ukrainian, Welsh and Zulu to name but a few.

Stevenson would write richer and subtler books, but *Treasure Island* appeals to me because it has all the speed and exhilaration and terror of the most brilliant cartoon film. It is entirely absorbing and yet pleasantly removed from the greyer complexities of real life. Its completion in just over a month of work was a marvel, but its survival a century later as a popular classic is a mark of genius.

HYÈRES

I

By the time *Treasure Island* was published as a book in November 1883, the Stevensons had already been living for eight months at a new home in Hyères-les-Palmiers, Var, France. I took a night train from Paris down to the Riviera.

I was reading *Newsweek* when an officer ordered four Foreign Legionnaires into my compartment. A brutal-looking soldier took off his white *képi*, sat down heavily beside me and stared at the magazine.

'By 'eck,' s nice to read summat in English, entit?'

Peter came from Yorkshire. He told me that his father was a senior police officer and his mother a nervous woman obsessed with cleanliness, the sort who emptied your ashtray after every tap of the cigarette. Neither of them knew their son was in the Legion. Peter showed me a photo of his former self: a fat unemployed biker with long hair and a leather jacket. Now all muscle and vigour, he was a depressingly good advertisement for military service. The romantic urge for adventure and excitement had led him to leave dole and booze at home for the Legion's Fort Saint Jean in Paris. He had signed on for seven years and thought it 'a great life'.

'What are you doing now?'

'I'm AWOL – Absent Without Leave. I were on me way back to England to sort out the girlfriend. Wouldn't hurt her, mind, just smack her a bit. Got picked up on the train to Calais 'cos I didn't have a passport. The conductor said, "With that haircut you must be in the Legion." They phoned Paris from the next station, and now I'm on me way back to the guardhouse. No trouble.'

There are many British soldiers in the French Foreign Legion, especially among the paratroopers. I asked what it was like to serve a foreign power.

'You feel a bit funny when they play the "Marseillaise" and you have to salute the old tricolour. And every one that's bought it has MORT POUR LA FRANCE on his grave. Dunno about that bit. Bastille Day parade soon, though, reet through the middle of Paris. That'll be great.'

'What are you going to do when you get out?'

'You can be a French citizen if you want. Reckon I'll take that and become a gendarme. Or maybe I'll join the CRS.' He looked to see my reaction to the initials of the riot police. 'Good fun that. A bit of stick, thwack, thwack.'

The big Finn opposite had a face yellowed by jaundice picked up in French Guiana, where the Legion guard the Kourou rocket-base. 'People go crazy on that posting,' said Peter grinning.

He leaned over towards the Finn, corkscrewing a finger round his temple. 'You fuckin' barmy, ay, ay?' The Finn nodded, and in an almost incomprehensible accent began to describe the leg ulcers men got from jungle rot.

The next compartment was full of new intake Legionnaires, and three of them were Scots. One from Glasgow had decided to join up after his sixteen-stone wife hit him over the head with a pressure-cooker. Peter said the hardest man in his section was a Scot. 'Alec's a real bampot, you know, a headcase, a nutter. Take on eight of the French and come out laffin'.'

A tense new recruit called MacGregor sat in our compartment. He had left the Territorial Army in disgrace after hitting a farmer whose crops he had just run over in a truck. He was anxious to impress us with the hardware he knew – the General Purpose Machine Gun, the Carl Gustav Rocket Launcher, and so on. Peter kept interrupting with jokes and MacGregor tried hard to control his irritation.

'I'll have to have a crack at them black women when I get to Djibouti,' said Peter cheerfully. 'No choice really. Had a couple of doses already. No sweat.'

Sniggering with excitement, MacGregor told how his drunken squad had gang-raped a prostitute during a Territorial Army night-exercise. The repulsive details haunted me as I tried to sleep.

When the Stevensons came to Hyères in 1883 it was already the oldest established Winter Station on the Côte d'Azur. The English had been coming here since Regency days, but the hotels started going up in the 1850s when Hyères became particularly famous for 'the wonderful effects of the climate on persons suffering from weak chests and lung disease'. In early 1861 George Sand wryly described Hyères as 'strongly prosaic, full of invalids or English awkwardly out of place'; it was pretty, but 'far from the sea, far from the mountains, far from the woods; an English town where one must always be dressed up to the nines'. In 1868 the Casino was opened and the winter spa was complete. The *Hyères Journal* was well worth fifteen centimes for the pleasure of seeing one's own name in the *Liste des Etrangers*, sharing a column with occasional nobility, gentry and solid citizens: Mr McCorquodale, the Hon. Mrs Grey, Mrs George Clive, Miss Farquahar, Miss Cockburn Hood, etc.

Hyères-les-Palmiers, called 'the Eden of Provence', had turned its flourishing micro-climate to advantage. At latitude 43.7 degrees North it was a place where anything would grow – native cork, cypress, olive, orange and lemon trees, many kinds of imported palms and, in the 1860s, seven varieties of eucalyptus seeds from Melbourne Botanical Gardens. Like everything else in Hyères they thrived.

The railway brought visitors and invalids. London–Dover–Calais–Paris–Dijon–Arles–Marseille–Toulon–Hyères was the route recommended in Adolphe Smith's 1880 guide-book, *The Garden of Hyères*. But there were dangers: the railway station was in an exposed position more than a mile from the town, and Smith warned 'very delicate persons' against arriving at night lest 'such a rare phenomenon as a fog or mist' should appear. The expensive hotels were solicitous of their guests: 'At the station a bath ambulance chair will be in waiting for invalids. In this the patient can lie down and . . . be drawn gently, without shock or exposure, to the hotel.'

The old medieval town, clustered under the castle-topped hill, was the most sheltered part, but suffered from 'insalubrious odours' of drains. A special quarter was constructed for the English; away from the town, it was exposed in winter to the Mistral, a cold dry wind. Smith's guide tries to make the best of a bad job: 'It must be borne in mind that the Mistral is a purifying wind . . . it oxydizes the germs of fever and reduces the danger of epidemic disease.'

Smith also recommended special precautions in clothing:

> The first essential is to protect the head and the back of the neck thoroughly from the rays of the sun, for sun-stroke even in mid-winter is to be feared. The body should also be protected with woollen cloth suits or flannel underclothes . . . The clothes should hang as loosely as possible, but should be thick, so as to ward off the hot rays of the sun.

For the sake of their lungs English invalids in hotel rooms would inhale benzoin, tar, tolu or turpentine, and it was to this warm oasis filled with shapeless glue-sniffers in bath-chairs that Mr and Mrs R. L. Stevenson came in March 1883.

3

The Stevensons 'house at Hyères was perfect, if small. Chalet la Solitude had been a Swiss show-house bought by a millionaire at a Paris exhibition and reconstructed on a road underneath the old castle. RLS wrote to his mother that it was 'healthy, cheerful, and close to shops, and society, and civilization . . . There are two rooms below with a kitchen, and four rooms above, all told.' He wrote to Gosse that it was 'sub-celestial', and to Jules Simoneau in California, he said he was in clover (apart from his health) with 'a beautiful large garden, a fine view of plain, sea and mountain; a wife that suits me down to the ground, and a barrel of good Beaujolais'.

*

In 1984 Hyères was having a bad summer. It rained; there were fewer tourists; it was a lean time for the service economy. The very nature of tourism in Hyères had changed; the First World War had marked the end of the old-style hotels, and not until years after the Second World War did a more modest and demotic form of tourism return to the camping sites and small *pensions*.

There are some reminders of the past. The Grand Hotel du Pare, formerly the Château du Fanoux, one of ninteenth-century Hyères's most lavish hotels with grounds encompassing all the fountains and palm-treed gardens of Stalingrad Square, is now the Lycée Jean Aicard. Idle bedrooms have turned into industrious school-rooms with scarred desks and scuffling kids; corridors where the gentleman-thief Moutone had tiptoed away with the jewels of European royalty and of aristocratic ladies, now see teachers hurrying for a Gauloise between lessons. There were pre-fabricated classrooms under the palm trees, rows of bike-sheds behind the rusting fence, and self-consciously careless youth revving scooters by the gate.

The old town of Hyères, wrapped round and rising up the southern flank of the Colline du Château, is still attractive. It is a cunning muddle of red-tiled roofs, twisting cobbled streets and bright patios. Pigeons explode into flight in the market square with its twelfth-century Templar tower, and the crooked streets angled through shadow and strong light still promise the unexpected. Often this means pressing against a wall as cars roar past, shuddering over the cobbles; or the whining noise that heralds an attack by a venomous scooter or motorcycle.

On my way to Stevenson's house, I went up to Rue Saint-Pierre, a narrow road that runs under the forested castle and above the roofs of the old town. There was an old rock carved with what a guide-book assured were neolithic cup-marks – to me it looked as if it had been battered and mugged by generations of vandals. Someone had hammered in metal spikes; others had carved names; it was impossible to tell what was natural and what ancient glyph. I sat on the bench and smelled the rosemary and thyme of the hill.

There was a hazy view south to the Mediterranean, the narrow peninsula of the salt-pans of Giens and the humps of the Iles d'Or – Porquerolles, Port-Cros, Levant. Barbary pirates, Saracens, French and English had fought for those islands. When Hyères had the Roman name Olbia, the dusty road on the hillside had been a route for salt and silver. Then an aircraft took off from the airport next to the sea; when I looked closer through the haze I saw that most of the plain was developed. One of (the Iles d'Or now holds a French missile-tracking station.

*

Joseph Conrad knew this coast as a young man, and his last novel *The Rover* (1923 – in French, *Le Frère-de-la-Côte*) is partly set on the peninsula south of Hyères, the Presqu'île de Giens.

Conrad and Stevenson never met but there is no doubt that Conrad, seven years younger than Stevenson, had read his work. He felt it an honour 'being placed, in such generous spirit, near Stevenson' in Sidney Colvin's *Memories and Notes of Persons and Places* (1921). In Colvin's view:

> Of those who had not begun to publish before he [RLS] had died, the man I imagine him calling for first of all is the above-mentioned Mr Conrad . . . How they would delight in meeting now! What endless ocean and island yarns the two would exchange; how happily they would debate the methods and achievements of their common art . . .!

4

I recognized the Stevensons' house at 4 Rue Victor Basch from old photos, but Chalet la Solitude had changed. A Second World War naval shell had knocked off some of the Swiss gingerbread: the ornately carved overhanging eaves and the wooden balcony that used to run right round the house were gone. There were still three tall front windows high over the road, but the whitewashed stucco walls and red-tiled roof looked modern. The front wall was overhung with bougainvillaea. As I went to the gate to read the blue plaque a huge dog leapt menacingly at the grille. After Fontainebleau I was cautious of French guard dogs and this was a real Baskerville hound. I copied the plaque into my notebook as the beast bayed.

HERE
DURING 1883–1884
LIVED THE ENGL ISH AUTHOR
ROBERT LOUIS STEVENSON
HE DECLARED 'I WAS
ONLY HAPPY ONCE:
THAT WAS AT
HYERES'.

I retreated across the road to calm the dog down and waited, wondering what Stevenson would have thought of being described as 'English'. He would probably swear a blue streak, as cursing was one of his fortes. Recuperating once in Hyères, he wrote to his cousin Bob:

> I am now shorn of my grog forever. My last habit – my last pleasure – gone. I am myself no more. Of that lean, feverish, voluble and whiskified zany Scot who once sparked through Britain, bent on art and the pleasures of the flesh, there now remains no quality but the strong language. That at least, I shall take grave ward; my last word, it is like, will be an execration   .   .   .

A car drew up and a tall, powerful man in a black leather jacket got out, carrying an attaché case. His head was shaved completely bald and he stared at me suspiciously.

'Monsieur Gibelin?' I inquired.

'Was it you telephoned last night?' he boomed.

'Yes, monsieur, it is because of Robert Louis Stevenson that I am here, and it is very courteous of you to . . .'

'Come on. Let's go in.' He cut me off brusquely, unlocked the gate and wrestled the dog's ears with a big hand. 'Chico, calm yourself, Chico.' The brute's name was a joke; *chico* means 'tiny' in Spanish. I was very glad when the front door closed on him.

We went up to the sunny first-floor sitting-room, whose three tall windows made it a miniature of the first-floor room at Heriot Row. I chattered about Stevenson while M. Gibelin fussed over newspaper clippings on the history of the place. He told me the plaque was fifty years old, and a protection order had been placed on the exterior of the house in 1976.

The Gibelins had restructured the interior, installed a metal circular staircase to save space, and modernized in bright colours. A downstairs wall held a rack of rifles and shotguns, chained through the trigger-guards. M. Gibelin shared the French terror of burglars, and brought out his 'special' protection from the bedside table. He unwrapped the cloth to reveal a semi-automatic pistol, then slid the ejector back and forth vigorously. Live 9mm cartridges bounced on the blue carpet at my feet.

He suggested lunch and we went into the kitchen. In Fanny Stevenson's tiny galley you ran the danger of 'being scorched by the range on one side, and at the same time being impaled by the saucepan hooks on the other'. But the Gibelin kitchen had space and every modern device. Claude Gibelin seemed like a man in unfamiliar territory as he hauled crocks, jars and plates on to a table dominated by a glowing yellow pumpkin; we sat down to an improvised spread of cold fish and meats, pickles, salad and morel mushrooms. He uncorked a bottle and poured. '*Coum menja, treballa,*' he boomed. It was a Provençal proverb – as you eat, so you work. We tucked in with gusto.

Eating, drinking and conversation thawed Claude Gibelin to geniality. He confessed that during our telephone conversation he had clapped his hand over the mouthpiece for a hurried talk with his wife, who feared I might be a crook casing the joint. 'But now I can see you are not like that.'

Claude opened another bottle. My French was getting better and better. I understood everything.

'Do you know why I shave my head like this? Because I would rather be ugly than infirm.'

'No, it's good. You look like Yul Brynner.'

We drank excellent coffee and he proffered a Seitane, and urged me to another glass of *génépi*, a fiery liqueur that his wife's family distilled from Alpine herbs. By the time we went into the garden everybody was my friend; Chico was my best friend.

There were seven terraces on the lower side of the house, and Fanny might have been pleased to see the variety and fecundity of her old garden. I picked and ate sweet fleshy cherries, wandered through lemon, apricot, olive, fig and medlar trees, past cacti, yucca, roses and mimosa. Claude pointed out a kumquat bush that yielded three to four kilos of fruit in November. On the other side of the house four old thick stumps of eucalyptus cut low to the ground were possibly the same 'plumed blue-gums' that Stevenson had seen and smelled at night. Across the road, trees and the modern rheumatism clinic hid part of the view, but you could still see across to the blue hills of Costabelle and Mont des Oiseaux, and catch glimpses of the sea. Stevenson had loved this garden; 'Angels haunt it', he wrote. He hated killing the snails that came, so collected them in a bucket and put them over his neighbour's wall.

*

Claude Gibelin was a Contrôleur in the Mutualité Sociale Agricole, and he invited me to visit a flower nursery he knew. We drove through tortuous streets with Johnny Hallyday blasting from the stereo.

The region had long been famous for flowers. Fanny wrote that she would never forget the day she and Louis drove 'through lanes of roses from which the attar of commerce is made. On either side of us the rose hedges were in full bloom; the scent, mingled with the fragrance of innumerable violets, was truly intoxicating.'

The Toulon region is still the flower and vegetable centre of France. The nursery had a hectare and a half of red and pink roses and heavy-headed yellow and white chrysanthemums. It was warm and heady inside the long greenhouses; there were heating pipes, lights and sprayers over netted straw beds, and arm-length gauntlets lay beside secateurs on a slatted table. Work began at three in the morning to get the flowers to the eight o'clock train to Paris. Ten roses a bouquet, 1500 bouquets a week. They would be wholesaled at night in the markets, and retailed on the streets of Paris next morning. The flower industry was vital to Hyères. Their economy depended, like the Stevensons', on other people's need for beauty and romance.

We roared back to Chalet la Solitude. I met Mme and Mile Gibelin, who declared themselves mortified at our rough lunch. I protested that it was excellent. They pressed cherries and wine on me to take away, and Claude Gibelin, ugly but kind, decanted a generous quantity of their precious *génépi* into a brown bottle.

5

Stevenson was often ill in Hyères, suffering from sciatica, ophthalmia, and occasional haemorrhages. Once, coughing blood, he wrote on a pad for Fanny who was clumsy with terror 'Don't be frightened. If this is death, it is an easy one.' Then he poured his minim glass of ergotin without spilling a drop. He could face his own death calmly, but not that of others.

Death came home to him 'like a thunderclap' with the news in September 1883 that one of his oldest friends, Walter Ferrier, had died of alcoholism and chronic Bright's disease. Among his youthful cronies, Ferrier had been 'the gentleman of the lot', a handsome courteous man, and a writer whose novel *Mottiscliffe* Stevenson once reviewed.

Stevenson's distress is evident in all his letters at this time. He wrote to Will Low, the American painter he had known at Barbizon:

> One of my oldest friends died recently, and this has given me new thoughts of death. Up to now I had rather thought of him as a mere personal enemy of my own; but now that I see him hunting after my friends, he looks altogether darker. My own father is not well . . . These things are very solemn, and take some of the colour out of life.

Ferrier's death prompted Stevenson's essay 'Old Mortality'. This death, like his marriage, marked his passing towards maturity, and RLS could look back on his own past with a new detachment.

*

At Hyères, Stevenson wrote from the early morning until noon, and after lunch read the work aloud to Fanny, who would criticize and suggest improvements. Then they walked in the garden, or up the hill with their bad-tempered little dog Bogue. After dinner they talked or read aloud in the Chalet that Fanny thought well-named, for it was 'almost a solitude *a deux*'.

Stevenson worked well at Hyères. In 1883 he earned £465 0s 6d, including the advance on royalties of 'a hundred jingling, tingling, golden, minted quid' for *Treasure Island*. He was now almost paying his way and during their stay wrote verses and essays, rewrote *The Silverado Squatters* and all but finished two very different novels.

Prince Otto was not published until 1885 but was mainly written over five consecutive months at Hyères in 1883. To Henry James it was 'the most literary of his works', 'a coquetry of artful inconsequence' with a 'hard glitter' that was almost 'inhuman'. It is a strange romantic comedy, the first 'Ruritanian romance' (set in a mythical state called Grünewald in 1848), a decade ahead of Anthony Hope's *Rupert of Hentzau and The Prisoner of Zenda*. As James remarked, *Prince Otto* is almost a homage to Stevenson's admired friend George Meredith. The curious dance of the four principal characters is observed with penetrating wit, and though the plot is artificial, the characters are entirely believable – like Marianne Moore's 'real toads in an imaginary garden'. The Prince is 'a plexus of weaknesses', and RLS felt the character was like himself, or perhaps Bob. The Countess Rosen, 'a lady of dishevelled reputation', is one of Stevenson's best women characters. Fanny made many interventions when he read her the book, and the Countess sounds like her:

> If she was not beautiful, she was vivid, changeful, coloured . . . given altogether to manlike ambition . . . Chafing that she was not a man, and could not shine by action . . .

The other novel, *The Black Arrow: A Tale of the Tuns tall Forest*, was a story of love and adventure set in the Wars of the Roses, written for *Young Folks* in two months. Fanny, 'the critic on the hearth', couldn't read it, and the author himself called it 'tushery', writing at such speed that he forgot about the fourth arrow and had to extricate himself from a jam in the proofs. This bright and brutal book was very popular with the readers of *Young Folks*, and in May 1919 the historian G. M. Trevelyan wrote to *The Times* to say that he read *The Black Arrow* every three years, finding it a book 'that teaches history in the highest sense'.

6

Fanny kept Louis alive at Hyères, and they grew closer together. 'I love her better than ever and admire her more', RLS wrote to his mother:

> This sudden remark came out of my pen; it is not like me; but in case you did not know, I may as well tell you, that my marriage has been the most successful in the world. . . . She is everything to me; wife, brother, sister, daughter and dear companion. And I would not change to get a goddess or a saint. So far, after four years of matrimony.

It was hard on Fanny, having to guard her husband against the over-excitement that brought on illness, and deadly germs that she perceived with a certain dramatic flair. When Baxter came to visit in January 1884, she warned him:

> *Drink no water* on the journey. A woman is just dead here from

drinking water in Paris. No siphon – abjure the siphon, if that is the way to spell it. St Galmier is the *only* safe beverage. Siphon is possibly made of poison water.

When Fanny took out a subscription to *The Lancet* she could diagnose even more perils. But her instincts were right: after the Municipality spread fresh sewage along their street, and cholera spread from Toulon, it was time to go. In July 1884 they returned to England, to a south coast resort with a Scottish feel to it – Bournemouth.

*

Years later, when a fitter RLS could weed his Samoan garden with sweat dripping from his nose, he enlivened the chore with imaginary conversation or correspondence with distant friends. He wrote to Colvin in 1891:

Methought you asked me – frankly, was I happy. Happy (said I); I was only happy once; that was at Hyères; it came to an end from a variety of reasons, decline of health, change of place, increase of money, age with his stealing steps; since then, as before then, I know not what it means . . .

BOURNEMOUTH

I

Bournemouth was beautifully sited on the Dorset coast, backed by a wild heathland of gorse, heather and broom. Creek valleys known as 'chines' led down to the sea, cutting deep into the white chalk cliffs. They had provided many a secluded spot for eighteenth-century smugglers to land their cargoes of tea, coffee, brandy and tobacco. The fishing-village also had pine woods, considered in the nineteenth century to be 'Bournemouth's best doctors'. Gradually it became a health-resort.

Bournemouth had around 1700 inhabitants in 1862, when Charles Darwin stayed in a cliffside cottage. 'This is a nice but barren country', he wrote, 'and I can find nothing to look at. Even the brooks and ponds produce nothing. The country is like Patagonia.' Twenty years later, after the railway came, there were 17,000 people in the town. It was a fashionable place to convalesce, with bath-chairs trundling along the front and scores of hotels and boarding-houses opening for residents. Today, Bournemouth still has more hotel accommodation than any other British city outside London.

The restless tribe of writers sent some notable members. The poet Paul Verlaine lived in a house now called Queenswood, about a third of a mile from where Stevenson would make his home seven years later; Verlaine had just completed a two-year sentence in Mons prison for wounding Arthur Rimbaud. The novelist Olive Schreiner, far from her African farm, loathed the sea-side landladies and thought Bournemouth in the 1880s 'the most awful place God almighty ever made'. Thomas Hardy renamed the town 'Sandbourne' in *Tess of the D'Urbervilles*; and P. C. Wren, the author of

Beau Geste and other tales of the Foreign Legion, retired to Bournemouth and an ugly house he had built himself, the replica of a mud fort in the Sahara.

*

Bournemouth is something of a private joke to the English. Like Cheltenham or Tunbridge Wells it evokes elderly fraying gentility, long hotel afternoons, and an orchestra in the Winter Gardens. My wife and I took a flat in eastern Bournemouth at the foot of Boscombe Chine, not far from the Pier View Hotel where Aubrey Beardsley came to recover from tuberculosis. I was pleasantly surprised by warm sun and clean air, cliffs with an almost Mediterranean vegetation – tamarisks, yucca, pampas grass, mesembryanthemums, many bright gardens and curious byways of history. My wife originally came to keep me company, but became so fascinated by Bournemouth she began writing a novel set in the town, *Light Years*.

2

The Stevensons first arrived in Bournemouth, where sixteen-year-old Lloyd was already at a school, in July 1884. They were under doctor's orders. Stevenson had a tapeworm removed at this time – Very like me in figure, in face there was only a family resemblance'. They lived for the first six months in a series of boarding-houses at Westcliff: Wensleydale, The Firs, Iffley Boarding House, and Bonallie Towers. The pine and heather were reminiscent of Scotland, something Walter Scott had also felt nearly seventy years before. If Stevenson could not experience the real place any more, this English hybrid of Scotland and the Mediterranean was the next best thing.

At first, Stevenson feared English bourgeois tedium, and longed for some dashing literary escape. In a Letter to Henley he sketched three romantic openings, pregnant with action. 'That is how stories should begin. And I am offered HUSKS instead:

What should be:	What is:
The Filibuster's Cache	*Aunt Anne's Tea Cosy*
Jerry Abershaw	*Mrs Brierley's Niece*
Blood Money: A Tale	*Society: A Novel'*

Clearly Bournemouth's old smuggling associations were more to his taste than its boarding-houses.

*

In early 1885 Thomas Stevenson bought Louis and Fanny a house of their own. It was a special gift – half a bribe to stay in the British Isles, and half a late wedding present to his daughter-in-law Fanny. The older Stevensons had grown very fond of her: Thomas nicknamed her 'Cassandra' because of her tendency to dramatic pronouncements. The house, Sea-View, had belonged to a naval man and stood at the head of Alum Chine in Westbourne, western Bournemouth. Alum Chine was a perfectly appropriate place for a writer to live; since the sixteenth century its alum had been used to treat paper and tan hides for binding, and its ferrous sulphate crystals had tinted Prussian blue ink.

The first proper house the Stevensons owned had a blue slate roof over ivy-covered yellow brick walls, and a view of the sea from the upper windows. The garden was full of hydrangeas and rho-dodendrons, apple, pear and plum trees. It had a dove-cot and a path leading down to the wooded chine at the bottom, where Fanny made a labyrinth of arbours with seats. In her kitchen garden Fanny planted raspberries and Indian corn, and she began growing tomatoes in the courtyard by the old stables. While many Victorians thought tomatoes were only decorative (the fruits were believed to be poisonous) the Stevensons ate them in salads.

They arrived in March 1885, in a chaos of packing-cases and Turkish carpets. Soon they re-named the house Skerryvore, after Uncle Alan Stevenson's greatest work of art – the lighthouse south-west of Tiree in Scotland. There were no streetlights in Westbourne then; so by their front door they erected a replica of the lighthouse, and its lamp was lit every night for two and a quarter years.

*

One of the Stevensons 'neighbours in Westbourne was a teenage girl called Adelaide Boodle. When she first heard the Stevensons were living at Skerryvore, she persuaded her mother to take her to visit them. At the time she had only read RLS's story 'The Treasure of Franchard' in *Longman's Magazine*, but she was to become a great friend of the family and its general factotum. She ran errands, did

[202]

copying work, took writing lessons from Fanny and RLS, and after they left looked after the house for them, feeding the doves and stray cats that Fanny had adopted. Much later, under the nickname they gave her, 'The Gamekeeper', she wrote a book about Louis and Fanny, *RLS and his Sine Qua Non* (1926).

It gives a vivid glimpse of the household – things getting lost, Stevenson's feverish moods and love of distraction, and his impetuous charm. There is also a wholly admiring portrait of Fanny. According to Miss Boodle, RLS trusted Fanny's critical judgement implicitly. But it was her 'quiet heroism . . . of self-restraint', deep sympathy and moral directness that the girl herself loved. As always, too much excitement made Stevenson ill, and Fanny had to protect him from it, thus alienating some of his friends.

3

The 1880s were a time of upheaval and social ferment in Britain; it was an era of discontent which some feared might lead to violent revolution. In this context, it is possible to read even a 'romance' like *Treasure Island* as a social parable of Britain at the time, written by a Tory. The Establishment – Squire, Captain, Doctor and loyal retainers – are threatened by the Pirates, who can organize a Black Spot ceremony ('"According to rules," said one. "Fo'c'sle council," said Morgan') like socialists or trade unionists, but who are liable to relapse into a superstitious mob, fuelled by drink and bent on violence. Social envy feeds the pirates' resentment: '"I want their pickles and wines, and that,"' says one; and Silver wants to be an MP.

The real, non-fictional unrest in Britain prompted two basic reactions to the perceived threat of violent revolution. The 'law-and-order' faction would have their turn when the police charged the crowd and broke heads in Trafalgar Square on 'Bloody Sunday' in 1887. There were also those, however, who thought the solution was to better the lot of the poor and the working class. To this end the Fabian Society was founded in 1884, dedicated to the gradual introduction of Democratic Socialism. The future Beatrice Webb, later a leading light of the Fabians, still lived as Beatrice Potter with her father in lodgings overlooking Bournemouth pier. Her first piece of journalism – on unemployment, for the *Pall Mall Gazette* – was written in the town.

Meanwhile, another less optimistic organization appeared in 1884 which would also help to shape the world we know today. The 'Special Branch' of the Metropolitan Police in London was set up to counter the 'Fenian Outrages' of the Irish Nationalists who planted bombs in English cities to further the cause of Irish independence. Newspaper reports of the bombs had reached the Stevensons when they were in Hyères, and inspired some of the stories Fanny told Louis while he was bed-ridden with sciatica. Now they were in Bournemouth and needed money, they wrote up these *More New Arabian Nights* as a volume, which was published the following year, sub-titled *The Dynamiter*. In the only tale that Stevenson wrote, 'Zero's Tale of the Explosive Bomb', he tried to show both the ridiculous and horrible sides of the dynamiter. This volume, dedicated to the Police Officers Cole and Cox who had courageously carried Fenian dynamite away from the public, marked the advent of a new form of political protest to mainland Britain – terrorist bombing.

4

Bombing became a fact of life for the towns along the south coast during the Second World War. Axis and Allied States both believed that aerial bombardment and the killing of civilians would win the war.

Bournemouth's second biggest air-raid came on the cold wet night of 15–16 November 1940. The siren went at 3.25 am on that Saturday and the bombers droned overhead less than half an hour later. Fifty-three people died in the raid and 125 were injured; 52 houses were seriously damaged, 6 required demolition and 6 were completely destroyed. Westbourne was hit by incendiary bombs and two parachute mines, which killed many soldiers billeted along Alum Chine Road. The bomb that landed in Denewood Road also destroyed Skerryvore, the Stevensons' first proper home.

Two elderly, Victorian ladies were in Denewood Road the night of the raid. A soldier found one sister sitting up in bed among the ruins of her home in the pouring rain. 'Come along, missus,' he said, 'I'm going to evacuate you.'

'Oh,' she cried, 'I can't go like this, I'm in my nightdress!'

'Never mind,' said the soldier, 'I'm in my underpants!'

*

Skerryvore was a ruin and its garden a jungle, but in 1954 Bournemouth Corporation acquired the site, and a memorial to Stevenson was proposed by C. J. Hankinson, son of Bournemouth's first Mayor. Hankinson wrote under the pen-name Clive Holland and knew Stevenson during his time in Bournemouth. He said he saw Fanny carrying the frail writer downstairs in her arms.

On the site of the demolished house stone-mason Wilfred House traced the outline of Skerryvore's original ground-plan in dwarf walls of Portland stone from the Purbeck Hills, and Bert Cray laid out the gardens of a small public park. In April 1957, the Mayor of Bournemouth unveiled a five-foot tall model of the Skerryvore lighthouse in the garden. Originally it had a glass dome at the top, but this was broken by vandals and never replaced. A plaque in front of the lighthouse tells the story of the house and ends with pride:

> Stevenson wrote many books while residing at 'Skerryvore', including Kidnapped and *The Strange Case of Dr Jekyll and Mr Hyde*.

5

Thanks to Fanny, Skerryvore was a pleasant home during their occupation. The drawing-room overlooking the south-facing garden was not cluttered with heavy furniture in the Victorian fashion, but had light wicker chairs and a long divan covered with cushions of yellow silk. On one wall hung the first of John Singer Sargent's two portraits of Stevenson, pacing up and down the room, spectrally lean, one hand twisting his moustache, with bare-footed Fanny sitting on a chair by the door in the background, an Indian shawl over her head.

The dining-room, known as 'The Blue Room', had an engraving of Turner's 'The Bell Rock Lighthouse' over the fireplace – Stevenson was obviously proud of his ancestors. It was here that he wrote his poem 'Skerryvore: The Parallel' that Borges was quoting when Greene pulled him back from the traffic in Buenos Aires.

On another wall of the dining-room, between two of Piranesi's etchings of Rome, was a portrait of Percy Bysshe Shelley. Under it hung a small portrait of his mother-in-law, Mary Wollstonecraft, the early feminist, and wife of the Enlightenment anarchist William Godwin.

*

The remains of the great radical Godwin family lie in the parish churchyard of St Peter, Bournemouth, and the town also has a strong connection with Shelley. I found the grave a few yards south of the Keble Chapel.

William Godwin
author of 'Political Justice'
Born March 3rd 1756 Died April 7th 1836
aged 80 years

Mary Wollstonecraft Godwin
author of 'A Vindication of the Rights of Women'
Born April 27th 1759 Died September 10th 1797

Mary Wollstonecraft Shelley daughter of the above
and widow of the late Percy Bysshe Shelley
Born August 30th 1797 Died February 1st 1851

Mary Shelley was the author of *Frankenstein or The Modern Prometheus* (1818). She and her poet husband had only one surviving child, a boy, Percy Florence Shelley, later Sir Percy Shelley. Together with his mother Mary and his wife Jane, Lady Shelley, he had moved to eastern Bournemouth in 1849, living in a large estate at Boscombe Manor. This third generation is now also buried at St Peter's.

Sir Percy and Lady Shelley befriended the Stevensons when they were living in Bournemouth (*The Master of Ballantrae* was later dedicated to them), and Fanny and Louis visited their home. The Shelleys had the death mask of Mary Wollstonecraft in their possession, 'over which Louis raves', wrote Fanny. One of Lady Shelley's great-nieces tells how in the drawing-room at Boscombe Manor there was an alcove fitted with silken curtains and a red lamp which was always kept burning; in front of it was a small urn which was a temporary resting-place for the remains of the poet Shelley's heart.

This heart had an active posthumous career. After Shelley's boat Ariel sank in a tempest off Italy in July 1822, his drowned body was burned on the beach, and his friend Trelawny, witnessed by Lord

Byron, plucked the poet's sizzling heart from the pyre to bring back to England. The relic then passed via Leigh Hunt to the widow Mary who kept what remained in a silken bag between the pages of a leather-bound copy of *Adonais*. Her daughter-in-law Jane found the fetish after Mary died in 1851 and enshrined it in her drawing-room. When Jane, Lady Shelley herself died in 1899, the heart was put back in the copy of *Adonais* and finally laid to rest with her body.

*

The Shelleys liked Stevenson. Lady Shelley was a semi-invalid who enjoyed her coca wine and was ready to plunge into any extravagance at a moment's notice; she took it into her head that RLS was a reincarnation of Percy Bysshe Shelley. This was not an unmixed blessing. She felt that any such reincarnation should by rights have been born to her, and accused Maggie Stevenson of purloining her rightful child. Stevenson wrote to Alice Taylor, another Bournemouth friend:

> I was uneasy at my resemblance to Shelley; I seem but a Shelley with less will and no genius, though I have had the fortune to live longer and (partly) grow up.

Sir Percy was an enthusiastic yachtsman, amateur playwright and amateur photographer. He took several portraits of Stevenson, his hair long and lank. In one of them RLS is straddling a chair, wearing a poncho that the Shelleys gave him which subsequently became his favourite garment for writing in bed. Perhaps it was the same red 'shawl' that Graham Greene remembered handling as a child.

6

The grounds of Boscombe Manor have long ago been sold into lots for villas and the house itself is now an art college. But there is a small Shelley Museum attached to it, run by the redoubtable Miss Margaret Brown MBE, a former radiographer and physiotherapist who was the founder and curator of the museum in its first incarnation as the Casa Magni Shelley Museum in Italy. She wore very brightly coloured clothes, and a youthful, radiant smile, and she knew all about the Stevenson connection.

The museum had hand-written labels and was quirkily interesting, a work of individual love and energy, amateur in the best sense. Miss Brown showed me a plastic folder with photocopies of some very early unpublished letters written from the school RLS briefly attended in London, Burlington Lodge Academy. The twelve-year-old was putting a brave face on boarding school: 'I am getting on very well, but my chief amusement is when I am in bed then I think of home and the holidays.'

Sir Percy had built the first theatre in Bournemouth, for his private amusement, at Boscombe Manor. He wrote and produced plays for it, designed scenery, sets and costumes. Miss Brown took me in to see it. The stage is still there, but the theatre has been turned into classrooms, a partition where the proscenium had been now cuts the stage off from the auditorium. Sir Percy's productions were often of a professional quality (but when he once tried charging admission to raise money for charity, he was fined one shilling). The most famous actors of the day came down either to act or join the audience, including the Kendals, Beerbohm Tree, and Henry Irving.

Lady Shelley's boudoir was just behind the auditorium, several floors up, with a hatch through the wall into the theatre so she could look down on the show from her bed. Her boudoir contained a recess known as the Sanctum where the rest of the Shelley relics were kept. She had painted its blue-domed ceiling with golden yellow stars, giving a new meaning to the theatrical term, 'the gods'.

7

One day at Skerryvore Adelaide Boodle walked into the aftermath of a domestic row. Fanny had just turned on RLS and some of his friends for gossiping about someone else's behaviour, and was still righteously indignant when she told Miss Boodle about it. The scandal itself is unrecorded, but it may have been Bournemouth's most illustrious secret, The Red House, at the corner of Derby Road and Knyveton Road, not far from the Shelleys' home.

*

The first owner of The Red House was born Emilie Charlotte Le Breton, daughter of the Dean of Jersey, but became famous as the actress Lillie Langtry. The man who paid for the house and visited his mistress there was Bertie, Prince of Wales, later King Edward VII. Lillie was a famous beauty of the day, painted by Millais and Burne-Jones, a friend of Oscar Wilde and Sarah Bernhardt; and her hairstyle 'the Langtry knot' was copied by countless women. She was presented to Queen Victoria wearing tight-fitting black velvet to show off her figure and flawless skin. More daringly, she wore three ostrich plumes (the Prince of Wales's emblem). Yet she remained a good friend of Princess Alexandra, the 'wronged' wife, and also seems to have managed a simultaneous affair with the Prince of Wales's nephew, Prince Louis Battenburg, by whom she had a daughter. Lillie Langtry was a remarkable woman, witty, well-read, and capable. At the time Stevenson was living in Bournemouth she was a regular visitor to The Red House.

It is now called the Langtry Manor Hotel, half-timbered and red-bricked, erotically lit in pink at night, and standing among pines. It specializes in four-poster beds and six-course Edwardian dinner parties at which a double of Bertie appears. It is popular with honeymoon couples and American servicemen stationed in Britain. The Lillie Langtry Suite offers 'a Romeo and Juliet south-facing balcony, refrigerated bar and colour television' and, of course, the lecherous afterglow of 'Turn Turn' and the Jersey Lily . . . nothing excites us proles quite like the concupiscence of princes.

In the 1880s however it was the sexual habits of the less eminent that gained newspaper attention. In 1885 the *Pall Mall Gazette* exposed child prostitution; in 1888 Jack the Ripper terrorized the East End. And in between the two, in 1886, the Crawford Divorce Scandal ended the career of the anti-monarchist Liberal MP for Chelsea, Sir Charles Dilke. The case prompted a letter from RLS to the *Court and Society Review* entitled 'Honour and Chastity'. RLS was interested in the first, the public in the second. Stevenson thought his age was 'morbidly preoccupied with sexual affairs'; to RLS, what mattered was that Dilke had broken the gentleman's code of honour by trying to save his own reputation at the expense of a woman's.

8

Stevenson's friend, Lord Guthrie, wrote:

On a difficult question of discretion and prudence, or of legal right, there are many men I would have consulted sooner than

Louis Stevenson; but on a nice point of personal honour, or on a question of generous treatment, I would unhesitatingly have placed myself without reserve in his hands.

This held true in public as well as private affairs. To Stevenson, Gladstone's abandonment of General Gordon at Khartoum in 1885 was above all dishonourable. In the political polarization of the 1880s, Stevenson appears to be on the right, a kind of romantic Tory. Sidney Colvin doubted that this Toryism had any theoretical foundation: 'He is the son of his father, and that's all.' But Stevenson was a far more idiosyncratic Tory than his father had been.

A sense of honour led Stevenson towards a Quixotic adventure in Ireland in April 1886. The 'Irish Question' was the political hot potato of the decade, but RLS's proposed intervention was neither for nor against Home Rule. He simply believed that 'populations should not be taught to gain public ends by private crime', as this was a threat to 'the whole fabric of man's decency'. Parnell's Irish National Land League were 'boycotting' farms in the pressure for Home Rule; in an obscure incident, the result of a local feud, a farmer called John Curtin was shot dead, and his widow and daughters were left unprotected. Stevenson proposed to go and live at the farm and defy all dangers on their behalf. 'If I should be killed, there are a good many who would feel it' – especially in America, he thought; 'writers are so much in the public eye, that a writer being murdered would . . . throw a bull's-eye light upon this cowardly business'. It is not unlike the principled bravery that would lead his distant relative Graham Green to brave *le milieu* – the gangsters – of Nice.

Fanny thought it was all nonsense, 'but if you go, I will go'. In the event he did not; the opposition of friends, illness, and the deterioration of his father's health all conspired against action. A sense of cowardice in this matter caused RLS some twinges during the rest of his life. The irony is that the Curtin women did not require his male chivalry to protect them in their helplessness: they shot John Curtin's assassin dead and later escaped to America.

Whatever the contradictions of his politics, Stevenson clung to a knotty cluster of ideals – decency, honour, justice – believing that 'the cheapest ideal is worth tending'. This is not to say he was a facile optimist: rather that he held to his ideals in defiance of his expectations of human nature. In the same year as he proposed his act of Tolstoyan idealism in Ireland, he wrote to John Addington Symonds after reading *Crime and Punishment*:

> Have you heard that [Dostoevsky] became a stout, imperialist conservative? . . . To something of that side, the balance leans with me also in view of the incoherency and incapacity of all. The old boyish idea of the march on Paradise being now out of season . . . a helpless desire to acquiesce in anything of which I know the worst assails me.

9

It was in Bournemouth that Stevenson developed his friendship with Henry James. The two men had met before, over lunch at the Savile Club in the summer before Stevenson went to America, in company with Andrew Lang and the feline *littérateur* Edmund Gosse. At first, James thought Stevenson a 'shirt collar Bohemian', and Stevenson found James a patronizing 'bland colossus'.

Their friendship, however, really began in the pages of *Longman's Magazine* in 1884. In the September issue, James wrote an essay called 'The Art of Fiction' in reply to a rather waffly piece by Walter Besant, who had founded the Society of Authors in that same year. James happened to praise Stevenson's book, *Treasure Island*, and Stevenson was inspired to reply, in the December issue, with an essay called 'A Humble Remonstrance'.

*

Their debate is important because it is one of the first serious discussions of fictional narrative by practising novelists in the history of modern English literature. Taken together with his almost contemporaneous essay 'On Some Technical Elements of Style in Literature', Stevenson's contribution is one of the earliest statements of the modernist position in writing.

Besant had proposed some rather crude categories for fiction, like 'novels of character' and 'novels of incident'. James however insisted on seeing the novel as a whole: 'What is character but the determination of incident? What is incident, but the illustration of character?' The 'least dangerous purpose' of a novel was 'the purpose of making a perfect work'. On this, Henry James and RLS were probably agreed, but at one point in his essay James says that the novelist, like the painter,' competes with life' in order to 'catch the colour, the relief, the expression, the surface, the substance of the human spectacle'. Stevenson's reply pounced on this notion:

> Life is monstrous, infinite, illogical, abrupt and poignant; a work of art in comparison, is neat, finite, self-contained, rational, flowing and emasculate . . . A proposition of geometry does not compete with life; and a proposition of geometry is a fair and luminous parallel for a work of art . . . The novel which is a work of art exists . . . by its immeasurable difference from life . . .

This is very like the symbolist and twentieth-century modernist view of the independent or autotelic art-work, a less indulgent formulation of 'Art for Art's Sake'. The nineteenth-century Realists deferred to 'reality', tried to transcribe it and ended up, in Stevenson's words, with 'mud and old iron', putting in so much substance that they missed the meaning.

It should be borne in mind that this discussion took place in 1884; Oxford did not found its Honours School of English until 1893, Cambridge until 1917. Stevenson was thus engaged in formidably intelligent literary analysis long before the establishment of the following century's academic English Studies industry – which would so often think him unworthy of inclusion in its 'canon'.

*

Henry James and RLS began corresponding. Stevenson's letter of 8 December 1884 ends with an invitation:

> Some day you may feel that a day near the sea and among pinewoods would be a pleasant change from town . . . my wife and I would be delighted to put you up, and give you what we can to eat and drink (I have a fair bottle of claret).

In spring 1885, James brought his sister Alice down to a sanatorium in Bournemouth and became a regular visitor to Skerryvore. The two men remained friends for life.

When Fanny and Louis Stevenson left Europe in 1887, Henry James saw them off with a case of champagne. Seven years later, when news of Stevenson's death came, James went crying to Fanny Sitwell 'It isn't *true*, it isn't *true*, say it isn't true.' To Fanny Stevenson he wrote:

how much poorer and shabbier the whole world seems, and how one of the closest and strongest reasons for going on, for trying and doing, for planning and dreaming of the future, has dropped in an instant out of life.

Stevenson's death was a major factor in the terrible depression James entered a month later when he was booed offstage on the first night of his play *Guy Domville*.

*

In Skerryvore's dining-room, the Blue Room, a cluster of buccaneer's weapons hung on the wall. Above them was Henry James's gift to Stevenson, a 'magic mirror' from Venice. It is the subject of RLS's poem 'The Mirror Speaks':

> Now with an outlandish grace,
> To the sparkling fire I face
> In the blue room at Skerryvore;
> And I wait until the door
> Open, and the Prince of Men,
> Henry James, shall come again.

RLS received the gift in early 1886, shortly after writing a story whose hero sees his face in 'a small cheval glass', terribly changed. It was the most famous story ever to come out of Bournemouth: *The Strange Case of Dr Jekyll and Mr Hyde*.

10

'In the small hour of one morning', Fanny Stevenson wrote, 'I was awakened by cries of horror. Thinking he had a nightmare, I awakened him. He said angrily: "Why did you wake me? I was dreaming a fine bogey tale."' She had interrupted Stevenson during the first transformation of 'Dr jekyll' into 'Mr Hyde'.

Stevenson wrote a draft of the story over three days in September 1885. But when he showed it to Fanny, she pointed out that this was more than just another 'crawler' – it should be an allegory, she said. He burned those 30,000 words and started again. In another three furious days he wrote a new draft. The whole process of writing *The Strange Case of Dr Jekyll and Mr Hyde*, from conception to delivery of final manuscript, took only six weeks.

Longman decided to issue it as a shilling shocker, but it was too late for the Christmas trade, and was published in January 1886. Little notice was taken of the book until an anonymous but perceptive critic in The Times of 25 January 1886 pointed out Stevenson's 'very original genius' and praised the novel as 'a finished study in the art of fantastic literature'. The book became a sensational success, selling over 40,000 copies in six months.

*

It is very possible that during his friendship with the Shelleys in Bournemouth, Stevenson borrowed a copy of Mary Shelley's *Frankenstein* to read. Both books had their genesis in nightmare dreams, but there are other parallels. Victor Frankenstein and Henry Jekyll are both well-educated men of science who make discoveries in the physical sciences but are reluctant to reveal exact details. Both become isolated from their friends and, unwittingly, unleash an evil that eventually destroys them. Frankenstein's monster has 'something so scaring and unearthly in his ugliness'; Mr Hyde has 'something abnormal and misbegotten in the very essence . . . something seizing, surprising and revolting'. But whereas Frankenstein's monster is an external creation, put together from bits of beasts and other men in the laboratory, Mr Hyde is the result of the scientist's chemical experiments on himself.

The respectable Dr Jekyll releases from his psyche a cruel *alter ego*, Edward Hyde. His intention is to separate the good and evil in himself; but gradually Jekyll loses control over these transformations. Finally, Hyde takes over completely, and the only solution for Jekyll is death.

Virtue, it seems, cannot be separated from Vice; evil is not external but within. The horror novel had moved forward from physiology to psychology. Perhaps it is no accident that the letter of the alphabet between H for Hyde and J for Jekyll is I.

[214]

'My name is Legion, for we are many,' says the 'unclean spirit' in the New Testament; 'I am large, I contain multitudes', wrote Whitman in 'Song of Myself'. Dr Jekyll's formulation in the book modernizes the notion of multiple personality:

> Man is not truly one, but truly two. I say two, because the state of my own knowledge does not pass beyond that point. Others will follow, others will outstrip me on the same lines; and I hazard the guess that man will ultimately be known as a mere polity of multifarious, incongruous and independent denizens . . .

There are multiple interpretations of *Dr Jekyll and Mr Hyde*. Some see it as an image of the Victorian age, of luxury and squalor living back to back, and of public respectability concealing private depravity. Dr Jekyll enters his house from the fine square; Mr Hyde slips out from the 'sordid negligence' of the rear. But though the book is firmly anchored in both time and place (Edinburgh, city of doctors, disguised as London) the book's inner meaning is more universal, or it could never have translated so easily and so widely.

'Jekyll-and-Hyde' has, of course, become an international cliché in journalism, a catchphrase for almost any kind of doubleness; more specifically it is popular shorthand for a 'split personality', the lay reading of schizophrenia. It is interesting that the psychiatrist R. D. Laing, author of *The Divided Self* among other works, claims a family relationship to RLS in his autobiography *Wisdom, Madness and Folly*.

According to Fanny Stevenson, one inspiration for the story was 'a paper . . . in a French scientific journal on subconsciousness', which 'deeply impressed' her husband. This article has never been identified, but a good place to search for it might be among the writings of Janet or Charcot. Nevertheless, *Jekyll and Hyde* was written a long time before (as Joyce put it) 'we were jung and afreud of the dark'. In 1885, Sigmund Freud had barely begun his life's work at 29, and Carl Jung was only ten.

II

Several scrupulous and self-conscious modern writers have shown an interest in *The Strange Case of Dr Jekyll and Mr Hyde*. The great Italian fabulist Italo Calvino admired Stevenson, and his own book *Il Visconte Dimezzato* (*The Cloven Viscount*: 1952) is a variation on RLS's themes. Vladimir Nabokov, in whose work doubles are a recurring motif, thought *Jekyll and Hyde* 'a masterpiece' that 'belongs to the same order of art as, for instance, *Madame Bovary or Dead Souls*'. He warned his students at Cornell University to

> . . . completely forget, disremember, obliterate, unlearn, consign to oblivion any notion you may have had that *Jekyll and Hyde* is some kind of mystery story, a detective story, or movie . . . You will ignore the fact that ham actors under the direction of pork packers have acted in a parody of the book, which parody was then photographed on a film and shown in places called theatres.

J. L. Borges made a similar point about the way film has distorted *Jekyll and Hyde* in a 1941 review for the magazine *Sur*. His witty demolition of the film by Robert Fleming makes several interesting points. Fleming, like most other cinematographers, had used one actor with two different sets of grimaces for the book's central character: Borges thought the only way to film *Jekyll and Hyde* was to use two different actors. This echoes G. K. Chesterton's view: 'The real stab of the story is not in the discovery that one man is two men, but in the discovery that two men are one man.'

Borges also observed that in the novel, Dr Jekyll is morally dual, like all of us, while his *alter ego* Edward Hyde is totally wicked. In the film, Dr Jekyll is merely 'a young pathologist who practises chastity', and Edward Hyde is 'a rake with sadistic and acrobatic tendencies'. So Fleming has narrowed down the ethics of the film to a struggle between chastity and sensuality. Borges points out that Stevenson himself never considered sexuality a sin, and adds 'I would contend that ethics do not encompass sexual matters unless they are contaminated by treason, covetousness, or vanity.'

This is very similar to Stevenson's own reaction after seeing an early theatrical production of *Dr Jekyll and Mr Hyde* in America in 1887. He emphasized, in a letter to John Paul Bocock, that Hyde was not

> Great Gods! a mere voluptuary. There is no harm in voluptuaries . . . The Hypocrite let out the beast in Hyde . . .

who is the essence of cruelty & malice & selfishness & cowardice, and these are the diabolical in man – not his poor wish to love a woman, that they make such a cry about . . .

12

Dr Jekyll's 'chameleon liquor', which triggers his transformation into Mr Hyde, is intriguing. There are echoes of De Quincey's *Opium-Eater* in the description of Jekyll's sensations after the draught of powders. And the book can also be read as a parable of addiction. In 1971, an American doctor suggested that Stevenson's prodigious energy in writing the first drafts of the story may have been aided by taking cocaine for respiratory problems. This seems a reductive view of the imagination; it is true that in the story Dr Hastie Lanyon observes a cocaine-like 'simple crystalline salt of a white colour' among the ingredients, but Stevenson did not discover coca until five years after he wrote the book; though he had tried coca wine.

On 20 January 1890 Stevenson wrote from Samoa to his old Bournemouth doctor with news of 'a medical discovery':

I find I can (almost immediately) fight off a cold with liquid extract of coca; two or (if obstinate) three teaspoonfuls in the day for . . . one to five days sees the cold generally to the door. I find it at once produces a glow, stops rigour, and . . . prevents the advance of the disease.

Stevenson erroneously supposed that 'perhaps a stronger exhibition – injections of cocaine for instance' would be useful in combating influenza. The drug was highly thought of then; in the late nineteenth century, Freud regularly used cocaine, and Conan Doyle thought he could sharpen the faculties of his brilliant detective Sherlock Holmes by administering cocaine in a seven per cent solution.

*

At Skerryvore, Stevenson lived surrounded by medicine bottles – some of them doubtless with psychotropic ingredients, laudanum, for example. Ergotin, which RLS took as a remedy for haemorrhage, came from ergot, the same rye parasite from which LSD was later derived. RLS's local Westbourne chemist, G. Taylor & Son, made his own cough linctus, probably containing powerful medicines. I once knew a drug addict who drank a bottle of cough mixture and observed his own face hanging six inches in front of him as he lay narcoleptic on the beach. I am not suggesting that Stevenson was a drug addict, but it is plausible that the disagreeable sensations produced by some of his medicines may have helped to inspire *Dr Jekyll and Mr Hyde*.

13

Everybody has a hidden Hyde. I was still thinking about the book when I volunteered to go up on the stage of the Winter Gardens in Bournemouth one Sunday night to make a public spectacle of myself.

My wife and I had bought tickets for a stage-show called 'Hypnotic Phantasy', starring the hypnotist Peter Casson, who had once so successfully hypnotized technicians on closed circuit television monitors that the BBC were convinced never to risk televising hypnotism, lest their viewers were left in a trance. When Peter Casson asked for subjects, I joined other willing volunteers on the stage.

I had never been hypnotized, and was curious. First came the initiation test: standing in front of the hypnotist, staring into his pale blue, unseeing eyes. We were asked to fall forward towards him, which required a certain degree of trust. Those who trusted and passed were sat in a row of chairs facing the audience.

Music was played, and we sat relaxed, our heads down, while he passed behind each person, touching our shoulders while telling us to relax. I acquiesced. The hypnotic trance was a strange state of double mindedness. I knew who I was, where I was, on the stage of a theatre with the audience laughing below me. I knew my wife was in the second row, taking notes. I could also observe the antics he was putting other subjects through. But there seemed no reason to resist what the hypnotist required.

In my case it was simple: every time a tune called 'So Tired' was played, I fell asleep. I could not help it. I rested my head on the nearest lap, my feet on another, and finally slid off my chair for a comfortable kip on the floor. I was asleep. And yet I was fully conscious, all through the delicious languor. It was even funny; I was smiling; but I could not help myself. It is odd to feel rational yet be helpless to resist another's will. Yet I suspect that Mr Casson anticipated just what each subject would or wouldn't be prepared to do: my hypnotic Hyde was just a blissful secret sleeper.

After the show, when all the subjects had been restored to their waking selves, I felt refreshed and cheerful as we walked home. He had made the others on stage simulate drunkenness, flirt, speak gibberish, and laugh hysterically at comedy shows only they could see. A woman had taken off one of my shoes and socks, and scratched my bare foot. 'His foot was itching me,' she said dazedly.

It was the kind of fun that is tinged with sadism and humiliation. Yet the audience, a big one for the low season, were not there for that reason. They were probably just fascinated, as I was a century after *Dr Jekyll and Mr Hyde*, by the hidden places in the mind.

On the way home, we passed a van-load of shrieking drag-queens outside a club, blonde hair and white hands waving at us in the ghastly street light. Contemporary Bournemouth has many such practitioners of the double life.

*

John Addington Symonds, a friend of Stevenson's from Davos days, was a married man with children who also pursued an active, though hidden, homosexual life. In Stevenson's essay 'Talk and Talkers', where he is disguised as 'Opalstein', it is clear that Stevenson had noticed something amiss: 'He is not truly reconciled either with life or with himself; and this instant war in the members sometimes divides the man's attention . . .'

Symonds thought Stevenson's early work 'a little forced and flashy' but *Dr Jekyll and Mr Hyde* made a deep impression on him. The letter Symonds wrote on 3 March 1886 is a raw acknowledgement of his own predicament.

> My dear Louis,
> At last I have read *Dr Jekyll*. It makes me wonder whether a man has the right so to scrutinize 'the abysmal deeps of personality'. It is indeed a dreadful book, most dreadful because of a certain moral callousness . . . a shutting out of hope . . .

The fact is, viewed as allegory, it touches me too closely. Most of us at some epoch of our lives have been upon the verge of developing a Mr Hyde . . . Your *Dr Jekyll* seems to me capable of loosening the last threads of self-control in one who should read it while wavering between his better and worse self. It is like the Cave of Despair in *The Faerie Queen.*

The denouement would have been even finer, I think, if Dr Jekyll by a last supreme effort of his lucid self had given Mr Hyde up to justice . . . The doors of Broadmoor would have closed on Hyde.

14

In his reply to Symonds in the spring of 1886, Stevenson wrote that 'Death is a great and gentle solvent; it has never had justice done to it . . .' But it was Death that would change Stevenson's fortunes in the following year.

In 1887, his father Thomas Stevenson went into his final decline. In early May, Fanny and Louis were summoned to Edinburgh by telegram and arrived the day before he died. Thomas Stevenson's mind was gone, but his willpower kept him up and dressed for visitors, at 17 Heriot Row.

THE LAST SIGHT

> Once more I saw him. In the lofty room,
> Where oft with lights and company his tongue
> Was trump to honest laughter, sate attired
> A something in his likeness. – 'Look!' said one,
> Unkindly kind, 'look up it is your boy!'
> And the dread changeling gazed on me in vain.

Stevenson wrote to Colvin:

I had no words; but it was shocking to see. He died on his feet you know; was on his feet the last day, knowing nobody – still he would be up. This was his constant wish; also that he might smoke a pipe on his last day.

Thomas Stevenson died on 9 May 1887, and was buried on 13 May in the Calton New Burial Ground. It was the largest private funeral Edinburgh had seen for many years, but his only son was too ill to attend.

*

There was no longer any reason for RLS to stay in Britain. His uncle, Dr Balfour, recommended either Colorado or the Himalayan foothills as a good place for his lungs, and they chose America so Fanny could visit her relatives. The widowed Maggie Stevenson was invited to travel with them, and accepted. In July they all bought tickets for New York City, and Skerryvore was let. Fanny left Adelaide Boodle and the gardener, John Phillips, in charge of her beloved plants. If Mr Phillips ever used a pruning knife on her creepers, Fanny said, then Miss Boodle was to snatch it from his hand and plunge it into his heart.

SARANAC LAKE

I

The SS *Ludgate Hill* sailed from London's Royal Albert Dock on 21 August 1887, and arrived in New York City on 7 September. The long voyage had begun which would take Stevenson away from Scotland and Europe for ever.

The ship carried Fanny and Louis, his widowed mother – 'Aunt Maggie' – young Lloyd Osbourne and Valentine Roch the French-Swiss maid who had been with them since Hyères, as well as a cargo of horses, cattle and monkeys. Stevenson made friends with a baboon called Jacko and the humans drained the vessel of everything from champagne to soda-water.

Stevenson wrote to Bob:

> I was so happy on board that ship, I could not have believed it possible . . . The mere fact of its being a trampship gave us many comforts; we could cut about with the men and officers, stay in the wheel-house . . . and really be a little at sea . . . I had literally forgotten what happiness was, and the full mind – full of external and physical things, not full of cares and labours and rot about a fellow's behaviour. My heart literally sang . . .

Seeing Newfoundland from a rolling ship was the greatest possible change from the indoor life of a writer in Bournemouth: 'like a weevil in a biscuit'. No wonder he told Bob that he 'could give it all up, and agree that – was the author of my works, for a good seventy-ton schooner and the coins to keep her on'.

When Robert Louis Stevenson arrived in New York he was famous. *Jekyll and Hyde* had been a sensational success, and was being busily pirated (the first copyright laws protecting British authors came in 1891). Newspaper reporters wanted interviews and 'human interest' stories; an American wife and stepson gave them a good angle. It was very different from arriving as a drenched anonymous passenger on the *Devonia* eight years before.

Stevenson 'nearly died of interviews and visitors', and fled New York for twelve days, to lie ill in bed on Rhode Island. When he returned, Auguste Saint-Gaudens came to his hotel to sculpt him, sitting pensively in bed. The sculptor thought him 'astonishingly young, not a bit like an invalid, and a bully fellow'. In a later version of the resulting bronze, now in St Giles's Cathedral, Edinburgh, the cigarette in Stevenson's hand has been transformed for propriety's sake into a pen.

At the age of thirty-six, Stevenson was, in our jargon, 'hot', and big circulation magazines and newspapers with syndication rights offered large sums for his by-line. The New York *World* bid $10,000 (£2,000) for fifty-two weekly articles – five times the income he had earned in an entire year at Hyères. He settled for *Scribner's Magazine's* deal of $3500 (£700) for twelve monthly articles, but even this was embarrassingly large. RLS wrote to William Archer that it was

> a scale of payment that makes my teeth ache for shame and diffidence . . . I am like to be a millionaire if this goes on, and be publicly hanged at the social revolution: well, I would prefer that to dying in my bed; and it would be a godsend to my biographer, if ever I have one.

*

Meanwhile, a New York City doctor had told them of a tuberculosis clinic upstate, in the Adirondack Mountains. Intrepid as ever, Fanny went off with Lloyd to scout for a house, and soon sent for the rest of the party to join them in Saranac Lake, New York. On 30 September 1887, Stevenson, his mother and the maid embarked on a boat that would take them up the Hudson River to Plattsburg. A black cabin-steward thought them an aristocratic group. 'Something royal, ain't they?' he remarked.

2

In August 1984 I took Amtrak Train 69, 'The Adirondack', north from NYC towards Montreal in Canada. 'The Empire State' of New York is big; its 50,000 square miles are little short of the combined areas of Scotland, Wales and Northern Ireland. At Albany, the capital, all the lights went out, garbage was hauled off and fresh bags of ice slung into the deep lockers of the bar. Life without ice is inconceivable in the USA; every year they consume a small planet of ice. We passed through Schenectady and Saratoga Springs, and at the foot of Lake Champlain, Fort Ticonderoga.

It must have been a curious experience for Stevenson to pass this place. Around the time of his father's death four months previously he had written a ballad called 'Ticonderoga: A Legend of the West Highlands'. In it, a Cameron highlander who refuses to avenge his dead brother is cursed with the name 'Ticonderoga', but cannot discover what it means. Eventually he travels as one of King George's soldiers to North America, to fight alongside painted and shaven Huron and Mohawk Indians. One dusk, on patrol with an Indian, he meets another captain: 'And he looked in the face of the man/And lo! the face was his own.' Seeing his ghostly double, he knows he is going to die and asks his Indian companion: 'Can you tell me the name of the place?' It is Ticonderoga.

> And far from the hills of heather,
> Far from the isles of the sea,
> He sleeps in the place of the name
> As it was doomed to be.

*

I hitch-hiked the forty-odd miles from Westport to Saranac Lake and was dropped outside a bar. 'It's got colour,' said the driver, and so it had. Wooden throughout, it was like the saloon in a western. I spent that evening drinking beer and watching the Los Angeles Olympics on television. The young men in the bar wore prole caps and drank from the bottle, whooping and hollering in the American way. The Russians had boycotted these Olympics, just as the Americans had boycotted the previous Games in Moscow, and the country seemed caught up in a fit of patriotism, yelling and flag-waving. From the television coverage you would not think any other nation was even competing.

A woman on the next barstool told me the story of her life. She longed to be an actress and took unreasonable encouragement from the tale of Faye Dunaway, who worked as a waitress in the town's Dew-Drop Inn. But Charlene had got fat, fallen pregnant and then given the baby away. At one point she disappeared, and came back bright-eyed and intensely eloquent. I suspected cocaine; recreational drugs are part of the American way of life. I had another beer. Two days out of England and I was disoriented: why was I on a barstool in upstate New York, drinking something called 'Old Vienna'? I thought of Stevenson's poem 'In the States':

> Youth shall grow great and strong and free
>> But age must still decay:
> Tomorrow for the States – for me,
>> England and yesterday.

3

The village of Saranac Lake, popularly called Saranac, is in the middle of Adirondack State Park – the largest in the Union. The old Adirondack Mountains, shunned by the Indians, were largely wilderness until the 1820s when trappers and hunters first started building log cabins. Parts of the area west of Lake Champlain are still wilderness: planes vanish, hikers disappear, and it is only years later that a hunter comes across the wreckage or the bones. Saranac itself is full of cars, TV aerials, lawnmowers, barbecue gear in backyards, and shady streets with big-porched wooden houses, fitted with large windows so the healthy cold air can circulate. But maybe a mile away where mosquitoes and midges hum in the undergrowth a black bear could be grunting through the choke-cherries. Europeans tend to think of the American wilderness as being Out West: in fact it has survived Back East too, right into the industrial age.

One book changed the history of Saranac Lake for ever. The Reverend William Murray's *Adventures in the Wilderness, or Camp Life in the Adirondacks* (1869) caught a post-Civil War desire for regeneration. He offered city-dwellers an escape from affluent angst; the message was 'Get out into the country and play Natural Man.'

Murray's book was half guide-book – how to get there, where to stay – and half an instructional moral fable to inspire depressed invalids in unhealthy cities. The first chapter tells the story of the sickly son of a wealthy New York family who has to be carried bodily into the woods. Here he meets a wise old hunter and guide who shows him the eternal truths of nature and generally makes a man of him. Five months later the once pallid youth emerges from the backwoods 'bronzed as an Indian, and as hearty'. The moral was clear: Nature Cures. 'The wilderness received him almost a corpse. It returned him to his home . . . as happy and healthy a man as ever bivouacked under its pines.'

*

At much the same time in Europe, Stevenson, with canoe and donkey, was playing his own small part in the growth of the back-to-nature camping and hiking movement, which would be commemorated in Edwardian pocket anthologies like E. V. Lucas's *A Book of the Road* – such collections nearly all contain lyrics by Stevenson. A reaction against industrial civilization would inspire the open-air paintings of the Impressionists, and artistic colonies like Barbizon; it would send forth the Boy Scouts with their brown knees and knapsacks; it would be distorted into the brutal heartiness of the Nazi Brown Shirts; it would also have innocent or irritating offspring like naturists and sun-bathers, George Orwell's 'bearded fruit-juice drinkers' and today's brown-rice-and-sandals brigade, including the admirable inhabitants of Earraid.

4

In 1873, four years after the Reverend Murray's book was published, a twenty-five-year-old doctor suffering from tuberculosis, Dr Edward Livingstone Trudeau, had come from New York City to stay at Paul Smith's rough and ready hunting lodge, deep in the forests and lakes of the Adirondacks. The man who carried the frail physician upstairs exclaimed 'Why, doctor, you don't weigh no more than a dried lamb-skin.' But in the wild country Dr Trudeau recovered and put on weight.

In 1876, the Trudeaus decided to live in Saranac all year round, even through the fierce winter. They would be sixty miles from the railroad, and he would be the only doctor. He fished and hunted and got his health back, but kept up to date with the latest medical journals. In 1882 he read about Dr Hermann Brehmer's Sanatorium at Gorbersdorf in Upper Silesia, which treated tuberculosis with rest, fresh air and a healthy regime. He also read of Robert Koch's identification of the tubercle bacillus in German, and went back to New York to learn how to stain slides and recognize the bacillus under his microscope. At that time tuberculosis – 'the White Plague' – killed more people than any other disease in the United States. In poor countries today it still kills about three and a half million people a year. Dr Trudeau became the first scientist in America to grow tubercle bacilli in an artificial culture in 1885, and could thereafter experiment on the disease's progress, treatment and prevention.

In 1884 he had established the Adirondack Cottage Sanatorium with special houses open to light and air, the first fresh air establishment for tuberculosis victims in the USA. Patients learned about rest and exercise, adequate nutrition, and hygiene. Trudeau took poor patients from the industrial cities as well as the wealthy. There were some deaths, but others survived and stayed on in the place which had cured them. Trudeau's Sanatorium was a kind of early, American 'Magic Mountain'. Bible-readers among his patients could take comfort from its location at the foot of a hill named Pisgah (it was on Mount Pisgah that Moses had been shown the Promised Land). And opposite Dr Trudeau's old home was the Episcopalian Church of St Luke the Beloved Physician, which has three fine stained glass windows depicting the ideals on which he based his life: Faith, Hope and Charity.

5

When Fanny Stevenson came on her advance expedition to Saranac Lake in late September 1887, the house she was to rent would have been the first she saw as the road from Bloomingdale curved round to run along the Saranac river.

'Baker's', built by the town's first postmaster, Colonel Milote Baker, was a white painted wooden house with green shutters standing on a knoll at the eastern end of town. The river ran below it and Mount Baker rose up behind it; the trees were the orange, magenta and yellow of the spectacular North American fall.

The house was inhabited by Colonel Baker's son, a hunter and guide, his wife and their twin daughters Belle and Bertha. They moved to one end of the house, vacating the rest for the Stevensons. On 27 September Fanny paid the deposit of $20 and four days later their first month's rent, $50.

Fanny was in her petticoat and jacket cooking supper when the rest of the party arrived. Stevenson, his mother and the maid Valentine had come the last twenty miles through mud and rain in a two-horse buggy with a button-up hood. Soon after arriving, RLS wrote to his cousin Bob that 'the whole scene is very Highland', except, that is, for the wooden houses, and lack of heather. He told Henry James that Baker's, 'emphatically Baker's . . .',

> has a sight of a stream turning a corner in the valley – bless the face of running water! . . . I like water (fresh water I mean) either running swiftly among stones, or else largely qualified with whisky.

RLS had come to Saranac determined to live an outdoor life and play the 'rank Saranacker and wild man of the woods'. Baker's was to be his 'Hunter's Home'. He refused both table-cloths and foot-stools, and it was only on sufferance that his mother was permitted a cut log to raise her feet above the cold draughts.

6

I recognized the house from a poster in a shop-window. 'Visit the Robert Louis Stevenson Cottage, Saranac Lake, New York' it said, 'in the quaint old cottage, still preserved in its original state, you will see the world's finest collection of Stevenson relics and personal mementos. Maintained by the Stevenson Society of America.' There was a white picket fence around the house on a small hill at the end of Stevenson Lane. I walked around the dark green verandah, following the sign-posted arrows to find a 1915 bronze bas-relief of Stevenson in a cap and heavy overcoat with the collar turned up, left hand in his pocket and his right holding his coat shut: an outdoor image that would probably have pleased him. 'Here dwelt Robert

Louis Stevenson during the winter 1887–1888.' The sculptor was Gutzon Borglum, best known as the man who carved the giant faces of US presidents into Mount Rushmore, South Dakota.

A bluff-looking young man with reddish hair opened the door. I introduced myself and he stuck out his hand.

'Hi! I'm Mike Delahant!' Mike was the third generation of his family to look after Baker's since his grandfather took it on in 1951. I paid my dollar and he showed me around.

The first room in the southern wing of the house had been Stevenson's work room; it had a specially made table for writing in bed that RLS would roll into position. Against the western wall was a pine desk and bookcase full of literary Stevensoniana. On the opposite wall hung a large oil-painting of Stevenson at Grez-sur-Loing by his friend Will Low: Louis, looking like a young David Bowie, sat under a tree, attended by a scantily clad Muse.

Mike was telling the story of Stevenson's life while showing some other visitors around the four rooms beyond. As I could not resist chipping in a few details through the open door, the tour soon became a double act and when one man tipped $5, Mike split it down the middle; 'Fair's fair,' he said.

Mike had rooms at the back of the house where the Bakers used to live, and he kindly said it was OK for me to unroll a sleeping-bag there for the weekend. My bag was across town. Mike offered me the use of his coat, and I found an old buckskin jacket on a hook, aged with grease and smoke, put it on and went into the rain. The weather was still mild in Saranac. Soon after RLS had arrived, in the fall of 1887, Fanny had gone up to Montreal and bought Amerindian buffalo robes, wolf-fur caps and sealskin boots or *mukluks* to help her little band of pioneers survive the winter cold.

*

When I got back to Baker's, three acquaintances of Mike's were having a beer. A brawny little tough with a twanging accent shook my hand. He was the proud owner of a Harley-Davidson motorcycle with side-car attachment which he drove wearing a paratrooper's helmet. He was a kind of rural American that RLS knew well. Mike called them 'Rufes' after that section in *The Silverado Squatters* where Stevenson described his neighbour Rufe Hanson and the whole class of 'Poor Whites' or 'Lowdowners':

Of pure white blood, they are unknown or unrecognizable in towns; inhabit the fringes of settlements and the deep, quiet places of the country; rebellious to all labour . . . Loutish, but not ill-looking, they will sit all day, swinging their legs on a field-fence, the mind seemingly as devoid of all reflection as a Suffolk peasant's . . .

Stevenson's particular *bête noire* at Silverado was Rufe Hanson's brother-in-law, Irvine Lovelands. 'I do not think I have ever appreciated the meaning of two words until I knew Irvine – the verb *loaf*, and the noun *oaf* . . .'

Nowadays, the Rufes and Irvines on the field fences or sitting with a six-pack on the old railroad trestle are as likely as not smoking pot. But so, perhaps, is the contemporary Suffolk peasant.

7

The Bakers liked having the Stevensons to stay. Mr Baker told a reporter that Stevenson was:

. . . about as fine a man as ever I saw . . . All our family thought the world of him, he was so kind and gentle. He seldom spoke a cross word, and when he did he followed it with so many kind ones that you forgot the first.

One of the twin daughters, Bertha Baker, had a pet cat, and in her autograph book RLS wrote 'All cats are born free and equal.'

Bertha wrote an essay about him for her school magazine, which reinforced her father's remark that RLS was 'the greatest smoker I ever saw'. Bertha said he never smoked a pipe or cigars, but was hardly ever seen without a cigarette, 'which he rolled himself. At night his room was a cloud of smoke. He threw the butts about indiscriminately – they would be found on chairs, on the table, on the floor – and often there were tiny holes burned into the bed-clothes.

Stevenson's friend, Will Low, wrote a whimsical little pamphlet about Stevenson's taste for tobacco: *Stevenson and Margarita: A Love Story*. He remarked on the 'extreme attenuation' of RLS's cigarettes; 'a few shreds of the soothing herb rolled almost to the diameter of twine in a wisp of rice paper'.

RLS was a true nicotine addict. At Saranac he was once reduced to picking shreds of tobacco out of the linings of his pockets and smoking them in the tissue paper that came between visiting cards. Smoking, and not the tuberculosis for which he came to Saranac, probably helped to kill him in the end. But smoking also fuelled his writing: Low said the cigarette 'served as a punctuation mark' in Stevenson's talk, and 'the pause in the research of his phrase as he wrote'.

In the Stevensons' sitting-room at Saranac – the coldest room in the house according to Fanny, for no fire could stop the wind howling down the chimney – I looked at the old mantelpiece. Cigarette burns still blacken the wood. They are said to be the careless marks of RLS himself.

*

I prowled around the deserted house that Mike had left in my charge. A museum at night is full of ghosts that vanish in the glare of electricity. Upstairs, where Lloyd and Valentine had lived, the wallpaper was now peeling and the rooms were cluttered with junk. The room at the front where Maggie Stevenson slept had a large bed and American primitive paintings of the Baker family. For all her dignity, fifty-eight-year-old Maggie was spritely. When she wanted to leave her room, she would climb out her window on to the verandah, so as not to disturb Fanny and Louis.

Their old bedroom was now the heart of the museum. Glass cabinets were full of relics, and the walls were covered with old photographs of ships, places, people. One of Stevenson's dark blue velvet jackets with silk piping hung in a case, a bunch of heather in the top pocket. In another cabinet was a creased red sash he had worn round his waist in the tropics, and his old white 'cheesecutter brim' yachting *képi*, so familiar in the late photos. There was a pair of yellow silk socks his mother had knitted for him in Honolulu, and next to them, the narrow-footed, high-laced boots that he wore in the last photo taken of him.

Perhaps he was wearing them when he died – Stevenson always wanted to die with his boots on. By moving the cabinet I could get the boots out and hold them in my hands. They were stuffed with newspaper, which I pulled out. It was the Sydney *Daily Telegraph* of Thursday, 12 August 1897.

The autumn colours of Saranac reminded Stevenson of the toy theatres he had played with as a child; but they soon turned winter-white. The thermometer plummeted, but it was the wind that was really cold, so every window and crack was plugged with cotton-wool. Temperatures sometimes plunged to forty degrees below. Stevenson's buffalo coat froze on its hook behind the kitchen door; a floor washed with hot water in a room with a blazing fire instantly glazed over with ice; ink, milk and water in the bedrooms all froze in the night; and even Valentine Roch's hankie froze under her pillow. There was ice in the bubbling stew, and the cooked venison on the table still had 'the ice *crunching* in it'.

Fanny did not enjoy Saranac and went to visit her family in Indianapolis. Maggie Stevenson went off to New York and Boston, where Professor William James 'talked much to me of Lou'. She was 'much provoked afterwards to find that he was the brother of Henry James, and I had not known it . . .'.

Only Stevenson seems to have really appreciated the dry, healthy cold; he felt well in it. Left on his own with Lloyd, he quickly settled into a routine. He would wake early; and once he woke from a dream of rats biting his ear to find he had mild frostbite. After his breakfast of oatmeal, toast and milk or *koumiss* (fermented mare's milk) he wrote in bed. In the afternoon he would go for walks alone in the woods, or sling a pair of skates over his shoulder and go skating on Moody Pond, not far south-west of the house.

*

The principal thing he had to write was the series of essays for *Scribner's Magazine*. The first of these was the beautiful 'Chapter on Dreams', which I would read nearly a hundred years later to Borges. Next came 'The Lantern-Bearers', in which Stevenson remembered childhood summers in North Berwick, and argued against 'Realist' books that miss the true joy of life:

> . . . no man lives in the external truth, among salts and acids, but in the warm, phantasmagoric chamber of his brain, with the painted windows and the storied walls.

The third essay, 'Beggars', argues that most beggars are frauds who sponge chiefly off the poor; that charity was best exercised by people paying their taxes, and that the very words 'charity' and 'gratitude' should be driven from the language. It is not a Tory essay, and William Archer thought it the work of 'a Fabian in disguise'.

*

Stevenson was probably still full of his day's writing when he went out one night through the snow in buffalo coat to visit Edward Trudeau at the Sanatorium. There he received a most unpleasant surprise. When he reached Dr Trudeau's kerosene-heated laboratory there was none of their usual jocular conversation. The scientist picked up a test-tube containing a vile liquid and showed it to Stevenson. This scum, he said, was consumption, which caused more human suffering than anything else in the world. Now they could produce it in guinea-pigs; perhaps they could learn to cure it in guinea-pigs, too. Enthusiastically the doctor showed the writer charts, cultures, stained slides, horrors under the microscope, stoppered bottles containing the tuberculous organs of dissected animals. Turning round, he saw his guest had vanished, and found him outside looking queasy on the verandah, breathing cold air under the glittering stars. Trudeau rushed to his side and asked him if he was ill; Stevenson attempted to smile but still looked sickly. He feebly tried to blame it on Dr Trudeau's lamp, which 'smells of oil like the devil'.

*

The experience in Trudeau's laboratory added an extraordinary charge to the fourth essay Stevenson wrote for Scribner's, the magnificent 'Pulvis et Umbra', which he himself called a 'Darwinian sermon'. It describes what science has to tell of the Kosmos – 'many doubtful things, and all of them appalling'. It is a measure of Victorian confidence that Stevenson in a mere essay takes on the entire universe: 'space sown with rotatory islands, suns and worlds and the shards and wrecks of systems: some, like the sun, still blazing; some rotting, like the earth'. He presents life and matter as 'revolting and inconceivable', the scudding planet as atrociously alien, 'loaded with predatory life, and more drenched with blood, both animal and vegetable, than ever mutinied ship', and man as a 'monstrous spectre', a 'disease of the agglutinated dust, lifting alternate feet or lying drugged with slumber; killing, feeding, growing, bringing forth small copies of himself; grown upon with hair like grass, fitted with eyes that move and glitter in his face; a thing to set children screaming'. Yet, in this vision of cosmic horror he retains one hope, that everything is striving to do better.

This did not quite console his mother, who was 'horribly depressed' when Stevenson first read the essay aloud. He was further surprised by others who thought it 'a nightmare'; to him it was bracing and he reassured Adelaide Boodle – 'There is nothing in it but the moral side and the great battle.'

9

Stevenson's stepson, Lloyd Osbourne, was a clumsy lad in his late teens who wore owlish gig-lamp specs; the Baker twins later confessed they had not liked him much. All his life he would be keen on technology – cameras and bicycles in the 1880s and motor cars in the 1900s. In his unlovely adolescence, he did better with the typewriter than with girls. In Saranac he taught himself to use that newfangled machine and by 6 December 1887 he had clacked and pinged a first draft of *The Finsbury Tontine*, a farcical romance that begins in Bournemouth. Stevenson found it 'not without merit and promise, it is so silly, so gay, so absurd, in spots (to my partial eyes) so genuinely humorous'. Stevenson helped to revise it, and the story was to emerge two years later as *The Wrong Box*.

A 'tontine' is a group fund which the lone survivor inherits. In *The Wrong Box* there are two surviving brothers, and their children have an interest in who wins. The comedy of the book is as deliberately artificial as that of *New Arabian Nights*; a corpse is shunted around the Home Counties in a grotesque version of pass-the-parcel, packed in a water barrel or a piano, always in 'the wrong box'. Rudyard Kipling, among others, thought it was a cult book, the 'Test Volume of the Degree of Eminent Master RLS'; and it is the only one of Stevenson's books that Kipling mentions in his 1937 autobiography *Something of Myself*.

*

Baker's also gave birth to one of Stevenson's greatest novels, *The Master of Ballantrae: A Winter's Tale*. In an essay on the book's genesis, Stevenson says the idea came to him as he walked on the verandah one night. 'It was winter; the night was very dark; the air extraordinarily clear and cold, and sweet with the purity of forests.' A story told by one of his Balfour uncles from India came into his mind, about 'a buried and resuscitated fakir', but he wanted to translate these happenings to the wild Adirondacks, 'the stringent cold of the Canadian border'. That gave him 'two ends of the earth' to string together. He worked at it feverishly and within weeks had produced ninety-two pages. He ordered books on Jacobites, American history, buccaneers, and further information 'as to the people in Hindustan who are buried alive'. When the original burst of inspiration died down he had not yet finished the book, and the manuscript travelled with him by land and sea for nearly two years before it was completed.

The Master of Ballantrae is a complex and subtle story of two Scottish brothers, dour Henry and dashing James, told by two similarly paired narrators, the repressed Ephraim MacKellar and the raffish Chevalier Burke. The brothers 'fortunes see-saw like the deck of the rolling *Nonesuch* and their characters reverse; the 'good' dull brother becomes devilish, and the 'bad' dashing one ultimately shows decency. Eventually, they kill each other, and end up lying together in the same grave. It is a great Scottish novel in the tradition of ambiguities begun by James Hogg's *Confessions of a Justified Sinner*. It is also a fascinating development of the psychological 'doubleness' that RLS had made his own in *Jekyll and Hyde*.

The act of fictional creation was 'double' too. In the Adirondacks he wrote scenes set in Kirkcudbrightshire, and when he came to write the final scenes set in the Adirondacks, he would be in Hawaii. Philip Larkin's 'the importance of elsewhere' is a consistent trait of Stevenson's writing. Only in the South Seas would he begin to write regularly of the age and space he was actually inhabiting.

10

I took a chair out on to the wooden verandah and sat reading, looking up occasionally at the late summer vegetation. Many trees had grown up in the intervening century and the river was now hidden from view. Some of these Adirondack trees were familiar – alder, aspen, birch and beech, oak, maple and ash; but others had names to be savoured – buckthorn, hickory, nannyberry, pignut, sourwood, staghorn sumac, and tupelo. I was temporarily in charge of the museum, and sprang to assiduous attention at the hollow footfall of visitors. A couple meant two dollars for the till.

The man had a small moustache and wore sandals with green socks. His adenoidal 'Hullo' told me he was English. We were in the room full of cabinets when he said self-importantly, 'I'm very interested in Robert Louis Stevenson because he was a fellow Freemason.'

'I'm very sorry but I don't think he was. You must be thinking of his friend, Charles Baxter.'

'Oh . . .'

The English couple were the only visitors that Sunday and they did not leave a tip: after all, I had probably wrecked the man's day. I found a copy of *An Inland Voyage* and located what Stevenson had to say about Masonry in the Maubeuge chapter:

> It is a great thing if you can persuade people they are partakers in a mystery. It makes them feel bigger. Even the Freemasons, who have been shown up to satiety, preserve a kind of pride; and not a grocer among them, . . . but comes home from one of their *coenacula* with a portentous significance for himself.

11

Mike drove me to the old Sanatorium, now no longer in use, and then down to the new Trudeau Institute overlooking Lake Saranac. There was a full-size bronze sculpture of Dr Edward Livingstone Trudeau, pioneer of tuberculosis research and fresh-air treatment in America. The statue by Gutzon Borglum portrayed him sitting up in bed with a blanket over his knees, and when viewed from the side his figure reminded me of the Saint-Gaudens sculpture of Stevenson. Trudeau was a Louisiana Cajun name but the doctor had a high-domed, Scottish-looking head. Dr Trudeau sat looking out over the lake where pine-covered islands floated in the mist, and behind him were the laboratories, opened in 1962, that continued the spirit of his research – studying the immune system and the immunology of cancer, but using tuberculosis, malaria and leishmaniasis as a model for their work.

*

E. L. Trudeau's grandson is the President of the Trudeau Institute, and I went to see him in what used to be E. L. Trudeau's old home, where the Medical Associates of Saranac Lake now practise. Dr Francis B. Trudeau uses the same study as his father and his grandfather who were village doctors here before him.

There were, alas, no anecdotes or mementoes of Robert Louis Stevenson, all gone with time, or lost in the fire of 1893. But Frank Trudeau, a handsome man with a leathery tan, vigorous grey hair and a wide smile, talked about the work of the Institute, and about his kids. He was proud of them all, especially his son Garry.

'Did you ever see a Pulitzer Prize?' Frank Trudeau asked.

I had not. The Pulitzer Prize is one of the most famous awards for journalism and letters, and I think I was expecting something grander, perhaps an Oscar statuette. He showed me a small framed diploma that his son G. B. Trudeau had won in 1975 for 'Doonesbury', his cartoon-strip that revolutionized the comics pages of newspapers. 'Doonesbury' spoke to a Vietnam generation; it is also a liberal chronicle of the 1970s that future social historians will refer to.

Frank Trudeau said he got on well with his son now, after some early difficulties. 'It's hard when the kids all blast you. My generation began to wobble with Vietnam, and we've been wobbling ever since. It was the first time the seniors were dead wrong, and were proved to be wrong. And there were fights in every American family, all across the country.'

I told Frank how much I enjoyed his son's work. 'Oh, you'd like my boy Garry too. He's a bit like you. Kinda scruffy.'

Garry Trudeau has not lost his roots. Every year he draws a coloured badge for the Saranac Lake Winter Carnival, when 'Walden Pond' is frozen hard, and Zonker can get his skates on.

12

Baker's had a photo of the Stevenson family on the porch in the winter snows. Valentine Roch and the local servant girl are in black dresses and white pinnies; gawky Lloyd Osbourne wears a woolly hat and moon-struck specs; Stevenson, by the thermometer, looking like a French trapper in his furs, strikes the pose that Borglum would model in bronze; and Fanny, her hands in a muff, is looking down at Sport, their half Newfoundland, half Irish setter mongrel. This dog, who was Stevenson's sole companion on his walks, was given them by George F. Berkeley of the Riverside Inn. A few months after Stevenson left, Berkeley was shot down after refusing to serve a drunken hunter called Charlie Brown, and died on the verandah outside the bar where RLS sometimes drank. Stevenson sent his widow, May, a letter of condolence.

The Riverside Inn is now Riverside Park, with 'a rock and a flagpole in the middle where four paths meet. The plaque says

'In Honor of Those Who Have Served Our Country In Time Of War.'

*

All winter in the frozen hills the Stevensons had been dreaming of tropical warmth and the South Seas. They pored over maps and Findlay's *Directory for the Navigation of the South Pacific Ocean*, which was full of curious lore. 'The best of reading', Stevenson thought, 'and may almost count as fiction'. Come spring, in April, they were itching to go. Stevenson had had no fever or haemorrhages and there were no tubercle bacilli in his sputum when Dr Trudeau checked, although he later added: 'It is a mistake to say [RLS] never had tuberculosis.' The remission was all they needed, and when both maids came down with heavy colds Stevenson had had enough. In a morning, he and his mother left Saranac Lake for good.

*

I stood with my bag packed on the verandah outside Stevenson's workroom. The Gutzon Borglum plaque had been unveiled at a ceremony on 30 October 1915. The audience sat in chairs on the lawn, among them Dr E. L. Trudeau, who was to die a few days later. A proxy read them a short address by Lloyd Osbourne. One paragraph stood out:

Once in this house Stevenson laid down the copy of *Don Quixote* he was reading, and said, with a curious poignancy that lingers still in my ears: 'That's just what I am – just another Don Quixote.' I think this was the most illuminating thing he ever said about himself.

RLS's life has been identified with idealism and romance; in fact, he knew how often they brought disappointment and deflation in their train. That did not *stop* him being an idealist – but he was Sancho as well as the Don, with a streak of matter-of-fact realism that allowed him to see his own gallantry as both tragic and comic. The reading of *Don Quixote*, which he did laboriously in the original Spanish, crystallized that self-perception. It cannot have been an entirely comfortable experience. It was 'the saddest book I have ever read' he told his stepson. And years later his faraway descendant Graham Greene would rework the noble story in his novel *Monsignor Quixote*.

Stevenson came for a short time to New York City, where he enjoyed a spring afternoon chatting to Mark Twain on a bench in Washington Square. Then he spent a few weeks pottering about in boats at Manasquan, New Jersey.

One day a cable arrived from Fanny – always the active partner and scout in their travels – sent from San Francisco, California:

Can secure splendid sea-going schooner-yacht 'Casco' for seven hundred and fifty a month with most comfortable accommodation for six aft and six forward. Can be ready for sea in ten days. Reply immediately – Fanny.

Stevenson's reply was brief:

Blessed girl, take the yacht and expect us in ten days – Louis.

RLS was taking his lance to the Pacific.

INTO THE PACIFIC

I

The Pacific is the largest and deepest ocean on our planet, stretching over a third of its surface. It is also an area where the great military and economic superpowers confront each other: China, Japan, the USA and the USSR. The thirty-four countries of the Pacific Rim are linked in the so-called 'Circle of Fire' of earthquake faults. Together with the twenty-three island states dotted across the vast expanse of ocean, these countries contain over half the world's inhabitants, nearly two and a half thousand million people. The differences in culture still gape – stone age to space age. But economically, the area is booming: the USA and Canada, Australia and New Zealand, Japan, Hong Kong and South Korea, the ASEAN partners (Singapore, Malaysia, Thailand, Indonesia, Philippines and Brunei) have accounted for more than half the world's growth since 1979. This zone is becoming the most important on earth.

*

It was very different some hundred years ago when Stevenson sailed into the great ocean. 'The Pacific is a strange place,' he wrote in June 1889, 'the nineteenth century exists there only in spots: all round it is a no-man's land of the ages, a stirabout of epochs and races, barbarisms and civilizations, virtues and crimes.' Stevenson would spend the last six years of his life, from 1888 to 1894, in the Pacific, and the time he spent there allowed him to be a witness to world history in a way he could never have been back home. He came on the scene soon after the signing of the Treaty of Berlin, in which Germany and Britain had carved out their respective spheres of influence in the Pacific and acknowledged French suzerainty over South-east Polynesia. Stevenson saw the French and German empires first hand, and pin-pointed the birth of the American empire: he did not like all he saw.

*

European maps of the world split the Pacific Ocean into two blue bits on corresponding sides of America and Asia. Partly because of its distance, partly because of its exotic and fragmentarily reported cultures, the Pacific has been seen as a 'romantic' place by Europeans. After Magellan, Bougainville and Cook, the Pacific islands entered European myth as paradise or inferno, with naked houris or savage cannibals. Modern tourism still markets this 'romantic' myth, but Stevenson's Pacific writings are the reverse of some readers' expectations. Oscar Wilde summed it up in a profound witticism:

> Romantic surroundings are the worst surroundings possible for a romantic writer. In Gower Street Stevenson could have written a new *Trots Mousquetaires*. In Samoa he wrote letters to *The Times* about Germans.

Marcel Schwob, one of Stevenson's admirers and a translator of his books into French, called RLS 'a romantic realist'. In his last years, realism dominates his work; not the 'Realism' of literary technique, but a realistic interest in the outside world, combining clear-eyed observation and political acuteness. While 1880s literary London wrung its delicate hands over Stevenson's exile, believing that the literary atmosphere was only to be found 'within a radius of three miles from Charing Cross', the realism of the Pacific period made it the most fascinating phase of Stevenson's writing career. He may have failed to write '*the* big book on the South Seas' as he had planned, but what remains in newspaper articles, letters and the published chapters of *The South Seas* is magnificent. Stevenson knew he had extraordinary material:

> . . . nobody has had such stuff; such wild stories, such beautiful scenes, such singular intimacies, such manners and traditions, so incredible a mixture of the beautiful and the horrible, the savage and the civilized.

In the Pacific he turned anthropologist, reporter and historian, as well as remaining a writer of short stories and novels. *The South Seas, A Footnote to History, The Ebb-Tide, The Wrecker, The Beach of Falesá*, The Bottle Imp 'and 'The Isle of Voices' catch the Pacific of his epoch as no other writer of his generation could, fixing it as if in a scan, showing us the future in embryonic form.

*

Stevenson visited over forty islands in the Pacific: 'High' (volcanic) islands and 'Low' (coral) ones. He visited Melanesia, Micronesia and Polynesia, without a passport. Like aerial bombing, passports are another unpleasant legacy of the First World War. A modern traveller scrupulously following the routes of RLS's three cruises in the *Casco*, the *Equator* and the *Janet Nichol* would return with a passport bearing the stamps of half the New Pacific's various countries, states and territories: including Australia, New Zealand, Hawaii, French Polynesia, New Caledonia, the Marshall Islands, the Cook Islands, Niue, Kiribati, Tuvalu, Tokelau, and both American and Western Samoa.

The Pacific Islands are all within the narrow band of the Tropics, 'the hot and healthy islands' as Stevenson called them. He noted, in *The Wrecker*, that for the whites at least the Pacific is 'a wide ocean . . . but a narrow world'; their conversation was of commerce – copra, shell, cotton – the semi-criminal activities: 'smuggling, ship-scuttling, barratry, piracy, the labour trade'; of schooners and their captains, and news of who had been wrecked where. Stevenson was a big fish in a small pond in social terms, yet he was peculiarly privileged as an apparently rich writer; he mixed with and met native chiefs and 'Kings' who treated him as an equal, or at least as a gentleman of great distinction. He met warriors, peasants, and witch-doctors as well as colonial officials, missionaries, nuns, priests, traders, ship-captains, naval officers and seamen, beach-combers, bums and maniacs. Stevenson was certainly not bored in the Pacific.

2 MARQUESAS

A month out from San Francisco, early on 28 July 1888, the schooner-yacht Casco approached landfall; it was Nuku Hiva island in the Marquesas. They dropped their anchor in Anaho Bay, which Stevenson thought was rather like a Highland loch.

He wrote later in *The South Seas*: 'The first experience can never be repeated. The first love, the first sunrise, the first South Sea island, are memories apart and touched a virginity of sense.' At last RLS, was 'out of the shadow of the Roman Empire', face to face in his own cabin with brown-skinned 'savages' with tattoos and knives, who swarmed over the white ship from their canoes. A woman rubbed her bare rump ecstatically on the velvet sofa. Stevenson felt a kind of rage to think they were beyond the reach of articulate communication, 'like furred animals, or folk born deaf, or the dwellers of some alien planet'. Stevenson was looking for 'a sense of kinship' with these Marquesans, whose language he could not speak, and found it in the parallels he began to detect between them and the Highlanders and Islanders of his native Scotland, a century or so before:

> In both cases, an alien authority enforced, the clans disarmed, the chiefs deposed, new customs introduced, and chiefly that fashion of regarding money as the means and the object of existence.

In Scotland kilts and plaids had been banned, here it was tattoing; in one country cattle-rustling was stopped, in another, cannibalism. Grumbling, fear, resentment, hospitality, and 'a touchy punctilio' were common to both races. He was not looking for differences, but similarities. And in the end he did hit upon 'a means of communication which I recommend to travellers': his own profession, telling stories, through an interpreter if necessary.

He told them of the savage customs and superstitious beliefs of Scotland, and was rewarded with legends and stories in return. 'The native was no longer ashamed, his sense of kinship grew warmer, and his lips were opened.' In this way the gentlemanly *Ona* (or owner) of the rich ship began the Polynesian career that ended six years later with Stevenson as a surrogate chief in Samoa, still pondering the history of a faraway homeland.

*

'Books are all very well in their way, but they are a mighty bloodless substitute for life.' Stevenson was very active in the Marquesas, meeting priests and gendarmes, the ex-'Queen' Vaekehu and her son, Stanislao Moanatini, while inquiring about cannibals and coconuts, opium and tattoos, custom, myth and the decline in population. As well as the anthropological interest of the beautiful and death-haunted islands, there were incredible sunsets and sunrises, and coloured sand along the bay. RLS would use Taiohae in the opening chapter of *The Wrecker*; here, too, they acquired the services of their brawny and loyal Chinese cook, Ah Fu.

From Nuku Hiva they sailed to Hiva Oa on 23 August, anchoring at Atuona. Stevenson thought it 'the loveliest, and by far the most ominous and gloomy, spot on earth'.

3 TUAMOTUS

In September 1888, the *Casco* sailed south towards the largest group of coral reefs in the world, nicknamed 'The Dangerous Archipelago' for its variable currents and unreliable charts. There are seventy-nine islands in what Stevenson called the Paumotus, today's Tuamotus, nearly half of which are still uninhabited. The contemporary islands have an added danger; in the south-eastern sector, the French test their nuclear weapons on and under Mururoa and Fangataufa atolls.

French Polynesia (comprising the Marquesas, the Tuamotu archipelago, the Society Islands and the Australs) is an overseas 'territory' of France, but to all intents and purposes it remains a colony whose inhabitants are bribed into acquiescence by material goods. The colonies were acquired in the nineteenth century when the British and the Germans were doing the same thing; the only difference is that the French are still there.

The ironically named Pacific Ocean has witnessed many of the world's nuclear explosions, including the atomic bombing of Hiroshima and Nagasaki, in 1945; the ninety-eight American test explosions at Bikini and Enewetak in the Marshall Islands from 1946 to 1958; and the nine British atom and hydrogen bombs exploded over Christmas and Maiden Islands in modern Kiribati from May 1957 to September 1958. France alone has the shame of continuing this tradition. The French nuclear weapon testers came to Mururoa in 1962 when the Algerian war made Saharan tests a potential target. Since the French Pacific tests began in 1966, there have been forty atmospheric explosions and nearly a hundred beneath the atolls.

Of course the tests are 'safe'. This is why France does not conduct them at home, and there are no public health records for this part of French Polynesia. *La mission civilisatrice* marches on; *Monsieur Tartuffe a sa bombe, et tout va bien.*

*

When he visited the Marshalls, the Gilberts and the Tuamotus, Stevenson could see the process of 'our shabby civilization' engulfing the islands. He was also a man who hated 'private crime for public ends'. The sinking of the Greenpeace ship *Rainbow Warrior* by the French secret service in July 1985, in an attempt to stop Greenpeace monitoring the tests, would certainly fit that definition. I believe he would be grieved by what has been done to the peoples of the Pacific, but as 'a student of his fellow man' perhaps not entirely surprised.

In French Polynesia, where the native inhabitants were dying out, Stevenson had his vision of universal extinction:

> In a perspective of centuries I saw their case as ours, death coming in like a tide, and the day already numbered when there should be no more *Beretani* [British], and no more of any race whatever, and (what oddly touched me) no more literary works and no more readers.

*

The *Casco* dropped anchor on 9 September 1888, in the lagoon of Fakarava in the Tuamotus. The Marquesas were 'High' islands; this was Stevenson's first 'Low' island, a narrow coral ring curving for thirty miles around a ten-mile wide lagoon. They spent a fortnight in the almost deserted town of Rotoava, hearing ghost-stories at night from the half-Tahitian Vice-Resident, and exploring the strange atoll life by day. Coconuts and pandanus grew from the broken coral; there were rats, crabs and mosquitoes. The ecologies of the sea beach and the lagoon beach, only a few hundred yards apart, were startlingly different, the lagoon shells pale and dead, the sea shells brilliantly alive. Fish were poisonous on one beach, healthy on the other; on other atolls this was reversed. It was mysterious – the natives put it down to the planet Venus – and the Fakarava chapters of *The South Seas* are full of superstition. Fanny thought that Stevenson's 1892 short story 'The Isle of Voices' was written with that bright sea-beach in mind. Fakarava was the place where the Hawaiian wizard in the story goes on his flying carpet to collect shells – and the shells turn into dollars.

4 TAHITI

On 27 September 1888, the *Casco* reached Papeete, the capital of French Polynesia, on the north coast of Tahiti, in the Society Islands. Stevenson did not enjoy it, spending his time writing letters from the Hotel de France, or laid up ill in a house across the road from the jail where Herman Melville had been imprisoned nearly half a century before. On 24 October they sailed clockwise round to Taravao on the south-east coast, a hot place full of mosquitoes. The redoubtable Fanny set off to look for a healthier place, bullying a Chinese into hiring them his horse and wagon. On 29 October they jolted the sixteen miles along the peninsula of Tahiti Iti to the village of Tautira, where Stevenson collapsed. The next day his life was saved by the ex-'Queen' of Raiatea, Princess Möe, who fed him strips of fresh mullet cooked in coconut milk, lime juice and red pepper. (This fairy story is true.) Stevenson recovered and wrote Princess Möe a poem; the family meanwhile moved into the bamboo and thatch house of the sub-chief Ori a Ori,' the very finest specimen of the native we have yet seen . . . more like a Roman Emperor in bronze'.

*

Stevenson spent a very happy two months in this isolated Tahitian village. He called Tautira 'the Garden of the World', and wrote to J. A. Symonds, 'we are *in heaven* here'. He never wrote a Tahitian section for *The South Seas*, only the ballad 'The Song of Rahéro', dedicated to Ori a Ori, 'my brother in the island mode'. He later told Sydney reporters: 'I should prefer living among the people of Tahiti to any other people I have come across'. Had he stayed, he might have met the painter Paul Gauguin, who first arrived in June

1891, two-and-a-half years after Stevenson left, and lived at Mataeia on the south coast about twenty-five miles due west of Stevenson's pleasant village of Tautira.

*

On Christmas Day 1888, the *Casco* left Tahiti for Hawaii. It was a sad parting, on a grey rainy day; Ori a Ori wept, and so did his wife. The *Casco* drifted out to the reef at two o'clock in the afternoon, and Captain Otis fired thirteen shots from his rifle as a salute. Life imitated art that Christmas Day: three days before, thousands of miles away in Britain, Henley's magazine the *Scots Observer* had published Stevenson's poem about a ship leaving harbour, 'Christmas at Sea'. It ends:

> But all that I could think of, in the darkness and
>   the cold,
> Was just that I was leaving home and my folks were
>   growing old.

After a month-long squally passage they reached the Hawaiian Islands.

HAWAII

I

It was a sunny Sunday afternoon. The middle-aged tourists on the flight from California, leathery necks poking out of fresh sportswear with Hawaiian Sunshine badges – 'Hi! I'm Samuel J. Ryan' – had done hollering and drinking. They sat with tables up and fastened seat-belts as the plane descended.

Flying into Honolulu International Airport on the south coast of the Hawaiian island of Oahu, you are bound to remember 7 December 1941, Roosevelt's 'day which will live in infamy'. Below, to the left, is Pearl Harbor, a key US Naval base since 1909, lying between the sea and the high spine of the green island. Pearl Harbor is a crude *fleur-de-lis* of three lochs, about five miles across, with a brown airfield on Ford Island to the right of the bay, and grey warships at anchor.

*

It had been a dull Sunday morning forty-three years ago when 360 Japanese planes suddenly attacked. The two-hour raid came in two waves of devastation, pounding the airfields at Kaneohe, Wheeler and Ford, destroying 188 US planes and damaging 159 more. They blitzed the harbour, sinking six ships and damaging twelve others beyond repair; they killed 2403 soldiers, sailors and airmen and wounded another 1200. The anti-aircraft shrapnel falling over Honolulu also killed and wounded American civilians. In one shocking morning the USA suffered the greatest naval and military disaster in its history. On the same day, the Japanese invaded Malaya and the Philippines; Singapore fell two months later.

Of the ninety-four vessels anchored in Pearl Harbor, one ship that escaped destruction by torpedo bombers was a cruiser anchored off McGrew Point called the USS *Phoenix*. Torpedoes did sink her, forty years later, in the South Atlantic, when she was flying the Argentine blue and white flag. The name on her bow was by then ARA *General Belgrano*.

The truth about that sinking is still an official secret in Great Britain, like the riddle of the astounding attack on Pearl Harbor. The British have never released their 1941 Japanese 'Ultra' intercepts – perhaps because they show that Britain knew Pearl Harbor was going to be attacked, but did nothing to prevent the US being drawn into the war as Allies.

And drawn they were. On 8 December 1941, an outraged Congress voted for war against Japan. It was passed *nem. con.* in the Senate, and almost unanimously in the House of Representatives. All save a Rankin. Congresswoman Jeanette Rankin, a Wyoming Republican, voted 'No' because she thought it was all a plot by F. D. Roosevelt.

*

The plane flew along Ewa Beach and you could see Barber's Point Naval Station and the US Naval Magazine where some of Oahu's 3000 nuclear warheads are stored. There were red roofs under green palms, ships, docks, cranes, a blur of hangars and helicopters at Hickam Air Force Base, the blackened tarmac rising up. As we touched down on the Fiftieth Star of the Union, 'the Aloha State', the wrinkled tourists cheered in the sunshine through the windows.

We were two thousand miles from California, but it was a domestic flight with no immigration hassles. Hawaii is a state of the USA, the only tropical one, on the same latitude as Laos, Cuba and Mecca. Over concrete buildings rose the gracefully-stemmed palm trees that Stevenson had called 'giraffes of vegetation'. The tops were like hairy spiders on the blue sky. It was sunny and warm and the hibiscus flowers were bright. I had a hunch I was going to like Hawaii.

2

No one was in a hurry on Sunday afternoon. The bus into Honolulu cost sixty cents, and the brown driver in a loud shirt gave no change.

A blonde, pink couple with a large suitcase also boarded, honeymooners still awkward with each other. Looking at the other faces on that first bus I wondered what a Hawaiian was. The one-time Sandwich Islands are more like a mixed salad of races, and people looked Chinese or Japanese or Filipino or Malaysian or just Eurasian. In the mid-nineteenth century, when sugar was king in Hawaii, Chinese, Portuguese, Japanese and Filipino workers were brought in to labour in the cane plantations. I had read that 40 per cent of the marriages in Hawaii were inter-racial; if America ever did have a melting-pot, it was here. And there was a new language among the kids, a Pacific patois called *da kine* which mixed Hawaiian, English and Japanese words, blending California surfer-talk with the intonations of Singapore.

The First World and the Third World have collided in Honolulu. There are huge motorways on concrete stilts, American shops and houses as well as rickety wooden places with peeling porches and shutters, the comfy squalor of green heat and slow decay, banana trees, rust, geraniums in tins and brown faces above bright shirts.

I got down in the deserted business area. The sun was hot on my back as I looked north from downtown Honolulu through towering canyons of steel and glass – black, white, blue, grey, ultra-modern office buildings – to the mountain that rises vivid green to a smouldering turban of cloud.

A bleating sound announced a police-vehicle; not a prowl-car, but a hooded scooter tricycle with a little pick-up at the back.

'Excuse me, could you tell me the way to Hotel Street, please?'

The police-officer did not stop sucking her McDonald's malted shake, but jerked a thumb north.

Hotel Street ran left-right. I turned west looking for the numbers. The street grew sleazier and the people odder. The porn-shops, bars and strip-joints looked shabby in the shameless sun, wild tramps shuffled about, and two men in an empty lot were furtive and urgent as dope-dealers. A startled Vietnamese, by a rack of lurid hardcore, knew of no YMCA. I walked east, away from Pearl City.

*

The Armed Forces YMCA stood back from the road with big trees in the car-park at the front. From a surprisingly spacious and gleaming lobby two staircases swept up to a first-floor, pillared verandah. I took a room on the fifth floor, and went up in the lift and along the spartan corridor.

As soon as I opened the door I liked my room. Sunshine flooded through the french windows from the balcony and lit up the pale lime walls. I stepped out on to the balcony under the red-tiled roof. Straight ahead, between palms and offices, there was a blue flash of Mamala Bay, the size of a little fingernail at arm's length. Leaning over the balcony you could see the fountains and pillars of the State Capitol, and through the palm trees across Richards Street, the grounds of Iolani Palace where the Hawaiian Royal Family once lived.

Other inmates of the YMCA seemed to have found their own version of the American Dream. On my corridor the door was always open on to one large room with a fridge, gas-stove, two beds and a pair of elderly fat men who sat there in their underpants. One of them never seemed to leave the room; he was either asleep on his stomach or sitting on the bed with his face buried in a paperback. He had silvery hair and pink flabby skin. The middle of the room was dominated by a huge table piled high with bags, boxes, cans, cartons and packets of food and drink.

The YMCA building used to be the old Royal Hawaiian Hotel, before they moved it to a pink, wedding-cake edifice in Waikiki, in 1927. It was the right place for me to be. This was where the Stevenson party had first come when the *Casco* docked in Honolulu on 26 January 1889.

3

I soon established a routine. I would breakfast at the lunch-counter downstairs, sitting next to fat, moustached men with the running-down bulk of taxi-drivers who would josh the waitress about the Filipino taste for cooked dog. 'You eat one black dog you gon' get TB,' she assured them.

Early morning is the best time in the tropics, when the sky is newly rinsed and the air cool. In Honolulu's lush parks and gardens the sprinklers were already spitting and whirling, and leaves and grass sparkled with drops. I never quite got used to the banyan trees in the grounds of Iolani Palace, thick and grey as baobabs but corded and hawsered by new growth. The banyan was a topsy-turvy tree: it grew up and out and the spreading branches dropped long hairy tendrils that swayed in the breeze like ropes till they reached the bare earth. Then they began re-rooting, tiny hairs burrowing and anchoring so the swaying rope became a tightened cable, a slender pillar, a stout mast, and so the whole tree moved outward from its centre in a widening circle, dying into its own rigging, a cycle of rotting and resprouting.

*

In the Pacific Room of the Hawaii State Library, the other side of Iolani Palace, I read up about the Hawaiian Islands. They began as volcanic eruptions out of the sea where life evolved slowly and selectively; there were no mosquitoes, no reptiles, no amphibians. Almost everything nasty in the Hawaiian Islands was brought in by man. The first to come were Polynesians, who sailed north from the Marquesas around AD 700. these first immigrants carried their food sources along with them in their redoubtable boats. Taro, bread-fruit, yams, bananas, sugar-cane, bamboo and gourds came along with pigs, chickens, and edible dogs.

All Polynesian languages and cultures are broadly cognate. In the Hawaiian Islands there was a feudal hierarchy of *ali'i* or chiefs, *kahuna* or priests, *maka'ainana* or commoners, and *kauwa*, slaves or outcasts. They were hard-working people, building stone walls for terraces, irrigation canals for taro fields, salt-pans, fish-ponds for mullet. Communities were small and scattered and wars were local; sometimes territorial disputes were solved by single combat, and there were special refuges for the defeated and for violators of *kapu*, the Hawaiian version of 'taboo'.

Some islands still had active volcanoes, but they were mostly rich and fertile land. Great waves rolled in on the beaches; the ancient Hawaiians invented the sport of surfing. Life went on much the same between the mountain and the sea until the last quarter of the eighteenth century.

*

On 30 January 1778, Captain James Cook, on his third great voyage, led the first Europeans to the Hawaiian Islands in HMS

[252]

Resolution: his sailors brought VD. Cook called the Hawaiians 'Indians' and he named their land the Sandwich Islands, after the First Lord of the Admiralty. He returned to the islands in early 1779; on St Valentine's Day he was stabbed and clubbed to death in Kealakekua Bay on the Kona Coast of the Big Island, Hawaii.

Cook died at a crucial point in the Hawaiian calendar, in a symbolic conflict he did not understand. Both his landings took place early in the New Year during the Hawaiian festival called *makahiki*, when the benevolent god of rain and agriculture, Lono, was in the ascendant. Afterwards, the war-god Ku took over, and it was politics as usual. Cook's ships sailed around the island clockwise; the sails of the *Resolution* looked like the poles and *kapa*-cloth. banners that the priests of Lono carried clockwise round the island. There was a prophecy that Lono would return from the sea – Cook seemed to fit the part. He was treated as a god. But *makahiki* ends with the Ku faction symbolically spearing Lono. When Cook led a party to retrieve a stolen cutter, the symbolic became bloodily real. A plaque in Kealakekua Bay marks the spot where the most notable explorer of the Enlightenment was hacked to death. The shore line has sunk, and his plaque now lies two and a half feet beneath the clear Pacific water.

*

The man who took and kept Cook's hair, thus gaining some of his *mana* or power, was a six-foot Hawaiian who became King Kamehameha I. He earned the nickname 'the Napoleon of Hawaii' by confiscating fire-arms and ships from passing seal-traders and uniting the eight islands in a twenty-eight-year campaign. Kamehameha deluded himself that he could resist foreign domination.

But he also liked the goods the American traders could bring, and he encouraged foreign trade. The Hawaiian Islands offered rich pickings – sandalwood trees to cut down, and whales in the seas. Foreign sailors also liked Hawaiian women and the living was easy. The Hawaiian flag came to incorporate the Union flag in one corner and elements of the Stars and Stripes. The Hawaiians' readiness to adapt would be their undoing.

After Kamehameha's death in 1819, a forceful woman, Kaahumana, his favourite among his twenty-one wives, made the next radical changes in Hawaii. Stevenson admired Kaahumana, who showed some of Fanny's independent spirit. Kaahumana broke the *kapu*-system for ever by eating pork and shark's meat with men and not being struck dead. She also provided a powerful protection for the first Protestant missionaries who arrived from New England with their leader Hiram Bingham in 1820.

*

The old joke about the Protestant missionaries is that they 'came to do good, and did very well'. In a newspaper article in the *Auckland Star*, 8 August 1891, part of *The South Seas*, but never reprinted in book form, Stevenson listed half a dozen objections to the Calvinist presence in Hawaii. One of the most important was that the Protestants

> showed a haste to get rich. Natural, because their children stayed with them and settled, but a scandal in a mission . . . The point felt in Hawaii, and justly felt, is this. The [Catholic] priest collects, he builds a church, he dies, and the church remains, a national possession. The married [Protestant] missionary makes money, he buys land, he builds houses; he dies, his son succeeds him, and the son is seen to till and sell the acres of disinherited Hawaiians.

RLS thought this difference might well explain the exceptional success of the Catholics in Hawaii.

For the second generation of whites to prosper they needed land, which meant they needed to break the old land tenure system. In traditional Hawaii, nobody owned land in the Western sense. Islands were divided into *ahupu'a*, or wedges like the spokes of a wheel. A community or group had access and usufruct rights to all the different ecologies of their wedge. The central point of the wedges was in the mountains where there were birds and rain-forest trees and plants; lower down there were agricultural areas, and the slice finally widened to include fish-ponds and wild fish out to the reef. Thus everyone benefited from their slice of the whole pie.

The Great *Mahele*, or land division of 1848–1850, was organized by the white Protestants. Land was redistributed and could be bought and sold for money. By the end of the century, the *haoles* or whites owned four-fifths of the land, and the *kanaka*, or Hawaiian islanders, were dispossessed.

It's an old story. Jomo Kenyatta told it in Kenya and Desmond Tutu of South Africa repeated it to the US Congress:

When the missionaries came, we had the land and they had the Bible. 'Let us pray,' said the missionaries. We closed our eyes. When we opened them again, they had the land and we had the Bible.

4

At dusk I would feel hungry. I often used to go down Hotel Street when the neon of the girlie bars was taking over the warm night and where there were cheap restaurants.

It's hard to say quite why I went so regularly to Cucumber Cool, a nondescript snack-bar run by a Chinese man of courteous gravity. I liked the place because it was small and scruffy and relatively quiet. I once watched an episode of *Magnum PI* there, on the TV over the counter. It is a private-eye series, filmed in Hawaii, and this episode had MI6 spies in Oahu, Patrick MacNee as an ex-SIS maniac dressed up as Sherlock Holmes being chased by Maurice Roeves of the Foreign Office. It is not the Honolulu where I eat my *won ton mein* with a doughball of spice-reddened pork.

Pairs of girls from the bars come into Cucumber Cool to buy cigarettes; girls with painted nails, naked backs and short skirts. There are men with congested faces hungry for relief, and drifting street-people – the black man who howls about Moses by the bus-stop, the bag-ladies with tropical tans, the young and the old crazies, with muddled hair and a look that jumps from fever to daze and back again, and the snarlers who must be watched, but without meeting their eyes.

A man in a T-shirt, grey with dirt, suddenly speaks in a loud grating voice.

'I read this book once, *How To Live Without Sex*. Didn't have no woman for six months. God, my body was *hot*! You know what I mean? Oh wow! No sex is *tough*!' He shambles out, feet grimy in sandals, his old pants terribly torn.

Everybody who is nobody goes to Cucumber Cool

5

The 1880s were a crucial decade in Hawaii, as white interests pushed the independent kingdom further towards annexation by the USA. A snapshot of Hawaii then is provided by James Anthony Froude MA, the biographer of Thomas Carlyle. Froude was a Tory imperialist, and his book of travels round the world, *Oceana, or England and Her Colonies* (1886), is also a meditation on the idea of Canada, South Africa, Australia and New Zealand federating with England to form a union of 'the British race'.

Froude spent a day – 13 April 1885 – in Honolulu. 'The whole Sandwich group is under the protection of the Americans', he wrote. The government were faintly preposterous puppets:

> There was a palace, a phantom army (of sixty warriors), a coinage with his majesty's face upon it, a parliament, a prime minister, an attorney-general, a chancellor of the exchequer, a minister for foreign affairs; how many secretaries of state I do not know.

Froude thought the natives 'flaccid and sensual-looking', given to 'lounging languidly about in loose European costumes'. The lush vegetation and flowering shrubs pleased him. He remarked on the number of telephone wires, which 'made a network against the sky. The people looked the laziest in the world. The wires would indicate the busiest.' He learned that an American speculator had palmed off a stock of unwanted telephones on the government, 'by a promise of the miracles which it would work'.

Colonization was a process that turned the simple and the splendid into the shoddy. The Tory Froude had his doubts:

> . . . our Anglo-American character . . . was spreading thus into all corners of the globe, and fashioning everything after its own likeness. The original, the natural, the picturesque, goes down before it as under the wand of the magician. In place of them springs up the commonplace and the materially useful. Those who can adopt its worship and practise its liturgy, it will feed, and house, and lodge . . . while those who cannot or will not bend, it sweeps away as with the sword of the destroyer.

*

When Stevenson arrived in Honolulu, four years later, he was already sympathetic to Polynesia's predicament in a century of competition. 'The island races,' he wrote, 'comparable to a shopful of crockery launched upon the stream of time, now make their desperate voyage among pots of adamant and brass.' He gained further insights into this destructive process with the help of the couple who met them off the *Casco* in Honolulu, those 'struggling cormorants', Joe and Belle Strong.

6

Fanny's daughter Belle and her painter husband Joe Strong came to Honolulu with their young son, Austin, in late 1882. Charles Warren Stoddard found them a house, and told them there were two mutually exclusive social sets: the 'Missionary' and the 'Royal'. It did not take them long to discover which was more congenial.

One of their earliest social functions was the great Coronation Ball at the opening of the brand-new Iolani Palace, on 13 February 1883. The throne-room was converted into a ballroom, dazzlingly lit by the latest modern import, vying with those ringing telephones, electric light. There were diplomats, naval officers, and a whole Royal Household. Belle, in her new golden kimono, thrilled to the romance of it all. Suddenly they were monarchists.

The Coronation celebrated King David Kalakaua's accession to the Hawaiian throne, some nine years after the actual event. In 1881, he had undertaken a ten-month world tour, picking up tips from other monarchs. He visited the Emperor of Japan, a viceroy of the Chinese Empire, the King of Siam, the Khedive of Egypt, the King of Italy, the Pope, Queen Victoria, the Prince of Wales and other European dignitaries. He was impressed; on his return he promptly ordered a new palace and had himself crowned in it. Apart from the Ball, there were two weeks of junketing, complete with fireworks, a regatta, horse-races at Kapiolani Park (named after his consort), and dancing by troupes of *hula* girls. Yankees of the missionary set fumed at this misspending, and the *Hawaiian Gazette* was shocked by the obscenity of the native dancing, 'the representative of all that is animal and gross, the very apotheosis of grossness'. Hawaii was horrible to some New England puritans, and Hawaiian traditions were best extirpated. Obscenity was everywhere in the warm moist air, in bare swelling flesh and sprouting fruits. Bananas were unspeakably provoking, and the thought of taking one in the mouth a torment.

Life was not all pleasure for the Strongs either. Their second son, named Hervey after Belle's dead brother, had died. Joe had a breakdown; Belle discovered a box of unpaid bills; and their marriage began to founder. Joe was a Mr Skimpole. 'He is a sweet, engaging, aggravating creature, refined, artistic, affectionate, as weak as water, living in vague dreams. One needs to be a millionaire to support him, and a philosopher to love him', wrote Fanny Stevenson, and she and RLS helped arrange the Strongs' divorce in 1892, after Joe had disgraced himself in Samoa with adultery, drunkenness and theft.

7

It was Joe Strong who met the *Casco* in late January 1889, and who arranged for Stevenson to meet the King. RLS and Lloyd Osbourne were formally presented at Iolani Palace on 27 January; three days later King Kalakaua returned the visit, coming aboard the *Casco* to demolish several bottles of champagne. Stevenson read 'Ticonderoga', Captain Otis played the accordion, Belle danced, and Lloyd sang the poem that Stevenson had written in Tahiti:

> But the dibbs that take the Hislands
> Are the dollars of Peru:
> O, the fine Pacific Hislands,
> O, the dollars of Peru!

Four days later they were to meet again when the King was guest of honour at a lunch in Waikiki. Henry F. Poor, a friend of the Strongs, offered his Waikiki house, Manuia Lanai, for a royal feast. King Kalakaua came with his sister, Princess Lili'uokalani, who was to succeed him and be the last monarch of Hawaii.

The meal in the beach-side house was emblematic of the mix of old and new in Kalakaua's kingdom. It was a traditional Hawaiian *luau* or feast with guests sitting on the floor with *leis* or wreaths round their necks. The *kaukau* or food was Hawaiian – one finger *poi* (mashed taro), *ulu* (breadfruit), *mahimahi* and other fish, chicken, pork and baked dog. But it was eaten off china, they drank flutes of French champagne, and the King wore a frock coat. A man called Arthur Richardson prowled about with his camera, fixing the scene. The Hawaiian flag, with its Union Flag in one top corner, was pinned over the model ships on the mantel. Henry Poor has a puffy face and a drink in his hand, Lloyd has glinting spectacles and sports a small moustache, while Belle is dark and exophthalmic. At the head of the *kapa*-cloth table-mat, Aunt Maggie is on the King's right and RLS on the Princess's left. There were speeches and toasts. Stevenson gave the King a yellow pearl from the Tuamotu archipelago and read a sonnet, 'To Kalakaua', whose final couplet was:

> To golden hands the golden pearl I bring:
> The ocean jewel to the island king.

The feast was also political; a writer could be useful to the King.

8

King Kalakaua was a man of two worlds. He had telephones and electricity and drank champagne: but he was also King of a people going under the new Anglo-American world, and he wanted to preserve tradition. Belle Strong, in her impressionistic memoirs *This Life I've Loved*, remembered him as a tall charming gentleman in white ducks and pipe-clayed shoes who wore a hat of braided peacock quills with a band of tiny sea-shells. He was kind to her son Austin, and some sixty years later, Austin Strong published a delightful autobiographical story about the King, 'His Oceanic Majesty's Goldfish'. The boy steals one of the Royal red carp, and tries to run home with it hidden in his hat; but he is overtaken by King Kalakaua in a carriage, and when the King tries to give him a lift home the guilty secret is discovered. Far from being angry with the terrified child, the King grants him a special permit to fish in the royal gardens. King Kalakaua was also an author. *The Legends and Myths of Hawaii: The Fables and Folk-Lore of a Strange People*, published in New York the year before the Stevensons arrived, is a melancholy book that prophesies the gradual death of the Hawaiian people.

Kalakaua did his best to prevent it. He had royal genealogists who reconstructed the family lines of old chiefs, and he preserved the bones and feather cloaks of the illustrious dead, supported the right of the *kahunas* to practise their traditional medicine, had the ancient chants recorded in writing, and formed a secret society, the *Hale Nuau*, for pure Hawaiians to keep the old ways. To many Americans then it seemed like heathen mumbo-jumbo, but a century later there has been a 'Hawaiian Renaissance' – the *Kokua Hawai'i* movement – whose spirit owes a lot to the best of King Kalakaua.

Stevenson judged him to be 'amiable, far from unaccomplished, but too convivial'. Kalakaua's enemies portrayed him as a buffoon – a monster of depravity – the bastard son of a Negro barber, and so forth. In fact, he stood in the way of American interests, and saw which way the tide was running. Hawaii was within the commercial orbit of the USA, and it was pulling the islands towards annexation.

As early as 1880, a US envoy reported, Kalakaua was 'inflamed with the idea of gathering all the cognate races of the Pacific into a great Polynesian Confederacy, over which he will reign'. In 1883, a 'Hawaiian Protest' was sent to twenty-six governments, opposing further annexations in the Pacific.

Kalakaua's next active step had wider repercussions. In December 1886 he sent a Delegation to Samoa proposing a Polynesian Confederacy to resist outside interference. The Delegation's secretary was Henry F. Poor, the man who was to hold the feast for Stevenson and the King, and the Official Artist and Cameraman was Joe Strong. They arrived in Apia, Samoa, on 3 January 1887.

Samoa, excluded from the Berlin Treaty, was still up for grabs, and the Americans, the British and the Germans were all interested in the islands as a strategic base. There were two contending Samoan chiefs to deal with; the Germans then favoured Tamasese, but on 17 February the Hawaiians signed a Deed of Confederacy with the other leader, Malietoa Laupepa. This was a threat to the Germans who suspected American interference. Alarm increased when a Hawaiian gunboat arrived on 14 June 1887. The German warship *Adler* was ordered to follow her everywhere.

The expedition ended in drunkenness and farce. The gunboat's crew mutinied, and the Hawaiian Delegation spent their time getting drunk; finally, they were all recalled in July.

In Stevenson's words, 'they returned from dreams of Polynesian independence to find their own city in the hands of a clique of shopkeepers'. In their absence, the whites had moved against Kalakaua's government. Under the so-called 'Bayonet Constitution', Kalakaua had been forced to obey the orders of a new white cabinet. That year the US gained its first exclusive rights to the anchorage at Pearl Harbor.

*

In February 1889, Stevenson had not yet seen the islands of Samoa, though he had been interested in them since June 1875 when a Mr Seed from New Zealand had dined at Heriot Row. Afterwards, RLS wrote to Fanny Sitwell that Mr Seed had talked about the islands 'till I was sick with desire to go there: beautiful places, green for ever . . . perfect shapes of men and women, with red flowers in their hair . . .'.

Now in Waikiki, RLS listened with interest to what the King, Joe Strong and Henry Poor had to tell him about the Samoan issue. Within a week he had fired off a letter to *The Times* in London about 'the present extraordinary state of affairs in Samoa'. He also wrote a sympathetic text to accompany a collection of photos Joe Strong had made of Samoa – the unpublished *Samoan Scrapbook*.

This was his first practical involvement with the place where he was to die five years later. By that time he would be rather cynical about King Kalakaua's ideas of a Polynesian Confederacy: he would also have exhausted himself in the separate cause of Samoan independence.

9

The *Casco* was paid off, Valentine Roch went home, and the Stevenson menage moved into a rented house a little east of Henry Poor's house on Waikiki Beach. Waikiki was three miles east of Honolulu, and their new residence was a rambling house surrounded by oleanders. Stevenson used a frowzy shack in the garden as his workroom, burning buhac powders to keep the mosquitoes at bay, feeding the cottage's mouse with scraps of cheese, piping on his flageolet and working hard in bed on *The Master of Ballantrae and The Wrong Box*. Sometimes, Stevenson went swimming off Waikiki Beach, as millions have done since.

The Honolulu bus map was written by a PhD graduate, and it takes another one to understand it. I had to ask which bus to take from downtown Honolulu to Waikiki. Once, a ten-cent ride in a horse-drawn tram took you through a couple of miles of country with taro patches, banana trees and rice paddies; nowadays, the trip along Kalakaua Avenue is all through American cityscape.

Stepping off the bus at Waikiki, I walk straight on to the beach, passing racks of surf-boards, brown bodies showering off salt, and sunbathers on white sand. It is very bright and the blue and green water sparkles. But I turn round to a vision of modern hell.

Huge tower-blocks rise beyond the beach like dead trees round a poisoned water-hole. Buildings pack Waikiki with people: 25,000 hotel rooms in less than a square mile, plus condos and non-stop shopping. Waikiki is no longer an escape from humanity, but an immersion in it.

There is only sandy beach where Henry Poor's house once stood.

'Wanna buy some good pot?' hisses a kid in shades. The Japanese endlessly photograph each other. A mad hippie curses me. I sit on a bench under a banyan tree and a mouse runs up my trouser-leg, panics and flees down again. A toothless old man in a T-shirt brandishing a plastic bag approaches. 'I'm Charley,' he chumbles, 'I collect.' A man dressed as a rooster hands out leaflets by the burger bar. There are signs and free magazines in Japanese. I stare at the water. This is where *The Master of Ballantrae* was written.

Travel-writing is tough, too. Research is hard, and there are sacrifices you owe the reader. Reluctantly I take my clothes off. The whitest man on Waikiki Beach, I walk over the hot sand into the warm water. Legwork counts in this business. I can report the conditions were very tolerable.

Later, I combed my hair with my fingers, walking along the beach with a damp towel. In Kapiolani Park, small Chinese pigeons pecked in the dust, a cardinal bird flashed vivid red, and men flew kites in the sea-breeze. There was no trace of Stevenson's house. The view stretched across the bay to the Waianae Range behind Pearl Harbor. I felt a long way from Scotland.

Stevenson found a Scots neighbour in Waikiki. Archibald S. Cleghorn was an Edinburgh-born Scots merchant in charge of the Customs and Excise, whose late wife, Princess Miriam Likelike, had been the King's sister. Cleghorn lived at 'Ainahau, just north of Waikiki, with his pretty daughter Princess Ka'iulani, then aged thirteen. Soon she was to leave for Britain, where she would be educated as a lady, and she was dreading it.

Stevenson was enchanted by the little Princess, and talked to her under her favourite banyan tree in the grounds of 'Ainahau, telling her stories of what she would find abroad. He also wrote her a poem beginning

> Forth from her land to mine she goes,
> The island maid, the island rose,
> Light of heart and bright of face:
> The daughter of a double race.

The Princess grew up to be a beautiful young woman: it shines from all her photos. Stevenson never saw her again after she left Honolulu, but her story would have saddened him. When her uncle David Kalakaua died, her aunt Lili'uokalani became Queen, but was soon deposed by an American coup d'état. Though Princess Ka'iulani went to Washington to protest on behalf of the Hawaiian people, the voice of a schoolgirl could not avert the Big Stick. In 1898 the United States annexed Hawaii: America had taken up 'the White Man's burden – The savage wars of peace'. Ka'iulani died the next year at 'Ainahau, of pneumonia. She was only twenty-six. Dispossessed Hawaiians grieved; her bereft father lived alone in his sorrow for another eleven years.

*

Jack London visited 'Ainahau on 29 June 1907, and noticed that white-bearded Cleghorn dated everything from her – 'before Ka'iulani left me, when Ka'iulani died, since Ka'iulani went away'. Her part of the house was locked up, untouched, and the great library was silent. Jack and Charmian London walked through the grounds with him, past lily-ponds, vines, arbours, eleven varieties of hibiscus, native and foreign trees, nurseries and vegetable gardens, 'real grass huts that have stood for years' and huge banyan trees.

'The white man is the born looter', London later wrote in *My Hawaiian Aloha* (1915):

> And just as the North American Indian was looted of his continent by the white man, so was the Hawaiian looted by the white man of his islands. Such things be. They are morally indefensible. As facts they are irrefragable.

*

When Stevenson returned to Hawaii from September to October 1893, he stayed once again at Waikiki, further east, at the Sans Souci Hotel. The Sans Souci Apartments, 2877 Kalakaua Avenue, now mark the spot.

'We feel RLS would have approved', ran the builders' press release. 'In its own way, the magnificent fifteen-storey reinforced concrete building that will rise on the spot RLS loved so well will preserve and enhance the charm that Stevenson found along this shore seven decades ago.'

In the car-park at the back of the unlovely building half a banyan tree survives the concrete. I thought of Ka'iulani's tree, where the peacocks once screamed at dusk and the last Princess had sat with the lean Scots man.

'Ainahau, Cleghorn's estate, which he left to the Territory to be turned into a park in 1910, was sold off a few years later for real estate lots. I walked along Tusitala Street where the Princess's banyan tree had stood within living memory. It had been cut down 'because of rats', and because it took up too much valuable space.

The few remaining old houses on the street, with their wooden shutters and cool verandahs, huddled in the shadows of giant towers. After Hawaii became a State of the USA, in 1959, the developers had been let off the leash.

A blonde man in T-shirt and shorts was watering his lawn and looking at me. I remarked what a bloody awful place Waikiki had become. He invited me into his wooden house.

John White Cater was an attorney with half-moon spectacles but also the Over-45 State Surfing Champion and winner of dozens of surfing trophies in his sixteen years in Hawaii. He was East Coast,

Ivy League and Upper Class; an ancestor had founded the Bank of London and South America, and he himself had been to Charter-house. He was a handsome man who looked fifteen or twenty years younger than his age. Surfing seemed to be the elixir of youth, and Waikiki is a mecca for the sport.

Walking back towards the beach with me, he greeted in passing a pair of muscular men and a beautiful girl, all in swimming costumes and carrying surf-boards. 'They,' said Mr Cater, 'are the most socially adept group of young people I have ever met. The guys are both male strippers and she's a high-class hooker.'

*

Waikiki's favourite commercial adjectives are 'ancient', 'authentic' and 'traditional'. One gem of the manufactured past intrigued me. When the old Cleghorn estate 'Ainahau was sold off in lots in 1917, Commander Rachel Payne of the Salvation Army bought one of the huts in the grounds 'whose walls were constructed entirely of plaited grass'. She had it moved almost three miles north, setting it up as a tourist attraction, suitably embroidered with legends of Princess Ka'iulani and Robert Louis Stevenson. The hut deteriorated under the sun, rain and wind, and by the 1970s had become 'dangerous for elderly people'; accordingly, it was 'reconstructed'. What emerged was broader, higher and lighter with added windows and a verandah. It is one of the authentic 'sights' of Honolulu – a fake replica of a house Stevenson was probably never in, standing behind the Waioli Tea Rooms at a place he never visited. Tourists happily take pictures of it and feel close to the spirit of the author of *Treasure Island*. A T-shirt costs $12 and says:

Robert Louis Stevenson
Memorial Grass House
Waioli Tea Rooms
Honolulu

11

I took a bus up to Waioli. We climbed up through hibiscus, frangipani, magnolia. Clouds rolled off the sheer slope of Puu Kakea and golden sun brightened the drenched bougainvillaea. It was an afternoon of Hawaiian 'liquid sunshine', wet asphalt steaming, the intense greens of wet vegetation in moody tropical weather. At school in Kenya we used to call sunshine during rain 'a monkey's wedding'.

The Salvation Army had been in Hawaii for ninety years, and the Waioli Tea Rooms were originally started to train 'unfortunates' and other wayward girls in the arts of domestic service. The RLS Memorial Grass House brought in a little cash for their work among the homeless, the missing, the elderly, and drug and alcohol abusers. More lucrative, though, was the Waioli Chapel, which the Salvation Army rented out to private enterprise.

The Chapel does big business in take-away nuptials for Japanese couples. The brochure explained:

A Japanese travel company (not connected with the Salvation Army), makes all of the arrangements. The couples fly to Hawaii, are greeted at the airport by local representatives, taken to their hotel, assisted in obtaining the wedding gown and tuxedo and then are transported to Waioli by limousine. And the total package cost is around $2500, much less than if they were to be married in Japan!

I stood in the Waioli Tea Rooms car-park watching the finale. The couple stood on the chapel steps, the stills photographer swooped and dipped, the video-camera-man backed away for a long-shot. He filmed the bride in the bridegroom's arms by the door of the limo after the stills man had darted in to pretty up the veil; he filmed the guitarist in the Hawaiian shirt and *lei*, the lady organist, the handsome Japanese-speaking missionary, all standing on the steps waving goodbye. The chauffeur spoke into his walkie-talkie and the camera-man filmed the limo sweeping away down the drive.

The preacher was grey with exhaustion. He had conducted ten weddings that day and seventeen the day before. It is all carefully organized, rather like a funeral, so that the couple do not see the one before or the one after. I watched the camera-man in the back of his van topping and tailing his video with standard shots and credits, professionally swift over his editing machine. I asked what happened next.

'They have a honeymoon in Waikiki, a couple of days, then take home an album of stills. The video is optional, but most take it. Retails around 250 bucks.'

It's only forty years since the Second World War; enemies are now customers, kamikazes have become camera-clickers. Most of the hotels in present day Waikiki are Japanese-owned, with AJAs (Americans of Japanese ancestry) encouraging the tourist-trade from home. Daily jumbos from Osaka and Tokyo disgorge package tourists who do not need a word of English. America and Japan meet in Hawaii. Its Governor, when I was there, was the AJA George Ariyoshi.

12

I went to the University of Hawaii at Manoa to find Professor Barry Menikoff, who was working on Stevenson. He was a small, neatly dressed man with a large intelligent head. His accent was still New York, though he had been in Hawaii for nearly twenty years.

Barry Menikoff had just produced a new edition of Stevenson's Pacific novella *The Beach of Falesá* for Stanford University Press, working from the manuscript in the Huntington Library in California. It was more than just an edition however – it was the scholarly version of an assault.

'The sub-title is *A Study in Victorian Publishing*, using what happened to the text of *Falesá* as a model. I trace how you can get a published book which does not reflect the author's intentions. From the evidence of changes that others made to the text you can make a historical, critical and stylistic study.'

Barry Menikoff did not like Sidney Colvin or his editorial style. He thought that when Colvin and others changed the punctuation, spelling and syntax of *The Beach of Falesá* they had diluted, and in effect censored, the novel's portrayal of white rapacity, racism and sexual abuse in the South Seas. There was an irony about this tale of thwarted authorial intentions. Menikoff himself had wanted to use, just once and with a precise meaning, the word 'fuck' in his 'Study' to convey the force that the trader Wiltshire's one-night wedding certificate might have had for Victorian readers. But Stanford University censored it.

'How do you rate Stevenson?' I asked.

'There is no doubt in my mind that he is a *major* writer. He has lived in the shadow of James and Hardy in English Studies. He should be taken out of that never-never land of the romance and the children's writer. In his time, he was the best educated and best equipped to interpret history, particularly in the Pacific. He had an almost scientific cast of mind.'

Menikoff thought that to understand *The Beach of Falesá* you had to live here in the Pacific: 'You have to experience it.'

*

In *The Beach of Falesá* the 'Beach' has a special meaning; it is the place where the whites lived and traded in Samoa, and was also shorthand for the whites themselves. The white trader Wiltshire lands on a South Sea island where trade is monopolized by a crooked gun-runner called Case, who controls the natives through force and superstitious terror.

On Stevenson's second visit to Honolulu in 1893, the whites had overthrown the monarchy and set up a 'Provisional Government' a few months before. One day Stevenson and a local man, Robert Gatton, were walking to the Royal Hawaiian Hotel for a drink. As they passed the grounds of Iolani Palace, a row was going on between Hawaiian monarchists and supporters of the Provisional Government. Robert Catton had just been reading *Beach of Falesá* and remarked: 'These Royalists and PGs remind me of Wiltshire and Case.' Stevenson looked at the shouting white men. 'Especially Case,' he said. In the novel, one of Case's nicknames is 'Tiapolo' – he is the capitalist as Christian demon among the communistic islanders.

13

I went over to the windward side of Oahu one Saturday morning. The bus went up the Nuuanu Pali through tunnels and cloud-fogged rain-forest, and came down the eastern slopes of the Koolau Range to blue skies, blue seas and a cool Pacific breeze.

It was invigorating to escape the humid grime of Honolulu. Stevenson had often felt out of sorts in the town, with headaches and 'blood to the head'. Over the mountain was another world, far away from urban Americana. The bus tootled north along Kaneohe Bay past rickety houses with little gardens, and I thought about cows.

A man called John Morgan had invited me out to Kualoa, the last working cattle ranch on the island of Oahu. The very first cattle came to Hawaii in 1793 when Captain George Vancouver brought some longhorns over from Monterey, California, as a gift for King Kamehameha. They ran wild and multiplied on Big Island and became a real danger to the unwary. Captain Cleveland brought the first horses ten years later, in 1803 – *mestaños* of the Berber-Andalusian breed, which developed into tough little 'kanaka mustangs'. In 1832, the first cowboys came from California, real *vaqueros* who spoke Spanish, *español*, which became corrupted into the Hawaiian word for a cowboy, *paniolo*.

Hawaiians took to horses like the American Indians had when the wild descendants of Cortez's horses drifted northwards. Killer cattle and fierce conditions made Hawaiian cowboys among the best in the world. North Americans had no idea how good the *paniolos* were until 22 August 1908, when islanders Ikua Purdy and Archie Kaaua walked off with the gold and the bronze medals at the World Championship Steer Roping at a big rodeo in Cheyenne, Wyoming. The principal beef ranches are now on Big Island, where the Parker Ranch (founded in 1847) has nearly a quarter of a million acres of range.

*

I got off the bus by the white gates of Kualoa Ranch. Behind it, a chunk of crumbly volcanic mountain, frothed with green, reared straight out of a field of dry brown grass. It was still early but there wasn't a cloud in the sky. It was going to be a hot day.

I walked up the dusty road towards grey sheds, and John Morgan whistled me over to the ranch office. He was vearing battered jeans and cowboy boots and had an honest Amercan face that belied a wicked deadpan humour. He handed me a rope and we went into the wooden corral where whickering horses Iran round in the soft pale dust. My horse was Wilē (pronounced why-lay) and John's was called Ehukai. We walked them to the barn and wrapped the halters round the hitching-post. Wilē was rolling-eyed and head-shy, and suddenly reared up to snap the old rope. Something was spooking the beast – maybe it was me.

I met John's pretty wife Carri, four months pregnant, and carrying their first son Jason on one hip. I met Abraham Akau, the ranch foreman, a big Hawaiian with *PANIOLO KUALOA* spelt out in studs on the back of his faded demin jacket. Abraham Akau was old *paniolo* stock, and had worked for over thirty years at Kualoa. He had started on the Parker Ranch and for four years he had been a full-time horse-breaker there. It's one of the toughest jobs going – getting on the back of wild horses up to sixteen years old who had never been ridden. 'Dey climbed the walls like dose motorcycle guys,' he chuckled.

We pulled out high-pommelled saddles from the tack-room that smelled of leather and sweat. John was hauling in the girth on my saddle when Wilē bit. A wild eye in a plunging head; I felt a blow and then a sharp pang; saw a strip of yellow shirt in big teeth, and Wilē had taken a morsel of my upper left arm. I peered in shocked curiosity at the blue and red wound. John stuck a plaster on, and we mounted up.

We rode by dry fields with Carri holding Jason on a pillow at her saddle-bow. Her saddle was seventy years old and had belonged to John's grandmother. We stopped under some acacia trees. Towards the sea were old taro-patches and the outline of an ancient Hawaiian fish-pond. I had been brought here to see history; a single palm and a clump of bougainvillaea marked the spot where the first family homestead had been. John Morgan was a descendant of Gerrit P. Judd, the medical missionary who had become physician to King Kauikeaouli and a Hawaiian nationalist into the bargain. His was an old *kamaaina* family, a word used to denote a long-time resident of Hawaii, rather than *malihini*, a newly-arrived stranger.

'We've held this land since the Great Mahele,' said John.

'Is that mountain yours?'

'Yes. The 4000 acres is on a flat map. You don't measure it up the mountain side.'

We rode back past the ranch and up the trail past the corral, heading north round the cliff that was hidden from the coast road below by thick *haole koa* scrub. There were caves in the cliff dug for Second World War gun emplacements against a possible Japanese attack on the windward side of the island. Round the corner we rode up the fine strath of Ka'a'awa Valley.

It was a beautiful place. Below to our right was the deep blue sea and lines of palm trees. I stood up in the creaking stirrups and followed the jagged line of mountain on the other side of the trough, volcanic rock furred with green, rising towards the central spine of Oahu, overhung by clouds. But Ka'a'awa was suffering the worst drought in six decades, and the stream had dried to a few pools and patches of hoof-pocked mud. Swaying on the horses' backs we walked *mauka*', 'toward the mountain', picking ripe strawberry guavas from the bushes and eating them in the hot sunshine.

Up Ka'a'awa Valley, where the two sharp sides narrowed together, there was cowboying work to be done, moving the herd browsing on the north side back down across the stream. The earth was red, the sun was hot on my arms and head; it was ten years since I had done anything like this.

'*Hele, pipi.*!' was the yell, '*hele, hele, pipi.*!' getting the Hereford steers flowing through the haole koa thickets, the pungent smell of cattle, dust and bruised vegetation, the feel of a horse between your knees, down the slope towards the flashing Pacific, moving *makai*, 'toward the sea'. '*Hele, hele, pipi*!'

*

'What's that?' I pointed at the small white chapel by the side of the stream in Ka'a'awa Valley. 'Missionary work?'

John explained it was a film set, the relic of an episode of the TV series *Magnum PI*, and it was supposed to be a chapel in Ireland. I looked round at the spiny mountains, the guava bushes, a white egret on a steer's back.

'This is *Ireland*?'

A Renegade jeep was parked on a bluff across from the 'chapel', and a crew of Japanese technicians with brutal spiky haircuts were shifting cameras and recorders for a languid director in dark glasses. The Tokyo TV programme *Do Sports*! was preparing to shoot the horse-riding episode of the series.

A model called Lisa came cantering up, with Abraham Akau and grinning ranch-hands. The director gave orders; a squat Japanese with headphones round his neck shouted '*Hai!*' with a short-range head-butt of obedience and ran bow-legged for the jeep.

Filming is like military life: boredom punctuated by hysteria; Hurry-Up-and-Wait. Everybody joined in – meaninglessly chasing cattle back and forth in front of the cameras, the Herefords crashing into the thickets, whooping yells and whistles in a haze of reddish dust, a posse of *paniolos* bunching the scattering cattle, with Abraham and Lisa cantering to the fore as the camera panned. Then there were more charges with tracking shots from the jeep;

John galloping after a bawling calf, the brim of his hat blown up, more dust and plaintive bellowing, going in circles.

We knocked off for *bento*, Japanese box lunch. The sun was high overhead, and John rode back beside me part of the way. He was carrying Jason asleep on the pillow, the way Abraham Akau had carried John himself thirty years before.

'Ka'a'awa is a fine valley.'

'I love it.'

'How do you feel about owning it?'

'I belong to the land as much as it belongs to me. It'll be here after I'm dead and gone. I am a steward of the land, and as it came to me so I shall pass it on.'

Seventh generation *kamaaina*, Jason slept peacefully in the hot sun as Ehukai clopped over his inheritance. I played Old Nick, the Developer, proffering a vision of a select hotel, tasteful condos, a golf-course; tempting John with millions of dollars in cash for Ka'a'awa.

'What would I do with the money?' he said, 'I've already got what I want.'

It was an appropriate answer. *Kamaainas* are the Creole aristocrats of the Hawaiian Islands, and Hawaii's motto is *Ua mau ea o ka aina i ka pono*: 'the life of the land is preserved in righteousness'.

*

The second smallest of the eight islands, Niihau, at the west of the chain was still privately owned by descendants of the New Zealand Robinson family, who bought it in 1864 for $10,000. You could not visit it, and its nickname was 'The Forbidden Isle'. And yet for all its paternalism it had preserved pure Hawaiian language, customs and blood. When an armed Japanese pilot crash-landed on radioless Niihau after Pearl Harbor and tried to take over the island, a Hawaiian called Benehakaka Kanahele killed him. Niihau was the only place to vote 'No' to statehood in 1959.

The smallest island, Kahoolawe, had been taken over by the US military as a bombing target. It was a sacred site and Hawaiians were outraged. Two islanders – George Helm and Kimo Mitchell – were drowned while protesting the desecration of Kahoolawe. *Ho 'iHo 'iHou*! was the cry of the monarchists after the overthrow of Queen Lili'uokalani in 1893, meaning 'restoration'. Now it had wider connotations – 'returning' and 'giving back'.

The Japanese film crew laid on a barbecue for all hands at the end of the day. A gay Texan ran the hired chuck-wagon, serving steaks on paper plates with coleslaw and beans. We sat under a monkey-pod tree and the cameras rolled.

'Talk about the day,' called the director, and Abraham told Lisa she had done real good, riding and roping, and we drank beer from the can, self-conscious and jolly, as the sun went down behind the mountain.

Later, the rubbish was bagged and the trucks rolled away with their freight of unreality, headlamps down the drive, and the quiet land remained. I helped John lay out light aluminium irrigation pipes in the dry field, shook hands with Abraham and the boys and rode in the back of the pick-up through the cool early night with palms black against the stars.

14

Tourism in Hawaii is intimately linked with prostitution and crime. Four million visitors a year fuel a billion dollar tourist industry. And Hawaii's principal cash crop, not far behind tourism in annual dollar turnover, is not sugar, pineapples, flowers or macadamia nuts but *pakalolo*, better known as marijuana. Hawaiian home-grown – Maui Wowie, Puna Butter, Kauai Buds, etc. – was fetching between $2200 and $4000 per pound on the mainland in the summer of 1984.

In Stevenson's time in Hawaii the drug problem was not *Cannabis sativa* but the derivative of *Papaver somniferum* – opium. In one extraordinary scene in his novel *The Wrecker*, desperate men disembowel 6000 sacks of rice in a search for 240 pounds of opium.

Stevenson had seen 'the vice of opium-eating' in California and noticed the crime which addiction brought in its wake in the Marquesan chapters of *The South Seas*. He was critical of French official acquiescence in the trade, but added: 'Those who live in glass houses should not throw stones; as a subject of the British Crown, I am an unwilling shareholder in the largest opium business under heaven.'

Opium came to Honolulu with the first Chinese immigrants and throve from then on. Sometimes the monopoly was licensed, and when it was not the drug was smuggled. In 1886, King Kalakaua rescinded two earlier vetoes and licensed its sale again. The next year the Opium Scandal broke; it was revealed that Kalakaua had sold the opium monopoly to a Chinese for $80,000 while pocketing the lower bid of another. Backhanders from drug-barons were the excuse the whites needed for 'Reform'; and the 'Bayonet Constitution' of 1887 was the result. Six years later, Queen Lili'uokalani was deposed; five years after that Hawaii was annexed by the United States. There's no smoke without fire.

15

Stevenson's present to himself after finishing *The Master of Ballantrae* at Waikiki was a week alone on Big Island, Hawaii. He went to the Kona Coast, where today the most powerful Hawaiian marijuana, Kona Gold, is grown in secret plantations from Thai and Colombian seeds. It was, he wrote to Charles Baxter, 'a lovely week, among God's best – at least God's sweetest works, Polynesians. It has bettered me greatly.' To Will Low he said it was good to live, 'the only white folk, in a Polynesian village; and drink that warm, light *vin du pays* of human affection and enjoy that simple dignity of all about you'.

Stevenson stayed at Ho 'okena, some ten miles south of the spot in Kealakekua Bay where Captain Cook had been killed, a century before. While he was there, he rode north to the City of Refuge – Hale o Keawe – near the village of Hōnaunau. It is possible that he began writing his story 'The Bottle Imp' at this time.

Certainly, the story itself begins near Hōnaunau. A 'poor, brave and active' seaman called Keawe goes to San Francisco and buys, for fifty dollars, a bottle with a magic imp inside that can make the owner wealthy and powerful by granting every wish – previous owners had included Prester John, Napoleon and Captain Cook. There is a twist to this familiar fable: the man who dies owning the bottle will burn in hell for ever, and the devilish container can only be got rid of by selling it for less than the buyer paid.

The Polynesian setting of the story is described with the vivid detail of familiarity – the Kona Coast, Honolulu, San Francisco and Tahiti all figure in the tale. There is an ironic contrast with *Treasure Island*, which ends in a proliferation of wealth in diverse coinages; 'The Bottle Imp' ends conversely, in a desperate search for coins smaller than an American cent.

'The Bottle Imp' travelled with Stevenson throughout the islands before it was finally finished. In 1891, the missionary Arthur Claxton, working with RLS, translated it into Samoan – 'O Le Fanga Aitu' – and it thus became the first Samoan short story. Stevenson later told Conan Doyle that native visitors who had read the story were liable to ask, when being shown over his large house at Vailima, 'Where is the bottle?'

16

At Ho'okena, on 1 May 1889, Stevenson came face to face with leprosy. Two women suffering from the then incurable disease were being deported, amid keening lamentations, to permanent exile in the lazaretto on the island of Molokai. Standing on the rocks at Ho'okena, watching their small boat being rowed out through the surf of the reef to the waiting ship, Stevenson knew he had to see their dreadful destination for himself. A Catholic priest, Father Damien, had died there from leprosy a fortnight before. On 22 May 1889, Stevenson stepped ashore at the leprosy colony's jetty at Kalaupapa.

*

In 'The Bottle Imp', Stevenson called leprosy 'Chinese evil'. This was the Hawaiian nickname – *mai pake* – for the disease which first appeared in the islands in the 1830s. Perhaps it did come on a ship from China, but no one knows. The ancient Chinese certainly knew the disease, and its folk name was 'Reward from Heaven'. One legend said it began as divine punishment for necrophilia. If ordinary Chinese believed leprosy was a scourge for all kinds of sexual licence, then Hawaii's Protestants, already disturbed by the polymorphous pleasures of Polynesians, were righteously convinced of the link. In the 1880s, many held that leprosy was an advanced form of syphilis. Of course, it is nothing of the kind, emphatically neither a venereal disease, nor particularly contagious. But Protestants saw both leprosy and syphilis as the outward physical manifestations of inward moral decay. It confirmed their neurotic belief that Hawaiian culture itself was contaminated.

There was no cure for leprosy until the end of the Second World War, and the discovery of the sulfone drugs, particularly DDS, known as Dapsone. So in the nineteenth century isolation became the policy.

In 1865, the Hawaiian Legislature passed 'An Act to Prevent the Spread of Leprosy' and the Board of Health chose a peninsula jutting out below the northern cliffs of Molokai as the best site. Kalihi Hospital in Honolulu tested people for the disease; the sick were sent, from 1866 onwards, to Kalaupapa Peninsula, never to return. Sometimes they had to be taken by force, for many Hawaiians did not dread the disease, nor understand the need for segregation. Some healthy volunteers accompanied the patients as *kokua* or helpers; other patients had to fend for themselves in the lawless conditions of a death-camp. In its first few years Kalaupapa was a fearful and desperate place.

*

On Saturday, 10 May 1873, a Catholic priest came ashore to join them. He had been born Joseph de Veuster, in Belgium, but was now called Father Damien. Originally, he was to stay a fortnight, and other priests were to be rotated through, but Damien, a strong peasant of a man, found plenty to do and wanted to stay. The smell was so bad that he took up pipe-smoking. He was thirty-three years old, and lived among the leprosy sufferers for the next sixteen years until he himself died of the disease.

Meanwhile, the Protestants in Honolulu were worrying about 'property values' and the safety of their own fair skins. Congregations were urged to segregate their infected members according to the laws of God and Caesar. No white Protestant minister went to live at the leprosy settlement in Damien's lifetime.

17

I had been to the museum at Father Damien's birthplace months before, on a side-trip from *An Inland Voyage*. It was in a place called Ninde, outside the village of Tremeloo, near Leuven, Belgium. There were poppies by the Flanders roadside, pollarded trees rising from the mist, and fields of potato and chicory. It was Ascension Day. Father Damien's coffin was in a small room directly under the one where he had been born – on 3 January 1840 – seventh child among four boys and four girls. Nineteen-year-old Joseph de Veuster joined the Congregation of the Sacred Hearts of Jesus and Mary, and took the name Damien. He was not yet ordained when he took his sick brother's place as a missionary to the Hawaiian Islands in 1863.

Old Father Vanfrachem projected a slide-show at Ninde and for my benefit the commentary was in English. It recounted the Judaeo-Christian opprobrium of leprosy, but pointed to those who had embraced the outcasts as an emblem of suffering humanity: Christ, St Francis, Gandhi. The commentary said that Damien had had to build over 6000 coffins in his sixteen years on the peninsula. Then he contracted leprosy himself. There were photos of him with his right arm in a sling, a pustuled left hand and a lumpy face. The photo of him on his death-bed showed him with half-opened mouth and fixed eyes. It is impossible to see what they are looking at: the horror of this world, or the certainty of the next. Damien died at the beginning of Holy Week in 1889.

*

The Belgian King and Government had asked to have Damien's body back in 1936. I hitch-hiked to Leuven to see his tomb in a crypt. Across the road from the church was the home of the Sacred Hearts' priests. Father Paul Aerts, a burly bearded man in ordinary clothes, offered me a cup of coffee and a cigar and gave me ten vigorous minutes of his time. He was a splendid man, outspoken and as honest as a rock, but the kind of rock the Lord would fit into a whirling combative sling. He had worked in the prisons of Peru, where the drug-barons and the bent military ruled through terror and violence, and was not the sort to keep his mouth shut. He was trouble, as good men sometimes must be.

'You must understand,' he said, 'that in Damien's time, leprosy was believed to be a moral punishment, like AIDS today. There is not only suffering, but guilt and shame and fear.'

I wondered why Damien was not a saint.

'Damien is a problem for two reasons. You remember the accusations of Hyde?' (The Honolulu Protestant C. M. Hyde had alleged that Damien contracted leprosy from his 'vices'.) 'Inter-course, breaking the vow of celibacy, would be too bad. And Damien was headstrong. They do not like a disobedient priest, one who says "no" to his superiors, one who is more concerned for the rights of the oppressed and poor. But we shall see. It is not yet a hundred years since his death.'

Father Aerts puffed on his strong cigar. 'You know, Damien is very Flemish in his stubborn character – the fighter, the obsessive.' He laughed uproariously, and banged his fist on the table so the coffee-cups jumped. He gave me the address of St Patrick's Church in Honolulu.

'Talk to Mrs Irene Litoto. She will help you.'

18

St Patrick's Church was on Seventh Avenue, a hot wide street in eastern Honolulu. Mrs Irene Litoto said it would not be possible to spend a night at Kalaupapa Settlement, but she would get in touch with the priest there, Father Fernández, to see if I could go for a day. You could not just turn up there, but had to have a 'sponsor' in the community.

The small museum by the church had photos of Damien in a dusty soutane at the bare-looking settlement. A tiny scrap of red paisley material had come from Damien's arm-sling. He was given it by Mother Marianne Cope, a Franciscan from a convent in Syracuse, New York, who in 1888 led the first party of nuns to settle at Kalaupapa, where they ran the Bishop Home for Girls.

Mrs Litoto called me at the YMCA early one morning. 'Father says it's OK for tomorrow. Book your flight – nine o'clock out, four-thirty return.'

*

I woke on 13 September around six as the sun was rising. It had been warm enough to sleep without a sheet. I lay thinking about the day ahead, and realized my mind had been shrinking from the idea of leprosy and the coming experience. Part of me was afraid; but it ironed out into a blank acceptance.

As the Royal Hawaiian Airlines ten-seater plane took off, a mushroom cloud of smoke uncoiled from the land beyond Pearl Harbor, and my heart jumped. But they were only burning sugar-cane trash. We flew east over Honolulu and Waikiki Beach and a view of roads and settlement eating their way up the green flank of Oahu's mountain ridge. Past Diamond and Koko Heads, we were over the sea, which gleamed in armoured plates wherever the sun broke through the grey clouds.

Stevenson left for Molokai on the afternoon of 21 May 1889 on the small steamer *Kilauea Hou*. Two nuns were also on the ship, going to join their Franciscan sisters at Kalaupapa. Sister M. Crescentia Eilers, travelling with Sister M. Irene Schorp, later told another nun what had happened to them.

> A very courteous gentleman . . . came several times to see if they were all right and if there was any service he could render them. Sister said they were as comfortable as could be expected and thanked him for his kind solicitude. Still he persisted – at last Sister said 'I should be very grateful if you would see if our cat is all right, I fear that some freight may have covered him up and perhaps be smothered.' So he started off to hunt up her cat. In a short time he came back saying 'Your cat is all right. I found him and gave him some milk.'

This gentleman was the great RLS.

It was a rough night, and Stevenson could hear the nuns being sea-sick. In the early morning they were wallowing under 'the stupendous cliffs' of Molokai.

*

Molokai is impressive from the air, rising sharply out of the sea into volcanic cliffs rimmed by white foam. Flying in from the west the peninsula is a smudge, then a finger, then a flat brown plain jutting out below cliffs now green with vegetation. The aircraft dropped below the cliff top as we came into land on the scorched brown earth.

*

Seeing the 2000-foot *pali* or cliff from sea-level made Stevenson's heart sink. Ships were allowed to land people at the settlement, but not to take them off, so his only way out was up the impossible looking cliff. But he could not back out now. He stared at the promontory as they approached Kalaupapa:

> . . . lowland, quite bare and bleak and harsh, a little town of wooden houses, two churches, . . . a landing-stair, all unsightly, sour, northerly, lying athwart the sunrise, with a great wall of the pali cutting the world out on the south.

Stevenson watched the first small boat disembarking new inmates for the leprosy settlement, 'about a dozen, one poor child very horrid, one white man . . .'.

*

The aircraft taxied to the wooden airport building – a shed with seats – and we got out to dry heat, scrub and few trees. There was no priest. I looked at the Lions Club sign

Kalaupapa Settlement
Established 1865
Area 12.17 sq ml
Population:
Residents – 111
Staff – 45
KALAWAO COUNTY

A white lighthouse tower stood at the northern tip of the peninsula. But here the rocks were lava and the grass was burned brown.

*

Stevenson got into the second boat with the two nuns. He was screwing his courage to the sticking point – 'my horror of the horrible is about my weakest point' – when he noticed one of the Sisters was crying quietly under her veil. He cried a little too, then felt better and tried to cheer her up. 'Ladies, God Himself is here to give you welcome. I'm sure it is good for me to be beside you . . . I thank you for myself and the good you do me.' Then they were at the landing stairs, 'and there was a great crowd, hundreds of (God save us!) pantomime masks in poor human flesh, waiting to receive the sisters and the new patients'.

*

The group of men in another plane included State Department of Health Officials and Federal Park Rangers. Kalaupapa had been made a National Park by President Carter in 1980. I asked a young doctor if he could give me a lift to Father Fernández's house in the Settlement. We set off along a rocky unpaved road with lava boulders by the side and reddish dust on the scrub. The cliff reared high ahead, a permanent wall. The priest's blue van appeared, trailing dust, the doctor waved it down and I changed vehicles.

[280]

The van was driven by Sister Dativr, a fifty-two-year-old Franciscan in nurse's head-dress and uniform. With her was Father Jim Nash, a retired priest. We bumped into the settlement. Busted cars were parked outside verandahs and wooden porches; the place seemed deserted. Sister Dativr told me how most of the patients were elderly – average age sixty; and though they were now free to leave, they had chosen to stay where they were cared for, among people they knew. At the Main Office I signed in, having read the 'Instructions for Visitors to Kalaupapa Settlement'. Photographs of patients may not be taken. Unescorted riding or walking about the Settlement will not be permitted.

We drove to the old Bishop Home for Girls (1888–1931), a white and green wooden building. A bare flagpole stood on the old croquet lawn.

'That's Mother Marianne's grave.'

On a stone nearby a patient had painted in white, 'Smile! It don't broke your face.'

19

Stevenson felt shame among the leprosy patients at the dock; he was 'useless and a spy'. I knew the feeling: I would have been ashamed to pursue the few patients I saw that day, who stepped back into the shadows on seeing a stranger.

RLS set off across the promontory from Kalaupapa to the guest-house at Kalawao where he was to stay. Everything soon changed; the fear had been imaginary. 'All horror was quite gone from me: to see these dread creatures smile and look happy was beautiful.'

As soon as he reached the guest-house he fell asleep. Writing that night to his wife, he believed his crushing fatigue 'was moral and a measure of my cowardice'. The next morning, 23 May 1889, he made his way to the Bishop Home for Girls. He had heard about them in Honolulu, and had sent them a new croquet set.

Sister Leopoldina Burns, a beautiful thirty-four-year-old nun, was passing through the cottages, attending to the sick around ten o'clock when she saw 'a strange looking man, hanging on the fence. I knew at once he was not a leper, and . . . I walked over to speak to him, and would not have been surprised had he told me he was a tramp and wanted help.'

Sister Leopoldina's account of that day and subsequent ones was written in a school-lined exercise book in the 1920s. It is a little-known glimpse of RLS at his best, and I quote it here in her spelling and punctuation

> . . . his thin pale face, locks of shining black hair had dropped on his broad very white forhead, beeded with prespiration for the morning was hot and he had walked far. his remarkable eyes were sunk with dark rings around them, he was a small man, dressed in gray, with a bright red silk scarf tied round his waste hanging far down on the side, his long bony fingers were clasping a large hat. I greeted him and asked, is there anything I can do for you? Oh! he said with a pleasant smile I was just admiring your cheerfull home, it is the only pleasant place I find in the Settlement, and wish to see the Rev. Mother if I am not too early. You are not too early I told him, come through the little gate and go around to the frunt door and you will find her. Had I known who he was I think I would have accompanied him to the house, but he smiled and bowed with his hat still in his hand, he disappeared around the corner of the home to the front door where our sweet gentle Mother welcomed him. When I told Mother how I took him for a tramp, she smiled and said, well he is the best tramp I ever met, and I know she said the tramping he is doing here is not good for him as the poor man is subjected to hemorrhages . . .

Mother Marianne Cope thanked Stevenson for his beautiful new croquet set and said how much she wished there was someone:

> . . . to teach the poor unfortunate girls as we are only three Sisters and the sick and sore require all our time. Why Mother if you allow me, I will teach them. No Mother told him, I will not allow you to be so exposed to this frightly disease remember they are lepers! but Mother how about you and the Sisters? he laughed and said they are to be ready tomorrow morning for their first lession your lawn is so nice I shall enjoy teaching them . . .

Stevenson saw round the Home:

the general impression . . . was one of cheerfulness, cleanliness and comfort. The dormitories were airy, the beds neatly made; at every bedhead was a trophy of Christmas cards, pictures and photographs, some framed with shells, and all arranged with care and taste. In many of the beds, besides, a doll lay pillowed.

He met some of the patients, who had not gone out guava-hunting with the rest:

One, I remember, white with pain, the tears standing in her eyes. But thank God, pain is not the rule in this revolting malady.

Sister Leopoldina writes:

Poor dear children could hardly believe that a fine well white man would not be afraid, and why he did not shrink from them and shun them as all other white men do. The next morning quite early he came, the girls were ready but they kept away thinking it could not be possible but when he called to them come girls I only have a few days to teach you, and you must know your game well so that you can beat me or I shall not be happy leaving you. In a few minutes they were all at ease they knew that he ment to be their friend in every way, and now each choose her color with mallet in hand ready for the game. Mr Stevenson with his mallet in hand looked as if his whole heart and mind was all interested. Now he said I will take the lead, he worked on until it was near noon and he seemed to enjoy teaching them, but how tired he was. He had learned nearly all their names, and it was remarkable how quickly they were learning and how very happy and interested they were. Mr Stevenson had become one of them so that they could forget at least for a little while that they were victomes doomed for life, unfortunate children 'God pity them.' When Mr Stevenson went to the house after his nearly three hours exite teaching he was tired out, his face flushed, and eyes sparkling. Mother told him in her sweet gentle way, it is not right for you to exert yourself it may be dangerous in your condition. His answer was Mother you have some very clever young ladies if I am not mistaken Waikahe will know the game better than I before the end of my visit I have had a very pleasant morning and I will be here tomorrow afternoon.

RLS had lunch with the Sisters – 'a little old-maid meal' – and rested afterwards, as Sister Leopoldina wrote 'injoying our Mother's edifing conversation her easy angelic maner refreshed him and he returned to the Doctor's house'.

The next afternoon he was back again, and soon on the lawn with the seven girls:

He put such excitement and life in the game that the time passed too quickly. It was interesting to watch them. Mr Stevenson stripped off his coat and hat and working so that every now and than he would throw himself on the soft grass to rest until it was his turn to play . . . he enjoyed playing with them and making belive he felt very sad when they beet him.

It was nearly ninety degrees in the shade, and when they stopped around five o'clock Stevenson was tired:

. . . he was so pale and his breathing so quick that Mother was anxious. What can we do she would say should he have hemorrhage in this dreadful place . . . not even ice we could get for him. He is not thinking of himself he is bound those girls must know how to play before he leaves them, and he succeede they all know the game so well . . .

He continued coming every day spending most of his time with the girls on the lawn, when the games were over he would have his tea, and a restful visit with our gentle loving mother before returning to the Doctor's home.

In the evening it was funny to hear the little girls talking about him. *Sister he only one howlie (white man) not scart of us all the other white man too much fraid he our good friend we like he stay with us he not fraid us leper.*

*

When he returned to Honolulu, Stevenson sent a 500 dollar Wetemayer piano, made in Tyrol, for the Bishop Home girls. He also sent a poem to 'Reverend Sister Maryanne, Matron of the Bishop Home, Kalapapa'.

> To see the infinite pity of this place,
> The mangled limb, the devastated face,
> The innocent sufferers smiling at the rod,
> A fool were tempted to deny his God.
>
> He sees, and shrinks. But if he look again,
> Lo, beauty springing from the breast of pain! –
> He marks the sisters on the painful shores,
> And even a fool is silent and adores.
> Robert Louis Stevenson

Kalawao, May 22nd 1889.

20

Sister Dativr's van bounced down the road through thick *haole koa* scrub, travelling over the hump of Makanula from Kalaupapa to Kalawao. The day was heating up, old lava absorbing the terrific sun, steaming the green cliff and making a shimmering haze of the distance. The bush was full of Java plums, sloe-like fruits which made your mouth pucker when you ate them. Sister Dativr parked the van across the road from St Philomena's, the church Father Damien had built. All the other buildings at Kalawao had gone, eaten by termites and overgrown by tropical vegetation. Cattle browsed among dry, fallen palm branches where the old Baldwin Home for Boys once stood. In the sea beyond the palm trees reared the volcanic loaf called Bread Island, and to the east huge black cliffs ran steeply into the Pacific.

We went into the pale blue interior of the simple church. I read a notice that $83,663.96c had been raised for repairs, and that Bishop J. J. Scanlan had denied a request that the Diocese of Honolulu turn over the church property on Kalaupapa to the State of Hawaii as it was 'a violation of the Church's role and not in keeping with the memory of Father Damien'.

13 September was St John Chrysostom's day. Father Jim said Mass with Sister Dativr assisting. He kissed the tiny cross on the white stole and put it round his neck.

I slipped out of the church. Where Damien's house had once stood, there was now a grove of waving palms. The graveyard was littered with dry brown fronds and rotting coconuts.

Damien's empty grave had rusting railings and black paint fading off the solid cross. I walked down towards the sea over scrubby grass and clinker. Kalawao Settlement had entirely disappeared; the guest-house where Stevenson had stayed with Dr Swift had gone, so had the big hospital that Jack London saw on his visit in 1907. At the edge of the plain, the rock dropped forty feet to gnarled black lava where the sea tore itself to tatters. The *pali* behind, Stevenson's 'viridescent cliff', was the home of wild deer and goats. It was a gloomy and spectacular coast, and deserted Kalawao had an unsettling presence.

I went back to the church. Father Jim was packing his chalice and paten, cruets for water and wine, purificator, folded stole and corporal into an old tartan night-bag. Outside St Philomena's Sister Dativr said, as straightforwardly as my Seychelles Nanny talking of ghosts:

'The voices were whispering this day, and you will hear them in your heart.'

21

At the Mother Marianne Library, Sister Dativr put a video on the machine, a 1982 TV documentary called *Kalaupapa: The Refuge*. It told how the settlement had gone from being a prison to a haven, through interviews with doctors and above all patients.

'First thing I saw was de lighthouse. Well, we in some sort of place now. Den a cliff. Dey told me I have leper. I didn't understand dat. A leper is contagious, contaminated to de family. Dey told me de long words. I hid. Dey kept coming. It was twenty years before I saw my family again.'

Things began to change in 1945 when sulfone drugs came to Hawaii. Ulcers and sores began to heal and disappear within three months. 'You become sort of human again.' With chemotherapy fewer patients were sent to Kalaupapa and new cases could be treated as outpatients in Honolulu. For the people who had spent most of their lives there, married there, had children there (though they were taken away) Kalaupapa became a refuge, where there were friends, 'people around like us'. It did not matter what the patients looked like, they were people; they had lived through an extraordinary and terrible experience, and they were funny, wise, grouchy, articulate, and sometimes sad about it. In the daily living of their lot, there was often a philosophical cheerfulness that was very heartening. My worries paled in comparison; if these people could cope, with humour and dignity, what on earth could I have to complain about? You could put your fear and pity away: they were just people.

22

I had lunch with Father Jim Nash and Sister Dativr in the priest's house. Father Fernandez was still out fishing. When Father Jim went for a rest, I looked into the bathroom where the shower was quietly running. In the bath lay a steely-blue four-foot wahoo fish, with a gash in its flank, cooling in the heat. There were fishing rods on the verandah, and one against the shelves in the yellow and orange sitting-room. There were fishy knick-knacks, game-fishing books next to *Reader's Digest, Catholic Digest, and Hawaiian Fishing News* on a small table.

I wondered what sort of man he was. In his cluttered office there was a plaque on the wall.

Det 2 1136 USAF SAS
Defense Nuclear Agency
↑　↑　↑
United States of America
Captain Nobincio Fernandez
August 75 – August 76
Johnston Atoll

It was near Johnston Atoll, a speck 900 miles south-west of Honolulu, that Stevenson had first conceived *The Wrecker* in June 1889. Now you were forbidden to get off the plane at Johnston Atoll; poison gas was said to be stored there. The Defense Nuclear Agency were the Lords of the Bomb. But maybe Father Fernandez had been the padre.

He came in through the door from the porch, a dark man in dark glasses, wearing a grey sweat-soaked sweat-shirt with a heart figure cut out of the shoulder, blue shorts and rubber flip-flops. He stuck out his hand.

'Nick. Sorry couldn't be wid ju. Help yourself to drinks, soda, whatever.'

In the kitchen he gathered knives from a drawer, got an ice-box and we drove down in his pick-up to a table with a tap under the palm trees south of the jetty. I threw an old coconut for a wildly excited dog called Illio, and watched the priest at work on the fish above the black rocks and the crashing surf. He was the sort of man who might have got on famously with St Peter. Expertly he gutted, scaled, sliced and dressed the wahoo, packing it into the ice-box to cook later for the patients, his parishioners. He showed me the Japanese way of slicing at an angle so there is no skin but good steaks of fresh fish. He was a tough, practical man, impatient with words but not with deeds. I was reminded of the robustness of Paul Aerts.

Father Fernandez also had an open sore on his ankle – dark skin broken by pink and white lumpiness, flecked with blood. Perhaps he had had some accident, but I did not dare ask him what it was.

'With suffering we become part of the Christian myth,' said Dr Colin of the leprosarium in Graham Greene's novel *A Burnt-Out Case*.

23

Stevenson, in his week at the Settlement, had toured the hospital with Dr Swift and Joseph Dutton as they dressed the patients' sores. He particularly asked after Father Damien, who had died in the community the month before. His comments on Damien, in a letter to Sidney Colvin, are interesting because they are those of an impartial outsider, a non-Catholic, who got first-hand accounts from those who had known the priest. Stevenson wrote:

> Of old Damien, whose weaknesses and worse I heard fully, I think only the more. It was a European peasant: dirty, bigoted, untruthful, unwise, tricky, but superb with generosity, residual candour and fundamental good-humour: convince him he had done wrong (it might take hours of insult) and he would undo

what he had done and like his corrector better. A man, with all
the grime and paltriness of mankind, but a saint and hero all
the more for that.

Stevenson spent some time talking with Mr Strahan, a Phil-
adelphia-born Scot and Pacific rover who was now blind from his
leprosy. Strahan called himself 'a hard old coon', 'an old tough'. He
had seen the guano, copra and labour trades in the South Seas when
they were no business for pretty gentlemen. Now blind, he wrote
poetry: 'It's dogg'rel, that's what it is. I'm not an educated man, but
the idea's there. You see I've nothing to do but sit here and think.'

After Fanny Stevenson was widowed, she treasured the letter she
got from Henry James, and one other. It was unsigned, in pencil, on
a scrap of paper that had come from Hawaii.

> Mrs Stevenson, Dear Madam: All over the world people will
> be sorry for the death of Robert Louis Stevenson, but none will
> mourn him more than the blind white leper of Molokai.

*

Father Nobincio Fernández, who was also a Lieutenant-Colonel in
the Air Force Reserve, drove me to the airstrip. He said Paul Aerts's
name had got me in, and I blessed the Flemish priest in Leuven. I
tried to say what the day had meant; fumbled a donation. Father
Fernandez stuffed the note back in the pocket of my white jacket.

'Don't worry about it, Nick.' He took off his dark glasses and
looked straight at me. 'Just write the truth, OK?'

A San Francisco journalist had recently written a damaging and
sensationalist piece about the community. Stevenson had known the
type, for whom 'any design of writing appears excuse sufficient for
the most gross intrusion'.

We shook hands. 'I won't forget.'

'Take care now.' Father Fernandez gunned the motor, and
disappeared down the dusty road to Kalaupapa.

24

I went to Leahi Hospital, near Diamond Head at the eastern end of
Oahu, and met the pathologist Dr Olaf K. Skinsnes, in the Leprosy
Atelier laboratory on the fifth floor. He was an alert sixty-

seven-year-old with a greying moustache and bright eyes. Even with his right arm in a sling from a recent fall, he could still manage to load and light his pipe. His Norwegian parents had been medical missionaries to China; he was born there and would soon return as Honorary Professor of Pathology at a medical college in Guangdong. Leprosy had been his work since the 1940s – he took the first batch of sulfone drugs into South China on a sampan from Hong Kong, and had published around 120 papers on the medical and social pathology of the disease. He had been part of the team in Hawaii that first grew *Bacillus leprae* on artificial media in 1975, doing for leprosy what Trudeau had done for TB.

Kalaupapa had changed; the old autocratic control of pre-sulfone isolation days with its zealous restrictions, fumigation of all mail etc. had been relaxed, partly thanks to the Citizens' Committee the patients themselves had formed. No new cases had been sent to Molokai for a long time. The old epidemic of leprosy had burned itself out in Hawaii and most new cases came in from Samoa and the Philippines, and were treated as out-patients.

Language was important to Dr Skinsnes. 'Hansen's disease' was not a useful euphemism for leprosy, but the noun 'leper' with its hostile connotations was now considered offensive. People with leprosy have contracted a particular disease, they are not defined by it.

Nobody really knew how many people in the world had leprosy: perhaps around ten million in 1966. But Dr Skinsnes told me that the World Health Organization once estimated mainland China's figure four times higher than it really was by extrapolating from Taiwan's statistics. The current world trend was stable, declining, or ready to decline, due to modern treatment and the rising standard of living which improved hygiene. Only about 4 per cent of the world was susceptible to leprosy, and basic hygiene could keep it at bay.

I left thinking about a story he told me. When his missionary parents were in China during the civil wars, the writer Agnes Smedley turned up at their door one day.

'I'm a Communist, not a Christian,' she said fiercely, 'but I'm sick.'

'I'm a Christian,' was the reply, 'and you are welcome.'

*

Dr Skinsnes's daughter, Anwei Skinsnes, was writing a two-volume book on leprosy in the Hawaiian Islands. A Norwegian, Gerhad

Henrik Armauer Hansen, had first identified and described *Bacillus leprae* in 1873, and now a woman of Norwegian descent was chronicling the historical drama of the disease in one important locale.

She was a friendly woman in her early thirties who was unaware of her clear beauty, or found it irrelevant. Anwei reminded me that leprosy figured in Stevenson's novel *The Black Arrow*, written long before he came to the Pacific. She thought he was attracted as well as repelled by the horrible; fear was mixed with a little desire. She entirely discredited one story Lloyd Osbourne had told of Stevenson's time in Honolulu. According to him, a French doctor came to see RLS at Waikiki in 1889, and confessed all his secrets to the writer. The next day, Osbourne claimed, they read in the newspaper that the Frenchman had shot himself in front of a mirror, unable to bear the fact that he had leprosy. The story was just sensationalism; the same sort of thing went on today, witness the crass journalist who had been in Kalaupapa recently. Stirring up prejudice and fear doesn't help anyone.

A more enlightened approach to leprosy began in 1949, with the opening of Hale Mohalu hospital near Pearl City. Its philosophy had been rehabilitation rather than isolation. From 1949 to 1969, only thirty-two patients were sent to Kalaupapa, and others were treated and discharged. Isolation had ended in 1969.

The new out-patients never lost their place in the community, but what about the old in-patients? Some at Kalaupapa wanted to live out their days there, but others wanted to come back into the world, 'have some fun' as one put it. This was why Hale Mohalu was important, as a bridgehead; the patients could get the varieties of food, friendship and family closeness that they couldn't at Kalaupapa, and the locals were accustomed to them.

But after a long battle, Hale Mohalu had closed, and the eleven acre site was up for 're-development'. A coalition had plans for a housing complex for the elderly and handicapped, which would include ten or fifteen units for long-term residents of Kalaupapa who wanted to come back into the world. The plan was enlightened and humane. But the other scheme for Hale Mohalu had money and political clout behind it, and public prejudice on its side – bulldoze the lot and turn it into baseball fields.

*

Anwei Skinsnes placed more hope in the patients than she did in some of the clever scientists who had learned to infect armadillos and monkeys with leprosy. The Great-White-Father syndrome still ruled generally – a lot of male doctors talking at conferences with no patients present. 'I want to get the patients talking,' she said, 'they know far more than I do. We should be learning from them.'

She had set up an oral history project at Kalaupapa; knowing some of the patients had been extraordinary. 'They're very special people: you get so much more than you can give.'

The world did not always value the victims of leprosy, however. The patients at Kalaupapa had been taught to be good Americans, to salute the flag and love their country. One patient, who believed it all with true simplicity, received one of those computer-personalized letters from Ronald Reagan, appealing for funds for the Republican Party. 'My President needs me,' he said, 'he's asking me for my money to save the country.' He sent his savings – $1200. Later he went to Washington DC, eager to be thanked, an innocent old guy from Kalaupapa Settlement. Not a single Republican official would see him.

25

Stevenson left Honolulu on the trading schooner *Equator* on 24 June 1889. He, Fanny, Lloyd and Ah Fu were joined by Joe Strong, who was going to take pictures for a money-making diorama. They were bound for the Gilbert Islands (then independent, not yet colonized by the British), and King David Kalakaua brought a brass band to the dock to see them off.

From the Gilberts they went to Western Samoa in early December 1889. In the new year, Stevenson purchased the land where he would later build his home Vailima. He and Fanny took the steamer to Sydney, Australia – 'this is like to be our metropolis' – for stores and supplies. Belle Strong was already living there, staying at a theatrical boarding house on the £15 a month allowance Stevenson had given her, and met them off the SS *Lübeck* on 13 February 1890. Stevenson liked Sydney, though Fanny saw 'the criminal stamp' everywhere, and he joined the Union Club in its fine building on Bligh Street. On 19 February, he wrote a calm letter to Henry James from there, praising his *Solution* as 'exquisite art'. A few days later his mood changed violently.

A man at dinner asked him if he had read the letter written by a Protestant clergyman about Father Damien of Molokai, published by the Sydney newspaper *The Presbyterian* the previous October. Stevenson had not seen it, but when he did his rage was incandescent. The letter was an outrageous libel: he determined to reply at once.

The Protestant missionary, Charles McEwen Hyde, had written to a San Francisco friend professing surprise at 'the extravagant newspaper laudations' of Father Damien. 'The simple truth is, he was a coarse, dirty man, headstrong and bigoted.' Hyde alleged that Damien had been disobedient and 'had no hand in the reforms and improvements inaugurated'. Worse still, Damien 'was not a pure man in his relations with women, and the leprosy of which he died should be attributed to his vices and carelessness'.

Hyde's son later admitted this was a mistake. There had been an unchaste priest in the Hawaiian Islands, but his name was Fabien, not Damien. In the meantime the dead man found a champion, who would speak for him.

It should be remembered that Stevenson had actually met the Reverend Dr Hyde, in his fine house on Beretania Street, Honolulu, when he was looking for passage on a missionary ship. He had seen his face, shaken his hand, and spoken his name. But it was not just the name 'Hyde' that recalled Stevenson's own parable of hypocrisy, *Dr Jekyll and Mr Hyde*. This Reverend Dr Hyde embodied the worst side of Protestantism in Hawaii, and the Presbyterianism that had suffocated Stevenson's own early life in Edinburgh. The vehemence of his reply to Hyde is extraordinary. Legend has it that he wrote his 'Father Damien: An Open Letter to the Rev Dr Hyde of Honolulu' in one day, 25 February 1890. It is passionately incautious and Quixotic; RLS had found a cause and an enemy – 'with you I rejoice to feel the button off the foil and to plunge home'.

The 'Open Letter' is *argumentum ad hominem*. Stevenson's target is the stout Reverend Dr Hyde, seated at ease in his fine home while Damien 'toiled and rotted . . . under the cliffs of Kalawao'. Stevenson does not try to refute the charges against Damien; he even supposes '– and God forgive me for supposing it –' that the worst might be true. It is not material. The real evil lies in Hyde's own envy and malice against a better man. The scorn is toe-curling. Stevenson is frank about Damien's faults – 'the truth that is suppressed by friends is the readiest weapon of the enemy' – yet insists he was a great man. For Stevenson, who had a stereoscopic view of humanity, dirt and stubbornness were no bar to a man's heroic saintliness.

RLS fully expected to be sued for libel; he thought the real Hyde would beat him down as the fictional Hyde had Sir Danvers Carew. But in the event the Reverend Dr Hyde only called Stevenson (in conversation) 'a Bohemian crank' and tried to brush him aside in print: 'His invective may be brilliant, but it is like a glass coin . . . shivered into fragments of worthless glitter when brought to the test of truthfulness.' Nevertheless the Hawaiian newspaper *Elele Poakolu* published Stevenson's letter as a broadsheet and Hyde won little support.

26

Molokai was one of the experiences that modified Stevenson's initial 'great prejudice' against missionaries in the Pacific, which became one of critical acceptance.

In 1893, in a paper read to the General Assembly of the Presbyterian Church of New South Wales, he urged that mission: aries should not overturn all native ways, but rather:

> . . . develop that which is good . . . in the inherent ideas of the race . . . Because we are, one and all . . . the children of our fathers . . . We make a great blunder when we expect people to give up in a moment the whole belief of ages, the whole morals of the family, sanctified by the traditions of the heart, and not to lose something essential.

This was his advice to members of his own Protestant denomination. Privately he considered the Catholics did a better job of adapting to island traditions; most of his servants at Vailima were Catholic boys, and Stevenson was a good friend of the French-speaking Catholic Bishop Broyer of Samoa. The white-bearded

Bishop confided to an Australian journalist his belief that Stevenson would have converted to Catholicism in time. He never did, but G. K. Chesterton and Graham Greene made the move in his place.

At all events, Stevenson did not forget Molokai, and in March 1893 sent a recent portrait of himself, with good wishes, to Mother Marianne Cope at Kalaupapa.

*

SACRA CONGREGAZIONE PER LE CAUSE DEI SANTI
Rome, 9 October 1985

Dear Mr Rankin,

Your letter . . . was recently forwarded to this Congregation for the Causes of the Saints. In that letter, you asked for information regarding the Causes of MOTHER MARIANNA COPE and FATHER DAMIEN.

In regard to Father Damien: he was declared to have lived an heroically virtuous life, worthy of imitation by the faithful, by Pope Paul VI on 7 July 1977 and thus has merited the title 'Venerable' Father Damien. For beatification, one miracle is required and yet to be verified.

In regard to Mother Marianna, her Cause was given the 'nihil obstat' of the Holy See on 28 July 1983. Thus, the investigation is at the diocesan level under the direction of the Bishop of Honolulu.

Hoping that this satisfies your request, I am

Sincerely yours in Christ,

Archbishop Traian Crisan

Secretary

27

My quest might have ended in the State of Hawaii, if Stevenson had been buried at Honolulu. He almost died at Waikiki on his second visit to Oahu in 1893. On 28 September, the day after giving a lecture on 'the long drawn out brawl of Scottish history', Stevenson took a cab from Waikiki into Honolulu. Quinn, the driver, had a new horse, which bolted. For eight terrifying minutes Stevenson sat white-faced in the back of the hurtling cab. It was like De Quincey's

'Vision of Sudden Death'. Soon afterwards RLS took to his bed, sharply ill.

Fanny came up from Apia to look after him, and she and Dr Trousseau forbade him to revisit the Scottish Thistle Club in Honolulu, who were going to make him their Honorary Chieftain. But he treasured the small silver thistle pin they gave him; he would be buried wearing it.

*

It was a gloomy farewell to Hawaii. The whites had deposed the monarchy nine months before, and Stevenson had several long talks with ex-Queen Lili'uokalani, then living under semi-house arrest at Washington Place. RLS was against the proposed US annexation and told Robert Catton he feared he 'should have to write about it'.

Archibald Cleghorn saw the Stevensons off on Friday 27 October 1893. When they shook hands for the last time on the *Mariposa*, Stevenson said: 'Now Cleghorn, if I can be of any service to the Royal cause in Hawaii, just drop me a line, and I will come right back here.'

But no one could stop Hawaii becoming a part of the Home of the Brave and the Land of the Free. Sanford 'Pineapple' Dole declared it a republic in 1894, and US annexation followed in 1898, in the summer of the year when the USA also declared war on Spain, invaded Cuba and the Philippines, gained Guam and Puerto Rico, and became an Empire.

SAMOA

I read the *Fiji Sun* on the aeroplane from Fiji to Western Samoa. It was very much a Murdoch tabloid with local variants – a primly buttoned-up Melanesian on page 3; an Indian film director talking about 'injecting box-office *masala*'; a '*Sun* says' editorial – 'Who the hell do our football referees think they are?'

The island of Savai'i appeared to port, and I folded the paper away. The westerly tip of the island was dark green bush sloping gently into pale green waters inside the reef. The Air Pacific stewardess handed out boiled sweets from a wicker basket and I filled in my Western Samoa immigration form. I was tired, nearing the end of my journey and my money, but also very curious. Samoa would be different from anything I had known, with a culture and liquidly euphonious language I could not hope to penetrate in the little time I had left.

OFU FAAOLA LALO IFO O LOU

Life Vest Under Your Seat

There were green and blue shallows to port and thousands of coconut palms in graceful ranks to starboard as we descended to the island of Upolu. The aeroplane taxied to tiny Faleolo Airport and stopped.

Through the window I could see strapping men wearing the Samoan wrap-around skirt or *lavalava*, and skinny horses tethered in the gloom of a coconut grove across the road. A bearded Samoan with *lavalava* and rubber flip-flops boarded the plane and walked down the aisle with two aerosol cans of insecticide fiercely spraying against Fijian bugs. There was a line of blue tattoos round his right wrist. I sneezed violently and looked out of the porthole with new clarity to see an advertisement for VAILIMA beer. So this really was *Samoa I Sisifo* – Western Samoa.

*

In bright sunshine I made my way through a mob of taxi-drivers, passengers 'friends and relatives to the white airport bus. It was a half-hour drive eastward along the northern coast to our destination, Apia. The narrator of *The Beach of Falesá* says that when he first stepped ashore in Samoa, 'The world was like all new painted.'

I felt as if I had been given new spectacles, looking out at Samoa on that first sparkling morning. Clear sky, pearly sea; vivid explosions of pink and red hibiscus and frangipani blossom; long curving palms on the beach; villages of beehive-thatched houses, *fale*, with wooden pillars open to the breezes; lava boulders by the road picked out in whitewash; brindled pigs wandering around like dogs; schoolchildren in bright uniforms (white shirts, scarlet *lavalavas*); a man fishing in the shallows; brown women with heavy black hair washing clothes in a stream; a white horse cantering on a lunge-line – all as strange and as familiar as a picture by Gauguin. Through Faleatiu and Faleasiu, Tufelele and Tuanoii, Malie and Vaitele, I rode open-mouthed with delight and happiness. The Western Samoan flag, red with one blue corner containing five white stars, snapped over every village green; the other huts clustered round the *fale* of the chief or *matai*, and the whitewashed church. We passed the Vailima Brewery and were into the scruffy outskirts of Apia. A Tarzan movie played at the Grand Theatre.

The bus began dropping off tourists at their hotels, beginning at the western end of Apia with the Tusitala Hotel, named after the writer of tales. Then we whirled east along Beach Road with the sunlight brilliant on the white-fronted buildings to our right and the water of the harbour to our left, where yachts rode peacefully at anchor.

Most of the passengers got off on the other side of Apia harbour at Aggie Grey's Hotel, still wreathed in the flowers they had been given at the airport. Aggie Grey's is the most famous hotel in the South Pacific, and she herself, at eighty-five years of age, is one of its best-known characters. Her father, William Swann, had been Stevenson's chemist in Apia. Half-Samoan and half-English, she still speaks with a German accent dating from the German occupation of the island. But her prices were not for the likes of me, and I was the last person left on the bus as it crossed the concrete bridge over the river to Matautu.

*

The Sea-side Inn, up towards the wharf, was mine; a bungalow with a corrugated iron roof the colour of dried blood. I left my bag on the verandah and peered into the cool darkness inside.

'Hallo?'

A Samoan girl emerged from the back, walking barefoot across the wooden floor. I could have any room I wanted; there was no one else staying. I took No. 1, at the front, an airy room with two windows and a double bed.

Ann, the half-Samoan manager of the Inn, lived with a genial Australian, called Rod, who had left a good job in Papua New Guinea because he was sickened by the violence – bodies draped over jeep-bonnets, continual blood-feuding, helicopters brought down by spears, the men inside burning to death.

'PNG's a bloody terrible place,' he said. His speech was tangily Australian: history happened 'Ages ago – when Jesus Christ played half-back for the Israelites,' and anything fishy 'smelled like the toilet on a crayfish boat'.

I stayed at the easy-going Sea-side Inn all the time I was in Samoa.

2

That first day I walked back into Apia to get something to eat: *The South Pacific Handbook* said the market was the cheapest place.

It was like being back in Bolivia again – large smiling brown ladies sat under wriggling babies behind piled mounds of fruit and vegetables, bananas, coconuts and pawpaw. At the back of the market, where the oily sea lapped and soggy trash floated, there were the same kind of tiny kitchens with benches and tables that you get in South American markets. A large matron beguiled me, holding up a package of green leaves tied with sennit.

'*Palusami, palusami!*' she exhorted, and picking up what looked like a grilled banana to go with it, '*talo, talo!*' We grinned at each other, the handsome Samoan huckster who spoke no English and the doubtless comical *papālagi* who spoke no Samoan. *Papālagi*, pronounced *palangi*, means foreigner; literally 'sky-breaker', from the sails that broke the horizon when the first whites came. We made our exchange: two grubby one *tālā* notes (a grand total of US$1) for the two items, complete with smiles and thanks.

The banana shape was a starchy tuber of *taro*, the Polynesian equivalent of potato. It went excellently with the *palusami* wrapped inside the green leaves: *palusami* turned out to be the top of the *taro* plant, a kind of spinach in creamed coconut.

'Delicious, madam!' I called out to the vendor and she laughed and smiled.

It was Samoan siesta time, with big barefoot peasants lounging in the shade on concrete sidewalks, the men in *lavalavas*, the women in green, yellow, red, purple dresses, sitting by small piles of produce for sale. I remembered the Aymara women in Bolivia, with their measured piles of beans on the pavement; if you bought one pile they would always toss in a few extra, the *yapa* which gave good luck, from the central hoard.

You could tell Western Samoa was a poor country. Garish buses went by with wooden seats and missing windows. The dusty square of the bus-park had booths selling sickly fizzy drinks – in California soft drinks proclaim their freedom from preservatives and artificial colours, but a poor country's products will be packed with them. You could buy single cigarettes from those booths – a whole packet was a luxury – and the heads leapt sulphurously off the cheap matchsticks.

I bought the *Samoa Observer* for fifty *sene* or cents from an old man squatting with a sleeping woman by a pile of bananas. 'Airport Project Continues At Crawling Speed' said the headline. The Government had run out of money to extend the airstrip to take wide-bodied jets. It was a developing country – but slowly.

3

There isn't a British Consul in Western Samoa, but there is an Honorary British Representative, c/o Armstrong and Springhill

(Samoa) Ltd; and I went along there to see if there was any mail from my wife. Klaus Kinski in a GI's helmet leered from a movie poster at the entrance to the wooden alley. A youth with wild frizzy hair and mirrored sunglasses scowled at me and laughed raucously with his mates. The Apia yob, no longer a villager, imperfectly cosmopolitan in his flared jeans, is also a product of development.

Armstrong and Springhill had a battered office in a wooden building. A secretary, with a hibiscus behind her ear, went to fetch the boss. Jack Warner from Aldershot came out of the back in white shirt, baggy shorts and long socks, looking like a tanned and wrinkled Norman Wisdom in tropical kit. He rummaged through a desk-drawer and produced an airmail letter in my wife's familiar black italic script, postmarked Bournemouth. It had taken just over a week to come 9000 miles, a miracle. Stevenson's mail – replies to the quantities of letters he fired off to friends and newspapers – took nearer a month, and was sometimes lost.

'Are you a relative of Bob's?' asked Jack Warner.

'Sorry?'

'Bob Rankin of Island Styles up at Vaoala.'

'No . . . I don't think so.'

'You ought to meet Bob, he's been here thirty years.'

He picked up the phone and within a few minutes I had an appointment to meet this Rankin of Samoa. We probably *were* all related somewhere along the line.

I asked Jack about his duties. Mostly he arranged things for visitors, whom he also seemed to see as part of an extended family. ('Bernard Weatherill was out recently. You know, the Speaker of the House of Commons. Very nice man, charming wife. Look him up when you go back to London.')

He told me there were forty-eight British in Samoa; the expatriates were mainly New Zealanders – 150 of them, a relationship dating from their days as colonial administrators under the UN mandate between 1920 and 1962.

'Any tips about Samoa? It's all new to me.'

'They used to call Samoans "the Irish of the Pacific". They're fighters, and some of them are very big chaps. So – respect their ways and don't mess about with their women. If you want to see the real Samoa, go to Savai'i. If you stay with people in the villages, and they'll invite you, they're very friendly, take tins of corned beef or canned fish as a gift. Oh, and don't forget to take your own bog-paper.'

'What about the language? I don't speak a word.'

'Well – *lay-eye* means "no", and that's important. *Talofa* is the greeting. *Faf-ay-tie* means "thanks", and *faf-ay-tie tay-lay-lava* is "thanks very much".'

I scribbled the words on the back of the envelope.

'Well, *faf-ay-tie* for the letter,' I tried, and went out into the sunshine.

*

I sat in a wooden stand watching a *kirikiti* match in progress. Cricket in Western Samoa is not quite MCC; they play it with a war club with the stabbing-spike knocked off. Each team has twenty or more players, and the competition is deadly serious. The *Samoa Observer* had a story at the foot of page 1:

Man Dies From Fractured Skull

A man died when he was struck on the head with a cricket bat at Siumu on 12 September, in a dispute during a cricket match.

Lauoletolo Inu, aged twenty-seven, was taken to Apia Hospital where he died from a fractured skull.

4

The Stevensons had left Honolulu on their roundabout route to Samoa in late June 1889 on the trading-schooner *Equator*, sailing via the Gilbert Islands. Three years before the British annexation the low islands were a haunt of white riff-raff who managed to stay one jump ahead of the law. They were also home to one particular native tyrant, the Winchester-wielding 'King', Tem Binok. He had, fortunately, been greatly taken with Fanny and Louis Stevenson, only partly because the Captain hinted they were close relatives of Queen Victoria. King Tem Binok, with his long black hair and screeching voice, who wore a lady's frock or a naval uniform as whim suggested and took pot-shots at retainers who displeased him, is one extraordinary character in the Gilbert Islands chapters of *The*

South Seas. Stevenson had intended to get to grips with his 'big South Seas book' after he had gained some understanding of recent events in Samoa. The *Equator* sailed into Apia only nine months after the historic typhoon of 16 March 1889.

*

The schooner ran into rough weather herself on the way south-east from the Gilberts; the fore-topmast broke off, and Ah Fu, the cook, was out with a knife cutting away the rigging. It was still blowing hard when they came into Apia Harbour on 7 December. The Reverend W. E. Clarke, of the London Missionary Society, happened to be walking that morning along the 'Beach', a sandy track lined with straggling stores and drink saloons. He describes a cloudless morning of relentless sun, but with 'the trade wind sweeping across the bay, driving the huge Pacific rollers against the barrier reef in great masses of foam'. Giant palms arched and creaked in the gale, their leaves 'crackling like musketry'. Clarke spotted three strange Europeans who had clearly just landed from the small schooner nearby.

Fanny was a remarkable sight in her patterned dress, big gold hoop earrings, and plaited straw Gilbert Islander's hat, 'encircled with a wreath of small shells', a scarlet silk scarf round her throat and a brilliant plaid shawl across her shoulders. She wore white canvas shoes, no stockings, 'and across her back was slung a guitar'. Lloyd Osbourne wore a striped pyjama suit, 'the undress costume of most European traders in these seas', a native 'slouch straw hat', dark blue sun-glasses, and a banjo. RLS carried a camera and wore shabby white flannels 'that had seen many better days', plus his prominently peaked white drill yachting cap. Both men were barefoot. The Reverend Clarke imagined they were wandering players *en route* for New Zealand, compelled by poverty to travel on a trading ship.

5

The Bohemian Stevensons had just seen for themselves the dramatic effects of the storm that had hit Apia nine months before, when a great typhoon had wrecked six out of the seven rival warships in Apia harbour.

Since 1879, Apia had been under the uneasy rule of the consuls of Germany, Great Britain and the United States, as the three powers jockeyed for control of the whole archipelago. In March 1889, all three powers had warships crowding the anchorages at Apia. Only the British HMS *Calliope* survived the typhoon; three German and three American warships were beached or sunk, with massive loss of life. Samoans who had been ready to fight the Germans the day before plunged into the surf to help rescue men in danger of drowning.

The German corvette *Adler* was lifted bodily on to the reef and her rusting red bones were visible there for the next seventy years. The symbol of German Imperial might now lies buried beneath the *kirikiti* ground.

*

The catastrophe had immediate and longer-term political consequences. Stevenson in 1892 called it 'a marking-epoch in world history'.

One immediate effect was the Berlin conference on Samoan affairs, 14 June 1889, whose final act RLS called 'the most dismally stupid production of modern diplomacy'. Supposed to provide for 'the neutrality and autonomous government of the Samoan islands . . . the free right of the natives to elect their chief or king and choose their own form of government according to their own laws and customs', it actually made way for two new foreign officials whose incompetence and dishonesty Stevenson was to lobby against. They were eventually recalled; but the three rival consuls started interfering again. There were more wars among the natives, made worse by white meddling and white weaponry; and finally in 1900, Western Samoa became wholly German. So much for neutrality and autonomy.

The longer-term effects of the 1889 typhoon were far more significant, as Stevenson perceived. The humiliating loss of the three US warships exposed the weakness of their maritime power, run down since the Civil War. American expansionists, who wanted 'Manifest Destiny' to roll on across the Pacific, lobbied for a big navy; and the Pacific was their new frontier. Hawaii saw the first push forward in 1893 with the overthrow of Queen Lili'uokalani; in 1898 the US took Guam and the Philippines from Spain, and formally annexed Hawaii; in 1889 the eastern Samoan Islands finally became American Samoa.

RLS showed remarkable insight in perceiving the global importance of that 1889 typhoon. It was 'a marking-epoch in world history' because it helped induce the birth of the US empire we live with today.

*

The *Equator* had to be paid off, and Stevenson gave a celebration meal for the crew.

Complimentary Dinner
given by
R. L. Stevenson and Party
to
Captain Reid, Officers and Passengers
of the
Schooner Yacht *Equator*
at the
Tivoli Hotel Dec 9 1889

MENU

Appetiser 'Strong' Punch
Oyster Soup, à la Josephus
Cambridge Sausage, Mashed Potatoes
Chicken Fricassee, French Beans
SALADE MARINEE
Roast Sucking Pig, Truffled Dressing, Sweet Peas
DESSERT
Cakes, Pie and Fruit
WINES
St Emilion Claret, Château Rabart Sauterne
Montaldo Sherry, Champagne
SCHLITZ MILWAUKEE BEER

Stevenson had written a comic song for Captain Reid, to mark their adventures on the voyage from the Gilberts. The fifth verse went:

The sail was the rotteness'd ever was bent
On board of the old *Equator*.
But blamed if it wasn't the stick that went,
On board of the old *Equator*.

Chorus:

Captain, darling, where has your topmast gone pray?
Captain, darling, where has your topmast gone?

6

Joe Strong, whose hand can be seen in the dinner menu, now left for Sydney, but Fanny, Lloyd and Ah Fu went to live in a rented house up behind Apia. RLS himself took up residence on 'The Beach' with a man who could tell him a lot about Samoa, the American trader, Harry J. Moors, who had formerly worked for the Hawaiian Government recruiting plantation labourers from the Gilbert Islands. Since 1884, however, he had been in business in Samoa, first with one E. A. Grevsmuhl – who was rumoured to have paid natives in whist counters – and now on his own. Not surprisingly, Stevenson was at first suspicious of Moors and his history in the labour trade; at its worst 'blackbirding' was a form of kidnapping and slavery. In fact, Moors had never been a slaver.

RLS said Moors's 'looks, his round blue eyes, etc. went against me, and the repulsion was mutual. However we both got over it, and grew to like each other.' Harry Moors, universally known as *Misimoa* (Mr Moors), had a Samoan wife, Fa'animonimo, and had supported one of the Samoan leaders against the German candidate in the last war. Moors was a highly intelligent man, and according to Stevenson, 'of all the scores of witnesses I examined about the war, HJM was the only one whom documents invariably corroborated'. He was very important to Stevenson as an informant for the book he was then writing, which would be called *A Footnote to History: Eight Years of Trouble in Samoa*.

This was a quite new departure for Stevenson. He felt he had a responsibility to history – and he was determined to discharge it conscientiously.

A Footnote to History is an invaluable work for anyone studying the history of colonialism in the Pacific.

*

The house where Stevenson stayed with Harry Moors still stands on Beach Road, Apia. The upper floor of the white wooden building juts over the sidewalk, supported by four slim poles; up there today is Faletupe O Le Atiinae O Samoa I Sisifo – the Development Bank of Western Samoa. Right round the building runs the first-floor verandah where, on 28 December 1889, Stevenson lay and wrote a letter to Charles Baxter.

I am writing this on the back balcony at Moors' . . . lying on the floor . . . 'clad in robes of virgin white'. The ink is dreadful, the heat delicious, a fine going breeze in the palms, and from the other side of the house the endless, angry splash and roar of the Pacific on the reef, where the warships are still piled from last year's hurricane, some underwater, one on her side . . . The island has beautiful rivers . . . pleasant fords and waterfalls and overhanging verdure . . . the people . . . are courteous, pretty chaste, but thieves and beggars . . . [Later he would come to understand this better.] . . . the women are very attractive and dress lovely; the men purpose-like, well set up, tall, lean and dignified . . .

In early January 1890, he travelled eastward along the coast to Falefa and Fagaloa, 'an enchanted bay'. Stevenson saw 'something indescribably Japanese' in one scene where a small stream ran into the sea between groups of coconut trees and below a bridge of palm-stems. The more he saw of Samoa, the more he fell in love with it; and the time was ripe for decisions.

*

Stevenson was born in 1850, so measuring the decades was easy for him. When 1890 began he was forty – entering his fifth decade. He had always believed in living through his ages. Now was the time to settle to maturity.

The 1890–93 accounts of his tailor, Wm Chorley & Co, George Street, Sydney, show quite a different Stevenson from the raffish Bohemian who had amused Henley and shocked Lang. Slovenly youth was all right, he opined, but 'not slovenly age. So really now I am pretty spruce; always a white shirt, white necktie, fresh shave, silk socks, O a great sight!'

There was a more fundamental change. Stevenson bought some land in Samoa, to build the house which would be his last and best home. Harry Moors sold him 314½ acres of uncleared bush north of Vaoala, charging ten Chile dollars per acre. At seven dollars to the pound, it was almost £450. RLS wrote to Baxter on 3 February 1890 an excited letter about his 'beautiful land':

We range from 600 to 1500 feet, have 5 streams, waterfalls, precipices, profound ravines, rich tablelands, 50 head of cattle on the ground (if anyone can catch them), a great view of forest, sea, mountains, the warships in the haven . . . a noble place.

Fanny added a long PS to the letter, repeating her husband's invitation to Baxter to come and visit; if he came they would ride up the hill together between hedges of lime:

> . . . through a little native hamlet where the dogs bark and my friends there call 'talofa' as we pass, into the sombre forest, out again, and only twenty minutes from the beach, and here we are at Vailima, the place of five rivers.

The Stevensons always thought that 'Vailima' meant the place of the five rivers, from the compound of *vai*, fresh water, and *lima*, five. But the true legend of the name was more precisely poetic. A Samoan couple once crossed over the mountains to visit the woman's relatives at Matautu. The husband, Soalo, was an old man, and after they had covered a dozen miles and were beginning their descent on the other side he needed to rest, and begged his wife Sina to find him some water. She found him a stream, but had no cup, and scooped up water for him with her hands. When Soalo had drunk he said that the place should be called *Vailima*, from *vai*, fresh water, and *lima*, a hand or hands. And so the name of Stevenson's last home recalled that gift – 'water from the hands' or 'a handful of water'.

7

The Stevensons were away from Samoa for most of 1890 while the land was being cleared; spending their time in Sydney and cruising on the cargo-boat *Janet Nichol*. In early February, Harry Moors gave a farewell dinner for Stevenson and his party who were leaving the next day. One speech came from Captain Hamilton, the Apia pilot whom the Samoans called *Samesoni* for his robust strength. 'The natives used to ask me,' he said, 'if white men ever did die. Their reason for such a question was that white men looked sick but none of them died of it.' During the *Janet Nicholas* three and a half month cruise through the Cook, Tokelau, Ellice, Gilbert and Marshall Islands, Fanny kept a diary 'to help my husband's memory when his own diary had fallen in arrears'. One of her observations confirms Captain Hamilton's:

> Natives have said that the first sight of white people is dreadful, as they look like corpses walking. I have myself been startled by the sight of a crowd of whites after having seen only brown-skinned people for a long time. Louis has a theory that we whites were originally albinos. Certainly we are not a nice colour . . .

Fanny's diary, published in 1914 as *The Cruise of the Janet Nichoi: Mrs Robert Louis Stevenson's Diary of a South Sea Cruise*, is a fascinating document in its own right. It is fast writing, vivid and dramatic, with a keen sense of the absurd, and shows the literary calibre of the woman whose critical judgement RLS trusted implicitly. Both this and her Samoan diary, published as *Our Samoan Adventure* in 1956, give a good idea of the drama Fanny's imagination added to the Stevensons' everyday life – probably only Fanny ever tried to make a Mexican *salsa* at sea, with Samoan chillies and onions grown in the soil of Niue graves.

For the Gilbert Island King, Tem Binok, who had made favourites of them on their way to Samoa, she had designed a flag (a shark, which Tem Binok claimed as his ancestor, rampant on bars of red, yellow and green; its motto was 'I bite triply'). This caused the King 'the keenest gratification' when the Stevensons flew it for him on their return visit. She carried with her on the *Janet Nichoi* quantities of artificial flowers she had bought in Sydney, and during the voyage wove thirty-eight wreaths, mixing the flowers with coloured feathers, as gifts for natives of the low coral islands where the indigenous flowers were rare and whitish. The ship's hold contained some 'immense' pure white rats with red eyes; and when the Captain spotted 'the loveliest rat in the world', Fanny ran to help catch and tame it.

She collected island curiosities, like the 'peace sticks', yellow-feathered clubs with which the women of Niue would break up fights among their menfolk; she did not shrink either from necklaces of human teeth. Her diary eagerly records gory head-hunting stories and tales of the supernatural, and she always catches the bizarre detail – the trader's hand blown off by dynamite, the man with elephantiasis tracking blood across the deck, King Tem Binok's wife suckling a puppy-dog, a lagoon the gold-green colour of chrysophrase.

*

It became a good year for literary voyages. The young Kipling, in 1890, was conquering London; Joseph Conrad, as yet unpublished, was venturing up the Congo, an experience which would lead to *Heart of Darkness* in 1902; and Stevenson, on the *Janet Nichol*, still working sporadically on *The Wrecker*, was gathering material that would be used in *The Beach of Falesá* and *The Ebb-Tide*, both of which deal with decivilized whites in the Pacific, the riff-raff living on the rough edge of Empire.

They met all kinds of traders on this trip; men who were destitute, anaemic, ill, and one with leprosy; men who had married natives, men who lived off natives, men who drank, and men who had murdered. They all provided good models for *Falesá's* Wiltshire and Case.

In her diary, Fanny was explicit about one source: June 27th – Arrived at Namorik. Louis went on shore and met a wicked old man who afterwards appeared in *The Beach of Falesá*.

Perhaps this is:

> Old Captain Randall, squatting on the floor native fashion, fat and pale, naked to the waist, grey as a badger and his eyes set with drink. His body was covered with grey hair and crawled over by flies; one was in the corner of his eye – he never heeded . . . He was nipping gin all the while; sometimes he fell asleep and woke again whimpering and shivering . . . 'My friend,' I was telling myself all day, 'You must not be an old gentleman like this.'

The Beach of Falesá was 'the first realistic South Sea story', as RLS wrote to Colvin in September 1891.

> Everybody else who has tried . . . got carried away by the romance, and ended in a kind of sugar-candy sham epic . . . You.. will know more about the South Seas after you have read my little tale than if you had read a library.

8

The Ebb-Tide's opening sentence is not exactly jingoistic.

> Throughout the island world of the Pacific, scattered men of many European races and from almost every grade of society carry activity and disseminate disease.

The 'Trio' that we meet in the opening chapter, 'Night on the Beach', are three bums stranded in Papeete, French Polynesia – Davies, the drunken skipper who has lost his ship through drink; Herrick the failed Oxford graduate; and Huish, the cockney rat. Huddled together on an island beach in a tropical rain-storm they are reminiscent of three other characters who did the same on a fictitious island nearly three centuries before: Stephano, Trinculo and Caliban in Shakespeare's *The Tempest*.

Stevenson's trio are outcasts of Empire during its heyday in the 1890s, before the twilight of decolonization, the ebbing of the tide. Herrick looks longingly back towards London, the Hub of the Empire. He spins a fantasy to amuse his broken companions; a disguised Arab offers him a flying carpet and a bottomless purse of gold sovereigns with the head of Queen Victoria, the international currency of British power. To please Davies, the American, Herrick changes sovereigns to 'Double-eagles', and lets the American 20-dollar coin into the dream. The magic carpet deposits Herrick in Trafalgar Square at noon and in one bound, he has gone from 'Hell' to 'the dandiest part of Heaven'. Actually, he cannot get back. The roar of London traffic is only the roar of surf on the beach. They are trapped in their characters, as in Shakespeare's *The Tempest*:

> Ebbing men, indeed,
> Most often do so near the bottom run
> By their own fear or sloth.

Still hoping to make their fortune, they get on a ship carrying stolen champagne, symbol of success and the good life – but most of the bottles turn out to contain water. They arrive at a Pacific atoll controlled by an extraordinary megalomaniac, William John Attwater, who rules with the Bible in one hand and a Winchester repeating rifle in the other. He variously destroys the three intruders: Herrick becomes an abject servant, Davies a religious maniac, and the vile Huish, 'perhaps as brave a man as ever lived', is shot dead as he is about to throw a bottle of vitriol at Attwater.

G. K. Chesterton was disturbed by the portrayal of Attwater; he felt that Stevenson admired his brutality, and detected Henley's influence – 'the swaggering cult of fear'. But did Stevenson really admire Attwater? We could similarly ask, did Joseph Conrad admire Kurtz? Both characters are solipsistic maniacs who think their will is the force of destiny: '"Oh, I can do anything . . . You do not understand: What must be, must,"' says Attwood in *The Ebb-Tide*. Likewise, '"By the simple exercise of our will we can exert a power for good practically unbounded,"' says Kurtz in *Heart of Darkness*.

Attwater achieves victory through the crushing power to break of a godlike father, perhaps an ultimate echo of Thomas Stevenson. The emotions that Attwater generates are far more complex than admiration.

9

A hundred years after Stevenson was born a most illuminating book was published, Dr O. Mannoni's *Psychologie de la Colonisation*. In 1955 it appeared in English as *Prospero and Caliban*, with an introduction by Philip Mason, who developed some of those ideas further in his 1962 book *Prospero's Magic: Some Thoughts on Race and Class*.

Mannoni thinks that colonials often suffer from a 'Prospero complex'. Prospero is a man who has failed in his own country and sails away to an island, where he continues his studies in magic – essentially an exercise in dominion over others. He tyrannizes his daughter Miranda and treats Caliban, the original owner of the island, as a slave. Prospero's excuse is that Caliban has tried to rape Miranda; in fact, it is Prospero himself who has incestuous feelings for his daughter. Sexual Miranda, sex-mad Caliban, and sexless Ariel are all projections of Prospero. In the colonial situation, which is a breeding-ground for fantasy, his unconscious blooms in new ways. Sexual guilt leads to a hatred of the other, and is at the root of colonial racialism.

Mannoni has a footnote which he does not develop: 'A particu-

larly interesting traveller to study is R. L. Stevenson. In his story
Ariel and Caliban are called Jekyll and Hyde. In the remote Pacific
he found courage to grapple with the image which had driven him
that far, and began writing *Weir of Hermiston*.'

*

Weir of Hermiston is Stevenson's last great Scottish novel, which he
would leave unfinished. Weir – a 'hanging judge' – terrorizes his
weak, sensitive son, Archie. There are parallels between Weir's
relationship to Archie, Attwater's relationship with the poor whites,
and Prospero's to his creatures on the island – all are father-figures,
who have not relinquished power over their adult children and
cannot accept them as they are.

In the extended family of white relatives and servants that
Stevenson would establish at Vailima during the last years of his life,
he would in many ways transcend the archetype of the bad father. A
writer need not repress his unconscious and project it on to others;
he can express it in his writing. Within the limitations of their status
as rich foreigners, Fanny and Louis were able to look at the South
Seas' indigenous peoples with unsentimental curiosity. The natives
often seemed extraordinary; they might be good or bad; but they
were not their hapless children, to be loved or hated, broken,
betrayed and owned.

*

The South Seas produced one flawed paternalist whose writing skills
and admiration for Stevenson did little to redeem him. After the
Second World War, the Gilbert Islands became well-known in
Britain when a retired District Officer of the Colonial Administration Service, Sir Arthur Grimble KCMG, began giving talks on the
BBC Home Service. In the 1950s his book *A Pattern of Islands* became
a best-seller. Grimble had gone to the Gilbert Islands in 1913 with
the words of an old man at the Colonial Office ringing in his ears:
'Do we stake our lives on Stevenson, *not* Kipling? Do we insist on the
dominion of romance, *not* the romance of dominion? I should
appreciate your answer.'

Grimble's answer was a joyful 'Yes' to Stevenson – but his
subsequent behaviour proved him a prime example of the 'Prospero
complex'.

A *Pattern of Islands* is a charming and deeply romantic book, with many references to Stevenson. His anecdotes of island life must have seemed paradisal to British people in the bleak post-war years. But Grimble omitted to mention his role in cheating the Banaban people out of their land on Ocean Island, thus enabling the British Phosphate Commission to earn millions of pounds. In 1976, the displaced Banabans tried to get compensation, and a 1928 letter-cum-proclamation from Grimble to the islanders was read out in court. Mr Justice McGarry called it 'disgracefully threatening' and said it could not be read without 'a sense of outrage'.

Arthur Grimble said he wrote *A Pattern of Islands* 'to record that, for all its admitted faults of principle, the old system of British imperialism did not always work out in practice as ruthlessly as some of its accusers . . . would have the world believe today'. But the Prospero who enchanted us with tales of the myth and magic of Ariel turned out to be another sad bully, abusing Caliban.

10

I took a taxi up to see my honorary uncle Bob Rankin at Island Styles. You could always get a cab outside Aggie Grey's Hotel, where the richer tourists stayed. There was a thatched hut across the road where large taxi-drivers in *lavalava*, shirt and sandals played noisy games of checkers.

A driver barrelled across the road, and I haggled a price. His taxi was ankle-deep in bits of multi-coloured foam rubber and the seat slid about and twanged. 'Vaoala, OK!' roared the driver as he hitched his sagging door into place.

Falealili Street is the road up to Vailima and runs over the mountain. Just above Tanugamanono we ground to a halt with smoke pouring over the bonnet. Delicately, the driver lifted the battered lid. The plug of wood and cloth that served as an oil-cap had blown out and he hammered it back in; then the engine would not start until it was set off downhill back to Apia in third gear. Finally, the driver managed to persuade the vehicle uphill again, rocking and crooning over the steering-wheel. I was using so much will-power to help him that I missed the gates of Vailima.

At Island Styles I paid off the moonfaced perspiring driver.

'You want me wait?' he asked eagerly from the fuming jalopy.

'No. No, thanks. Thank you very much.'

*

Bob Rankin came out of the rambling wooden building to greet me, a grey-haired man with dark eyebrows, wearing an old shirt and khaki shorts.

'Reckon we must be cousins,' he said with a broad, snaggy-toothed grin. We sat in his small office and he waved a dismissive hand at the clutter of papers. He was too impatient a man to be tidy.

Bob Rankin had been in Samoa for the length of my life. His grandfather had gone from Scotland to New Zealand, and Bob first came to Samoa in 1950, as a teacher. He married a Samoan called Sophie (they now had six children), and in 1960 started a newspaper called *Samoana*. This paper was closed down after six years because the other shareholders felt Bob should not criticize the fledgeling government during the first stage of Samoan independence. Then he read a few books on silk-screen printing and began his enterprising career in business.

Bob and Sophie set up a company called Island Styles Ltd in 1967. It began with clothes; these days they import cotton cloth from China and Poland and print over 275 metres a day with local designs for the tourist trade. His next project was wine – Talofa Tropical Fruit Wines, which come in dry, medium, sweet and sparkling. Grapes would not grow in Samoa so he used bananas, papaya and passion fruit. Then he bought a solar still to make 80° proof alcohol. That created a new series of products: cacao and passion-fruit liqueurs, jasmine and frangipani perfumes, and aftershaves.

Fanny Stevenson, in similar pioneering spirit, had made perfume in Samoa from armfuls of *moso'oi* flowers, though her attempts at banana beer exploded. Bob's ideas seemed inexhaustible; he also made soap from coconut oil and papaya leaves, and manufactured billiard tables, one a week, which went for a thousand *tālā*, plus cues and balls.

It's not easy to be an entrepreneur in the 26th Least-Developed Country in the world. Western Samoa was in dire straits with the International Monetary Fund at the time, who dictated devaluations, local taxes, heavy interest on overdrafts, etc. The cost of living was high, wages were low and taxation on the enterprising steep.

The currency itself was a problem; when the oil companies presented a bill for 14 million *tālā* (the Western Samoan dollar) they wouldn't accept the local currency in payment, so most of the foreign exchange disappeared in repayments. In the decades of development when roads, schools, hospitals, clean water all had to be provided, most of its precious foreign exchange was used to clear debts.

If a poor country just exports raw material it will tend to stay poor; local processing is one way forward. But the local copra mill needed $800,000 just to pay its oil bill. Bob said the potential of Samoa was tremendous; you could grow just about anything there, but the island was still crippled by poverty. If the airport couldn't take even a fully loaded 737 it wasn't possible to ship out perishable fruit and flowers in commercial quantity.

Grandiose dreams of tourism also depended on the airport. There were plans for jumbo jets of rich tourists to fly in direct from Los Angeles and stay at the Royal Samoan Hotel at Apia Park. A thousand Samoans could be employed in food, flowers and entertainment, and dollars would pour in. But the airport project was stalled, and the hotel was still a chimera. So was the projected cable-car. If it ever gets built it will whisk eager tourists up Mount Vaea to see Stevenson's grave. Perhaps there is something to be said for slow progress at the airport.

Bob showed me round Island Styles; a dog had cracked the solar still but the wine-bottling plant was busy, with the radio on. Half-printed T-shirts lay on long tables. They were to publicize the launching of Western Samoa's home-produced bully-beef, *Pisupo*. Samoans were mad about corned beef; their exotic name for it arrived with the first traders in the nineteenth century who brought with them cans of Pea Soup. Thereafter tinned meat was also *Pisupo*.

*

I asked my putative cousin about the Samoan extended family.

'Yes – the *'ainga* system. That's the real strength of Samoa. If somebody gets into trouble, even in New Zealand, everyone kicks in and helps. Everybody belongs to some family or other. Get married and you marry the whole lot of them.'

There was a lot of generosity to balance the aggression – and the big arguments were usually over land. The whole system was based on which family owned which land. It was always owned by the family, not the individual. Each family had its *matai* or chief, and so did each village: these *matais* held the political power. 'That's the *fa'aSamoa* – the Samoan way.' Apparently a change in the suffrage was being proposed so that sub-*matais* could be appointed. 'But they're very cautious about change. In Samoa, tradition is everything.'

11

In the lobby of the Nelson Memorial Library, by Apia's town clock, there were 'Nuclear-Free Pacific' posters and an announcement of the next meeting of the Samoan Natural History Society; Dr A. R. M. Mendoza would speak about 'The Sex-Life of the Coconut'.

The library had a good Stevenson section. It even contained a faded and stained copy of *The Stevensonian*, the journal of the defunct RLS Club of London edited by Ernest Mehew. It was strange to read it in the hot Pacific Room with broken fans and sweat dripping off the tip of my nose on to my lined notebook.

My notes were scrawled in pencil; a farrago of legends, customs, myths, dates, 'facts' and fancies as I grappled with Samoan history, my mind ballooning in the sun. I did not want to be just one more wrong-headed, blundering *palangi*. Stevenson, who was good in the heat and had five whole years to learn about Samoa, said:

> Foreigners in these islands know little of the course of native intrigue. Partly the Samoans cannot explain, partly they will not tell.

*

Stevenson's little-read *A Footnote to History: Eight Years of Trouble in Samoa* (1892) is still invaluable in trying to understand modern Samoa. The first two chapters, 'Elements of Discord: Native' and 'Elements of Discord: Foreign', are a masterly summary of the misunderstandings involved in its colonization. 'We have passed the feudal system; [the Samoans] . . . are not yet clear of the patriarchal. We are in the thick of the age of finance; they are in a period of communism.' What Stevenson called 'communism' is a traditional society which was essentially 'pre-capitalist'.

Outside Apia, the *fa'aSamoa* is still, in the 1980s, not wholly dependent on the money economy. It is also based on the mutual support of the extended family network. Even the Samoan word for money – *tupe* – had to be imported; it is a loan word derived from 'to pay'. Pigs, breadfruit, *taro*, fine mats, etc. could be given as gifts or exacted as fines, but there was no indigenous means of exchange as such.

Westerners, who can buy and sell everything for the right amount of cash, naturally have a strong sense of property and possession. The Samoan notion was and is far more fluid. Stevenson explains how in 'the loose communism in which a family dwells', it was not the custom to refuse requests for anything:

> The man who (in a native word of praise) is *mata-ainga*, a race-regarder, has his hand always open to his kindred; the man who is not . . . knows.. always where to turn in any pinch of want or extremity of laziness. Beggary within the family – and by the less self-respecting, without it – has thus grown into a custom and a scourge, and the dictionary teems with evidence of its abuse.

Stevenson then tells of a Samoan pastor who bought a boat for $100, paying $50 down. His relatives turn up, take a fancy to the boat, and ask for it. The pastor has to sell some land and beg mats from other relatives to finish paying for the boat he has already given away. Not content with that, a few months later, 'the harpies' broke a thwart on the boat and brought it back to the pastor, demanding that he repair and re-paint it.

This Polynesian system had a depressive effect on individual industry. 'You will get men to work with difficulty if those that do not work come down like locusts and devour the harvest.' Moreover, in the end begging led to what we call theft:

> From applying for help to kinsmen who are scarce permitted to refuse, it is but a step to take from them . . . 'without permission'; from that to theft at large is but a hair's breadth.

This explains Stevenson's remark in the early letter to Baxter that Samoans were 'thieves and beggars'; he had not yet understood that 'the idea of theft itself is not very clearly present to these communists'. It also explains the frequent references I heard in modern Apia to pilfering – everything from cassettes and chickens to cattle.

The open-handed *fa'aSamoa* can be abused on either side. Some innocent travellers return from places like Savai'i stripped of all possessions, which the Samoans have begged from them with a pleasant *fa'amole* or 'please'; whereas the cynical and well-informed travellers may go empty-handed and live for weeks on the generosity of their hosts in the villages.

*

Thieving infuriated the meticulous Germans in the nineteenth century. The principal German company on the island set up its own private enterprise jail to confine malefactors, and Samoan feelings ran high against it. Prison, isolation from family and friends, was an alien notion. Even today many Western Samoan prisoners go home for the weekend.

The German firm also protected its investments by the manipulation of puppet 'kings', whose very existence was based on an imperfect understanding of the complexities of Samoan titles – they could not all belong to one 'king', as Stevenson explains:

> The successful candidate is now the *Tupu o Samoa*, much good may it do him! . . . He can summon parliaments; it does not follow they will assemble . . . in so far as he is king of Samoa, I cannot find but what the president of a college debating society is a far more formidable officer.

The 'king' reigned, but the Germans ruled, from 1879 through to 1914. No wonder that Stevenson's Samoa was a land 'full of war and rumours of war'. Nearly every year one or other province was in arms, or at least 'sits sulky and menacing, . . . disregarding the king's proclamations and planting food in the bush, the first step of military preparation'.

12

Stevenson saw Apia as 'the seat of the political sickness of Samoa'. In the 1880s, the villages around Apia bay were a special zone, the

'*Ele'ele Sa*, the 'Forbidden Soil' of the treaties. 'The handful of whites have everything; the natives walk in a foreign town', wrote Stevenson. At the western end of the bay, the 'Long Handle' German firm – *Deutsche Handels und Plantagen Gesellschaft der Süd-See Inseln zu Hamburg* – had its headquarters; there were German stores and bars, and the German consulate. Heading east, the stores, bars and mission were all English and American, and their consulates stood at the far eastern end of the zone. The rest of the island might be Samoan, but Apia was European by law.

RLS found this:

> a singular state of affairs: all the money, luxury, and business
> of kingdom centred in one place; that place . . . administered
> by whites for whites; and the whites themselves holding it . . .
> in hostile camps, so that it lies between them like a bone
> between two dogs, each growling, each clutching his own end.

The whites were in Apia to make money and selling arms was part of the business. Stevenson described one episode in which Germans sold guns to the Gilbert Islanders, who paid for them in money or in labour. The islanders 'misused' the guns 'as it was known they would be misused'. The Germans consequently disarmed them by force, and re-sold the guns at a handsome profit to a new set of belligerents, this time Samoan.

Apia seethed with intrigue and gossip. Many of the events Stevenson records in *A Footnote to History* would make a good knockabout farce with pith-helmets and coconut palms – except that it all actually happened; because of 'horrid white mismanagement' people were killed, natives were cheated, and houses were burned down.

Yet Apia was and is fundamentally unreal, a toehold of capitalism on a communistic island, a downmarket Shanghai or Hong Kong. In the 1980s, only Apia offers electricity, bright lights, and a ticket to booze and dope in New Zealand. Once 'the seat of the political sickness', Apia is now the focus of the cultural enemy: money.

For some, money offers a kind of freedom in the form of an escape from the traditional hierarchy. The '*aumanga* or untitled men of a village no longer have to obey the dictates of an authoritarian elder if they can earn and own in the Western way. Of course, many recycle goods and cash back into the *'ainga*, whose more traditional members still work on the land or fish out on the reef. They try to blend the old and the new; *taro* and Toyotas; breadfruit and ghetto-blaster.

But the money-dream, what Stevenson called 'the dollar-hunt', is not as easily satisfied in Samoa as hunger for food. These desires never stop.' Nobody would die for Western capitalism', Graham Greene once wrote. Many would kill for it, though. Even the *fa'aSamoa* may be killed.

13

Western Samoa was the first island state in the Pacific to become independent, in 1962. Stevenson had longed for this to happen nearly seventy years before, in 1893, when he was still in Honolulu:

> I can see but one way out – to follow the demand of the Samoan people that the Berlin Act be rescinded, while the three Powers withdraw absolutely, and the natives be . . . allowed to govern the islands as they choose . . . it might affect commerce, and certainly the present standing of all foreigners . . . but . . . it is the patient and not the doctor who is in danger . . . If left alone, the Samoans would continue fighting, just as they do under the tripartite treaty . . . but at least they would fight it out among themselves, without their wars being turned to the advantage of meddling foreigners.

The domed Western Samoan Parliament House lies up Mulinuu Peninsula, just beyond the tomb of Mata'afa, the Samoan leader who resisted German imperial ambitions, and who was supported by both Stevenson and Harry J. Moors. A clear line links him with the later *Mau* movement, who resisted the ham-fisted New Zealand administration that took over from the German colony at the beginning of the First World War. One of the founders of the *Mau* was O. F. Nelson, Harry Moors's son-in-law. Later, one of the first Prime Ministers of Western Samoa (after independence) was O. F. Nelson's grandson – Harold Moors's great-grandson – the wholly Samoan Tupuola Taisi Efi.

14

Waking one morning in the early sunlight at the Sea-side Inn, Apia, I thought I was a child again in Africa. The Samoans outside the window were speaking Swahili, and I was back in the colony of the past, not a *palangi* but a little boy called *Raikorosi*, the African pronunciation of Nicholas.

Samoan had adopted English loan-words in much the same way as the East African *lingua franca* did, adding the same 'i' on the end – the Swahili for blanket was *blanketi*; biscuit bisikoti. In Samoa, you could listen to a programme, *polokalame*, on the radio, *leikio* (or wireless, *uaealesi*), read the *niusipepa*, and write a report, *lipoti*, on *pepa* with a *peni*. Samoa had to import the concept as well as the word for time, *taimi*, and its industrial offshoot *ovataimi*. In the West, Time is Money; in Polynesia, both are alien signifiers.

*

The early mornings are lovely in Samoa, the sort of mornings I will remember at incongruous moments all my life. It was in the morning that Stevenson did most of his writing up at Vailima, waking early when the air was cool and the rest of the house was still; writing in bed when his mind was as fresh as the new day.

I would breakfast on the verandah, on fresh pawpaw, bread, butter and guava jam, and lots of coffee, looking west from Matautu across the smooth, milky harbour. Over the road, whose verge was spiked with yellow-green striped crotons, there was a pair of chestnut trees. A rotting wooden boat called the *Tautua* was beached between them, and a desultory crew of shipwrights worked on new timbers. Further up the beach towards the wharf was a rusting pilot-cutter called *Lady Perse*, and two piles of hardwood tree-trunks – the timber was immobilized until the right 'export tax' was paid. Korean and Japanese companies were keen to log out Western Samoa's hardwood, offering to replace it all with eucalyptus. If this happens the traditional ecology that Fanny described will be ruined: 'numbers of magnificent timber-trees, very hard and beautiful in colour'.

Walking down Beach Road towards Apia, the long green hill straight ahead of you is Mount Vaea. In the flush of early morning, when the shadows are still long and everything glows, you pass chattering Samoans on their way to work or school. And at the mouth of the Vaisingano river beyond the concrete bridge there is a man in a wet *lavalava*, thigh-deep in the pellucid water, waiting stock still – then with a single graceful sweep he casts a net for fish. It is almost eight o'clock.

Hurry past Aggie Grey's and the Protestant Church to reach the Court House, that white-painted relic of the German Empire, virtually unchanged from the old photos of eighty years ago with its pillared verandahs and gables of red corrugated iron. Stand on the corner where Ifiifi Street meets Beach Road; this is where New Zealand policemen fired on the *Mau* in 1929. After Sergeant Horatio Waterson, an ex-First World War machine gunner, opened up with his Lewis gun, hundreds of Samoans lay wounded on the street and eleven were killed. Down Ifiifi Street, the old Police Station and Barracks still stands. Instruments are tuning up. Suddenly, into the sunlight step the Apia Police Band, playing a triumphant version of 'Colonel Bogey', which seems to demand the alternative words:

> Hitler has only got one ball
> Goering has two but very small
> Himmler is somewhat similar
> But poor old Goebbels has no balls at all.

Behind the band, the Apia police come smartly marching, in black leather sandals, pale blue *lavalavas* and bushshirts, and white Mr Plod helmets on their proud Polynesian heads. Every morning the flag of Western Samoa is reverently raised up the flagpole outside the Court House, the band plays, and another day has begun.

15

You have to go to the Prime Minister's Office, up on the first floor of the rambling wooden Court House, for a permit to visit Robert Louis Stevenson's old house at Vailima.

The PM's Office was more appealing than Downing Street; a breeze off the sea came through the windows and half a dozen attractive Samoan girls in blue skirts and white blouses sat behind old-fashioned manual typewriters, each one with a fresh frangipani, hibiscus or jasmine blossom behind one ear, bright against her dark hair. You write your name in a big book on the wooden counter and receive a handwritten chit to give the policeman at the gate.

*

In Stevenson's day, the road up the hill was a rough track through the forest, and at night decaying wood on the ground glowed phosphorescent. Now the road is paved, a pleasant uphill drive. The bus drops you right at the curving white walls which frame the blue gates of the estate. I could hear children's voices singing from the Vailima Primary School across the road; at break time the children run out and buy a roll of bread or copra pie, *pai*, from Mrs Filemoni's little wooden store in the shade of the trees. It's a typical Samoan store, a hut with a hatch, tins in a gloomy interior, a mongrel snoozing against muddy white planks outside. Mrs Filemoni sold bottles of Innes Tartan Lemonade ('contains preservatives'), a 'Product of Innes Tartan Ltd, Bottled by Apia Bottling Co.'. It was a marvel of authentic Samoan – Scots pedigree.

*

Just through the gates of the estate there is a small white and red house. It is the police post. On a hot day you may catch the policeman asleep over his desk, bare of everything but a black bakelite telephone, as he guards against all danger the Official Residence of the Western Samoan Head of State, His Highness Malietoa Tanumafili II – such is the current august function of Vailima.

PC 989 Romani Smalley and PC 941 Filemoni Elisara were obliging and friendly. They took my chit and posed for a photograph outside their post in their *lavalavas* and safari shirts. (Later I delivered a copy to each of them at the police station; but on my last morning I met one of them again and he said he hadn't got it – possibly, he said, the desk-sergeant had torn them up, because he was jealous.) They told me only Apia had actual police; local *fonos* or councils dealt with minor matters outside the capital. They both strongly disapproved of firearms and said Samoan policemen only needed a stick.

What was Stevenson's house in his own country like? they asked. I drew them a picture of 17 Heriot Row in my notebook, but *Peretania* or Britain seemed a long way away.

*

The long shady drive to the house, lined by *kiki* trees with peeling bark, leads between two meadows, one rising to a grove of coconuts, one with cattle browsing and a skinny white horse. I remembered Stevenson's favourite horse, Jack, on which he used to ride down to Apia. A group of gardeners stood by an orange Toyota pick-up, at work with axe and machete on four big logs. I was a good excuse for a break.

Uale was ready to talk. He wore a torn T-shirt that said 'Here Comes Trouble' on the front and 'Excuse Me While I Kiss The Sky' on the back. On his upper right arm there was a tattoo of the letters AJOBA, underneath a crest.

'What does that mean?'

'Avele Junior Old Boys' Association,' he said proudly.

Uale spoke English, his mates didn't. He told me he had read three Alastair Maclean novels, and was keen on Brooke Shields; the remake of *The Blue Lagoon* had been a big hit in Samoa. I asked if His Excellency was at home today, and was told he didn't actually live at Vailima but over by Apia Park. Vailima was used for government parties and distinguished guests. 'Like the Queen,' said Uale, grinning. Queen Elizabeth II and the Duke of Edinburgh lunched at Vailima during their Jubilee Tour of 1977.

We squatted in the road, smoking. I picked up Uale's *naifi*, the cutting tool I knew as a *panga* in childhood. There was a picture of a crocodile on the blade. Martindale. Birmingham. Made in England.

'Tell me something,' said Uale, the Vailima gardener in his ragged T-shirt. 'What do you think of Margaret Mead?'

Western Samoa is a surprising place. The people have great dignity; you don't patronize them; they patronize you.

16

In late September 1890, the Stevensons moved in at Vailima, squatting, rather as they had at Silverado, while the big house was built. The bush was already cleared and Fanny began making a vegetable garden. They lived temporarily in a two-storey building they called Pineapple Cottage; Stevenson continued to write, though he also worked on the estate.

This life was a great change from the sick-rooms of Europe. He could be out with his *naifi* (which he called by its swashbuckling Caribbean name, 'cutlass'), clearing paths in the forest under

Mount Vaea, following the river, finding old banana patches; alone in the spooky forest with its strangling lianas and whistling birds.

*

Very little has changed today beyond Vailima Stream. The forest is hot, silent and alive, the air still, as if waiting. You understand why some of Stevenson's servants disliked going into the bush where *o aitu*, ghosts, were supposed to lurk; and it still feels haunted. Stevenson had twinges of superstition: 'Am I beginning to be sucked in? Shall I become a midnight twitterer like my neighbours?'

In those thick jungly woods I was startled by a crack like a pistol going off and a thumping tatter – a heavy coconut dropped through thick leaves. RLS wrote to Colvin in 1890: 'I have taken refuge in a new story, which just shot through me like a bullet in one of my moments of awe, alone in the tragic jungle.' It was called at first *The High Woods of Ulufanua*, it would become the first, and possibly still the greatest Samoan novel, *The Beach of Falesá*.

*

Fanny was the real pioneer at Vailima. 'I was never a coward in my life,' she wrote of herself, 'and never lost my presence of mind in any emergency.' This is borne out by her experiences at Vailima: out of a jungle of amazing plants and vampire bats she fought to wrest a home and a garden. She could make a pig-pen and battle the pigs inside it, and she could mend a draughty stove and cure canker in a dog's ear or a machete wound. She was eminently practical and her real love was her garden. As soon as they moved in she planted potatoes, tomatoes, sweetcorn, peas, onions, lettuce, radishes and melons on the cleared jungle floor where they had never grown before.

Yet she was hurt when her husband said she was a peasant not an artist. In her marvellous diary she wonders why she was so hurt, when she really believed that the peasant life was the happiest. Louis thought she dug 'like a demented beast' because she had the peasant's love of her own land. But it was not ownership that spurred her on. 'When I plant a seed or a root, I plant a bit of my heart with it . . . when the tender leaves put forth I know that in a manner I am a creator.'

Her diaries show her to have been creative in the widest sense. It can never have been easy to have RLS as a husband, and they kept each other on their mettle with scorching rows. Part of her chafed for an independent source of income, which she could do with as she wanted. Her diary is ironic about men's behaviour; she did not want to be 'kept' and 'protected', lying under the table and handing out cartridges to a buffoon like Bazett Haggard, if war came. She was a powerful and remarkable woman.

'A violent friend, a brimstone enemy', her husband wrote of her, 'is always either loathed or slavishly adored; indifference impossible.' So it is with accounts of her spells of illness, which some call madness, at Vailima. Many biographers of her husband dislike her, and ascribe a malign influence to her. They are not apt to be sympathetic to what ailed her. Living in the storms of creative elation and depression, few people suffer quite like a writer's wife. And their marriage was happy, in its rich, strange way.

17

On this island full of voices, Vailima underwent its sea-change. There was no timber-mill on Upolu so the lumber was imported, some of it redwood from California. The house with its great verandah and polished floors went up; it would be comfortable and airy, but not exactly empty. Crates of linen and china and books and pictures came up the road from Apia, in all seventy-two tons of crated furniture, which had come round half the world from Heriot Row and Skerryvore. Stevenson ordered all the lamps kept lit at night so that he could see his mansion ablaze through the trees when he came back up the road on horseback from Apia.

*

Slowly, a household grew up. In May 1889, Stevenson had written to R. D. Blackmore that 'the family is the only natural moral fact, and a movement towards a larger sense of family relations, or generous sense of clanship, is the only road to safety for troubled mankind as a race'. At Vailima he built a circle of Samoan kith and four generations of Anglo-American kin, an extended family of between thirteen and thirty-one members which fitted well with the Samoan sense of 'ainga.

*

On the verandah of Vailima today hangs a copy of a well-known photograph that the Apia photographer A. J. Tattersall took on the same verandah on 31 July 1892. On this copy Stevenson wrote the names of all fourteen people in the picture, and signed it to Charles Warren Stoddard 'with the compliments of all hands'.

On the left, Joe Strong leans his elbow against a pillar. Joe has a puffy, drinker's face, a cockatoo on his shoulder, and wears a flowered *lavalava*, with belt and purse, over stockinged legs. On the right is the fierce-faced Tomasi, their Fijian assistant cook, a bandolier of flowers across his bare chest, holding an axe at port arms with the blade uppermost. Between these two are the Stevenson family and retainers. Maggie Stevenson sits in profile on a chair in her white starched widow's cap, looking like a thinner version of Queen Victoria; below her sits her peaky-looking white maid, Mary Carter, probably the only woman in the picture wearing corsets. Lloyd Osbourne, called 'Loia' by the Samoans, stands on the verandah with arms folded, very much the overseer of the estate. There is something arrogant and sensual in his stance. Stevenson sits beside Lloyd, extremely thin, almost gaunt, his hair, now cut short by Belle, slicked over his narrow head. The family had dubbed him 'The Tame Celebrity'. Fanny sits beside him, her hand against her cheek, with two large flowers pinned to her dress, her mouth rather turned down. She is as RLS described her to J. M. Barrie: 'infinitely little, extraordinary wig of grey curls . . . insane black eyes . . . tiny bare feet, a cigarette, wild blue dress usually spotted with garden mould'. But she has laid aside the cigarette for the photographer. Fanny, 'the weird woman', was known behind her back as *O le Fafine Mamana o le Maunga*, 'the witch woman of the mountain'.

Belle sits below her mother on the verandah steps, dark hair pulled back off dark-toned face, full-lipped and dreamy-eyed, seemingly more Russian than European. To the Samoans she was *Teuila*, because she would garland them with flowers of that name. Belle holds her eleven-year-old son Austin, a barefoot boy in a striped shirt – he has a painful 'photograph face', screwed up in the bright sunshine. And there are the other servants: Lafiele the muscular cattle-man; slim Simi, the butler; Talolo the chief cook, a *matai*'s son, with flowers in his hair; Auvea, the plantation hand; Eelene, the laundress, wearing an elaborate casque of leaves and buds; and Arrick, the Solomon Islander, an escapee from a German plantation, who Stevenson described as 'Pantry Boy cannibal'. It is the clan of Ona, the rich man.

Stevenson was a quite different kind of patriarch from his father; he took a broader view. RLS's 'Vailima Prayers', written for the Sunday evening service in which the whole extended family participated, are not narrowly pious, but part of a ceremony of clan bonding and reflection.

Household order was not lax: Vailima was run like a good ship, with discipline and fairness, and everyone knew their duties. Stevenson knew that he could, on the instant, be 'the old man virulent, stumbling into anger', and so justice was ceremonial and never on the same day of the offence. Small breaches of the Vailima code resulted in fines: the Protestants' fines went to Roman Catholic coffers, and vice versa. This shows a sense of humour, at least. Serious offences merited a *suenga* or trial. And the Samoans responded; you knew exactly where you were with Tusitala.

Stevenson was the *matai* of his *'ainga*. He was the earner for the whole household, and he cared for those in his responsibility. One man, Elinga, had a tumour on his back, for which he was mocked: Stevenson arranged for the wen to be surgically removed, and Elinga was accepted once again by his village, and earned titles and land.

Stevenson did not suffer from the 'Prospero complex' because he was not a self-deceiver. His people were not Calibans or Ariels, and he did not try to make them into little Britishers. He respected Samoan ways, and adopted some of their modes: household *kava* was served at 2.30 (with Tusitala taking the first coconut shell of it) much as tea might have been taken elsewhere and at other times in the Empire. In the endless dance of presents that make up Samoan courtesy, his were neither too big nor too small. He earned respect, made not a few white enemies, and many Samoan friends.

When Adelaide Boodle, the 'Gamekeeper' of Skerry vore, told him she wanted to become a missionary among 'natives' he advised her:

> Remember that *you cannot change ancestral feelings of right and wrong without what is practically soul-murder.* Barbarous as the customs may seem . . . always find in them some seed of good; see that you always develop them . . . In fact what you have to do is to teach the parents in the interests of their great-grandchildren.

It is paternalism, for he lived in a paternalistic epoch, but it is also tolerant and far-sighted.

18

Vailima today is like a large plantation mansion set in huge lawns. Rich Germans, and later New Zealand High Commissioners and their green-fingered wives, followed the Stevensons here, and each subsequent set of inhabitants 'improved' and domesticated the house and grounds. So many wings and extensions have been built on that you can no longer clearly see where the original spare colonial house begins and ends. At the end of the long drive a hand-painted sign under the large portico tells you to 'Enter on Official Business Only.' Mine must have been Official, for the Head of State's daughter-in-law, Mrs Malietoa Laupepa, allowed me to wander around the empty, rambling house. The ground floor is ringed by a long windowed verandah with woven Lloyd Loom wicker chairs and tables. The Stevensons' dark dining-room and staircase are as they were, but painted white. Upstairs is the same tropical ministry of works furniture, very much government guest house. Fans hang like silent propellors from the light blue ceiling. Five volumes of the Vailima Edition are missing from a bookcase.

Stevenson's room was tucked away at the west end of the upstairs verandah, like a port-side pilot's cabin on the bridge of his house, over-looking the lawn they had made and the thick forests of Mount Vaea to the left; in the distance he could see every ship that steamed into Apia harbour. Stevenson always liked to work in a small, bare room. 'A deal kitchen table and a small bed are all I require. Chairs are an unnecessary luxury, a mat flung on the floor is all one wants.' The grand house was for show and entertainment; its engine room was a spartan cell, with a rack of Colt's rifles on the wall in case the wars ever came their way. Here he wrote almost unstoppably; *Catriona, St Ives, The Wrecker, Weir of Hermiston*, his remarkable letters, the *Fables* and much more.

It was an extraordinary life, divided between Samoan business and physical activity and the realm of the imagination which could take him thousands of miles away. One day a particular smell of rain on earth made him literally stagger, overcome with emotion, as he stood on the verandah outside his workroom.

I knew I had found a frame of mind and body that belonged to Scotland . . . highland huts and peat smoke, and the brown swirling rivers, and wet clothes, and whisky, and the romance of the past, and that indescribable bite of the whole thing at a man's heart which is – or rather lies at the bottom of – a story.

This is very Scottish, having the ability to settle well in a foreign country while retaining a strong sense of the old homeland. They were not just day-dreams for Stevenson; he wrote them into his work. Distance, memory, and great literary skill – all these things made him a forerunner of those twentieth-century modernist exiles who lived abroad in order to write better about home.

19

On the last day of February 1891, the American Consul-General invited Stevenson on a *malanga*, or trip, to the eastern islands of Samoa, those that now comprise American Samoa. Stevenson was in Apia on 1 March when all the flags were lowered to half-mast: *Samesoni*, Captain Hamilton, the Apia pilot, was dead. That evening, a hot night with a full moon, Stevenson offered his condolences to Mary, his Samoan widow, and went in to see the body at Matautu:

> . . . the Captain's hands were folded on his bosom; he looked as if he might speak at any moment; I have never seen this kind of waxwork so express or more venerable; and when I went away, I was conscious of a certain envy for the man who was out of the battle.

There was one jarring note: the horribly hearty Dr Bernard Funk, lover of strong cocktails and young girls, came pounding in with a lighted cigar in his mouth, filling the room with his strident voice. Three-and-a-half years later, this same Dr Funk would pronounce Robert Louis Stevenson dead.

Stevenson had the image of the dead man in his mind all night on the boat. When he reached the land-locked loch of Pango Pango harbour, 'Captain Hamilton's folded hands and quiet face said a great deal more to me than the scenery.'

*

My 'cousin' fixed me a ticket to Tutuila, the principal island of American Samoa. Bob's son Danny Rankin was a pilot with Polynesian Airlines, the national airline of Western Samoa; when Danny introduced me to people in Apia as a relative, it felt good to be part of an *'ainga*.

The fourteen-seater Nomad flew back east from Faleolo directly over Mount Vaea and the pale blue roofs of the house at Vailima. There was still a lot of forest on the island. From the air, I lusted over the tiny uninhabited islands of Nu'ulua and Nu'utele, green croissants at the eastern end of Upolu.

Pango Pango International Airport is on the south coast of Tutuila island in American Samoa. Coming in to land, you can see waves shocking into the black volcanic rocks and collapsing in gouts of foam. Storm clouds hang over the mountains.

*

I soon discovered that they did not accept Western Samoan *tālās* in American Samoa, and nor would anyone change them. The US dollar rules. Tutuila is only eighty miles from Upolu and though the Samoans speak the same language and share the same culture, they have had a different currency, flag and politics since 1900, when the US got the eastern islands and the Germans the western.

The public lavatories at the American Samoan airport said *Tane* and *Fafine* (Men and Women) whereas ones in Western Samoa were signed *Ali'i* and *Tama'itai* (Gentlemen and Ladies). Chiefly titles were higher in Western Samoa; it was one reason why the eastern Samoans didn't want to rejoin any Samoan confederation. They thought they were better off as a US Territory. They were 'US Nationals', which meant they didn't have the status of citizens, but did have free access to mainland USA, and dollars flowed into their economy.

I made some calls from the airport. Somebody told me that a Joe Theroux, who wrote for *Pacific Islands Monthly*, was worth talking to. I rang him to arrange a meeting the next day and asked:

'Are you related to Paul Theroux?'

'He's my brother. Three of us are novelists. You should read my book, *Black Coconuts and Brown Magic*'

'I will.'

Stevenson came to American Samoa from a funeral, and I arrived to one. The dance floor of Herb and Sia's Motel had been transformed into a mourning *fale* and an elderly Samoan woman, surrounded by friends, rocked and keened quietly over a pile of fine mats. A *matai* had died, and kegs of beef were being trundled in for the wake. A shirtless lad said I could have a bunk in a dormitory for $5. In the small room next door a crop-headed German in wire-framed spectacles lay reading on the bed clad only in a pair of shorts. A *Wandervogel*.

I went out to have a look at Fangatongo, the principal town of American Samoa. It's on the south side of Pango Pango harbour, a long loch ringed by high volcanic hills clothed in forest. Mount Pioa, the Rainmaker, dominates it to the east. I walked west, looking for a great-grandson of Stevenson's friend, H. J. Moors.

The duty free shop was crammed with Japanese electronic gadgetry, an avalanche of goods compared to the stores of Western Samoa. I asked the fat Samoan guy behind the counter if Wayne Moors was in.

'Who's lookin' for him?'

I introduced myself and he admitted he was Wayne. 'I wondered if you could put me in touch with your uncle Oliver. I gather he's got some papers to do with H. J. and Stevenson.'

A smaller man butted in: 'He's an asshole. We ain't speakin' to him. The old guy's paranoid, lives down at the beach with a big dog and a shotgun.'

I looked at the new speaker. 'This is my brudder Lyle,' explained Wayne. We shook hands, and they made it clear it would be hard to talk to Oliver. 'He ain't got no papers anyway.' Later I heard that Oliver had left Western Samoa after threatening, in his cups, to assassinate the Head of State.

'So,' said Lyle, 'you're interested in Stevenson, huh? I been workin' as an adviser for that TV film they're gonna make next year. ABC TV from Sydney. They're gonna rebuild Vailima up the hill like when he was livin' there. Big production.'

Lyle changed some *tālās* into dollars for me. 'Why'd'ya change your money into *tālās*? It's a con-trick. You can get everything you want in Apia for dollars, too. *Tālās* are shit, man.'

A cable car runs across Pango Pango harbour up to the giant TV transmitters on Mount Alava. The early sixties idea was that everyone would be educated through television: you could see kids on the floor of a *fale* illuminated by the blue glow, and hear the inane voices or gunfire. Below the TV towers are the wharves and factories of Star Kist Tuna, American Can Company, Van Camp Seafood Company. Tuna chunks and fish for petfood were the main exports of American Samoa. A cable car slid down the wire towards me. Two unsmiling white Americans got out, wearing dark glasses and Hawaiian shirts. Maybe I watch too much TV myself, but they looked like cartoon CIA men in tropical camouflage.

I stared across at Mount Pioa, the Rainmaker, furred with green against a clear blue sky. Stevenson had seen the mountain making rain one Saturday night when rats had woken him from sleep. He watched the moonlit clouds

> flashing from dusk to silver, and thrusting forth strange horns and promontories . . . Even as I gazed, a cloud grounded on the summit of Pioa; it seemed to hang and gather there, and darken as it hung: and I was scarce fled to shelter ere the rain struck and roared about the house.

*

Back in the motel, I lay on my bunk reading Joseph Theroux's first novel, *Black Coconuts and Brown Magic*, devouring it in a few enjoyable hours. It's a tropical comedy of cultural misunderstanding, which sometimes made me laugh out loud. But there was a darker vein of murder and violence, and some startling facts. One of the characters, a woman psychiatrist, is writing a paper on the toll of Vietnam:

> American Samoa is third in the world in per capita beer consumption, just behind Australia and West Germany. Veterans are a part of that group . . . American Samoa lost more men in Vietnam per capita than any American community of similar size. The volunteers, who believed the recruiters' speeches, became not officers or technicians but mere cannon fodder . . . These were American nationals, not citizens, and so not subject to the draft. Volunteers.

Four of the six bunks were occupied. Francis was fully Samoan, and Peter was half. Both of them wanted to join the US Armed Forces. Francis had four brothers in the service and he was keen to sign up too. Samoa has a warrior tradition and they esteem bravery. Uncle Sam has a ready supply of grunts for the future; half of American Samoa is under sixteen.

It was a dire night, warmth turning to cold, the old sailor in one bunk coughing, then snoring; a dog fighting its way into a dustbin outside, rooting in frenzy. I woke from a nightmare where I was in freezing rain, wrapped in white bandages, laid out like a corpse.

22

Stevenson had a fine trip in March and April 1891. He went along the northern coast and in the bay of Oa saw a whole tree fluttering alive with butterflies. He camped on the beach, and was first up in the morning, as was his habit. He noticed how the Samoans slept like old-time Scots used to:

> The Highlander in his belted plaid, the Samoan with his *lavalava*, each sleep in their one vesture unfolded.

Later that morning, Stevenson sat in a shed overlooking the lovely bay, with the buhac powder burning beside him against mosquitoes:

> . . . and read Livy, and compared today and two thousand years ago, and wondered in which of these two epochs I was flourishing at that moment; and then I would stroll out and see . . . the arcs of beaches, curved like the whorl in a fair woman's ear, and huge ancient trees jutting high overhead out of the hanging forest, and feel the place belonged to the age of fable and awaited Aeneas and his battered fleets.

The fleets of the US Navy took over eastern Samoa in 1900. The United States, officially and rhetorically anti-colonial, had no Department to administer its own colonies, and so the Navy administered the Territory of American Samoa until 1951, when the Department of the Interior took over. Stevenson recorded in 1891:

Pango Pango is not popular with the gentlemen of the American navy. They say it is hot, feverish and dull, and are said to languish for the joys of poker.

As a guest of the American Consul-General, Stevenson took part in negotiations with a group of *matais*. The Americans wished to buy the land between Swimming and Observatory Points in Pango Pango harbour, and turn an ancestral Samoan burying-ground into their Naval 'establishment'.

Negotiators sat in a *fale* with their backs against wooden pillars, lit by a petroleum lantern, smoking banana-leaf cigarettes. The deal was agreed, the chiefs would sell the land. The bag of money was there; mixed, like the coinage at the end of *Treasure Island*, 'Chile dollars and half dollars, English shillings, American twenty cent pieces, the maddening currency of the islands'. Then a scrupulous chief spotted a snag: if they took the money before the bones were dug up, were they not selling the remains of their ancestors? Eventually it was agreed that the money should be given to a trustee until disinterment was over. *Kava* was made and drained bravely: it was made in the old way, by girls chewing the *Piper methysticum* roots before soaking in water (salivary enzymes help extract the active ingredients). Stevenson thought it 'an offensive process' and called it 'spit-kava'.

Now it was time for my lunch.

23

Joe Theroux looked almost Samoan on his dust-cover photo: a big man with folded arms, thick hair and a black Mexican bandit moustache. I climbed into his battered white jeep and we shook hands.

We ate hamburgers in a restaurant. I stared at my plate when Joe said: 'Stevenson was just a romantic.'

I remembered the advice of a character in *Black Coconuts*: 'Stay away from Stevenson and the poets. They didn't know the Pacific from a doorknob. Stick with the guys who lived it.' Of course, Stevenson *had* lived it. Perhaps it was the aura of 'romance' that irritated Joe, or perhaps he just disliked Stevenson's Britishness. Joe kindly gave me an offprint of his from *The Journal of Pacific History*, 'Some Misconceptions About RLS', which may have cleared up some, but also perpetrated others.

Joe Theroux knew Samoa at any rate. He had come to Western Samoa as a volunteer in the Peace Corps, the *Pisikoa*. He spoke Samoan and it was a family joke back home in New England that he told them off for saying 'S'moa' instead of the correct 'Sārmoa'. He was currently working on another Pacific novel.

Joe had researched Harry Jay Moors for some good articles in *Pacific Islands Monthly*. The descendants of Harry Moors and Stevenson's solicitor, Hetherington Carruthers, were Samoan now, and the white ancestors had been assimilated into a Polynesian past that is not so concerned with papers and written records – the basis of European history. It was an oral culture, not a literate one, and genealogy was more likely to form a chant than a chart. Paper, of course, has a shorter life in the tropics, and writing is hard in the heat. Looters from outside had sometimes stolen what written records there were. One of the Moors aunts had lent some manuscripts to a collector in naive trust, but they had disappeared. When Oliver Moors lent a picture of Stevenson he had inherited to an exhibition in Apia, it came back with the signature cut out. But even the oral culture was adapting: it was interesting to hear that the first novel written completely in Samoan had only recently appeared. The author was an orator, a *tulafale* or 'talking-chief' from Savai'i.

24

I didn't really like the American version of Samoa; Pango was oppressive and a faint threat of violence hung in the air. I didn't like the policeman with his black uniform, gunbelt, nightstick and handcuffs, and I wanted to get back to Western Samoa where people seemed both poorer and prouder, and the policemen strolled about in blue skirts and didn't even bother to carry their stick.

I went to the airport. But I had not confirmed the flight clearly marked on my ticket, and there was no seat.

'But I've got to get back. I must get a flight today.'

'All fully booked I'm afraid.'

'What about tomorrow? I've got to . . . '

'Fully booked.'

'*Oh no!*'

'You'll have to try standby from the early morning. Might work.'

'I'm running out of money. I've got *tālās* but no one will change them. The banks just laugh.'

'Can't help you, I'm afraid.'

*

God bless Joe Theroux for rescuing the whimpering Limey. He picked me up from the airport and took me home, where he and his wife Diane made an excellent dinner. During an entertaining evening – he is a savagely funny mimic –Joe and I discussed the controversy over Derek Freeman's book, *Margaret Mead and Samoa: The Making and Unmaking of an Anthropological Myth* (1983), which is a demolition job on the work that made Margaret Mead famous: *Coming of Age In Samoa* (1928). Mead saw life in the eastern Samoan islands as gentle, loving and free from stress. Freeman, by contrast, saw Samoan society as rigidly authoritarian, ruled by protocol and puritanism, with frequent outbursts of aggression and rape and a high suicide rate. For Freeman, Mead was a naive dupe, and the pleasant smiling mask of the islanders was a mask of deception. He regularly quotes 'the incomparable Robert Louis Stevenson' with approval. But Stevenson's evidence does not always confirm Freeman's thesis that the Samoans are profoundly puritanical, and esteem virginity above all. RLS quotes one song Samoan boatmen sang on the very island where we were.

> *Leaga lava te fafine Samoa*
> *A faitai faasee le oloa*
>
> 'Tis shameful in the Samoan maid
> To sell herself for the white man's trade

I translate with delicacy, the other verses of the song scarce support the moral promise of the first; and become indeed extremely skittish.

RLS also saw erotic dances in Tutuila, with children of all ages applauding the indecency; and the lewd models of the human anatomy that a small boy made in the sand, and which he explained to Stevenson, left nothing to the imagination. RLS commented: 'the Samoan loves the business like pie'.

There is another point in Mead's favour – she did her fieldwork research from 1925 to 1926 in Luma village on the easternmost island of the Samoan archipelago, Ta'ū. This island is part of the Manu'a group, about eighty miles east of Tutuila and Pango Pango.

'Manu'a was always different,' said Joe Theroux, 'They used to worship the sun.'

Freeman treats all of Samoa as a unity and discredits Mead's observations of life on Ta'ū with statistics and incidents from other islands. Manu'a's paramount title – *Tui Manu'a* – was the highest in the archipelago. Tangaloa-a-Langi, the supreme god and creator of everything, including the chief system, was supposed to live on Ta'ū's highest mountain.

Stevenson had been eager to see Manu'a and made several unsuccessful attempts before he managed to get there in June 1894, courtesy of the Royal Navy warship, HMS *Curaçoa*. He found a complete break with tradition. A girl called Margaret Young had been installed as the ruler Tu'i Manu'a. Stevenson wrote about his Ta'ū visit to Henry James:

> The three islands of Manu'a are independent and are ruled over by a little slip of a half-caste girl about twenty, who sits all day in a pink gown, in a little white European house with about a quarter of an acre of roses in front of it, looking at the palm trees on the village street, and listening to the surf. This, so far as I could discover, was all she had to do. 'This is a very dull place' she said.

Stevenson also noticed that the kava ceremony had

> some very original features. The young men who run for the kava have a right to misconduct themselves *ad libitum* on the way back . . . they came beating the trees and posts of the houses, leaping, shouting and yelling like Bacchants . . . My name was called next after the captain's, and several chiefs (a thing quite new to me, and not at all Samoan practice) drank to me by name.

It is possible that there might have been other cultural differences on Ta'ū, and Margaret Mead may not have been so wrong as Professor Freeman so fiercely insists.

25

Joe Theroux lent me $20 and drove me back to Herb and Sia's. I took the same bunk. Richard, the American seaman, paced the room talking endlessly, his speech all oaths and curses, genitals and bowels. He was an avid newspaper reader and collector of 'facts'. He remembered a New York barkeeper who was keeping a cutting to show to his son when he grew up. It gave the cost of the Vietnam war as $634,000,000,000. Richard was an angry veteran, bitter about government duplicity; a confused populist in a $5 bunk.

It was a terrible night. What if there was no plane tomorrow? I saw the connecting flights all collapsing like a row of dominoes, the project falling apart, pages shredding and scattering, tickets invalid, money gone, trapped in American Samoa for ever, begging from tourists along the wharf.

A fitful sleep was broken by dogs fighting, the chanting of hymns, a distant hysterical TV; an idiot in a baseball cap rummaging through my clothes for 'cigarettes'; a fat lady moving mysteriously through the darkness; snoring; cold; the whining of mosquitoes; and the depressing smell of old blankets and sweat.

I got up early and walked through faint drizzle to my usual place, the Ala Moana lunch counter, for Breakfast No. 1. To my right was the hatch from the kitchen to the outside world, serving take-away customers. A young Samoan male looked sullenly in.

'*Palangi!* . . . fucking this island!' The bitter speech continued in Samoan which I didn't understand; but body language is universal, and he meant me. The nervous glances of the women in the kitchen confirmed it. I looked at him; hard face, crazy eyes. 'What you fuckin' starin' at?' he shouted. 'Don't you look at me!'

I stared down at Breakfast No. 1. It was not yet seven o'clock, and after a rough night, I had a drunk to deal with, one who was beyond roaring and staggering but on the cold plateau of mad lucidity and long-fuelled violence. I tried to prong a moody forkful of toast and egg, and saw that my hand was not quite steady. The hectoring tirade went on and an agitated woman hissed, 'He's stupid.'

I had not been in a fight for seventeen years, and yet part of my mind computed the moves if he stepped inside, right leg back off the stool, the innocent breakfast knife and fork transformed into weapons of defence. It was ludicrous. A woman slipped out the back as the harangue continued: I thought I heard 'CIA'. The man was going to waste a spook, a TV fantasy, and I was it.

Then a door behind me opened, and a large Samoan in a brown *lavalava* entered. I say large; he was huge, with the sort of traditional build that has made Polynesians good sumo-wrestlers in Japan. He moved *fa'aSamoa*, a purposeful walk of dignity and presence.

'Good morning,' he said in a deep brown voice, and his huge hand rested lightly on my damp shoulder as he passed by me. Then he blocked out the light in the door.

The drunk's voice rose and I saw his white-knuckled hand gripping the edge of the hatch. The big man moved him back, gentle as a strolling mountain. A vehicle door slammed and an engine roared off. The relief in the diner was palpable; the women smiled, one said: 'Some people crazy in the head.'

I apologized in the English way. The big man sauntered back, 'Sorry about that. He had one too many last night.'

*

Sullen weather, surly faces. I took a series of buses heading west to the airport – they are travelling juke-boxes. The driver sits very low in a nylon fur seat, eyes just above the rim of the crude dashboard; by the gearstick is a rack of cassettes and a stereo sound system wired to strings of tiny bulbs that wink and flash to the beat of reggae, rock or soul.

The rain wept over the bay; green mountains shugged past, banana trees gleamed. At the airport turn-off I ran splashing for shelter on the porch of a store, joining a group of Samoan high school kids. Some of the boys had the absurd body-armour of American football under their team sweaters. A youth said something in Samoan and others grinned and sniggered. I smiled at the joker – 'Good morning to you, too' – and he looked away sheepishly.

The last bus had a furry dashboard, a necklace of miniature vodka bottles clanking across the windshield, and a Church of Prophecy decal plastered on a Pioneer speaker, wedged at the head of the aisle. The driver had thick sideburns and shades, and his head bobbed as the lights flashed and the music boomed. You get a lot for your quarter.

I ran into the airport at ten to eight. Four hours of desperation and embarrassment followed, pitiful threats and bluster, new stratagems, devised sitting on the concrete floor, fresh pleadings, too many cigarettes, and gnawing anxiety. It was a betrayal of all the lessons I had learned when I fancied myself 'a traveller' in South America, all the stoicism and patience and fatalistic acceptance. I was just another wretched white tourist, desperate to get off US territory.

I almost wept when I got a boarding card for Western Samoa.

26

In July 1893, Stevenson saw his first and last war; the thing he had so longed for as a young man in Europe. 'Shall we never shed blood? The prospect is too grey . . .'. He had had to wait till his life was nearly over before he actually saw what he had once envisaged as drums and trumpets.

In the event, war sickened him. Villages were burned, fruit-trees cut down, warriors with blackened faces danced in the ruins with bits of pork in their teeth to signify severed heads. The warriors of the German-backed Laupepa brought in fourteen heads to display to their chief, including (and this was a new barbarism) those of three women. Mata'afa, the Samoan leader backed by Harry Moors and the Stevensons, was defeated in the skirmish.

Stevenson rode down on Sunday 9 July to visit the wounded at the mission. 'I found Apia, and myself, in a strange state of flusteration; my own excitement was gloomy and (I may say) truculent; others appeared imbecile; some sullen.' It was not a glorious affair.

The ten wounded lay around the walls with their helpers. One man, shot through the bowels, was 'dying rather hard in a gloomy stupor of pain and laudanum, silent, with contorted face'. Though depressed by the war, Stevenson was surprised by his lack of squeamishness at 'hospital sights, etc.; things that used to murder me'. He made himself useful: 'I held some of the things at an operation, and did not care a dump.'

*

This war was wholly unnecessary. It caused fierce arguments between Fanny and Louis; she thought they should support Mata'afa even more strongly. They blamed themselves that in counselling Mata'afa to strive for peace, they had led him to be outmanoeuvred and defeated. The nervous excitement of war affected everyone; Rider Haggard's brother, Bazett, who was then a Land Commissioner, drank too much, grew wildly romantic and got into a punch-up at the Tivoli Hotel.

War brought out the Scots choler in RLS; he sulked when Fanny refused to stay at home; snapped savagely at a Naval officer and later, at a missionary's wife. Fanny behaved badly at a dinner by calling all the whites in Samoa, save H. J. Moors, 'cowards'. But they were desperately uncertain days, full of rumours and wild allegations, and with so many armed men about and feelings running high a massacre seemed on the cards.

Both Fanny and Louis Stevenson blamed the war on the three consuls: Bierman (Germany); Blacklock (USA); and Cusack-Smith (Great Britain). 'Well,' wrote Fanny bitterly in her journal, 'there was a woman's head for each great power, or, if one likes better, for each consul.'

It was the Great Powers that had insisted on supporting Laupepa and unseating Mata'afa, even though Laupepa had already ceded to Mata'afa and agreed that he should be king. Mata'afa had been clearly chosen by the Samoan people as their leader; but the consuls had overruled the vote because Laupepa was more malleable by foreign masters. No one behaved with any credit. Mata'afa surrendered to the British and they promptly handed him over to the Germans. He was then condemned to live in exile with a dozen other chiefs in Jaluit, the German headquarters in the Marshall Islands.

Exile was a draconian punishment for a Polynesian. RLS took up Mata'afa's case, badgered *The Times* and a Westminster MP with his very small, very far away grievance:

> . . . it is only the case of under a score of brown skinned men who have been dealt with in the dark by I know not whom. And I want to know. I want to know by whose authority Mata'afa was given over into German hands . . . In its small way, this is another case of Toussaint L'Ouverture . . . with circumstances of small perfidy that make it almost odious.

27

The chiefs that had supported Mata'afa were held in Apia jail. Stevenson visited them there and brought gifts of kava and tobacco. The chiefs feasted him; it was clearly a political demonstration, a studied affront to the ruling powers. He continued to visit and lobby for them, and managed to get hospital care for one sick *matai*. Stevenson paid for their food until the authorities were finally shamed into action.

A little over a year after the war had ended, the last of the imprisoned chiefs, old Po'e, was released. Po'e came up to Vailima with eight other chiefs who had also been in jail. Stevenson had *'ava* made; they all sat down on the floor, together.

These titular chiefs or *ali'i* did not speak in council themselves; they had a special 'talking chief', an orator called a *tulafale*:

> His face was quite calm and high-bred as he went through the usual Samoan expressions of politeness and compliment, but when he came on to the subject of their visit, on their love and gratitude to Tusitala, how his name was always in their prayers, and his goodness to them when they had no other friend . . . he warmed up to real, burning, genuine feeling. I had never seen the Samoan mask of reserve laid aside before, and it touched me more than anything else.

The chiefs said they wanted to work on his road that joined the house to the public highway. Stevenson was at first suspicious:

> I should have to lay out a great deal of money on tools and food and to give wages under the guise of presents to some workmen who were most of them old and in ill-health.

But he was quite wrong; the chiefs meant to come back with their families and bring their own food. They asked to borrow tools, 'but it was specially mentioned that I was to make no presents'.

On the day appointed, 'bright and early up came the whole gang of them . . . and fell to on my new road'. It was an unprecedented event:

Now, whether or not their impulse will last them through the road does not matter to me one hair. It is the fact they have attempted it, that they have volunteered and are now trying to execute a thing that was never before heard of in Samoa.

Road-making was not popular in Samoa; it was normally a task the Germans tried to impose on the natives, and they hated it as much as German taxes. 'It does give me a sense of having done something in Samoa after all,' mused RLS.

The road, a third of a mile long, did get finished, and Stevenson invited all the chiefs responsible to a feast at Vailima which would celebrate and dedicate the road. He was going to put up his own sign, but the chiefs begged him to use their own inscription, which was duly painted on a finger post.

O LE ALA O LE LOTO ALOFA

Ua matou mafautau i le alofa sili o Iana susuga Tusitala i lana tausi alofa i le puapuagatia o i matou i le fale puipui a matou sauni ai se mea alofa ua sili e la pala e oo i le faavavau o le ala matou elia.

The chiefs put their names underneath, and the places they came from (i means 'of or 'from'), for example: Lelei i Palauli, Tupuola i Lotofaga, Ifopo i Lepa, Po'e i Siumu, and so on, seven in all.

There are several translations of ' *O Le Ala O Le Loto Alofa*' Literally, it means 'the road the heart love'. So Road of the Loving Heart – or Hearts – is a fair version many books use. But Stevenson's own translation was 'The Road of Gratitude'. Here is his version of the inscription that followed:

Considering the great love of Tusitala in his loving care of us in our distress in the prison, we have therefore prepared a splendid gift. It shall never be muddy, it shall endure for ever, this road that we have dug.

28

Everyone sat together on the verandah, and there were traditional speeches from the chiefs. Then Stevenson read aloud, in their own language, a long speech that he had written and sent to a missionary for translation into good Samoan. Though he did not know it, it would be his last public speech. And as Graham Balfour observed, it was also his most outspoken talk on Samoan affairs.

In his speech, Stevenson crowned a lifetime of support for the underdog and opposition to the 'Big Battalions', going back to *The Pentland Rising*, which he had written as a boy of sixteen. In the Samoan mode, it is like a sermon; ever since the influence of the different Christian churches had spread through the islands biblical quotation had become a notable feature of Samoan rhetoric.

Stevenson referred to the parable of the 'Talents':

> What are you doing with your talent, Samoa? Your three talents, Sava'i, Upolu and Tutuila? Have you buried it in a napkin? . . . You have rather given it out to be trodden under feet of swine: and the swine cut down fruit trees and burn houses, according to the nature of swine, or that much worse animal, foolish man . . .

Stevenson warned the Samoans: 'If you do not occupy and use your country, others will.' He told them how it had happened before, in Ireland, and in his own country Scotland, through occupation and subsequent depopulation; 'other people's sheep who graze upon the foundation of their houses'. He warned them too of the fate of Hawaii, and of the desolation of the empty villages 'in the midst of the white men's sugar fields'.

> I do not speak of this lightly, because I love Samoa and her people. I love the land, I have chosen it to be my home while I live, and my grave after I am dead; and I love the people, and have chosen them to be my people to live and die with. And I see that the day is come now of the great battle . . . whether you are to pass away like these other races of which I have been speaking, or to stand fast and have your children living on and honouring your memory in the land you received of your fathers . . .
>
> Now is the time for the true champions of Samoa to stand forth. And who is the true champion of Samoa? It is not the man who blackens his face, and cuts down trees and kills pigs

and wounded men. It is the man who makes roads, who plants food trees, who gathers harvests . . . using and improving that great talent that has been given him in trust. That is the brave soldier. That is the true champion . . .

And Stevenson praised the exiled Mata'afa, 'king over the water':

When he was still here among us, he busied himself planting cacao; he was anxious and eager about agriculture and commerce, and spoke and wrote continually; so that when we turn our minds to the same matters, we may tell ourselves that we are still obeying Mata'afa. *Ua tautala mai pea o ia ua mamao* (We continue rendering service though he has gone far away).

Mata'afa did not forget Stevenson's loyalty. A dozen years after RLS's death, the old chief spoke of him with emotion. 'After I am dead, men will connect our names,' he said. 'His wisdom was great and he was always for peace. His words have come true, all of them. God bless the spot where Tusitala lies!'

29

Robert Louis Stevenson died suddenly, three weeks after his forty-fourth birthday. He had foreseen something like it in a late poem, 'An End of Travel'.

> Let now your soul in this substantial world
> Some anchor strike. Be here the body moored;
> This spectacle immutably from now
> The picture in your eye; and when time strikes,
> And the green scene goes on the instant blind –
> The ultimate helpers, where your horse today
> Conveyed you dreaming, bear your body dead.

He had worked in the morning on *Weir of Hermiston*, a book which had a new kind of poetic density; 'its imaginative vision is hungry and tender just in proportion', wrote Henry James. RLS was writing about women in a new way; his last paragraph was about the young lovers 'quarrel at the Weaver's Stone. Archie is shocked by Kirstie's emotion:' In vain he looked back over the interview; he saw not where he had offended. It seemed unprovoked, a wilful convulsion of brute nature . . . ' The sentence remains unfinished.

*

A wilful convulsion of brute nature took him on the evening of Monday 3 December 1894. Fanny had been haunted by ominous dread all day, and they were together on the verandah as the sun went down. Stevenson was concerned for his wife and wanted to cheer her up; he had fetched up a bottle of Burgundy and was helping her to make a mayonnaise for the evening meal:

> . . . gaily talking, when suddenly he put both hands to his head and cried out, 'What's that?' Then he asked quickly, 'Do I look strange?' As he did so, he fell on his knees beside her.

Fanny and the servant Sosimo helped him to his grandfather's chair in the great hall, where he became unconscious. Fanny's cries brought Belle and Maggie Stevenson to his side.

Lloyd rode, coatless and hatless, pell-mell down to Apia. He found Dr Anderson of HMS *Wallaroo* at the Tivoli and gave him a horse. Dr Bernard Funk couldn't ride and a buggy had to be found. Dr Anderson arrived first, and quickly recognized the signs of 'thundering apoplexy', a stroke. The women had rolled up Stevenson's sleeves and were rubbing his thin arms with brandy. 'How can anybody write books with arms as thin as these?' said Anderson. Maggie Stevenson turned on him indignantly: 'He has written *all* his books with arms like these!'

Funk and Anderson both worked, but they could do nothing. Stevenson never regained consciousness and died at ten past eight in the evening.

Lloyd Osbourne carried out Stevenson's wish to be buried on Mount Vaea. 'Loia' called on all the chiefs he knew to send men for the work; an Apia store was opened to supply axes, mattocks, shovels and *naifis*, scores of white vests and bolts of black cotton cloth to make mourning *lavalavas*.

Stevenson's body was washed and dressed in a soft linen shirt, white tie, black evening trousers with dark blue silk sash, blue silk socks and patent leather shoes. Over his heart was the thistle pin from the Hawaiian Scots Club, and on his left hand the silver ring he had married Fanny with fourteen years before. The Red Ensign that had flown over the *Casco* covered his body and the Roman Catholics among his servants kept vigil by candlelight.

Work began on a path up the trackless steep mountain before dawn on Tuesday 4 December; the forty Samoans hewing and hacking did not sing. Below, early in the morning, chiefs brought their finest and oldest mats to the body lying in state in the hall at Vailima. The '*ie tonga* represented wealth, status and respect in Samoa, and these particular mats were so valuable that Fanny returned them to their donors afterwards.

Early in the afternoon the coffin began its journey up the mountain. It was a steaming hot day, and the box was relayed from shoulder to shoulder with difficulty. *The Samoa Times* reported: 'The bearers in some places could do no more than retain their hold of ropes.' The mourners, some of them elderly, struggled to get up the hill after them, holding on to roots of trees.

The burial took place at two o'clock. Reverend Clarke, who had seen them on their first day ashore in Apia five years before, read the burial service and one of Stevenson's prayers. Sixty Samoans and nineteen Europeans saw Stevenson's coffin laid in a grave dug and filled in by his own men from Vailima. Then they left him alone on the mountain. '*Aüe!*' ran the Samoan lament, 'for Tusitala who sleeps in the forest.'

30

The road goes on for ever. *O Le Ala O Le Loto Alofa* is today a grassy track below the gates of Vailima which runs to the foot of Mount Vaea. It is the road you take to go up to Stevenson's grave. The true name seems to have been forgotten; on the 1980 map of Apia and environs it is *Ala O Le Alofa* (the Road of Love). And on the 1965 plaque of the cairn at its start it is called *O Le Ala O Le Agaalofa*, which means the Road of Loving Behaviour.

At the end of the Road of Gratitude, you cross Vailima Stream on a beam of wood. To the right the trickle drops forty feet into the pool where the Stevensons used to bathe. The forested mountain is ahead. I took the short track; a steep walk, and even though it was early morning, hot work. The reddish earth and the lizards scuttling over the buttresses of hardwood trees reminded me of Silverado. Mosquitoes whined in the gloom, birds whistled. My heart was galloping, the pebble gripped in my hand felt slippery, and the half hour to the top made my torn yellow shirt wet.

A sign in Samoan and English says 'All Plants, Trees and Other Animals Are Protected. No Shooting. No Cutting Trees.'

The grave is on the crown of the hill, surrounded by mown turf, and Louis and Fanny Stevenson's tomb is a slab of concrete with a raised bier, like a blunt green and white ship with a cabin. Most of the names scratched on it are Samoan. You can look down on the pale roofs and coconut groves of Vailima, some 700 feet below.

The tomb points north-east, and at 1350 feet above sea-level you can see Apia harbour, the wharf at Matautu and the crescents of reef. Way over the curve of the earth are nearly 3000 miles of Pacific Ocean to Hawaii and beyond. You are 10,000 miles from Scotland.

I spent a lovely few hours up there. It rained a warm rain, and then the sun came out again and I stood on the raft of tomb and sang Stevenson's words to the old Jacobite tune:

> Sing me a song of a lad that is gone,
>   Say, could that lad be I?
> Merry of soul he sailed on a day
>   Over the sea to Skye.
>
>   . . .
>
> Billow and breeze, islands and seas,
>   Mountains of rain and sun,
> All that was good, all that was fair,
>   All that was me is gone.

*

When Jack London came up here, he said it was one of the only graves in the world that he wanted to visit. The sailors from the Russian cruise ships used to come too; scores of matelots from Murmansk and Vladivostok as well as their counterparts from the USA. Travellers and tourists of every nationality had come to visit him, for, despite some decades of neglect by a few English academics, Stevenson is a world writer, read and responded to by ordinary readers in their millions. And he was read by other such writers: Borges, Buchan, Calvino, Chesterton, Conan Doyle, Conrad, Forster, Gide, Greene, James, Kipling, London, Nabokov, Owen, Schwob, Woolf, the list goes on.

Of my special triangle of writers, two were still busy that day. I had Borges's stone in my hand; perhaps he was at home in his apartment near Plaza San Martin, in Buenos Aires, with his cat Beppo and the Stevenson volumes bound in red, dictating a poem or being read to. Graham Greene was in London to give the Second Annual Jorge Luis Borges Lecture to the Anglo-Argentine Society; an elusive man's rare public appearance.

Stevenson had lain buried on that mountain for ninety years, and yet he was still alive in his pages, a friend to people who had never known him. The dead are not really dead while there is someone alive who remembers or reads them.

I lit a cigarette for Fanny and Louis, and stood it on the table in the grass-roofed hut near the tomb. It is a rite from Bolivia where they believe that spirits can still smell – and they were both avid smokers. A yellow butterfly came floating from the direction of the grave, fluttered through the wreathing smoke, and danced down the hill toward Vailima.

*

On the east side of a concrete bier was the epitaph Stevenson wrote for himself, on a plaque with his name and dates.

> Under the wide and starry sky,
> Dig the grave and let me lie.
> Glad did I live and gladly die,
>   And I laid me down with a will
>
> This be the verse you grave for me:
> *Here he lies where he longed to be,*
> *Home is the sailor, home from the sea,*
>   *And the hunter home from the hill.*

(Lord Cobham, Governor-General of New Zealand, once gave a £50 cheque to have that extraneous definite article in the penultimate line removed, but it has never been done. The 'all-round literary man' has a literal on his tomb.)

On the west side the plaque has a quote from the Book of Ruth, Chapter 1, Verses 16 & 17, in Samoan:

> . . . whither thou goest, I will go; and where thou lodgest, I will lodge . . . Where thou diest, I will die, and there will I be buried.

Fanny died of a cerebral haemorrhage, too, twenty years after her husband, and Belle brought her mother's ashes from California to be buried here. Her plaque, on the north end, has a tiger-lily and a hibiscus above the lines Stevenson wrote for her:

> Teacher, tender comrade, wife,
> A fellow-farer true through life . . .

I had seen the place of the name. Now it was time to take the lucky stone home and write the book that you hold.

SUGGESTED FURTHER

READING

BIOGRAPHIES

Balfour, Graham, *The Life of Robert Louis Stevenson*, Methuen, London, 1901

Furnas, J. C., *Voyage to Windward*, Faber, London, 1952

Pope Hennessy, James, *Robert Louis Stevenson*, Jonathan Cape, London, 1974

MEMOIRS

Guthrie, Lord, *Robert Louis Stevenson: Some Personal Recollections*, Green, Edinburgh, 1920

Hammerton, J. A. (ed.), *Stevensoniana: An Anecdotal Life and Appreciation of Robert Louis Stevenson*, Grant, Edinburgh, 1910

Masson, Rosaline (ed.), *I Can Remember Robert Louis Stevenson*, Chambers, Edinburgh, 1922

Strong, Isobel, and Osbourne, Lloyd, *Memories of Vailima*, Constable, London, 1903

LETTERS

Adam Smith, Janet (ed.), *Henry James and Robert Louis Stevenson: A Record of Friendship and Criticism*, Hart-Davis, London, 1948

Colvin, Sidney (ed.), *Letters of RLS to His Family and Friends*, London, 1911

Colvin, Sidney (ed.), *Vailima Letters*, London, 1899

Ferguson, D., and Waingrow, M. (eds.), *RLS: Stevenson's Letters to Charles Baxter*, Yale University Press, 1956

BIBLIOGRAPHICAL

Swearingen, Roger G., *The Prose Writings of Robert Louis Stevenson: A Guide*, Macmillan, London, 1980

Booth, Bradford A., Mehew, Ernest (eds.), *Collected Letters of Robert Louis Stevenson*, vols 1–8, Yale University Press, 1994–1995

Mehew, Ernest (ed.), *Selected Letters of Robert Louis Stevenson*, Yale University Press, 1997

CRITICAL

Calder, Jenni (ed.), *Stevenson and Victorian Scotland*, Edinburgh University Press, 1981

Maixner, Paul (ed.), *Robert Louis Stevenson: The Critical Heritage*, Routledge and Kegan Paul, London, 1981

MISCELLANEOUS

Chen, Jack, *The Chinese of America*, Harper and Row, San Francisco, 1981

Daws, Gavan, Holy Man: Father Damien of Molokai, Harper and Row, San Francisco, 1973

Daws, Gavan, *Shoal of Time: A History of the Hawaiian Islands*, University of Hawaii Press, Honolulu, 1968

Freeman, Derek, Margaret *Mead and Samoa: The Making and Unmaking of an Anthropological* Myth, Harvard University Press, 1983

Hanley, Sister Mary Laurence, and Bushnell, C. A., *A Song of Pilgrimage and Exile: The Life and Spirit of Mother Marianne of Molokai*, Franciscan Herald Press, Chicago, 1980

Jacobs, Michael, *The Good and Simple Life: Artist Colonies in Europe and America*, Phaidon, London, 1985

Mair, Craig, *A Star for Seamen: The Stevenson Family of Engineers*, John Murray, London, 1978

INDEX

edits RLS's work, 68, 267
first meeting with RLS, 63–4
friendship with RLS, 69, 81, 82,
  114, 121
letters to, 73, 120, 162, 179, 199,
  220, 288, 310, 326
on Conrad, 193
on RLS's politics, 210
Conrad, Joseph, 192–3, 310, 312,
  351
Cook, Captain James, 252–3, 274
Cooper, Lettice, 74
Cope, Mother Marianne, 278,
  281–5, 295
Cornhill Magazine, 58–9, 63, 111
Corot, Jean Baptiste Camille, 88
Cotier, Charles, 41
Crockett, S. R., 41
Cunningham, Alison, 19
Curtis, John, 210

Dalton, Alison, 125
Damien, Father, 275–8, 285–6,
  288, 293–4, 295
Darwin, Charles, 200
Dativr, Sister, 281, 285–7
Davies, Jack and Jamie, 175
Davos, 184, 186
Defoe, Daniel, 43
Delahant, Mike, 229, 231, 236
De Quincey, Thomas, 42, 217,
  295–6
Devonia, SS, 120–4, 126
Dilke, Sir Charles, 209
Disney, Walt, 76
Dole, Sanford, 296
Dostoevsky, Feodor, 211
Doyle, Sir Arthur Conan, 56, 105,
  217, 275, 351

'Dreams', see 'Chapter on
  'Dreams, A'
Drummond Street, 56–7
Durham, Katherine, 76, 172
Dutton, Joseph, 288

Earraid, 44, 46–52
Eastwood, Clint, 144
Ebb-Tide, The, 242, 310–12
Edinburgh, 6, 8–21, 27–8, 52–61,
  81
Edinburgh: Picturesque Notes, 10, 39,
  114
'Education of an Engineer, The',
  45–6
Edward VII as Bertie, Prince of
  Wales, 113, 209
Eelene, 328
Efi, Tupuola Taisi, 321
Eilers, Sister M. Crescentia, 279
Elinga, 329
Elisara, Filemoni, 324
Elko, 146–8
Emigrant Ship, The, 121
Emigrant Train, The, 121
'End of Travel, An', 347
Equator, Schooner Yacht, 302–3,
  305
Evans, Andrew J., 115

Fa'animonimo, 306
Fables, 1–5, 155, 330
'Father Damien: An Open Letter',
  293
Fergusson, Robert, 17–19
Fernández, Father Nobincio, 278,
  281, 287–9
Ferrier, Walter, 196–7

Hardy, Thomas, 200–1, 267
Hare, William, 54
Hart, James D., 121
Harte, Bret, 166
Hawes Inn, 42–3
Hazlitt, William, 6–7
Helm, George, 272
Henley, William Ernest:
    character, 58–9
    friendship with RLS, 59, 120,
        307
    letters to, 127, 136, 140, 154,
        161, 163
    London magazine, 112
    Scots Observer, 247
    Treasure Island, 59, 186
'Henry David Thoreau: His
    Character and Opinions', 163
Heriot Row, Edinburgh, 14–16,
    39, 44, 100, 220, 261
High Woods of Ulufanua, The, 326
Hogan, Elodie, 180
Hogg, James, 235
Holland, Clive, 205
Holmes, Richard, 115
Honolulu, 248–61, 268, 273–4,
    276, 293–6
'Honour and Chastity', 209
Hope, Anthony, 82, 197
'House of Eld, The', 60
House, Wilfred, 205
Howard Place, Edinburgh, 13–14,
    76
Hyde, Charles McEwen, 277,
    293–4
Hyères, 31, 37, 154, 190–9

Ide, Annie, 76
Ide, Marjorie, 76–7

Inland Voyage, An:
    account of, 100, 105, 111, 124,
        236
    publication, 100, 114
    Wattie Simpson, 16, 55,
        99–100, 107
'In the States', 225
Inverleith Terrace, 13
Iona, 44–6
Isherwood, Christopher, 113
'Isle of Voices, The', 242, 246

Jack the Ripper, 209
James, Alice, 212
James, Henry:
    compared with RLS, 267
    friendship with RLS, 172,
        211–13
    Greene on, 74
    letters to, 228, 292, 339
    on *Kidnapped*, 49–50
    on *Prince Otto*, 197
    on RLS, xi, 59, 105, 154
    on *Weir of Hermiston*, 347
    opinion of Lang, 82
James, William, 232
Janet, Pierre Marie Félix, 215
*Jekyll and Hyde, see Strange Case of
    Dr Jekyll and Mr Hyde*
Johnson, Dr Samuel, 44, 46
Johnston, Mrs (at Colinton
    manse), 29
Judd, Gerrit P., 270

Kaahumana, 253–4
Kaaua, Archie, 269
Ka'iulani, Princess, 263–4, 265
Kalakaua, King David, 257,

Made in the USA
Las Vegas, NV
02 March 2021